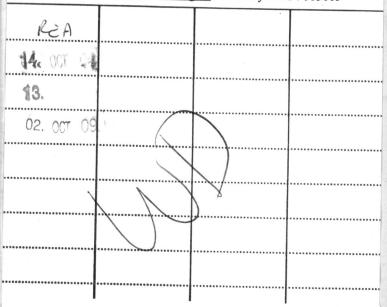

PENGUIN TWENTIETH-CENTURY CLASSICS

THE PENGUIN BOOK OF
SPANISH CIVIL WAR VERSE

Valentine Cunningham is Fellow in English Literature at Corpus
Christi College, Oxford. His books include Spanish Front (1986) and
British Writers of the Thirties (1988).

The Penguin Book of

SPANISH CIVIL WAR VERSE

EDITED BY
VALENTINE CUNNINGHAM

PENGUIN BOOKS

PENGUIN BOOKS

Published by the Penguin Group
Penguin Books Ltd, 27 Wrights Lane, London W8 5TZ, England
Penguin Books USA Inc., 375 Hudson Street, New York, New York 10014, USA
Penguin Books Australia Ltd, Ringwood, Victoria, Australia
Penguin Books Canada Ltd, 10 Alcorn Avenue, Toronto, Ontario, Canada M4V 3B2
Penguin Books (NZ) Ltd, 182–190 Wairau Road, Auckland 10, New Zealand

Penguin Books Ltd, Registered Offices: Harmondsworth, Middlesex, England

First published 1980
Reprinted with minor revisions 1996
1 3 5 7 9 10 8 6 4 2

Contents

(P) = prose piece

5

CONTENTS

JUNKER ANGELS IN THE SKY 155

HE IS DEAD AND GONE 173

8

CONTENTS

9

THE INTERNATIONALS

UNHEROIC NOTES

For Joseph and Willoughby

It is the logic of our times,
No subject for immortal verse,
That we who lived by honest dreams
Defend the bad against the worse.

(C. Day Lewis, 'Where are the War Poets?',
Penguin New Writing, No. 3 (February 1941),
p. 114)

Preface

A couple of major promptings led me to start preparing this anthology of poems and prose of the Spanish Civil War. In the first place, exasperation with a publisher for suggesting that yet another anthology of First World War poems might possibly be useful, especially when this request brought it so firmly home that while the poetry of the First and Second World Wars was very well served by numerous anthologists there was not only no Spanish War anthology in print at that time in Britain, but there *never had been* a full collection of the work of the British writers of that war. And in the second place I had begun to realize that my students, especially students who were interested in the important relationship between literature and society in the 1930s and as evinced during the Spanish Civil War period, were unable to make informed judgements because most of the material they needed was uncollected, had been subjected to authors' emendations and other changes of heart, was scattered in numerous magazines in widely located libraries, and so was extremely difficult of ready access.

To be sure, there have been, and for that matter still are, collections of some of the literature of the Spanish Civil War. The Americans were promptest off the mark with *From Spanish Trenches*, a gathering of letters edited by Marcel Acier, and . . . *And Spain Sings: Fifty Loyalist Ballads, adapted by American Poets*, a set of romanceros in translation, edited by M. J. Benardete and Rolfe Humphries (both books published in New York in 1937). *Poems for Spain* followed, edited by Stephen Spender and John Lehmann (1939): the first and only British attempt at anything like even a full-ish collection of British poems but, thanks not least of all to the modest reluctance of Spender to bulk out the book with his own stuff, many available poems still remained ungathered. Alvah Bessie, Civil War veteran and victim of the McCarthyite witch-hunts, brought out *The Heart of*

15

Spain: Anthology of Fiction, Non-Fiction and Poetry in New York in 1952. None of these volumes was ever republished, though, and they've all long been out of print. More recently there have been a French anthology in two volumes (*Le romancero de la résistance espagnole*, compiled by Dario Puccini (Maspero, Paris, 1970), itself a translation of *Romancero della resisteriza Spagnola*, Milan, 1960), and Murray Sperber's admirable (but largely prose) collection *And I Remember Spain* (Hart-Davis, McGibbon, 1974). The most useful, and most available gathering of British poems of the Spanish War has been in Robin Skelton's handy Penguin *Poetry of the Thirties* (1964). But here, necessarily, the Spanish material makes just one quite small section of thirties poetry.

So my anthology is something quite new: for the first time, a comprehensive assembly of British poems (as every Eng. Lit. syllabus does, I'm assuming, however gratuitously, that Irishmen belong under the 'British' banner) which have to do with the Spanish War, together with some supporting prose – reports, letters, stories, reviews – by the poets. In order not to omit an important part of the flavour of the War as it was mediated at the time to the readers of literary journals and, even, of the daily newspapers, I have included some poems, particularly but not exclusively Spanish romanceros, in translation – usually translations by British authors, but on a few occasions translations by Americans which appeared in British papers or papers available in Britain. Special, too, about this collection are the previously unpublished things it contains: several poems by Miles Tomalin; several by Clive Branson, among them his unique concentration camp verses; a poem 'Two Days', and an insert previously unknown to print, for his Mass Declamation 'On Guard for Spain!', by Jack Lindsay; several translations of romanceros by Sylvia Townsend Warner; and an epigram by Valentine Ackland. My Introduction is also the first account of this War's relation to English literature that's been able to draw on the valuable new Archive of the International Brigade Association (including the I.B.A. correspondence, a copy of the unpublished diary of Harry Stratton, and the only copy I've seen of *Volunteer for Liberty*, the paper published for its members by the International

Brigade in Spain), housed at the Marx Memorial Library, Marx House, Clerkenwell Green, London ECIR ODU.

Some of the poems in this anthology are extremely well-known, others, of course, deserve rather to be known only to readers with a particular interest in the literature of this War. Some authors, it will be noticed, often fairly unknown ones, have been deliberately represented in some quantity. For one prime intention of this anthology is to put firmly on the map the work of those undeservedly too-little-known poets Charles Donnelly, Ewart Milne, Clive Branson, Tom Wintringham and Miles Tomalin. Another is to reveal the considerable (in every sense) extent of Stephen Spender's contribution, in verse and prose, to the literature of Spain. I want others to be impressed, as I have been in discovering it, by Spender's great bulk of serious and sensitive, often anguished, always would-be honest, writing of this period.

Naturally enough I've had to seek, and have been gratified to find, considerable assistance. I'm very grateful to Noreen Branson for letting me have the previously unpublished poems of her late husband Clive Branson, as well as the correct version of his poem published in *Poetry and the People* No. 17 and copies of his two poems which appeared in the elusive *Poetry and the People* No. 11. The late Sylvia Townsend Warner kindly supplied me with original typescripts of her romancero translations and (she was her literary executor) of the squib by Valentine Ackland. Jack Lindsay not only generously gave me his unpublished poems but also much helpful information about Mass Declamations and a tip-off about the existence of *New Lyrical Ballads* (1945). Ewart Milne alerted me to his stories in the (then unknown to me) magazine *Ireland Today* – in which, I then discovered, Charles Donnelly was also published – and generously lent me several of his own copies of that periodical. J. Skelley, Esq., Managing Director of Lawrence and Wishart (publishers of *Left Review* and the first series of *New Writing*), first told me about Clive Branson, and Alan Ross first mentioned to me T. C. Worsley's *The Fellow Travellers*. The officials of the International Brigade Association – William Alexander its Chairman, Alec Digges its past secretary, and Nan Green its present secretary and heroic toiler in the new Archive – have been unfailingly helpful, as has Margaret Kentfield, Librarian of the Marx Memorial Library. Alvah Bessie corresponded most informatively and cheerfully between, as he put it, 'the anniversary of the International Brigade's successful defence of Madrid', 1975, and the death in November of that year of the dictator Franco. I've also been much assisted by kind attention and information from Humphrey Carpenter, Tina Carpenter, J. L. Gili, A. S. Knowland, Geoffrey Grigson, Bernard Gutteridge, Margot Heinemann, J. C. Hall, A. L. Lloyd, Mrs F. L. Lucas, the late Christopher Grieve (Hugh MacDiarmid), H. B. Mallalieu, Mrs Hugh Miller ('Sagittarius' of the *New Statesman*), Eric Southworth, Rex Warner, Miles Tomalin, Claire Tomalin and the library assistants at the Bodleian, the British Museum, the London School of Economics, and Marx House.

VALENTINE CUNNINGHAM

6. x. 1978.
Corpus Christi College,
Oxford.

NOTE ON TEXTS OF PREVIOUSLY PUBLISHED POEMS. Wherever possible this anthology has sought to reprint the first published version. Where this has not been allowed, the notes indicate which other text has been reproduced.

LINE NUMBERS 'N THE TEXT indicate textual variants: listed in the Notes at the end of the book.

SPANISH PROPER NAMES were variously accented in England in the 1930s — another measure of Spain's foreign-ness, its distance. The titles and texts of the poems in this anthology attempt to preserve these oddities.

Preface to the 1996 printing

I have corrected a few errors of fact in the Introduction and a few misprints in the texts of the occasional poem. If the Preface and Introduction were written now, the elegiac ending of the latter would have been more pronounced and the occurences of the grim phrase 'the late' would have been more numerous in the former. Since 1978 so many more of the people who contributed to this anthology and helped shape its thinking have, sadly, died – Roy Fuller, Nan Green, Geoffrey Grigson, Margot Heinemann, Jack Lindsay, A. L. Lloyd, Ewart Milne, Stephen Spender, Julian Symons, Miles Tomalin, Rex Warner, to name no others. Happily, their words, and their hopes, will live on, though they do not.

VALENTINE CUNNINGHAM
January 1996

Acknowledgements

For permission to reprint copyright poems and pieces of prose the editor makes grateful acknowledgement as follows:

For VALENTINE ACKLAND: 'Instructions from England (1936)', to Sylvia Townsend Warner.

For RAFAEL ALBERTI: 'A Spectre is Haunting Europe', translated by A. L. Lloyd, to the *Morning Star*.

For MANUEL ALTOLAGUIRRE: 'My Brother Luis' and 'Madrid', translated by Stephen Spender, and 'I Demand the Ultimate Death', translated by Inez and Stephen Spender, to A. D. Peters & Co., Ltd.

For ANON: 'Salud, Brigade – Salud!', to the International Brigade Association.

For W. H. AUDEN: 'Spain, 1937', from *Collected Shorter Poems 1930–1944*, to Faber & Faber Ltd; for 'Epitaph on a Tyrant', and 'Impressions of Valencia', to the *New Statesman*.

For GEORGE BARKER: 'Calamiterror', Section X, and 'Elegy on Spain', from *Collected Poems 1930–1955*, to Faber & Faber Ltd; for 'O Hero Akimbo on the Mountains of Tomorrow', to John Johnson, Authors' Agent.

For CLIVE BRANSON: to Mrs Noreen Branson.

For ROY CAMPBELL: 'A Letter from the San Mateo Front', from *Flowering Rifle: A Poem from the Battlefield of Spain* (1939), to the Bodley Head; for the letter 'Flowering Rifles', to the *New Statesman*.

For MAURICE CARPENTER: 'Lament for a Lover', to Tina Carpenter and Jack Lindsay.

For CHRISTOPHER CAUDWELL: 'Last Letters of a Hero', to Associated Newspapers Group Ltd.

For RICHARD CHURCH: 'The Hero' and 'Grief's Reflections', to the Estate of the late Richard Church; for 'The Madrid Defenders', to the *New Statesman*.

For ELIZABETH CLUER: 'Analogy in Madrid', to the *New Statesman*.

For JOHN CORNFORD: 'Poem' ('Heart of the Heartless World'), to Lawrence & Wishart Ltd; for letters to Margot Heinemann,

ACKNOWLEDGEMENTS

'A Letter from Aragon', 'Diary Letter from Aragon', and 'Full Moon at Tierz: Before the Storming of Huesca' (from *John Cornford: A Memoir*, ed. Pat Sloan), to the Estate of John Cornford, Pat Sloan and Jonathan Cape Ltd.

For NANCY CUNARD: 'To Eat To-day', to the *New Statesman*; for Nancy Cunard's translations of Pablo Neruda, 'To the Mothers of the Dead Militia' and 'Almeria', and of Jacques Roumain, 'Madrid: to Ramon Sender', to Lawrence & Wishart Ltd; for 'Sonnet in Five Languages: the Internationals', from *Nancy Cunard: Brave Poet, Indomitable Rebel 1895–1965*, copyright © 1968 by the editor Hugh Ford, to Chilton Book Company, Radnor, Pa., U.S.A.

For ERIC EDNEY: 'The Battalion Goes Forward' and 'Salud!', to the author and the International Brigade Association.

For A. M. ELLIOTT: 'Jarama', to the author.

For EDGAR FOXALL: 'Spain and Time', to Charles Skilton: The Fortune Press.

For ROY FULLER: 'Times of War and Revolution', from *Collected Poems*, to André Deutsch Ltd; for 'Poem (For M. S., Killed in Spain)', to Lawrence & Wishart Ltd.

For GEOFFREY GRIGSON: 'The Non-Interveners', from *Several Observations*, to the author.

For BERNARD GUTTERIDGE: 'In September 1939' and 'Spanish Earth', to the author.

For HANS HAFLIN: 'The News', to the *Morning Star*.

For CHARLOTTE HALDANE: 'Passionaria', to Lawrence & Wishart Ltd.

For J. C. HALL: 'Postscript for Spain', to the author.

For MARGOT HEINEMANN: 'For R. J. C. (Summer, 1936)', 'Grieve in a New Way for New Losses', and 'On a Lost Battle in the Spanish War', to Lawrence & Wishart Ltd.

For J. F. HENDRY: 'Picasso: for Guernica', to the author.

For MIGUEL HERNÁNDEZ: 'Hear This Voice', translated by Inez and Stephen Spender, to Lawrence & Wishart Ltd; for 'Winds of the People', translated by A. L. Lloyd, to A. L. Lloyd.

For LANGSTON HUGHES: translation of Anon, 'Spanish Folk Song of the War', to the *Morning Star*.

For T. A. R. HYNDMAN: 'Jarama Front', to the author.

For W. B. KEAL: 'For the Fallen' and 'But no Bugles', to the *Morning Star*.

For H. M. KING: 'Cold in England', to the *Morning Star*.

For A. S. KNOWLAND: 'Guernica', to the author.

21

ACKNOWLEDGEMENTS

For LAURIE LEE: 'A Moment of War', and 'Words Asleep', from *The Sun My Monument*, to the author and the Hogarth Press Ltd.

For C. DAY LEWIS: 'The Nabara' and 'The Volunteer', from *Collected Poems* (1954), to the Executors of the Estate of C. Day Lewis and Jonathan Cape Ltd; for 'Bombers', from *Collected Poems* (1954), to the Executors of the Estate of C. Day Lewis, Jonathan Cape Ltd, and the Hogarth Press; for 'Newsreel', to Lawrence & Wishart Ltd.

For JACK LINDSAY: to the author.

For L. KENDALL: 'To the Heroes of the International Brigade in Spain', to the International Brigade Association.

For F. L. LUCAS: 'Proud Motherhood (Madrid, A. D. 1937)', to Mrs F. L. Lucas.

For SOMHAIRLE MACALASTAIR: 'Ballyseedy Befriends Badajoz', to Lawrence & Wishart Ltd; for 'Battle Song of "Irish Christian Front"', from Peadar O'Donnell, *Salud! An Irishman in Spain* (1937), to the author and Methuen & Co. Ltd.

For HUGH MACDIARMID: 'An English War-Poet', to the author.

For DONAGH MACDONAGH: 'He is Dead and Gone, Lady . . .', to Mrs I. McGuiness.

For ANTONIO MACHADO: 'The Crime Took Place in Granada' (translated by D. Trevor), to Lawrence & Wishart Ltd.

For LOUIS MACNEICE: 'Today in Barcelona', to the *Spectator*; for 'Autumn Journal VI', from *Collected Poems*, to Faber & Faber Ltd.

For H. B. MALLALIEU: 'The Future is Near Us', to the author; for extract from 'Poem in Spring', and for 'Spain' and 'In the Interval', to Charles Skilton: The Fortune Press.

For EWART MILNE: to the author.

For T. E. NICHOLAS: 'In Remembrance of a Son of Wales (Who Fell in Spain)', to the *Morning Star*.

For GEORGE ORWELL: 'The Italian soldier shook my hand', to Mrs Sonia Brownell Orwell and Secker & Warburg Ltd.

For GEOFFREY PARSONS: 'Lorca', to the author.

For JOSÉ HERRERA PETERE: 'Against the Cold in the Mountains', translated by A. L. Lloyd, to Lawrence & Wishart Ltd.

For KATHLEEN RAINE: 'Fata Morgana', from *The Year's Poetry* (1937), to The Bodley Head.

For HERBERT READ: 'Bombing Casualties in Spain', 'The Heart Conscripted', and 'A Song for the Spanish Anarchists', from *Collected Poems*, to Faber & Faber Ltd.

ACKNOWLEDGEMENTS

For EDGELL RICKWORD: 'To the Wife of Any Non-Intervention Statesman', to the author and Carcanet Press Ltd.

For SAGITTARIUS: 'Dulce et Decorum Est...' and 'They Got What They Wanted', to the author, Mrs Hugh Miller.

For BERNARD SPENCER: 'A Thousand Killed' and 'A Cold Night', from *Collected Poems* (1965), to Alan Ross and London Magazine Editions.

For STEPHEN SPENDER: 'The Landscape', 'War Photograph', 'The Moment Transfixes the Space Which Divides', 'The Bombed Happiness', 'At Castellon', 'Till Death Completes Their Arc', 'Heroes in Spain', and 'The Talking Bronco', to A. D. Peters & Co. Ltd; for 'To a Spanish Poet', 'In No Man's Land', 'The Room above the Square', 'Thoughts during an Air Raid', 'A Stopwatch and an Ordnance Map', 'The Coward', 'Ultima Ratio Regum', 'Fall of a City', 'Two Armies' and 'Port Bou', from *Collected Poems*, to Faber & Faber Ltd; for 'The Word Dead and the Music Mad' and 'Pictures in Spain', to the *Spectator*; for 'Spain's Air Chief in a Mechanic's Blue Dungarees', to the *Morning Star*; for 'The Will to Live' and 'Guernica', to Stephen Spender and the *New Statesman*.

For RUTHVEN TODD: to the author.

For MILES TOMALIN: 'Wings Overhead', 'May Day', 'Self-Destroyers', 'Christmas Eve 1937', 'The Gunner', 'After Brunete', 'Nicholas', 'To England from the English Dead', and 'Aftermath', to the author; for 'Down the Road', to the author and the International Brigade Association; for Miles Tomalin's translation of Zofia Schleyen, 'Plaza de España', to the translator.

For GONZÁLEZ TUÑÓN: 'Long Live the Revolution', translated by A. L. Lloyd, to Lawrence & Wishart Ltd.

For LORENZO VARELA: 'Poem', translated by A. M. Elliott, to the *Morning Star*.

For REX WARNER: 'Arms in Spain', to the author; for 'The Tourist Looks at Spain', to Lawrence & Wishart Ltd.

For SYLVIA TOWNSEND WARNER: 'Waiting at Cerbere', 'Barcelona', and 'Benicasim', to the author; for Sylvia Townsend Warner's translations of Francis Fuentes, 'Revolutionary Madrid'; Julio D. Guillén, 'La Peña'; Felix Paredes, 'Encarnacion Jimenez'; and José Herrera Petere, 'El dia que no vendra', to the translator; for "Harvest in 1937", to the *New Statesman*.

For TOM WINTRINGHAM: 'Barcelona Nerves' and 'Comrades of Jarama', to the International Brigade Association; for 'Monument'

23

ACKNOWLEDGEMENTS

and 'British Medical Unit – Granien', to Lawrence & Wishart
Ltd.

Every effort has been made to trace authors and owners of copyrights.
Occasionally these efforts have failed. The editor and publisher
apologize for these unwilling cases of copyright transgression and
would like to hear from any copyright holders not acknowledged.

INTRODUCTION

Cornford is immensely significant not merely because he was young and brave, but because he lived and died with the courage of a purpose which reaches far beyond himself and which effectively challenges the barbarism and defeatism of the age we live in. One may feel, as I do, that the pattern of this young hero is over-simplified; his vision of life is impatient and violent, it leaves too many questions unanswered, he burns out too quickly, rushing headlong to his death; but nevertheless it is a pattern which in other lives may take on a greater richness without losing Cornford's power and determination. The spirit of Cornford and some of his comrades rises like a phoenix from the ashes of Spain, which are the ashes of Europe.

(Stephen Spender, 'The Will to Live' (a review of *John Cornford: A Memoir* ed. Pat Sloan, 1938), *New Statesman*, (12 November 1938), p. 772)

Clauson's gesture stirred the bottom of Garner's memory – a public meeting years ago at a hall somewhere in Holborn in aid of Republican Spain and Philip Clauson, his head tilted back and the lights burnishing his hair, holding up both his hands at the end of his speech. Garner, too, had been on the platform. It was another world.

(Roy Fuller, *The Second Curtain* (1953), Ch. 9)

With a deference to Marxist expectations much kinder than history often manifests, the 1930s were marked by a pronounced series of crises and more-than-marketable rumours of crisis. It was 'this hour of crisis and dismay', as Auden described his times to Christopher Isherwood in his poem 'To a Writer on His Birthday' (1935). At home there was deep economic trouble and political uncertainty, abroad there was political opportunism and territorial aggression by the Fascist forces of Japan, Italy and Germany. The period began and ended in crisis. 'Crisis' was the front page article by Oswald Mosley in the very first number of his New Party's new organ *Action* (8 October, 1931); the Penguin Special on *Britain* opened the last year of the decade with Mass-Observation's analysis of public opinion about the Czech 'crisis'. But if, out of such an appallingly tense decade, it is possible to select one particular year as the most disturbing and turbulent, that year would have to be 1936.

To read through the newspapers of 1936 – particularly the crisis-expectant Communist Party organ the *Daily Worker* – is to realize what a frenetically hectic helter-skelter of a year that was. The old king, George V, had died in January, leaving a country still blighted by economically dead areas and with nearly two million unemployed, and in doubt over the qualities of the heir to the throne. In March Hitler pushed German soldiers into the demilitarized Rhineland; on 1 May Emperor Haile Selassie had to flee Abyssinia to escape the invading Italian armies; a week later Mussolini declared that a new Roman Empire was now established. For some years, of course, there had been plenty of Fascists much nearer home, and both their determination and the resolution of the anti-Fascist Left were yet again vividly demonstrated on the afternoon of Sunday 4 October. Between 2,500 and 3,000 of Mosley's Blackshirts were intending to march provocatively through the heavily Jewish quarters of the East End of London. Between 6,000 and

7,000 police turned out to protect them while they did so. But they weren't enough: thousands of anti-Fascists had gathered to stop them, and when serious street-fighting broke out between the opposition and the police trying to clear a road for Mosley, the march was diverted. A victory, perhaps, for the Left, but the following week mobs of Mosley's thugs returned to smash and loot Jewish shops in the Mile End Road. And anti-Jewish activity by the British Union of Fascists in the East End was so intense in October and November that 300 police had to be daily drafted into the area.[1] In this autumn too the new king's domestic problems were being made public, and his intent to marry the divorced Mrs Simpson became widely known. It led to his forced abdication on 11 December. Many of the depressed and unemployed were angered: they thought, rightly or wrongly, that the sympathetic noises Edward had uttered while visiting impoverished Welsh mining districts had made the ruling capitalist class hostile enough to want to engineer the king's departure. Ironically the Abdication Crisis itself, it was thought, masked the impact on government and public opinion of the arrival of the 'Jarrow Crusade' in London. This was the most respectable of the many thirties hunger marches, consisting of officially chosen representatives, including town councillors and Jarrow's M.P. Ellen Wilkinson but excluding Communists, sent to publicize the plight of the town where two-thirds of the working population had no work. This plight wasn't unexceptional for the North East nor for parts of Lancashire and for South Wales, but Jarrow became famous, through the Left Book Club title, as *The Town That Was Murdered*.

But if the press had difficulty keeping up with all this, how much more shocking to democratic, liberal, and left-wing opinion was the biggest crisis of the year, the putsch in July, planned and spearheaded by right-wing generals, against the Popular Front, Republican government of Spain.

It was not that literary people, predominantly leftist-liberal if not actually fellow-travellers or members of the Communist Party, had been idle that year in promoting what was effectively a kind of literary equivalent of the Popular Front against Fascism.

1. Robert Benewick, *The Fascist Movement in Britain* (1972), Ch. 10.

The first number of *New Writing*, edited by John Lehmann, had appeared in the Spring of 1936. The new periodical was self-declaredly 'independent of any political party' but, characteristically of the period, it did 'not intend to open its pages to writers of reactionary or Fascist sentiments'. The would-be revolutionary organ of British surrealism, *Contemporary Poetry and Prose*, first appeared in May 1936. Just prior to the Spanish outburst the Left Book Club had been founded. 'The Club *is* a United Front', ran its *Daily Worker* advertisement: it was to stand '*for* World Peace' and '*against* Fascism'. But suddenly, in Spain, was a more direct challenge and opportunity: almost on Britain's doorstep. 'For us,' writes T. C. Worsley in his documentary-novel *Fellow-Travellers: A Memoir of the Thirties* (1971), 'at the start of it, there was practically no other topic of conversation. To us the issue seemed as clear as anyone could possibly want. The Spanish Popular Front Government had been elected by democratic processes and was clearly entitled to receive every support. The Generals' rebellion was obviously Fascist-inspired. Here was the whole European issue at its most naked and pure, Democracy versus Fascism.' If the new Republic's struggle for life should succeed, the reverses democracy had suffered for years would at least be halted; if not, the freedoms British writers and artists enjoyed might, in their turn, go the way of German and Italian and Japanese writers' liberties. '[E]verything,' John Lehmann has recalled, 'all our fears, our confused hopes and beliefs, our half-formulated theories and imaginings, veered and converged towards its testing and its opportunity, like steel filings that slide towards a magnet suddenly put near them.' Not surprisingly, then,

When the full significance of what was happening in Spain gradually became apparent, and all the political parties, organizations, the un-attached liberals, intellectuals and artists who had become aware that their own fate was deeply involved in the battles developing in front of Madrid and Barcelona, had banded themselves together to organize the International Brigade and the Spanish Medical Aid, I think every young writer began seriously to debate with himself how he could best be of use, by joining the Brigade, or driving an ambulance, or helping the active committees in England or France, or in some other

INTRODUCTION

way. The pull was terrific, the pull of an international crusade to the ideals and aims of which all intellectuals ... who had been stirred by the fascist danger, felt they could, in the hour of apocalypse, whole-heartedly assent.[1]

No wonder, given this heady mixture of fear and wish and the prevailing sense of apocalypse at last really come, that the Spanish Civil War has passed into myth, and furnished a hardy set of myths. In the first place there is the possibly excusable myth that this was a 'poets' war'. So Stephen Spender labelled it in his essay in *the God That Failed* (1950). So later commentators have chimed in: 'It had been a poets' war,' concludes Stanley Weintraub at the end of *The Last Great Cause: the Intellectuals and the Spanish Civil War* (1968). Upton Sinclair thought the foreign volunteers formed 'probably the most literary brigade in the history of warfare. Writers and would-be writers had come to live their books, journalists to make their news.' And, to be sure, a large number of young and not-so-young intellectuals and writers did go from Britain and Ireland, as well as from many other countries, to add to the Republic's war-effort. W. H. Auden volunteered as a medical worker. Stephen Spender hoped (unsuccessfully) to help with English broadcasts from Valencia's Socialist Broadcasting Station. Arrived in Barcelona he was surprised to hear the voice of the surrealist poet David Gascoyne (an already published twenty-two-year-old) broadcasting in English through loudspeakers attached to upper-storey windows. Roger Roughton, the still more youthful surrealist, and editor (he was only nineteen) of *Contemporary Poetry and Prose*, shut up shop, his back cover blaring starkly 'ARMS FOR SPAIN', but with a coyly hintful insert informing that the editor was 'going abroad for some time'.[2] Ewart Milne, the Irish poet, stayed on with a British Medical Unit until the last months of the year. George Orwell fought and was wounded. Clive Branson, the painter and poet, volunteered late (apparently at the end of 1937 or early in 1938)

1. John Lehmann, *The Whispering Gallery* (1955), pp. 273-5.
2. Robin Skelton (ed), *Poetry of the Thirties* (Penguin, 1964), p. 20.

and was captured to endure eight months in a Franco concentration-camp (he was repatriated at the end of 1938).[1]

Writers held important political posts, like the English novelist Ralph Bates, or rose to positions of high command, like the Hungarian, Mata Zalka (who fought under the name of General Lukacz), or the Germans Gustav Regler and Ludwig Renn and the French novelist André Malraux.[2] Some English writers, Cecil Day Lewis in particular, were conspicuous by their absence: perhaps Day Lewis was too valuable a propagandist at home for the Communist Party to allow him to risk getting killed. Rex Warner volunteered to drive an ambulance, but was rejected after making a flippant remark about 'Russian gold' to the 'rather solemn Communists' who interviewed him.[3] Louis Macneice, though sympathetic, only visited Barcelona in the closing days of its drama, at the end of 1938: he left on 9 January; twenty-five days later the city fell to the rebels. Still, 'At least five of the best young English writers gave their lives', Spender claimed in *The God that Failed* He was referring, presumably, to Ralph Fox the Communist novelist, critic and journalist, to John Cornford the recent Cambridge graduate and budding poet, to Christopher St John Sprigg the novelist, aeronautical writer and (under the pseudonym of Christopher Caudwell) perhaps England's most distinguished practitioner of Marxist literary criticism, to Charles Donnelly the young Irish poet, and to Julian Bell, nephew of Virginia Woolf, a minor belles-lettrist and would-be poet who was fatally wounded while driving his ambulance. These weren't the only writers the war claimed. Mata Zalka was killed in action. The Spanish poet Antonio Machado died at Collioure, of an old asthmatic complaint fatally exacerbated by his evacuation from Spain at the end of the war. Miguel Hernández the Spanish shepherd-poet died a little while after Machado in a Franco jail in Alicante.

1. *British Soldier in India: The Letters of Clive Branson* (1944), introd. Harry Pollitt, pp. 4–7.

2. Hugh Thomas, *The Spanish Civil War* (Penguin, 1965), pp. 413–14.

3. Quoted by Stanley Weintraub. *The Last Great Cause: The Intellectuals and the Spanish Civil War* (1968), pp. 83–4.

And most notable of all, of course, was the murder on the night of 18–19 August 1936, during the Terror that marked the right-wing upsurge in Granada, of Federico García Lorca, a man of well-known Republican sympathies and now regarded as one of Spain's most important modern poets and playwrights. [1]

But for all this, it was hardly a poets' war. Even within the Communist Party, which was ever anxious for whatever advantageous publicity could be gleaned from the support of distinguished men and women of letters, there were cautioning voices. The disclaimers, though, sat ill on a Party which craved the respectability its middle-class 'heroes' gave it. The slippery contradictions in Harry Pollitt's Introduction (Pollitt was a founder member of the Communist Party of Great Britain and for about forty years its General Secretary) to *David Guest: A Memoir* (1939) are pretty evident:

David Guest and men of similar type would not have us be unmindful of those hundreds of other young men, labourers, dockers, railwaymen, engineers, clerks, seamen, miners and textile workers who have also made the supreme sacrifice. Men whose family circumstances make it impossible for any special Memoirs to be published about them, but who were David's comrades in life, in arms and in death, and to whose immortal memory this volume is as great a tribute as it is to those from the public schools and universities.

For his part Tom Wintringham is at some pains to disavow what he takes as the slur that the British volunteers for the International Brigades consisted of lots of the unemployed or Jews. They weren't, he insists in his account of his Spanish experiences in *English Captain* (1939), 'the lowest dregs of the unemployed' (only between an eighth and a quarter of the British joined up because they were out of work), and only about 3 per cent were Jewish. And to prove many of them weren't 'the sort of people usually labelled "unemployed"' he lists some of them: the Carritts (of Boar's Hill, Oxford), the son of Lady Dunbar, a musician, an architect, a descendant of Clive of India, a cartoonist, a 'Boxing Parson' from Killarney, and a Cambridge

2. See Ian Gibson's careful and enthralling detective work in *The Death of Lorca* (1973).

scientist. On this kind of reckoning it was a graduates' war at least. And, of course, he also puts in the writers Ralph Fox and Hugh Slater, the poets Cornford, Bell, Sprigg, Donnelly, Branson and Tomalin, making it out to be an intellectuals' and writers' scrap if not precisely a poets' one.

But the facts are clear. Of the 2,762 Britons who fought with the International Brigades it has been estimated that about 80 per cent were working-class. Certainly many of them were out of work; certainly many bore Jewish names and came from strongly Jewish areas like the East End of London. The lists of the dead (543 of these volunteers were killed, and only 456 survived without wounds of some sort) indicate a cosmopolitan crowd, largely proletarian, predominantly from the big cities like London, Glasgow, Manchester, Leeds and Liverpool. But the myth of a poets' war is hard to shake loose even where the ideological pressure isn't of Wintringham's kind. Peter Stansky and William Abrahams, the American biographers of Cornford and Bell, are undisarmingly frank:

One of our first considerations was to ask why it was, and how it was, that young men like John Cornford and Julian Bell, both of them poets and sons of the intellectual aristocracy of England, went out to Spain to fight for the Republic. But we had no sooner begun our researches than it became evident that in our phrasing of the question we had been misled by legend, which has tended ever since 1939 to overpopulate the Spanish conflict with poets, especially young English poets, 'exploding like bombs'. In fact some eighty per cent of the English volunteers for the International Brigades came from the working class, and they were simply and precisely that: workers, many of them out of jobs, not worker poets. Yet John Cornford and Julian Bell, and a handful of others – Ralph Fox, Christopher Caudwell, George Orwell – were more or less what the legend claimed.

Their received myth was indeed a narrow one (by 'English' they mean more strictly 'British', and there were considerably more British poets and writers in Spain than they name) but instead of challenging the myth, or even inspecting why it was that those trade-unionists and out-of-work workers went to Spain, they proceeded simply to bolster a legend and reinforce a prejudice:

'Accordingly we rephrased our question: Why, and How, had John Cornford and Julian Bell gone out to Spain? We were launched . . .'[1]

There is also another myth, it too carefully fostered by the Communist Party, the myth of the International Brigades as the and uniquely glorious expression of volunteer overseas support for the Republic. This myth is there, encapsulated *tout court* in just a couple of exclamations in Hugh MacDiarmid's long poem *The Battle Continues* (1957): 'Spain! The International Brigade!'[2] Stephen Spender's clear assumption in his Introduction to the *Poems for Spain* anthology that he edited with John Lehmann in 1939 is that to be a poet, and being in Spain to fight, are the same as being part of the International Brigades: 'The fact that these poems should have been written at all has a literary significance parallel to the existence of the International Brigades.' The *Daily Worker* refuted some *Daily Mail* charges about British volunteers with the calming assurance that *they* knew what was what because their man, Wilf Macartney (author of *Walls Have Mouths* – an account, published in 1936 by the Left Book Club, of his imprisonment as a convicted spy) handled all the recruits: 'Every man who came from Britain to Spain, said Mr Macartney, reported to him personally' (*Daily Worker*, 1 March 1937, p. 5). No doubt it was with equal mindfulness that Pat Sloan, the Communist editor of *John Cornford: A Memoir*, pointfully altered line 40 of Cornford's poem 'Full Moon at Tierz' from 'Now, with my party, I stand quite alone' to 'Now, with my Party . . .' And one wonders whether it wasn't the presence in the poem of 'an Anarchist worker' that kept 'A Letter from Aragon' out of *Poems for Spain*. According to Tom Wintringham, the best answer to the questions 'Who were these "English" . . . ? How had they come to be here, part of an international army . . . ?', 'is to trace the growth of this fellowship's vanguard, the International Brigade, of which "these English" were solidly part. We do not know how to

1. Peter Stansky and William Abrahams, *Journey to the Frontier* (1966), p. xviii.
2. Hugh MacDiarmid, *The Battle Continues* (1957), p. 86.

answer such questions about our three companies that are not also questions about the Brigade . . .'[1]

But the Communist-organized International Brigades (or International Legion, or International Column, as they were variously dubbed earlier in their career) weren't the only auspices under which foreign volunteers might fight in Spain. George Orwell was evidently deemed 'politically unreliable' by Harry Pollitt, who interviewed him, especially since Orwell refused to undertake to join the International Brigade before he had seen at first hand what was happening in Spain (Pollitt's *Daily Worker* review of *The Road to Wigan Pier* a little later, 17 March 1937, sneered at its author as 'a disillusioned little middle-class boy' who would 'have to try again'). Pollitt wouldn't give Orwell his Party's help in getting into Spain. But Orwell managed to obtain Independent Labour Party backing, and indeed went out with the I.L.P. contingent, so he was not only enabled to enter Spain under a non-Communist banner but inevitably joined a militia of the anti-Stalinist, revolutionary Marxist party the P.O.U.M. when he arrived. (The P.O.U.M. was a member of the London Bureau of 'Revolutionary Socialist Parties', led in 1936 by Fenner Brockway, a leader of the British I.L.P., hence Orwell's and his comrades' easy passage into the P.O.U.M.)[2]

Nor was international Communism very prompt in organizing the International Brigades. Doubtless, early in the summer when the Republic did urgently need help, especially aeroplanes, and when obvious sources of arms like France and even Britain were quickly blocked because of the non-interventionist policies these countries succumbed to, international Stalinism was reluctant to assist a government and country where anarchism and anti-Stalinism, not to say even Trotskyism, appeared strong and were

1. Tom Wintringham, *English Captain* (1939) pp. 17–18. Cf. Bob Cooney, Commissar of the British (57th) Battalion of the Brigades: 'The first British volunteers arrived in Spain in October 1936'. 'The British Volunteers', *Volunteer for Liberty*, II, No. 35 (Barcelona, 7 November 1938), p. 8.
2. Leon Trotsky, *The Spanish Revolution (1931–39)* (New York, 1973), p. 209.

widely condoned. So at first many foreign volunteers simply went on their own initiative and under their own steam to aid the Republic, including, most notably, André Malraux who organized the buying of arms, the running of guns, and a small air-force. Some of the early volunteers simply happened to be in Barcelona for the Workers' Olympiad. Set up as a rival to the Munich Olympics, the Barcelona People's Olympiad was planned for 19–26 July, and it was rumoured, certainly in the *Daily Worker* (see the issue of 23 July 1936, p. 6), that the uprising had been timed to frustrate this international anti-Fascist protest. The first English volunteer to be killed was the London Communist Felicia Browne, a painter who had been working on the Costa Brava and had gone to Barcelona for the Games. She had joined in the street fighting in which the Generals' coup had been successfully resisted in the city, and she carried on fighting – to be shot dead in Aragón on 25 August. The very first English volunteers were a couple of East End tailors, Sam Masters and Nat Cohen, both Communists, who were on a cycling holiday in France at the time of the revolt and carried on to do their bit in Barcelona.

The case of John Cornford sets the myth of the International Brigade most instructively in focus. When the Generals revolted he had just graduated with a First in History at Trinity College, Cambridge, and had been awarded a research studentship. He and his latest girlfriend Margot Heinemann had been planning anyway to go to France in August, when he 'suddenly' decided to go on ahead and look in on the Civil War. Within three days of getting to Barcelona on 8 August he was being driven to the front with the Austrian journalist Franz Borkenau. Cornford was a committed Communist activist, already at twenty an experienced and even important member of the British Party, but whether out of ideological naivety or, more likely, because he was still just a young and romantic revolutionary, he promptly joined the wild, ragged, but exhilarating P.O.U.M. column led by the Austrian miner Grossi. Borkenau returned to Barcelona; Cornford stayed to fight.[1] What's more, when Cornford returned

1. Franz Borkenau, *The Spanish Cockpit* (1937; Ann Arbor paperback 1963), pp. 93ff.

briefly to England in the middle of September (he'd been wounded and was tired out), it was with the stated intention of returning to the same P.O.U.M. militia, with others who would provide an exemplary stiffening in the ranks. He wrote to his college tutor on 4 October 1936, to resign his scholarships 'as by the time this reaches you I shall already be on the way to rejoin the unit of the Anti-Fascist Militia with which I have been fighting this summer'.[1] Even for a Communist Party insider, then, the kind of innocence about the seamless unity of the anti-Fascist cause that at first possessed Orwell was a possibility. It does appear strange, though, that when he left London on 5 October Cornford had been told nothing of the International Brigades, already, since Maurice Thorez's visit to Moscow on 22 September, forming. Cornford had seen Harry Pollitt before he departed: it's not at all inconceivable that Pollitt was suspicious enough of this P.O.U.M. militiaman not to have told him what was already afoot.[2] In Paris, of course, Cornford and his chums threw in their lot with the new Brigades. Later, however, when the Communist view of the P.O.U.M. as a party, 'objectively' viewed, of Fascist traitors, had hardened and any contribution by volunteers outside the International Brigades was being assiduously minimized, Tom Wintringham spent a deal of time in his *English Captain* (1939) explaining away Cornford's apparent aberration in not joining the United Socialist Party (the P.S.U.C.) militia instead of that column of the wicked P.O.U.M.:

The policy of this party, which called itself the Workers' Party of Marxist Unity, was not so clear in August 1936 as it later became. They claimed to be not only Communists but super-Communists, more 'red' than Moscow. They were known to include Trotskyists, but how far these strangely twisted dogmatists controlled P.O.U.M. could not have been clear to John Cornford. He could not know that the militia he joined would serve more to disorganize and disunite the Republic's forces than to strengthen them; would produce a stillborn abortion of a revolution, a rising in the contradictory names of libertarian anarchy and proletarian dictatorship against the Republic at one of the tensest hours of the Republic's struggle with Fascism.

1. *John Cornford: A Memoir*, ed. Pat Sloan (1938), pp. 181–2.
2. Stansky and Abrahams do not agree: *Journey to the Frontier*, p. 361.

37

All that story of treachery and sheer silliness and disaster was hidden in the future.

Nevertheless Cornford is blamed for not being vaticinatory enough about these 'political surrealists' who couldn't wait for the revolution. And most uncomplimentarily so. If he had enjoyed a realist's eye ('a soldier's eye or a worker's') Cornford wouldn't have joined these impatient adventurers:

But those who look with a poet's eye, or that of a desperate petty-bourgeois revolutionary, search Europe in the hope of a hopeless, a suicidal advance. They want to counter-attack before achieving such disarray of the opponent as makes counter-attack possible. The rank and file of the P.O.U.M. were often of this type. . . John Cornford was not in any way in sympathy with the P.O.U.M. except in this deep impatience.[1]

So perhaps it wasn't just because his best poems were yet unpublished that so little fuss was made over Cornford when he was killed. The Party rallied round later and got up a *Memoir*. But though Ralph Fox and Cornford had been killed in the same battle in late December 1936 it was the death of Fox that made all the running in the *Daily Worker* early in January 1937. Pages of tributes were published. But then he had worked on the paper and he could spot a 'Trotsky-Fascist' when he saw one. Precisely at the time Cornford was spiritedly collaborating with those Fascists in sheep's clothing, Fox had been dutifully informing *Daily Worker* readers that 'Trotsky was No Great General' (*Daily Worker*, 28 August 1936, p. 3: apparently Stalin did all the work at the fronts while Trotsky skulked cowardly in his train) and that 'He was always a Base Double-Crosser' (*Daily Worker*, 1 September, p. 3). When Cornford's death was eventually noticed by the paper (3 February 1937) he was described as 'typical of the finest of the intellectuals'. There was no mention of any writing. Ten days later the wounding of Wilfred Macartney was heralded under the banner 'Famous Author Wounded'.[2]

Still, Wintringham did, after a fashion, try whitewashing

1. Tom Wintringham, *English Captain* (1939), pp. 45–7.
2. The official biography of Harry Pollitt by John Mahon (*Harry Pollitt: A Biography*, 1976) makes mention of Ralph Fox, but not of Cornford, nor even of Caudwell.

Cornford. He claims that in Barcelona Cornford did attempt to enlist in the P.S.U.C. militia but was baulked by precision Germans who wouldn't accept his anti-Fascist standing without some documentation and, alas, Cornford hadn't brought his Party card out from England with him. So the 'restless', 'impatient' poetic temperament 'flung off to join a rival party's militia'. An odd concoction of a story, this. Apparently Cornford made no efforts to enlist in anything at all in Barcelona, but when, a few days later, he found some appealing anti-Fascist fighters who just happened to be P.O.U.M. he joined them, and – as he wrote to Margot Heinemann – 'on the strength of my Party card'.[1] So much for his having forgotten to take it to Spain. But evidently the notion that foreign volunteers, even Communist Party members, might be quite confusedly naïve romantics rather than completely clear-sighted people, in Spain for only the most politically pure and publishable motives, had vigorously to be quenched.

And the presence in Spain of many volunteers did have fairly muddy motivations. Miles Tomalin has freely confessed that his 'personal life was in flux, and this seemed the best thing to do with it' (he left a five-year-old son behind).[2] No less confiding, Julian Bell included among possible reasons he might have for going to Spain 'the prestige one would gain in literature and – even more – left politics'.[3] In a bit of his memoir of his son that the editor of *John Cornford: A Memoir* chose not to publish, Professor Cornford claimed that in Spain John found an escape from 'personal responsibilities': by that he presumably meant his tangled relationships – ex-mistress, illegitimate child, new girlfriend.[4] When, in T. C. Worsley's *Fellow Travellers*, Martin Murray (Stephen Spender) ditches his boyfriend Harry Watson (the ex-guardsman T. A. R. Hyndman who appears in *World*

1. Stansky and Abrahams, *Journey to the Frontier*, pp. 317–19. See below, p. 118.

2. 'Memories of the Spanish War', *New Statesman* (31 October 1975), p. 542. See his poems, 'After Brunete' and 'Nicholas', below, pp. 364–7.

3. Letter to Quentin Bell, 24 December 1936. *Julian Bell: Essays, Poems and Letters*, ed. Quentin Bell (1938), pp. 175–6.

4. The father's memoir is quoted in Stansky and Abrahams, *Journey to the Frontier*, p. 330.

Within World as Jimmy Younger) to get engaged to a girl, the peeved Harry joins Gavin Blair Summers (Giles Romilly) in enlisting. And what unstated domestic rifts lay behind Harry Stratton's decision to sneak off to volunteer in London on the pretext of looking for a job in Southampton, leaving his pregnant wife in Swansea (thrown onto the unreliable mercies of Charlotte Haldane's fund for volunteers' dependents)?[1]

As for murky promptings, the middle-class fellow-traveller was in any case a guilty man. 'I was driven on,' Spender later wrote in *The God that Failed*, 'by a sense of social and personal guilt which made me feel firstly that I must take sides, secondly that I could purge myself of an abnormal individuality by co-operating with the workers' movement.' And Spain amply intensified the guilt. Far away from that particular battle and editing *New Writing* in Vienna, John Lehmann says that the guilt he felt at not being in Spain, especially 'as the fortunes of the long-drawn-out war moved gradually against the Republicans, as news came of the deaths of Ralph Fox, and Julian, and John Cornford', the guilt burnt in 'ever-smouldering fires'.[2] Jack Lindsay 'suffered extremely from a bad conscience at not being in the International Brigade'.[3] Cecil Day Lewis 'believed I ought to volunteer for it, but I lacked the courage to do so'.[4]

'[G]uilt-feelings among those who stayed at home,' T. C. Worsley wrote in 1939, 'were pretty widespread among the vocal democrats at the end of 1936.'[5] In *The Fellow Travellers* he expanded the point: 'I think, in the minds of all those of us who were single and free, there was the nagging question – should we not, instead of merely demonstrating, join the International Brigade and fight.' And Spender at least was to suggest in 1939 that for poets to join the International Brigade indicated desperation, a fundamentally alienated state, an unhappy incapacity to accept their own lives and the existing relationship between their

1. Harry Stratton's Diary: copy in International Brigade Archive, Marx Memorial Library.
2. Lehmann, *The Whispering Gallery*, p. 284.
3. Jack Lindsay, *Fanfrolico and After* (1962), p. 264.
4. Quoted by Hugh Ford, *A Poet's War: British Poets and the Spanish Civil War* (Phil., 1965), p. 129.
5. T. C. Worsley, *Behind the Battle* (1939), p. 12.

art and their society: how else could one 'renounce everything, and try to merge oneself in an alien and violent environment'?[1] 'If you read Cornford's Memoir,' he wrote to Day Lewis (26 November 1938),

you will find that he tended to become less and less interested in poetry, and that he was certainly in a position in which he was willing to abandon poetry altogether for a revolutionary action. Doesn't it strike you that he'd been forced out of the position in which it was possible for him to create, into a position which was a complete denial of it, into a position indeed in which he denied his own creative self and attacked violently all the poets who had 'collapsed into subjectivism' – so that finally, in despair, he was driven into the life of action in which he was killed.[2]

But murkily guilty and alienated or not, the support of writers was diligently sought out by the Communist Party. Cecil Day Lewis appealed in the *Daily Worker* (25 August 1936, p. 3) 'particularly to writers – to do all in their power to counteract the contemptible campaign of innuendo, falsehood and atrocity-mongering which is being carried on against the Spanish Government by certain sections of our Press. Neutrality is not enough.' And martyred writers gave the cause especial credit. The story of Harry Pollitt advising Spender that the best contribution he could make to the Party would be 'to go and get killed, comrade, we need a Byron in the movement', may be apocryphal,[3] and A. L. Rowse's insinuation that Ralph Fox's death was deliberately sought ('He was ordered to Spain by the Party, which wanted martyrs for the cause') may be unjust.[4] Nevertheless, when Fox had been killed Pollitt did speedily claim for him Byronic status in thus dying for liberty in a foreign

1. 'Poetry and Politics', *Spectator* (28 July 1939), pp. 154–6.
2. Letter exhibited in *Young Writers of the Thirties*, National Portrait Gallery, London (25 June–7 November 1976).
3. Thomas, *The Spanish Civil War*, p. 436, n. 3.
4. A. L. Rowse, *A Cornishman at Oxford* (1965), p. 57. Cf.: 'In Harry Pollitt's opinion, I was told . . ., I was an ordinary, decent, working class chap who had got into the hands of the kind of intellectuals the party could do without.' T. A. R. Hyndman in *The Distant Drum, Reflections on The Spanish Civil War*, ed. Philip Toynbee (1976), p. 128.

cause.[1] Fox was joining, chipped in John Strachey (*Daily Worker*, 5 January 1937, p. 1), 'the great tradition of English writers who have fought and died for the ideas of which they had written'. And when Kitty Wintringham went to Pollitt to try and get her husband, twice wounded and a typhoid victim, sent home, Pollitt is alleged to have replied: 'Tell him to get out of Barcelona, go up to the front line, get himself killed and give us a headline.'[2]

Dead or alive, but especially dead, the writers and artists on its side were exultantly laid claim to by the *Daily Worker*. The adjectives 'great' and 'famous' got quickly diluted by over-use. The most tenuous connection with literature was apparently worth exploiting. Leslie Maugham of Kettering, killed on 14 January 1938, is picked out as Somerset Maugham's 'great-nephew' (8 February 1938, p. 2). One Emmanuel Julius, reporter and ex-medical student, killed in action, is described as a poet – 'some . . . published' (21 October 1936, p. 1). And the *Worker* even had the gall to describe Christopher St John Sprigg after he had been killed as 'the well-known author' (14 April 1937, p. 5): so well known had he been in the Party's King Street headquarters that when his brother had pleaded his literary importance as grounds for his recall from the battle-front, Communist officialdom had been fatally tardy in being convinced.

To be fair, the *Daily Worker* did make much of non-writing stars who went to Spain, such as Clem Beckett the Speedway champ (his death was reported with Sprigg's), but that a special value was placed on writers is shown by the fuss made over Spender. 'Spender for Spain' crowed the *Worker*'s front page, 19 February 1937: 'Stephen Spender, the British poet and author of *Forward from Liberalism*, is leaving England for Spain to broadcast regularly from the Valencia radio station which is engaged in combating propaganda sent out from the Spanish rebel wireless stations, and is giving a true account of conditions in Spain. He has joined the Communist Party of Great Britain

1. In *Ralph Fox: A Writer in Arms*, ed. John Lehmann, T. A. Jackson, C. Day Lewis (1937), p. 6.
2. Quoted by Weintraub, *The Last Great Cause*, p. 43.

. . .' And alongside Spender's inside page article 'I Join the Communist Party' is an editorial box affirming that 'The Communist Party warmly welcomes Comrade Spender to its ranks as a leading representative of the growing army of all thinking people, writers, artists and intellectuals who are taking their stand with the working class in the issues of our epoch . . .' Netting Spender was such a coup that Pollitt had not only allowed in the poet despite his still having reservations, but was willing to publicize this unwholeheartedness; for the editorial comment continued '. . . and [the Party] is confident that in life and work with our Party, Comrade Spender will reach complete unity with the outlook of Communism'.

That the Spanish Fascists were barbarians was proved by their having had Lorca murdered. Spanish Fascism was clearly no better than the Nazi kind which had had books burned and caused the intellectual and cultural élite of Germany to flee for its life. For its part the Republic diligently advertised its extensive campaign to eradicate illiteracy and spread reading materials. Claud Cockburn, using his alias of Frank Pitcairn, fostered this on the whole accurate picture with an impossibly exaggerated scenario: 'We stood in a front-line post among the German bombs, and saw a young Communist poet, with books under one arm and a bag of bullets under the other, distributing books and pamphlets to men hungry for knowledge, who read them aloud to one another between the shell fire and the air raids.'[1] The Republic's careful safeguarding of national art treasures, the Goyas and El Grecos and Velasquezes, was also carefully publicized: photographs of rescued works of art were published as 'documents which prove the spirit in which we are fighting this war; they, our enemies, burn and destroy; we rescue and save.'[2] So publicity was given to any writer or artist who would stand up for the Republic: each one of them helped emphasize the Republic's cultural concern and conservatism and, by contrast, the Nationalists' barbarity. '"Fascism is Death to Art": Statement by Epstein'; 'Famous Artists [Vanessa Bell, Eric Gill, Paul Nash, Henry Moore, Ben Nicholson, Rex Whistler] Aid

1. Frank Pitcairn, *Reporter in Spain* (1936), p. 85.
2. *Nine Rescued Works of Art* (booklet in International Brigade Archive).

Spain by Giving Works'; 'Famous Poet [W. H. Auden] to Drive
Ambulance in Spain'; 'Film Stars [Chaplin, Gable, Dietrich,
Bette Davis, Joan Crawford] all back Spanish Republic'; 'Why
Renn is fighting in Spain'; 'Charles Laughton to open Exhibi-
tion in Aid of Spain'; 'Artists [Picasso, Heinrich Mann, Pablo
Casals, Paul Robeson] to Speak for Spain'; 'With Paul Robeson
on the Spanish Front'; over 700 British writers, artists and
musicians petition the Prime Minister to restore to the Spanish
Government the right to buy defensive arms; and so on: thus
the *Daily Worker*'s headlined stories ran during the Civil War.
And sympathetic writers and artists were kept busily scurrying
about the country, speaking in Aid Spain rallies, helping raise
cash at Medical Aid for Spain assemblies, and appearing for
Spain on Left Book Club platforms to speak up against Britain
and France's Non-Intervention policy. And not only poets were
directly useful. Poetry itself also had a quite concrete contribution to make. At least the Mass Declamation had its propaganda
uses.

So-called Mass Declamations had come into prominence in
Britain early in 1936 when Unity Theatre's premises in Britannia
Street, London WC1, were opened on 19 February. On that
memorable Sunday night the programme included Ernst Toller's
poem 'Requiem', a commemoration of Karl Liebknecht and
Rosa Luxemburg, 'performed as a massed chant with stylized
movements'.[1] Group recitation, like this, of poetry written in the
cause of the proletariat was one of the characteristic (and more
successful) attempts by left-wing poets and sponsors of socialist
commitment in art to achieve forms of a 'non-bourgeois' kind.
It at once reflected the new and growingly anti-bourgeois consciousness of writers and, since it was a group activity, it made
a step at least towards the dearly wished-for 'mass' art of
Marxist literary theory. And Jack Lindsay, who had already
tried his hand at a Mass Declamation ('Who are the English?')
produced one for Spain, called 'On Guard for Spain!', at the
request of a Unity Theatre Group. 'The method,' Jack Lindsay
told me in a letter,

1. See letter from Bram Bootman (who was one of the chanters on the
night), *Listener* (12 April 1973), p. 483.

was to break up the poem into a number of voices, allotting suitable passages for choric effects. The effect of a multiple set of individual voices, now and then brought together in a collective outburst, was given a dramatic effect by continual movement among the group – again a movement of individuals which at moment[s] came together in a collective pattern. Though not directly dance, yet the effect of grace and purpose had its dance-quality, and was the work of a girl who had given much thought to dance mime. The result was a distinctive type of mass-declamation which I think I am correct in saying was quite different from the forms developed by Brecht in the early thirties of Germany, and in the U.S.A. during the New Deal.

Jack Lindsay's Declamation now seems un-urgently lengthy and even turgid, but at the time its impact was wide and powerful. 'It was,' its author says in *Fanfrolico*,

continually done all over England by Unity Theatre or groups connected with the Left Book Club. It was performed in Trafalgar Square and at countless rallies; the typical meeting in support of the Spanish Republic consisted of speeches by Victor Gollancz, Harry Pollitt, and the Duchess of Atholl, with a performance of *On Guard*. Harry once felt impelled to write to me after such a meeting that he had never in all his life seen an audience so powerfully affected as by the declamation.

The intellectuals, reports Lindsay, didn't altogether approve the poem's emotional effect on audiences (Spender, for one, took exception to it), and the *Daily Worker* was apparently averse to mentioning Lindsay's name in reports of rallies featuring 'On Guard' (although he was a convinced socialist he jibbed at joining the Communist Party lest he be 'hurried' into joining 'the many activities of the day', including the International Brigade). But memories of the poem held hard. In an article 'On Mass Declamations' in *Our Time*, 11, No. 11 (May 1943), R. Vernon Beste recalls one revivalistic occasion of its reciting:

'Badajoz!!'
'The word was bitten off short like the involuntary cry caused by an unexpected lash of a whip; it expressed hurt surprise and anger, anger so quick that it scarcely preceded the action it stimulated.
A long pause followed. The audience looked steadily at the little

cluster of dungaree-clad figures on the platform, unconscious of its tautened muscles and stertorous breath.

'Malaga!!'

It was a deep growl of fury rather than a name, not just a place in Southern Spain, but a word to give vengeance a sharper meaning, a banner rallying the defenceless and shaming the cynical.

Another pause.

'Teruel.'

This time it was a woman's voice, full and vibrant speaking slowly with a falling cadence that was half-sigh, half-sob.

Infinitely slowly the drawn-out vowels went beating down the smoke-filled hall gripping every stomach with sorrow, the awful sorrow that comes with the first realization of the loss, irretrievable and irreplaceable, that is death.

Even now, all this time after first hearing Jack Lindsay's 'On Guard for Spain', the impression is still extraordinarily vivid. I recall that when Isabel Brown [the activist] came on to the platform to make the appeal three minutes afterwards there was hardly need for her to speak – one was ashamed of being able to give no more than money . . .

I not only knew *intellectually* that the Spanish People's fight was my fight, but for the first time *felt* that it was.

Place-names echo through the version of 'On Guard!' published in *Left Review*, but no passage resembles Beste's description. He's closer, in fact, to the 'adagio passage' added by Lindsay 'at the request of the Unity producer so that there would be a period of rest, a slow dirge, as contrast with the movement of the rest of the declamation'. This passage has not been published before, but is now, through the kindness of Jack Lindsay, published for the first time in this anthology.[1]

Victor Gollancz, the Duchess of Atholl, Isabel Brown, Unity Theatre, a poem: as Claud Cockburn put it, describing the strings of celebrities who put in, and were encouraged to put in, an appearance close to, if not always actually on the battlefields of Spain, 'everyone turned up'. If for no other reason this was, in another of Cockburn's memorable phrases, a photogenic war.

Everyone was very happy to have Mr Hemingway there, partly because he was obviously a fine man to have around when there was war and

1. Information about it comes in a note, written for me, by Jack Lindsay.

trouble, and partly because to have so famous an author there, writing on behalf of the Republic, made people feel less alone in the world – in a sense, which was no fault of Mr Hemingway, it helped to foster the illusion that sooner or later the 'world conscience' would be aroused, 'the common people' in Britain and France would force their Governments to end non-intervention, and the war would be won.[1]

And Benny Goodman played his clarinet at a Spain benefit, and Shirley Temple did her bit,[2] and Professor J. B. S. Haldane would drop in on the trenches during university vacations (once he arrived during a stand-to and 'he stood to with us, revolver at the ready'[3]), and, in July 1937, the Second Congress of the International Association of Writers met in Valencia and Madrid, and was feted there and in Barcelona (where Pablo Casals gave a concert in its honour) and at points in between. The Congress was organized from Paris by Pablo Neruda who had been the Chilean Consul in Madrid. Eighty writers from twenty-six countries (or at least over sixty delegates, according to which reporter you read) turned up, including Neruda, Malraux, André Chamson, Julien Benda, Hemingway, Renn, Eric Weinert, Rafael Alberti, José Bergamin, Ilya Ehrenburg, Machado, Hernández, Spender, Alexei Tolstoy, Mikhail Koltzov, Altolaguirre, Octavio Paz, Sylvia Townsend Warner, Cockburn, Edgell Rickword, Valentine Ackland, and René Blech. They were there, of course, to demonstrate (in Edgell Rickword's words in his account in *Left Review*, 111 (August 1937), pp. 381–3) that 'the continued existence of human cultural activity is dependent upon the Spanish people's successful defence of their freedom and political independence'. They also focussed the touchingly misplaced faith of the Spanish people that 'los intelectuales' could help alleviate their plight. '*Viva la Republica! Viva los intelectuales!*' they cried, to the delight of Valentine Ackland: 'that extraordinary, unbelievable greeting from even

1. Claud Cockburn, *In Time of Trouble: An Autobiography* (1956), pp. 252–8.
2. *The Republic and the Civil War in Spain*, ed. Raymond Carr (1971), p. 125.
3. Harry Stratton's Diary, International Brigade Archive.

the smallest village, the most isolated group of peasants: 'Viva los intelectuales!'[1] Spender felt much less chuffed about what this salutation implied:

This circus of intellectuals, treated like princes or ministers, carried for hundreds of miles through beautiful scenery and war-torn towns, to the sound of cheering voices, amid broken hearts, riding in Rolls-Royces, banqueted, fêted, sung and danced to, photographed and drawn, had something grotesque about it. Occasionally we were confronted with some incident which seemed a reproach, a mockery, emerging with a sharp edge from the reality which had been so carefully disguised for us. One such occurred at a little town called Minglanilla on the single road connecting Valencia with three-quarters – surrounded Madrid. Here we were as usual banqueted, eating *arroz a la valenciana*, followed by sweets, and washed down with excellent wine. The meal was (as nearly always happened) delayed. Waiting for it, we stood on the balcony of the town hall while the children of Minglanilla danced and sang to us in the brilliant sunlight of the square below. Suddenly Señora Paz, the beautiful wife of an equally beautiful young man, the poet Octavio Paz, burst into hysterical weeping. This was a moment of realization. There was another one, for me, after the meal. We had all walked out of the banqueting room into the square, when a peasant woman seized my arm and said imploringly: 'Sir, can you stop the *pájaros negros* machine-gunning our husbands as they work in the fields?' By the 'black birds' she meant the Fascist aeroplanes. Somehow the villagers of Minglanilla thought that the Congress of Intellectuals was a visitation which would save them. The same peasant woman invited the Chilean poet Pablo Neruda and myself to her house, where she showed us photographs of her two sons, both of them fighting at the front. Then she took from a cupboard some sausages and pressed these on us, insisting that we would most certainly need them on the journey. We accepted them in order not to offend her, for she was convinced that we would go hungry.[2]

The photogenic circus was clearly capable of backfiring. And backfire it went on doing, not least when some of the glamorous fighting writers got killed. It wasn't only growing suspicious

1. *Daily Worker* (21 July 1937), p. 7.
2. Stephen Spender, *World Within World* (Reader's Union edn, 1953), pp. 208–9.

about whether the Spaniards really wanted the volunteers there that started disillusioning Ewart Milne, but resentment at what came increasingly to look like the fruitless sacrifice of promising young writers like Charles Donnelly.[1] The Communist Party itself caught on quickly. After the deaths of Fox, Cornford and Caudwell it would have been relatively safe, says Jack Lindsay, for him to have joined the Party, for by then 'every barrier was put in the way of intellectuals sacrificing themselves'. And suddenly, around March 1937, the *Daily Worker* starts reporting the arrival back in Britain – for no publicly stated reasons – of key cadres. With the war not being won, the Party couldn't afford to go on being thinned of its best men.[2]

Supportive publicity from intellectuals, though, was still desirable and, what's more, copiously available. In June 1937 a group of writers, including Aragon, Heinrich Mann, Pablo Neruda and, from Britain, Auden and Spender, addressed – apparently at the instigation of Nancy Cunard – a letter from Paris 'To the Writers and Poets of England, Scotland, Ireland and Wales'. Its overtones, indeed its tones, were plainly Audenesque:

It is clear to many of us throughout the whole world that now, as certainly never before, we are determined or compelled, to take sides. The equivocal attitude, the Ivory Tower, the paradoxical, the ironic detachment, will no longer do.

We have seen murder and destruction by Fascism in Italy, in Germany – the organization there of social injustice and cultural death – and how revived, imperial Rome, abetted by international treachery, has conquered her place in the Abyssinian sun. The dark millions in the colonies are unavenged.

To-day, the struggle is in Spain. To-morrow it may be in other countries – our own. But there are some who, despite the murder of Durango and Guernica, the enduring agony of Madrid, of Bilbao, and Germany's shelling of Almeria, are still in doubt, or who aver

1. Statement in a letter to me. See 'Thinking of Artolas', below, pp. 177-9.
2. ' "We discussed very thoroughly. Pollitt advised us to think it over very seriously, to remember that we needed revolutionary intellectuals here and could not afford to send everyone to Spain." ' Evidence of one of the Oxford volunteers on the reception afforded young intellectuals after Fox's death: Mahon, *Harry Pollitt: A Biography*, p. 212.

that it is possible that Fascism may still be what it proclaims it is: 'the saviour of civilization'.

This is the question we are asking you:

Are you for, or against, the legal Government and the people of Republican Spain?

Are you for, or against, Franco and Fascism?

For it is impossible any longer to take no side.

Writers and Poets, we wish to print your answers. We wish the world to know what you, writers and poets, who are among the most sensitive instruments of a nation, feel.

The responses – or most of the responses – to this extremely Romantic appeal to what Pound called the 'antennae of the race' were published by *Left Review* in a 6d. pamphlet entitled *Authors Take Sides on the Spanish War* (an American go at the same sort of poll was published in 1938 under the title *Writers Take Sides*). Less than completely honestly, some replies weren't printed. Like Joyce's (he simply phoned Nancy Cunard to say 'I am James Joyce. I have received your questionnaire') and, most notably, Orwell's. In correspondence with Spender, Orwell revealed just how unfriendly had been his riposte to 'that bloody rot which was afterwards published in book form (called *Authors Take Sides*) ... that damned rubbish of signing manifestos to say how wicked it all is'. He'd 'sent back a very angry reply' in which he'd mentioned Spender 'uncomplimentarily', in the vein of '"parlour Bolsheviks such as Auden & Spender"'.[1]

Presumably this reply was omitted because it too spoilingly upset the otherwise fairly predictable groupings. Sixteen authors chose to be neutral (though whoever edited their replies only allowed them to be 'Neutral?'). Among them, T. S. Eliot was 'naturally sympathetic', but still felt 'convinced that it is best that at least a few men of letters should remain isolated, and take no part in these collective activities'. Less sympathetically neutral were Ezra Pound ('Questionnaire an escape mechanism for young fools who are too cowardly to think; too lazy to investigate the nature of money, its mode of issue, the control of such issue by the Banque de France and the stank of England.

1. (April 1938.) *The Collected Essays, Journalism and Letters of George Orwell*, ed. Sonia Orwell and Ian Angus (Penguin, 1970), I. pp. 345–8.

You are all had. Spain is an emotional luxury to a gang of sap-headed dilettantes') and Vita Sackville-West ('I hate these sub-terranean forms of propaganda'). Only five replies 'Against the Government' were published, again predictable ones. Edmund Blunden thought it was 'necessary that somebody like Franco should arise – and although England may not profit by his victory I think Spain will. The ideas of Germany, Italy, etc., in your document do not square with those I have formed *upon the whole* of the recent history of those countries.' And Evelyn Waugh insisted crabbedly: 'If I were a Spaniard I should be fighting for General Franco. As an Englishman I am not in the predica-ment of choosing between two evils. I am not a Fascist nor shall I become one unless it were the only alternative to Marxism. It is mischievous to suggest that such a choice is imminent.'

On the other side, however, 127 authors failed to interpret things Waugh's way, and were prepared to make a pro-Govern-ment choice. The roster of their names is simply a star-studded reminder of much that was good in the immediate past, and most that was good or promising in the present, of British thought and letters. It included Lascelles Abercrombie, Valentine Ackland, Mulk Raj Anand, Auden, George Barker, Beckett, Arthur Calder-Marshall, Cyril Connolly, A. E. Coppard, Aleister Crowley, Nancy Cunard, Day Lewis, Havelock Ellis, Ford Madox Ford, David Garnett, David Gascoyne, Victor Gollancz, Geoffrey Grigson, James Hanley, Tom Harrisson, Laurence Housman, Brian Howard, Aldous Huxley, Storm Jameson, C. E. M. Joad, Arthur Koestler, H. J. Laski, John Lehmann, Rosamund Lehmann, Jack Lindsay, Eric Linklater, F. L. Lucas, Rose Macaulay, Hugh MacDiarmid, MacNeice, Charles Madge, Naomi Mitchison, Ivor Montagu, Raymond Mortimer, John Middleton Murry, Sean O'Casey, V. S. Pritchett, Herbert Read, Edgell Rickword, T. S. Moore, Randall Swingler, Sylvia Town-send Warner, Helen Waddell, Rex Warner, Rebecca West, Clough Williams-Ellis, Leonard Woolf.

Samuel Beckett's response, '¡UPTHEREPUBLIC!', was perhaps the nicest; it was certainly the most succinct. Among the rest it's noticeable that replying affirmatively was taken to be completely natural by very many of the group. 'Of course,' replied Victor Gollancz, Aldous Huxley, John Lehmann and Sean O'Casey. 'No question,' replied Naomi Mitchison. And comparing the three groups, one is bound to agree with Ivor Montagu's prescient summary: 'Fox-hunters, people who shoot down birds, dukes, bankers, like Franco. Cocktail parties are given for him. If there were no other good reason – with the Republic you find better company.'

The Right wasn't, of course, completely represented by the questionnaire's little bunch (which also embraced Arthur Machen, Major Geoffrey Moss and Eleanor Smith). But even if letters had been sent to, or replies received from, Roy Campbell, or Yeats, or the Count Potocki de Montalk, Montagu's point would still hold. Not only were right-wing opinions held by comparatively few writers at the time but the rightist fringe was an unpleasantly lunatic one. Even Yeats, who rejoiced to see any government, including a Fascist one, controlling Spain if that would upset the British Empire, and who gave the Irish Fascist Blue Shirts their marching song ('Three Songs to the Same Tune'), fell out with General Eoin O'Duffy, their leader. O'Duffy's Irish Christian Front, 700 volunteers who went to join the Moslem Moors in fighting for Franco's holy and Catholic Crusade, retired to Ireland pretty smartly (they only lasted in Spain from November 1936 to May 1937).[1] More nastily pretentious and still less effective militarily, Roy Campbell, English verse's most bullying blusterer, was in words at least pugnaciously anti-Red and, a Catholic convert, anxious to pass himself off as a 'Catholic soldier of Spain'. His actual soldierly exploits in the Civil War seem to have been somewhat restricted to functioning briefly as war-correspondent of the *Tablet*. In his violently ranting autobiography, *Light on a Dark Horse* (1951), he does boast about smashing the glasses, watch and dentures of a 'German communist', a Dr Meyerstein (the Communists, Campbell alleges, were setting up 'sex-clinics' in his part of Spain and interrupting Catholic church services), but that was before any real fighting began. But after the Second World War, in which he had insisted on seeing somewhat aged

1. See Ford, *A Poet's War*, pp. 148ff., and Weintraub, *The Last Great Cause*, pp. 153ff.

service, his boldness in the anti-Red struggle continued on about the same plane as when he was putting the boot into the Jewish doctor's false teeth and specs: he brought himself to strike another actual physical blow against the Left, or at least against the erstwhile Left, by punching Stephen Spender at a poetry reading. Lover of weak opponents that he clearly was, he was even ready (in a footnote to *Flowering Rifle* (1939)) to countenance the bullet the Nationalists put in the back of the neck of 'the cowardly Lorca': 'when the Nationalists entered Granada the unbelievable babooneries perpetrated by the Reds made them trigger-happy as they rounded up and shot all corrupters of children, known perverts and sexual cranks. A normal reaction . . .' 'The Sodomites are on your side,/The cowards and the cranks', he had jeered in one of the poems ('Hard lines, Azana!') that he contributed to Mosley's Fascist journal the *British Union Quarterly* (I, No. 1 (January–April 1937), p. 104).

But Campbell's fantasy of himself as a Crusader didn't depend on realities. And no wish-fulfilling leftist fantasist ever got close to rivalling Campbell's bizarre claims to prophetic powers. No reader of Campbell is convinced by his story of foreseeing the surrender of the International Brigaders at San Mateo in a vision, still less by the blurry lines that he repeatedly claims as a dedication of 'his prisoners to his wife in a poem printed before the war!'[1]

A characteristically careless bout of posturings (the poet imagines himself firing a machine-gun at the Reds – from the saddle of a horse!), Campbell's poem 'The Singer' found an apt home in Potocki's *Right Review*. Geoffrey Potocki de Montalk (the 'Apostate Humanitarian' of Edgell Rickword's poem to him published in *Twittingpan* (1931)), a claimant to the Polish throne and astrologer, who had been imprisoned for publishing 'pornography' and who was jailed again in the Second World War for disclosing uncomfortable Polish claims about what happened in the Katyn Forest, added overt anti-Semitism to his Francoism. 'Communism is Jewish Fascism,' his scruffily hand-printed paper declared in its 'Eclipse 1937' number. 'The Japanese and Spanish Wars against international Yiddish money

1. See footnotes to Part One of *Flowering Rifle*, below, pp. 427, 433 and 435.

tyranny are getting on very nicely, thank you,' he noted in September 1937. He published several poems by Campbell, and produced that decided rarity, a laudatory review of *Flowering Rifle*. Better than Pope's, 'more like Byron' in their 'verve and readability', 'Heroic couplets such as these can be written only by a Hero'. Campbell's 'immense tirade' makes him England's 'greatest poet'.[1]

With chums like Potocki Campbell scarcely needed hostile reviews like Spender's in the *New Statesman*, nor Hugh Mac-Diarmid's lengthy but marvellously kept-up heaping of ironic and scornful abuse (in *The Battle Continues*) – in something not altogether dissimilar to (though it's altogether clearer and more controlled than) Campbell's own bluff-tough mode:

Campbell boasts he is the first English poet who has dared to give
Bleary old democracy a sock in the jaw.
He might as well brag of pinching errand money from a child
Or filching the coppers from a blind man's tin with his monkey paw.[2]

Nor is it difficult, looking at Campbell's and Potocki's bombastic and curious offerings, to become still more warmly appreciative of the liberal-left solidarity of most of the intellectuals.

There certainly was considerable consistency about the reasons for supporting the Republic that they gave in response to Nancy Cunard's poll. It was necessary to stand up to barbarity in Spain before it encroached any closer. Fascism's domino-expansion had already claimed for it Italy and Germany, and was now bidding high for Spain – where might it next turn? So the Republic's defence was the defence of all civilized decency – what Orwell meant when he insisted (while calling John Sommerfield's *Volunteer in Spain* (1937) 'a piece of sentimental tripe') that the International Brigades, of which Sommerfield was a member, were 'in some sense fighting for all of us – a thin line of suffering and often ill-armed human beings standing between barbarism and at least comparative decency'.[3] And those questioned felt, as writers, specially implicated since

1. *Right Review* (June 1939).
2. MacDiarmid, *The Battle Continues*, p. 26.
3. (31 July 1937.) Penguin *Collected Essays*, I, p. 311.

Fascism had proved a direct and explicit threat to their craft and its practitioners: by killing Lorca the Spanish rebels had shown their hand, revealed inescapably their pedigree. 'As writer,' replied Arthur Calder Marshall, 'I oppose Fascism as the enemy of the arts.' In Fascist states, Cyril Connolly wrote in his reply,

Those who will not make soldiers are not required; those who are not required are eliminated. What we can learn from Spain is the order and extent of that elimination before the stultifying of the human race can proceed. Intellectuals come first, almost before women and children. It is impossible therefore to remain an intellectual and admire Fascism, for that is to admire the intellect's destruction . . .

Auden's answer summed up the generally accepted position:

I support the Valencia government in Spain because its defeat by the forces of International Fascism would be a major disaster for Europe. It would make a European war more probable; and the spread of Fascist Ideology and practice to countries as yet comparatively free from them, which would inevitably follow a Fascist victory in Spain, would create an atmosphere in which the creative artist and all who care for justice, liberty and culture would find it impossible to work or even exist.

'We believed,' Miles Tomalin – once described by the *Daily Worker* as 'the' poet of the British Battalion[1] – has written, 'we were enrolling to defend not only democracy but world peace and the basic human decencies . . . We were indeed fighting for these things.'[2]

Spender's Introduction to the *Poems for Spain* anthology indicates just how much this noble cause was felt to mean for poetry. In the first place, Spain has been a stimulant to poetry partly because the war has vitally to do with the survival of poetry:

The fact that these poems should have been written at all has a literary significance parallel to the existence of the International Brigade. For some of these poems, and many more which we have not been able to publish, were written by men for whom poetry scarcely existed before the Spanish War. Some of these writers, first awakened

1. *Daily Worker*, 16 July 1938, Supplement, p. 2.
2. Miles Tomalin, 'Memories of the Spanish War', *New Statesman* (31 October 1975), p. 541.

to poetry by Spain, died before they had the opportunity to cultivate their talent.

Poets and poetry have played a considerable part in the Spanish War, because to many people the struggle of the Republicans has seemed a struggle for the conditions without which the writing and reading of poetry are almost impossible in modern society. . .

No doubt Spender was thinking of what D. Trevor heralded as the revival of Spanish poetry, particularly in the form of the 'romancero', the very popular, loose-limbed Spanish medium formally adaptable to carry simple rhetorical exhortations and celebrations, hundreds of which were composed for recitation in the Republican cause (and many examples of which appeared in translation during the Civil War, not just in Spender's anthology). 'Poetry is now being poured out, poetry of a quantity and quality that justifies the term "renaissance".'[1] The war came as an immense stimulus to men like Miguel Hernández, an illiterate shepherd (according to Spender) or goatherd (according to Lehmann), who was taught to read and write by a priest and joined the Republican army when war broke out. 'Poetry then seemed suddenly to pour out of him as if a rock had been struck and a spring leapt out of it.'[2] And, like Lehmann, Spender too was probably thinking of the British volunteers from whose dry rocks poetry had also been struck. And not just of men like Charles Donnelly, whose distinction as poet rests entirely on his few lines about the war, or like Cornford, whose poetically arid period of political activism was transformed into a fine creativity by the fighting, but of men like Tom Wintringham whose poetry writing enjoyed a noticeable blossoming in this war. Or T. A. R. Hyndman, Spender's ex-boyfriend, and John Lepper, who appear to have produced only the single poem each that appeared in Spender's collection.[3] Or the author of the now famous couple of verses about 'Eyes', found scribbled on a leaf of some unknown International Brigader's notebook:

1. D. Trevor, 'Poets of the Spanish War', *Left Review*, III, No. 8 (September 1937), pp. 455–60.

2. Spender, *World Within World*, p. 208; Lehmann, The *Whispering Gallery*, p. 280.

3. Hyndman recalls John Lepper, and both poems, in his piece in *The Distant Drum: Reflections on the Spanish Civil War*, pp. 121–30.

Eyes of men running, falling, screaming
Eyes of men shouting, sweating, bleeding
The eyes of the fearful, those of the sad
The eyes of exhaustion, and those of the mad.

Eyes of men thinking, hoping, waiting
Eyes of men loving, cursing, hating
The eyes of the wounded sodden in red
The eyes of the dying and those of the dead.

Secondly, Spender finds in Spain a resolution of the guilt middle-class left-wing poets had felt about the frivolity and irrelevance of indulging in poetry while the workers stood in dole-queues and a revolution beckoned. For in the Republic poetry seemed to matter to the ordinary people: little magazines flourished, crowds of workers and soldiers thronged to hear poets like Alberti declaiming their romanceros. Suddenly, amidst all this manifest popular care for culture – and poetry was just one factor, to be set beside the literacy drive, and the safeguarding of the Grecos – the 'impossible' dream of a truly popular culture looked that much nearer. It's easy to exaggerate poetry's role in Spain, just as it's easy to inflate the importance of poetry to the Brigades' wall-papers and their magazine *Volunteer for Liberty*. David Guest's letter to Vivian de Sola Pinto probably gets the right perspective: 'one is always glad to read books here, poetry is especially popular. But . . .' And he went on to ask his friend to send him some binoculars and a prismatic compass.[1] Nevertheless it's possible to grant that there was some basis for Spender's enthusiasm:

In a world where poetry seems to have been abandoned, become the exalted medium of a few specialists, or the superstition of backward peoples, this awakening of a sense of the richness of a tomorrow *with* poetry, is as remarkable as the struggle for liberty itself, and is more remarkable than the actual achievement. The conditions for a great popular poetry are not yet obtained; what we note is the desire for such a poetry.

Thirdly, Spender finds in the poetry of the Spanish cause a viable alliance between politics and poetry: propaganda and

1. (21 June 1938). *David Guest: A Memoir*, ed. Carmel Haden Guest (1939), pp. 165-6.

poetry are coming together as appropriately as in Wordsworth's sonnet against Napoleon's invasion of Spain, 'Indignation of a High-Minded Spaniard'. The political subject, a focus of considerable attention in the critical writings of the early thirties and clearly a constant worry for committed poets, appears to have at last come properly into its own:

The ideas that inspire such poetry [as Wordsworth's sonnet] are fundamental, political and moral ideas of liberty, justice, freedom, etc. Usually policy, although it is continually invoking these ideas – which are only kept alive and separate from their prostitution to public interests by the poets – is entirely removed from them. But occasionally, in a revolution, a national resurgence, a war against an aggressor, there is a revival of the fundamental ideas and there is actually an identity of the ideas of public policy and poetry. This is the sense in which poetry is political; it is always concerned with the fundamental ideas, either because they are being realized in action, or, satirically, to show that they are totally removed from public policy. In the one case, we get a poem like Auden's *Spain* discovering the poetry in the Spanish Republican Cause; in the other, satire, like Edgell Rickword's on Non-Intervention, in which the fundamental ideas are turned against the politicians . . .

Certainly, at least in the first few weeks and months of the war, the sudden alliance between what left-wing intellectuals and writers had longed vainly for in England and the tangible hopes for poetry incited by the Spanish revolution and its defence of culture, produced a 'bliss was it in that dawn to be alive' kind of élan and exuberance. No wonder Wordsworth and Byron kept getting invoked. Catalonia in particular presented the spectacle of a country in revolution, a romantically gladdening new world that was bracingly welcome to the new arrival. On the night of 5 August 1936 Franz Borkenau wrote excitedly in his diary about his tour of Barcelona's Ramblas. It was like going into a new continent: 'before our eyes, in a flash, unfolded itself the revolution'. Proletarians, in civvy clothes, went about armed in an impressive display of the power of the factory workers. Bourgeois clothing – in particular, garb like hats – had disappeared. The hotels and shops had been expropriated; the churches had been gutted by fire; girls, some armed, walked around (emancipatedly for the times) publicly wearing trousers. And the city was filled with volunteers, many of them exiles from totalitarianism elsewhere in Europe, eager to spar with Fascism: 'All languages are spoken and there is an indescribable atmosphere of political enthusiasm, of enjoying the adventure of war, of relief that sordid years of emigration are passed, of absolute confidence in speedy success.'[1]

Philip Toynbee's diary received the same inspiriting news during the Christmas season of 1936:

The streets [of Barcelona] were full of these sweet, slovenly uniforms, and the buses and trams had U.G.T. and C.N.T. written on them – so had the trains. The place had a sort of carnival atmosphere, 'en pleine révolution'. It is a workers' city at war, fighting to keep its trams and cinemas and industries in the workers' hands. I felt so wildly excited and yet so wretched at being a 'student delegate'. A French anarchist militiaman asked us which front we were going to, and it was bloody to have to say, to Madrid, to look around ... Anyway it was intoxicating being in a city which is ours and seeing uniforms which one can delight in.[2]

The same excitement breaks through even the propagandistic tones and phrases of Ralph Fox's published letters ('The whole atmosphere is revolutionary, the very streets full of people, few signs of any bourgeoisie, and out of all this talking, gesticulating, variegated crowd, the energy of the workers will surely create something firm and stable in the end. The Party here grows daily ...').[3] And for once, in Valencia, even Auden failed to keep up his usual cool distance:

And everywhere there are the people. They are here in corduroy breeches with pistols on their hip, in uniform, in civilian suits and berets. They are here, sleeping in the hotels, eating in the restaurants, in the cafés drinking and having their shoes cleaned. They are here, driving fast cars on business, running the trains and the trams, keeping

1. Borkenau, *The Spanish Cockpit*, pp. 69ff.

2. Philip Toynbee, *Friends Apart: A Memoir of Esmond Romilly and Jasper Ridley in the Thirties* (1954), p. 89. Extensive extracts (with some variation on the previously published bits) appear in *The Distant Drum: Reflections on the Spanish Civil War*, pp. 144-61.

3. 10 December 1936. *Ralph Fox: A Writer in Arms*, p. 16.

the streets clean, doing all those things that the gentry cannot believe will be properly done unless they are there to keep an eye on them. This is the bloodthirsty and unshaven Anarchy of the bourgeois cartoon, the end of civilization from which Hitler has sworn to deliver Europe.

For a revolution is really taking place, not an odd shuffle or two in cabinet appointments. In the last six months these people have been learning what it is to inherit their own country.[1]

Orwell's impressions of Barcelona in late December 1936 form the most famous and powerful account in this enthusiastic vein:

It was the first time that I had ever been in a town where the working-class was in the saddle. Practically every building of any size had been seized by the workers and was draped with red flags or with the red and black flag of the Anarchists; every wall was scrawled with the hammer and sickle and with the initials of the revolutionary parties; almost every church had been gutted and its images burnt. Churches here and there were being systematically demolished by gangs of workmen. Every shop and café had an inscription saying that it had been collectivized; even the bootblacks had been collectivized and their boxes painted red and black. Waiters and shop-walkers looked you in the face and treated you as an equal. Servile and even ceremonial forms of speech had temporarily disappeared. Nobody said 'Señor' or 'Don' or even 'Usted'; everyone called everyone else 'Comrade' and 'Thou', and said 'Salud!' instead of 'Buenos días'. Tipping was forbidden by law ... There were no private motor-cars, they had all been commandeered, and all the trams and taxis and much of the other transport were painted red and black. The revolutionary posters were everywhere, flaming from the walls in clean reds and blues that made the few remaining advertisements look like daubs of mud. Down the Ramblas, the wide central artery of the town where crowds of people streamed constantly to and fro, the loudspeakers were bellowing revolutionary songs all day and far into the night. And it was the aspect of the crowds that was the queerest thing of all. In outward appearance it was a town in which the wealthy classes had practically ceased to exist. Except for a small number of women and foreigners there were no 'well-dressed' people at all. Practically everyone wore rough working-class clothes, or blue overalls, or some variant of the militia uniform. All this was queer and moving. There

1. 'Impressions of Valencia', *New Statesman* (30 January 1937), p. 159. See below, pp. 100–102.

was much in it that I did not understand, in some ways I did not even like it, but I recognized it immediately as a state of affairs worth fighting for.[1]

'Going over' to the workers' side, according to Cyril Connolly, was, for middle-class writers, not so much a matter of political parties. 'I think a writer "goes over" when he has a moment of conviction that his future is bound up with that of the working classes', and this means a change of life-style – not wearing a hat or a stiff collar, not being rude to taxi-drivers or waiters, not being polite to young men with umbrellas or bowlers or 'Mayfair men' moustaches, and tolerating no longer 'the repressive measures of his class'. And in that atmosphere of Spain so eagerly discovered by Orwell and his kind, heady with the absence of bowlers, stiff collars and tipping, it's unsurprising that writers should 'go over': 'it is clear that Spain has done a great deal for writers, since many have had that experience there, and have come back with their fear changed to love, isolation to union, and indifference to action.'[2] Of course those who, like Borkenau and Orwell, lived or stayed long enough saw the bourgeois re-emerge from their hidey-holes and hierarchy and élitism re-established. Already by early 1937 Borkenau was shocked at the disappearance of all signs of a 'workers' dictatorship' from Barcelona. With the ascendancy of the Communists and Socialists over the P.O.U.M. and Anarchists and the taming of the revolutionary impetus, hats and pretty clothes returned to the streets, just as army officers now wore separate uniforms from their men. The petty-bourgeoisie was now installed back in the saddle – or at least in the reopened fashionable restaurants and dance-halls. But there's little doubt that while the revolutionary atmosphere persisted – and it obviously lasted longer in some areas and in some militias – it provided the British middle-class, public-school educated author with what he'd long been seeking, and was crucially barred from finding in England: equal and open contact with the working classes.

In his long essay, 'Revolution in Writing', in *A Time to Dance*

1. George Orwell, *Homage to Catalonia* (1938), Ch. 1.
2. Cyril Connolly, *Enemies of Promise* (1938), pp. 136–7.

(N.Y., 1936), Cecil Day Lewis insisted – and it was characteristic of a middle-class author's concern in 1936 – that contact with the workers, though difficult to manage, was essential to strive for. It wasn't enough, though, to stand on the football terraces or walk in a demonstration of the unemployed: 'A living contact means the relationship between men living together, working together, sharing the same economic conditions and the same language. To be able to express the life of the workers – as opposed to merely exploiting it for literary purposes – the bourgeois writer must share it. He must work, eat and sleep with them.' But in England this was far easier said than done, as Orwell, classically, found out. For the insignia of class – names and accents in particular – marked the bourgeois, instantly singling him out as a mere slummer. And none of the stratagems so widely adopted made a truly effective mask. Ralph Winston Fox (born in 1900 and doubtless named after the Boer War celebrity), Humphrey Slater, Rupert John Cornford (conceived in the month of his mother's friend Rupert Brooke's death at Skyros), Cecil Day-Lewis, Christopher William Bradshaw-Isherwood, Christopher St John Sprigg, all changed or modified their names as part of their shedding of odious class attachments. As Ralph Fox, Hugh Slater, John Cornford (or Dai Barton, the pseudonym Cornford took up for his poem 'Unaware' in the *Listener*, 25 April 1934), Cecil Day Lewis, Christopher Isherwood and Christopher Caudwell they were attempting the same kind of disguising break as Eric Blair sought when he went among the down-and-outs as Edward or P. S. Burton and hit finally on the name Orwell. But changes of name, or of voice (Orwell is alleged by Empson to have affected a 'formalized Cockney';[1] Isherwood has himself attempting something similar in *Lions and Shadows*), or even changes of clothes (like Weston, i.e. Wystan Auden, in *Lions and Shadows*, with his clutch of hats, including 'a workman's cap, with a shiny black peak, which he bought while living in Berlin, and which had, in the end, to be burnt, because he was sick into it one evening in a cinema', or Orwell carefully dirtying-up an old suit of clothes before going

1. William Empson, 'Orwell at the B.B.C.', *The World of George Orwell*, ed. Miriam Gross (1971), pp. 94-9.

among the destitute[1]), were decidedly ineffective. The boatmen he met poked fun at Isherwood's pseudo-cockneyisms ('Well Marmaduke, and how's the trahsers'), and Orwell was compelled to acknowledge that he was irrefutably *different* from the coal-miners who befriended him. 'Whichever way you turn, this curse of class-difference confronts you like a wall of stone. Or rather it is not so much like a stone wall as the plate-glass pane of an aquarium; it is so easy to pretend that it isn't there, and so impossible to get through it.'[2] But the insignia of class that demarcated one so irrefutably at home meant little or nothing to the Spanish proletariat or to other foreign volunteers. Old Etonian tones didn't offend many ears amid the polyglot babble of the Internationals. And this is clearly why the Italian soldier with whom *Homage to Catalonia* begins (and who is celebrated in Orwell's poem 'The Italian soldier shook my hand') mattered so much to Orwell: he symbolized acceptance, in a common proletarian cause, of a kind Orwell had never found before. 'It was as though his spirit and mine had momentarily succeeded in bridging the gulf of language and tradition and meeting in utter intimacy. I hoped he liked me as well as I liked him.' Interestingly, Christopher Caudwell, whose career as a serious novelist writing under the name Caudwell – as opposed to the unawakened St John Sprigg of the aeronautical books and the pot-boiling thrillers – coincided with his becoming a Communist, appears to have been confident enough to go by his real name in Spain. There, it would seem, 'Christopher St John Sprigg' lacked the instant bourgeois recognition it carried in England. 'I have often seen it written,' writes Jason Gurney in his *Crusade in Spain* (1974), 'that he used the name of Caudwell while in Spain; in fact he was always known as "Spriggy" among his companions.'

And the combination of revolutionary fervour, the unsullied conviction of rightness in the cause, and the sense these writers clearly shared of having unshackled themselves, and of being now perhaps enabled to free their art, from the old bourgeois

1. See Peter Stansky and William Abrahams, *The Unknown Orwell* (1972), pp. 228-9.
2. George Orwell, *The Road to Wigan Pier* (1937), Ch. 10.

bonds produced, as far as English literature is concerned, some revolutionary art of a high order. At the very least, this is true of Cornford. Very commonly, though, one finds Cornford highly valued, on the one hand, for striking his personal note – in 'Heart of the Heartless World' or in the third, most personal, section of 'Full Moon at Tierz' – while being rebuked, on the other hand, for talking Communist history (he doesn't waive casual mention of the Seventh Congress of the Comintern, or Dimitrov, or Maurice Thorez) and resorting to what are dismissed as slogans ('Our fight's not won till the workers of all the world/Stand by our guard on Huesca's plain'). But the various elements of his poetry can't be separated out like this; what makes 'Full Moon' noteworthy is precisely its combination of autobiography and personal confessions of fearfulness with a dialectical consideration of the past, present and future and with political reflection and aspiration. The author writes and sounds, in fact, like a whole man, and each part of his poem works interdependently to bring home the force of the other sections and aspects. In Cornford at least there is an indication of the possible scope of the political subject in modern English poetry, and a revelation that there could be ample justification for it.[1]

Spain provided, then, a situation where the dreams and aspirations of the thirties generation of critics and writers could be tested. It was in fact a place where, willy-nilly, you were tested. Here, all the talk everybody had indulged in about resisting Fascism was suddenly translated into an inevitable and challenging reality. Christopher Caudwell wrote very perceptively in *Illusion and Reality* (published posthumously in 1937) of the Romantic revolutionaries, the fellow-travelling poets, that they enjoyed the idea of violence and that this imparted a 'Fascist tinge' to 'even the revolutionary element in their art'.[2] Auden's Airman in *The Orators* (1932) could be taken, as Spender very revealingly did take him, as being 'in much the same position as the contemporary writer who hates the social system under

1. For a fine, admiring discussion see Roy Fuller, 'Poetic Memories of the Thirties', in *Professors and Gods* (1973), pp. 144–5.
2. Christopher Caudwell, *Illusion and Reality: A Study of the Sources of Poetry* (new edn, 1946), p. 284.

which he exists, and lives, and writes in a dream of violence on behalf of himself and his friends'.[1] And the characteristic poetic diction of the early thirties, with its hankering for frontiers and combat and struggle and for what Isherwood has labelled the 'test', was exactly a 'dream of violence' that Auden, 'the boy bushranger' with the 'cruel handshake' (as Dylan Thomas and Herbert Read described him in the Auden Double Number of *New Verse*, November, 1937), persuaded all his chums to condone and join in. A morally dubious world of arbitrary brutalities that the perpetrators are also trying to pass off as jokes, it appealed particularly to thuggish revolutionary schoolboys like Esmond Romilly and Philip Toynbee, who in 1934 had kitted themselves with knuckle-dusters at an ironmongers in Drury Lane before proceeding to the Mosley Rally at Olympia.[2] Toynbee was beaten up by Fascist thugs, but Romilly had his own unscrupled beating-up to do: 'Then, during the fighting outside the building, I recognized a boy I had known slightly at Wellington. He was wearing a black shirt, and we came almost opposite each other. Everyone around me was fighting, so as he came towards me, I punched hard with my fist into his face. Recalling the incident half an hour later, I had an idea that perhaps he might have been trying to shake hands with me.'[3] About as irresponsibly and unfunnily violent, that, as the deplorably 'unspoilt' childhood of Julian Bell who was given to drowning newly hatched ducklings by throwing them repeatedly into a pond, or to pushing unwanted governesses into ditches, or letting off his airgun at Roger Fry's kneecaps.[4] John Cornford was another such young tough whose 'highest enjoyment', we're told, was 'to break up a Fascist meeting', and who recounted to Victor Kiernan 'with genuine relish, a story of Bela Kun machine-gunning five thousand prisoners during a forced retreat in the Russian Civil War'.[5] It's not at all surprising to find that Cornford was schooled on Auden (to whom his early poems were sent

1. Stephen Spender, *The Destructive Element: A Study of Modern Writers and Beliefs* (1935), p. 273.
2. Toynbee, *Friends Apart*, p. 21. Toynbee has recently disclaimed the knuckle-dusters.
3. Giles and Esmond Romilly, *Out of Bounds* (1935), pp. 288–9.
4. *Julian Bell*, pp. 3ff. 5. *John Cornford: A Memoir*, pp. 119, 124.

for approval by the English master at Stowe) and was producing at sixteen Audenesque lines like: 'At the street corners they were selling papers,/Told us what teeth were broken in what riots,/Where fighting on the frontier is unsuccessful/But causes as yet no panic in the city.'[1]

And from many accounts it's clear that several of the younger English volunteers were still inhabiting an Audenesque school-boy dream of metaphorical violence when they arrived in Spain. Cornford had gone in his summer vacation 'with the intention of staying a few days, firing a few shots, and then coming home'.[2] 'It's really rather fun,' Julian Bell wrote to his mother, 'and all's boy-scoutish in the highest.'[3] And while it may be simply from poverty of other experience to draw on, school analogies are to be found springing curiously constantly to these volunteers' minds. Esmond Romilly, in his account in *Boadilla* (1937), finds 'a merry atmosphere, like the last day at school' in the Thaelmann Battalion; returning to the battle for Madrid is 'like going back to school'; battle-fatigued, he remembers having experienced 'that same feeling of tingling dizziness once at the end of a long cross-country run four years before, coming down the long avenue of the grounds of Wellington College'. Gavin Blair Summers (Giles Romilly) in *The Fellow Travellers*, who is writing a novel about his experiences, thinks of school when he joins the Brigade: it will be cold and awful, 'like an afternoon run prolonged for months'. And it *is* like school: '"Back at school, back at school, back at dreary old bloody old school". That's what we used to chant on the first day of term, and the chant is singing in my head.' T. C. Worsley has, of course, the advantage of reflective hindsight, but at the time Cornford was confessing to dreaming, at the front, of fighting and holding his own with 'an oaf called D—', the captain of rugger who had bullied him as a small schoolboy.[4] And even the mind of Orwell, as he was chasing a half-naked soldier down a trench, 'leapt backwards twenty years, to our boxing instructor

1. ibid, p. 66. 2. ibid.
3. (10 June 1937). *Julian Bell*, pp. 188–9.
4. 'Diary letter from Aragon', *John Cornford: A Memoir*, p. 199. Below, p. 119.

at school, showing me in vivid pantomime how he had bayoneted a Turk at the Dardanelles' (*Homage to Catalonia*, Ch. 7).

But Spain was not, for all the ready analogies with school that might strike the former public-schoolboy, simply a theatre for schoolboys to play violent games in; it was a veritable theatre of war. And Cornford, for one, quickly realized that he must grow up: 'You can't play at civil war.'[1] Here was a very literal struggle, across a very literal frontier; the familiar metaphors had suddenly snapped out of the pages of the poetry books into a very certain and grim reality. And some who had lightheartedly embraced the metaphor couldn't square up to the reality. This appears to be at least partly the trouble with Auden. The obscure struggle, not unakin to civil war, that's going on in his early poems, in *Paid on Both Sides* (1930) and *The Orators*, is a set of tough-sounding enough but still essentially juvenile doings, a monstrous game actually quite distinct from the realities Auden encountered when he went to Spain. And, unlike some others, he flinched away from those realities.

Not that he didn't *try* to face Spain's realities realistically. 'I shall probably be a bloody bad soldier,' he confessed to Professor E. R. Dodds, but he did nonetheless decide to 'go out . . . to join the International Brigade in Spain. I so dislike everyday political activities that I won't do them, but here's something I can do as a citizen and not as a writer, and as I have no dependants I feel I ought to go, but O I do hope there are not too many surrealists there. Please don't tell anyone about this. I shan't break it to my parents till after Xmas.'[2] But what Auden actually did when he got to Spain remains rather mysterious. Spender says that 'He had offered his services in Spain as a stretcher bearer in an ambulance unit'.[3] The *Daily Worker* reported, 12 January 1937, that Auden had left for Spain to 'serve as an ambulance driver'. And he was certainly quite strongly associated with the cause of Medical Aid for Spain, to raise money for which his poem 'Spain' was sold at one shilling a time.

1. See below, p. 121.
2. Two letters (one 8 December, the other about Christmas, 1936), to E.R. Dodds: exhibited in the *Young Writers of the Thirties* Exhibition, National Portrait Gallery, London, (25 June–7 November 1976).
3. Spender, *World Within World*, p. 213.

(Anne Fremantle recalls seeing him 'at meetings to raise money to send a hospital ship to Spain'.[1]) But Cyril Connolly remembered meeting him in Valencia where he 'was working for the government radio'. As for the 'very short visit' that Spender mentions in *World Within World*: Connolly claimed he met Auden in Valencia in May 1937, that they 'soon met again in Barcelona' (where Auden was indignantly accosted 'by two militia men – or were they military police?', for peeing behind a bush in the Monjuich Gardens), and then Connolly and, apparently, Auden left Spain 'a few days later'.[2] Edward Mendelson, in the same volume as Fremantle and Connolly, has Auden in Spain only until March.[3] We know he was in London by 4 March ('Spain' was published 29 May). Did he make a second visit to Spain? Probably not. But the blurs and mythics are characteristic.

In comparison with, say, Spender, Auden wrote very little indeed about his Spanish experiences. What he did produce suffers from a failure of tone as crucial as that incautiously inept peeing behind the people's shrubbery. The main impression afforded by Auden's article 'Impressions of Valencia' (*New Statesman*, 30 January 1937) is, in the phrase Geoffrey Grigson deployed in the Auden Double Number of *New Verse*, of 'Auden as a Monster', unable to respond to the actualities of war except in a mood of bland flippancy. 'In the centre of the square, surrounded all day long by crowds and surmounted by a rifle and fixed bayonet, 15 ft high, is an enormous map of the Civil War, rather prettily illustrated after the manner of railway posters urging one to visit lovely lakeland or Sunny Devon.' Already the tone is going badly awry; the reader is impressed less by the bad taste of the Spaniards in having made a war map *pretty*, than by Auden's bad taste in having noticed it, in not, in fact, having declined to be mindful of Sunny Devon at such a time. And Auden's brutal lack of feeling is quickly confirmed by his further animadversions on Valencia's posters: 'Altogether it is a great time for the poster artist ... in photomontage a

1. 'Reality and Religion', in *W. H. Auden: A Tribute*, ed. Stephen Spender (1975), p. 89.
2. 'Some Memories', in ibid., pp. 69–70.
3. 'Chronology', in ibid., p. 10.

bombed baby lies couchant upon a field of aeroplanes.' The heraldic image is a sharply adroit but impressively unfeeling one: other reporters, e.g. Cyril Connolly in his article 'Barcelona',[1] preferred more tactfully straightforward accounts. But Auden is evidently commanded by his own style, the Audenesque ('the foreign correspondents come in for their dinner, *conspicuous as actresses*'), to a slick management of words that wilfully rebuffs any human connection with what is being described. And this refusal to connect – it amounts to a debilitatingly inhuman standoffishness – is clearly what is wrong with his poem 'Spain'.

Even among Auden's friends, as their muted responses show, 'Spain' was a disappointment. John Lehmann whispered of 'the suspicion of rhetoric that clings' to it.[2] Spender's immediate reaction tried hard to explain away the poem's impersonality. It's

an occasional poem in the same sense as are the poems by Wordsworth, Byron and Landor on the struggle of the Spanish people against Napoleon, and it is worthy of a great tradition. The poet has confined himself to an abstracted view of the fundamental motives of the struggle and a bird's-eye view of Spain ... Within these limits, in which the element of personal experience and direct emotional response is rigorously excluded, the poem is a remarkable interpretation of the issues and implications of the struggle in Spain.[3]

What Spender is hedging about is in fact the poem's crucial self-distancing from the conflict. 'Spain' is evasive in a way that's quite characteristic of Auden, the writer who needed constantly to pose and hide, the lover of dressing up and disguise, the book-reviewer whose tactic from first to last was to shun commitment by venting a sentence or two of general approval or disapproval and then talking about something else. The poem dotes lengthily on the past, it welcomes the future, and it nearly succeeds in fending off all but a mention of the present ('today the struggle'): an attempt at striking a Marxist note about History that impresses one as being as faked as Cornford's similar attempt in

1. *New Statesman* (21 November 1936), pp. 801-3.
2. Lehmann, *The Whispering Gallery*, p. 281.
3. *Left Review*, III, No. 6 (July 1937), p. 361.

'Full Moon at Tierz' is the real thing. There are, to be sure, some admirable, revelatory moments when the poet does, as it were, commit himself, albeit crankily, to the cause, frankly uniting his hypochondriac, cossetted, very bourgeois but nevertheless personal neuroses ('the fears which made us respond/To the medicine ad, and the brochure of winter cruises': lines deleted in 1940) with Spain's fearful actualities ('Our thoughts have bodies; the menacing shapes of our fever/Are precise and alive': lines altered in 1940). But there just aren't enough of these moments – queer as they are – of commitment.

Edgell Rickword, in his piece on 'Auden and Politics' in the Auden Double Number of *New Verse*, spotted one reason for the poem's slippery evasiveness. Speaking as a Communist demanding greater commitment of the poet, Rickword attacked the 'flat ephemeral pamphlet' lines as

an extraordinary example of what used to be accepted as the aloofness proper to the intellectual, in one who has recently been to Spain and had the opportunity of observing the immense vitality which the people are bringing to the task of simultaneously defeating the invaders and creating a free culture. 'Today the struggle, tomorrow the poetry and the fun', that attitude of Auden's would be completely incomprehensible to the Spanish intellectuals today.

This can be put another way: Auden's 'Spain' is a poem seeking to be enthusiastic about a cause its author cannot work up much except despondency about. Having fudged and reserved his position as much as he dare in the course of what is after all a fund-raising venture, he tries at the end to make the best of a grim situation and face up to the present in Spain, but simply comes on briskly touting the old schoolboy-revolutionary attitudes that refuse, or are unable – once more, as in the 'Valencia' piece – to connect with the human actualities they touch on.

The stanza that includes the notorious line 'The conscious acceptance of guilt in the necessary murder' has been defended (for example by John Fuller[1]), but surely Orwell was right to attack it (in 'Inside the Whale') as symptomatic of the kind of uninspected inhumanity that is so visible in the 'Valencia'

1. In his *A Reader's Guide to W. H. Auden* (1970), pp. 258-9.

article. Auden is only able to cope with real war as if it were one of his juvenile war-games. The offending stanza is, Orwell jibes,

intended as a sort of thumb-nail sketch of a day in the life of a 'good party man'. In the morning a couple of political murders, a ten-minutes' interlude to stifle 'bourgeois' remorse, and then a hurried luncheon and a busy afternoon chalking walls and distributing leaflets. All very edifying. But notice the phrase 'necessary murder'. It could only be written by a person to whom murder is at most a *word*. Personally I would not speak so lightly of murder. It so happens that I have seen the bodies of numbers of murdered men – I don't mean killed in battle, I mean murdered. Therefore I have some conception of what murder means . . . To me, murder is something to be avoided. So it is to any ordinary person. The Hitlers and Stalins find murder necessary, but they don't advertise their callousness, and they don't speak of it as murder; it is 'liquidation', 'elimination' or some other soothing phrase. Mr Auden's brand of amoralism is only possible if you are the kind of person who is always somewhere else when the trigger is pulled. So much of left-wing thought is a kind of playing with fire by people who don't even know that fire is hot.[1]

Everyone knows, of course, that Auden emended the offending phrase, 'the necessary murder', to 'the fact of murder', and eventually discarded the whole poem from the canon. And the impression is often given that this change of heart was effected very shortly after the poem's first publication. Certainly, 'the fact of murder' had within three years come into the poem (in *Another Time*, published in 1940); but 'the necessary murder' had been allowed to stand in *Poems for Spain* (1939), and, more astonishingly still, the poem, including 'the fact of murder', was allowed to appear in *Collected Shorter Poems* – and that didn't come out until 1950. That was by no means a rushed job of execution.

1. What kind of frivolity, also, led *Left Review* on the back cover of the number containing Edgell Rickword's terrifyingly harsh poem 'To the Wife of Any Non-Intervention Statesman', to run an advert like 'Win Your Friends and Influence People to read *Left Review* and to subscribe to it'?: 'This Month's Tip for WYFIPs. Win Over Non-Intervention Statesmen through their wives. Send copies to them. Make dates with them. Special Offer: We undertake to publish immediately any photographs we receive of little groups of them reading this month's *L.R.*' *Left Review*, III (March 1938).

Nor is another common impression – that, as Spender put it in *World Within World*, Auden 'returned home after a very short visit of which he never spoke' – quite the case. He did not, as he wrote to Hugh Ford, 'wish to talk about Spain when I returned because I was upset by many things I saw or heard about. Some of them were described better than I could ever have done by George Orwell ... Others were what I learned about the treatment of priests.'[1] Nevertheless Auden did talk, particularly about the treatment of churches and priests. When he met Anne Fremantle again in the forties (she doesn't specify precisely when) he included in the reasons he gave for returning to Christianity the fact that 'when I was in Spain during the Civil War and all the churches were shut, I realized I didn't like it. I wanted them to be open. I didn't at that point want particularly to pray myself, but I wanted people to be able to.'[2] And by the mid-fifties he was being quite public about this, in his personal testimony in James Pike's *Modern Canterbury Pilgrims*:

On arriving in Barcelona, I found as I walked through the city that all the churches were closed and there was not a priest to be seen. To my astonishment, this discovery left me profoundly shocked and disturbed. The feeling was far too intense to be the result of a mere liberal dislike of intolerance, the notion that it is wrong to stop people from doing what they like, even if it is something silly like going to church. I could not escape acknowledging that, however I had consciously ignored and rejected the church for sixteen years, the existence of churches and what went on in them had all the time been very important to me. If that was the case, what then?[3]

But this frankness about his feelings in the matter of the pillaged Barcelona churches wasn't all. The outburst given to the right-wing Valerian in Act III, sc. ii of *On the Frontier* (written with Isherwood, and presented by Group Theatre, 14 November 1938) must be taken as pertaining to Spain:

1. Quoted by Ford, *A Poet's War*, n. 8, p. 288.
2. 'Reality and Religion', in *W. H. Auden: A Tribute*, p. 89.
3. James Pike, *Modern Canterbury Pilgrims: The Story of Twenty-Three Converts and Why They Chose the Anglican Communion* (English edn, 1956), p. 41.

'You poor fish, so cock-a-hoop in your little hour of comradeship and hope! I'm really sorry for you. You don't know what you're letting yourselves in for, trying to beat us on our own ground! You will take to machine-guns without having enough. You will imagine that, in a People's Army, it is against your principles to obey orders – and then wonder why it is that in spite of your superior numbers, you are always beaten. You will count on foreign support, and be disappointed, because the international working-class does not read your mosquito journals. It prefers our larger and livelier organs of enlightenment, which can afford snappier sports news, smarter features, and bigger photographs of bathing lovelies. We shall expose your lies and exaggerate your atrocities, and you will be unable to expose or exaggerate ours. The churches will be against you. The world of money and political influence will say of us: "After all, they are the decent people, *our* sort. The others are a rabble." A few of the better educated may go so far as to exclaim: "A plague on both your houses!" Your only open supporters abroad will be a handful of intellectuals, who, for the last twenty years, have signed letters of protest against everything from bi-metallism in Ecuador to the treatment of yaks in Thibet . . .'

The passage doesn't at all imply total hostility to the Spanish Republic's cause; indeed its tone is not only sympathetic but suggests that the authors had themselves once had some definite commitment to the cause. But it is a despairing passage, nothing less, in fact, than Auden's despondent farewell to the thirties dream as it foundered in Spain, a rejection of the aspirations and tactics in which he himself – star of the mosquito journals, arch-participant in round-robins of protesting intellectuals, and, however briefly, volunteer – had once put his trust.

Spain was, then, in more ways than one a test. Above all, it was a test for truthfulness, and truthfulness in poetry. The propaganda case – that this was an heroic, righteous cause, a just war fought for democracy and freedom – was, at least at first, in fact the case, and so 'propaganda' poems, as many of them were, have a pointful role, for they bear pertinently on the truth of the matter. But even here propaganda could be overdone, and become simply ludicrously and hagiographically immoderate – as in Charlotte Haldane's address to La Pasionaria, or in John Sommerfield's characteristically exaggerated respect for Russian lorries:

It was a good lorry, tremendously strong, built sensibly, and we were pleased, because there were so many of them and that they were so good. It was grand that the Russian workers had been able to send them, and that they were so strong and efficient. *Viva Rusia*![1]

A lorry is only a lorry: but not, it appears, when it's a Soviet lorry. Still, Sommerfield's propagandizing can be put down simply to over-enthusiasm; it's probably not too wilful or malicious. And MacNeice's absolutely drawn (and often quoted) distinction between 'writing good propaganda (dishonest poetry) and honest poetry (poor propaganda)'[2] won't altogether hold for poets like John Cornford who do make propagandistic points but whose poems certainly don't impress one, in the reading, as dishonest. There were doubtless some dishonest manipulators about, and poets who kept up, or like Auden tried to keep up, appearances on issues they had quietly personal doubts about. But there's certainly a world of difference between deliberately distorting the truth and making honest mistakes, or believing other people's lies because you are (as were so many poets contemplating Spain) too far from the action to be able to do any personal checking.

The truth was, indeed, as everybody sooner or later learned, being deliberately and cynically distorted. Some of the fiction-mongering, of the kind Koestler and Claud Cockburn later admitted to promoting and condoning, can be excused as a natural part of any war-effort – the sort of deception and counter-deception scarcely anyone despises Western Intelligence for exploiting later, in the war against Germany. But the main agents of distortion in Spain, the Communists, seem from the first to have been infected with a queerly total disregard for truth. It was, for instance, the *Daily Worker*'s custom (and not just on the Spanish issue) to serve up any old caption to go with its limited stock of photographs, and it clearly expected its readership not to care. On 3 August 1936, for example, it carried a snap on page 5 of some 'young anti-Fascists marching beside

1. John Sommerfield, *Volunteer in Spain* (1937), pp. 61–2.
2. Louis MacNeice, 'The Poet in England Today', *New Republic*, 102, (25 March 1940), pp. 412–13.

an armoured car through the streets of Barcelona'. A mere twenty-three days later, on the front page, the very same picture appeared, but this time purporting to be a 'Young Workers' Militia' setting out 'for the Front'. Deception, self-deception and lies – already, on a massive scale, an essential characteristic of Stalin's politics, a regular result in fact of the 'unmechanistic', 'dialectical' thinking that turned whatever suited the Party into 'the truth'[1] – were from the start, then, just a mental habit for Communists in their presentation of the war. And this habit of untruth-telling is particularly evident in the furtive refurbishing for public consumption of what became the International Brigade's Song.

After enduring immense casualties on the Jarama River the International Brigades had nevertheless been kept on unconscionably long (over three months) in the line, and then, at last relieved and removed to the rear, they were within twenty-four hours shunted back again into their old trenches. Their natural disaffection was naturally even further increased, and Alec (or Alex) McDade (it was said), who was later killed at Brunete in July 1937, composed some wryly discontented lines to be sung to the tune of 'Red River Valley':

> There's a valley in Spain called Jarama,
> That's a place that we all know so well,
> For 'tis here that we wasted our manhood,
> And most of our old age as well.

> From this valley they tell us we're leaving,
> But don't hasten to bid us adieu,
> For e'en though we make our departure,
> We'll be back in an hour or two.

> Oh we're proud of our Lincoln Battalion,
> And the marathon record it's made,
> Please do us this little favour,
> And take this last word to Brigade.

1. See, for example, Arthur Koestler's testimony in *The God that Failed*, ed. R. Crossman (1950).

> You'll never be happy with strangers,
> They would not understand you as we,
> So remember the Jarama Valley
> And the old men who wait patiently.[1]

The authorities naturally didn't take to the words but, with slight variations, the song became very popular and was, according to Jason Gurney, 'particularly favoured to bait Political Commissars' with.[2] This more or less authentic version of 'The Valley of Jarama' survived into *The Book of the XV Brigade: Records of British, American, Canadian, and Irish Volunteers in the XV International Brigade in Spain 1936–38*, first published in Madrid in 1938 by XV Brigade's Commissariat of War. '[I]ts humorous cynicism made it popular in all Battalions,' the *Book* informs: so much so that 'our Lincoln Battalion' is sometimes 'our British Battalion' and sometimes 'our Dimitrov Battalion'.[3] But at some stage some anonymous political functionary cleaned up the song. At a wartime rally in London's Cambridge Theatre organized by the International Brigade Association (*The International Brigade Association Salutes the Allied Armies*) the printed programme supplied the audience with what had clearly become the more official version of the song. It's called 'Jarama!':

> There's a valley in Spain called Jarama,
> It's a place that we all know so well,
> For 'twas here that we gave our manhood
> And most of our brave comrades fell.

> We are proud of our British Battalion,
> And the stand for Madrid that they made.
> For they fought like true sons of the people,
> As part of the 15th Brigade.

> With the rest of the international column,
> In the fight for the freedom of Spain,
> They swore in the Valley of Jarama
> That fascism never would reign.

1. Jason Gurney's version in his *Crusade in Spain* (1974), p. 150.
2. ibid., p. 151.
3. *The Book* . . . (republished Newcastle upon Tyne 1975), p. 97.

We have left that dark valley for over (*sic*),
But its memory we ne'er shall forget,
So before we continue this meeting
Let us stand for our glorious dead.[1]

In the Memorial Souvenir for the *British Battalion XV International Brigade* (sold for 6d. at the Empress Hall Memorial Meeting) the words of (this time) 'Jarama Valley' are much the same, if, perhaps, still more heavyhandedly romantic. For 'true sons of the people' this version has 'true Sons of the Soil', and for 'that dark valley for [e]ver' it has 'that dark valley of sorrow'. In other words, an ironic, extremely authentic-sounding trench-grumble has been transformed by Party hacks into a slogan-laden celebration. But it's still attributed to Alec McDade. As slim a regard for the truth, this, as for his memory and for his widow's feelings on the truth about her husband and his literary efforts. A photo, in fact, of Peggy McDade appeared on the front page of the *Worker* (6 January 1939), where she's described as the widow of Alec McDade, composer (in the trenches, it's stressed) of the 'Valley of Jarama' which 'will for ever be the song of the Brigade'. 'The Song', the *Worker* goes on, 'will be sung by the Brigade at the Memorial Meeting', two days hence on Sunday 8 January in the Empress Hall. Reporting the Memorial Meeting on 9 January the *Worker* confirmed that the song 'had echoed many times on the roads of Spain'; now, it claimed, the same song had echoed through the Empress Hall. The next day the *Worker*'s account had become still more embroidered: 'In the trenches near Jarama . . . Alec McDade, of Glasgow, wrote the words of a song. Members of the Battalions took it as their own, and they sang it now, accompanied by Clapham Accordion Band.' But it was not, as we've seen from the Memorial Souvenir, McDade's song that they sang.[2]

1. International Brigade Association Archive.
2. Some of the differences between poems in *Poems for Spain* and their more orthodox versions seem like the result of propagandizing editing. For instance, 'riches or repression', line 18 of MacNeice's *Autumn Journal*, Part VI, becomes 'riches and repression' in the anthology. But the clearest case of all is Donagh MacDonagh's 'He is Dead and Gone, lady . . .': in Mac-Diarmid's (Communist) periodical *Voice of Scotland* it's robbed of its piously Christian subtitle ('For Charles Donnelly, R.I.P.'), and its last line,

If McDade had lived he might no doubt have obstructed this mishandling of his verses. He died, like so many, before the full story of Stalin's betrayal of the Spanish revolution could be told. At least those who died kept their illusions and their dreams more or less intact. It's true that there were many like Clive Branson who remained loyal to the Communist Party after having fought in the War (though his speedy capture 'in almost his first battle',[1] followed by lengthy imprisonment, make him rather a special case). But for many others, what were often naïve enthusiasms quickly gave way to something else. When even C.P. apparatchiks like John Cornford would be so naïve as to look on the P.O.U.M. as possible brothers it's scarcely surprising that somewhat less committed politicos – the Jimmy Youngers and Harry Strattons and Jason Gurneys – might have illusions to shatter. Their innocence about what modern war entailed seems incredible. Spender confesses that he mistook the paper-strips, stuck across Barcelona window-panes as an air-raid precaution, for 'some kind of sign with a political significance, so that they excited me with a feeling of Republican ardour'.[2] It was small wonder, then, that faced with trench arduousnesses and military discipline many volunteers got disgruntled and wanted simply to go home to Britain, or that many fellow-travelling liberals felt sickeningly betrayed by the political ruthlessness they witnessed or heard about. Nor is it good enough for Hugh Ford to declare that his discussions with Spender, Day Lewis, Jack Lindsay, Randall Swingler, Edgell Rickword, Nancy Cunard, Miles Tomalin and others, had shown that few of the poets 'really felt that they had been betrayed, that they had been duped or cheated by the Soviets or anyone else', and that only Koestler and Orwell expressed a sense of betrayal.[3] Auden, as we've seen, said he agreed with Orwell. Spender has been emphatic in print about his disillusionment. Ewart Milne

---

'Something has been gained by this mad missionary', is rewritten as 'Time will remember this militant visionary'! See Notes, below, pp. 470 and 498.

1. H. Pollitt's Introduction to *British Soldier in India: The Letters of Clive Branson*, p. 4.

2. Spender, *World Within World*, p. 187.

3. Ford, *A Poet's War*, p. 257, and n. 4, p. 291.

said (in a letter to me) that he 'came to the conclusion that Peadar O'Donnell and others in Ireland were right: that it was waste of young Irish lives, and that the Spanish people should be allowed to decide this matter entirely for themselves.' 'In any case,' Milne went on, 'I do *not subscribe* to the opinions which may come through the poetry now, and entirely reject . . . in fact, that aspect of them.' Miles Tomalin talks of the rightness of the convictions that impelled him to Spain, but he doesn't attempt to deny 'those grimmer realities that might otherwise have had a brutalizing effect' (*New Statesman*, 31 October 1975, p. 541). Jack Lindsay (again in a letter to me) reaffirmed the principle of the struggle 'of the people against power . . . and in this sense we have the Spanish situation with us'; but while 'the essence of the matter' wasn't, he thought, altered by them he wouldn't deny 'the many betrayals or distortions that have beset the struggle for a newkind of democracy'. Even the Chairman of the International Brigade Association, Bill Alexander, was declared at the opening of the I.B.A. Archive (22 November 1975) to be intent on 'the writing of a history of how it really was – "warts and all" – the mistakes and muddles as well as the heroism and the glory'.[1] Orwell's kind of truth-telling can no longer be shrugged off as the account of a gutless liberal ('The value of the book is that it gives an honest picture of the sort of mentality that toys with revolutionary romanticism but shies violently at revolutionary discipline. It should be read as a warning,' according to John Langdon-Davies's limply sneering review in the *Daily Worker* (21 May 1938), Supplement, p. 4).

The case of Orwell, and the case Orwell puts, set the issue of truthfulness firmly at the centre of any discussion of the literature of the Spanish Civil War. The deepest impression he carried with him from Spain was of the insidiousness of propaganda – not just the anti-revolutionary horror-mongering of most of the British press, but the distorting Communist and International Brigade line against the P.O.U.M. with whom he had fought, a line swallowed and diligently put about by the periodicals and

1. 'Priceless Records of the War in Spain – International Brigaders Donate their Archives', *Marx Memorial Library Quarterly Bulletin*, No. 77 (Jan/Mar 1976), p. 5.

spokesmen of the Left. Of this latter kind of propaganda Orwell had first-hand knowledge. The *New Statesman* refused to take an article and a review by him which supported the P.O.U.M. (Later on, in the second volume of his autobiography, *Editor* (1968), Kingsley Martin tried unrepentantly and with conviction to excuse himself for this editorial blunder: his wriggling arguments serve only to show what Orwell was up against.) Victor Gollancz turned down the book that became *Homage to Catalonia* before it had even been written. No wonder that at times Orwell despaired of the truth:

During the Spanish Civil War I found myself feeling very strongly that a true history of this war never would or could be written. Accurate figures, objective accounts of what was happening, simply did not exist. And if I felt that even in 1937, when the Spanish Government was still in being, and the lies which the various Republican factions were telling about each other and about the enemy were relatively small ones, how does the case stand now? Even if Franco is overthrown, what kind of records will the future historian have to go upon? And if Franco or anyone at all resembling him remains in power, the history of the war will consist quite largely of 'facts' which millions of people now living know to be lies.[1]

So he became obsessed with telling what he knew to be the case about the Communists in Spain, not only in *Homage to Catalonia* (1938) and 'Looking Back on the Spanish War' (in *England Your England*, 1953), but in a persistently kept-up roster of articles and reviews. 'Spilling the Spanish Beans' as he called it (*New English Weekly*, 29 July and 2 September 1937) became a mission: 'There has been a quite deliberate conspiracy ... to prevent the Spanish situation from being understood. People who ought to know better have lent themselves to the deception on the ground that if you tell the truth about Spain it will be used as Fascist propaganda.'[2] It was better, he thought, that the truth be told whatever the immediate cost to the cause: '... the dissensions on the Government side were never properly thrashed out in the left-wing press, although they involved fundamental

1. George Orwell, 'As I Please', *Tribune* (4 February 1944); Penguin *Collected Essays*, III, pp. 109–10.
2. George Orwell, Penguin *Collected Essays*, I, pp. 308–9.

points of principle. To discuss the struggle between the Communists and the Anarchists, you were told, would simply give the *Daily Mail* the chance to say that the Reds were all murdering one another. The only result was that the left-wing cause as a whole was weakened.'[1]

And his reflections on the tribulations of truth and of the truthteller led Orwell straight to *Nineteen Eighty-Four* and *Animal Farm*, classic defences of truth-telling, of keeping the language clean from the distortions politicians want to keep sullying it with, and of the need to strive for historical objectivity against the totalitarian attempts to reshape the past. It was Spain that fashioned for Orwell the major lesson of his writings after the Civil War, the point that if you abandon 'the idea that history *could* be truthfully written' you enter 'a nightmare world in which the Leader, or some ruling clique, controls not only the future but *the past*. If the Leader says of such and such an event, "It never happened" – well it never happened. If he says that two and two are five – well, two and two are five. This prospect frightens me much more than bombs . . .'[2]

Orwell wasn't the only one to find truthtelling a problematic business. T. C. Worsley's *The Fellow Travellers* has Martin Murray (Spender) very creditably rebutting the political commissars' arguments about the need for socialist writers to spread 'the *useful* truth':

'I told them pretty strongly that I wasn't – never had been – interested in the "useful truth". But in the truth good or bad. "If there's brutality, silliness or wastefulness on our side, it's as much a part of the truth as the same thing on the other side. People have a right to know how we're behaving, as it is, not as they imagine. Make no mistake, Comrades", I told them straight, "I shall report exactly what I've seen and exactly what's been said . . ." '[3]

And after he got home Spender claims that he had no desire to be (in Stendhal's phrases) either an 'enthusiastic simpleton' or

---

1. George Orwell, 'As I Please', *Tribune* (9 June 1944); Penguin *Collected Essys*, III, p. 201.
2. George Orwell, 'Looking Back on the Spanish War', Ch. 4.
3. T. C. Worsley, *The Fellow Travellers*, pp. 219–20.

an 'adroit hypocrite': 'I wanted to know what was going on, and why, and who was responsible for it'.[1] But even for Spender the truth didn't come easily. His poems refuse admirably to go in for heroics. He explained why in his Foreword to *The Still Centre* (1939): 'a poet can only write about what is true to his own experience, not about what he would like to be true to his experience'. So Spender's poems about Spain simply register his feelings, his fears, in a quite personal way, and often inhabit regions and report incidents in which the war crops up only incidentally, with a kind of inevitable naturalness:

Crossing the Spanish frontier from France, I spent a day in Port-Bou, alone. This was a charming little port, with two headlands like green arms stretched into the sea and almost embracing, but leaving a little gap between, which was the harbour mouth. Port-Bou had been bombed, though the quay was intact. Having nothing to do while waiting for my connection to Barcelona, I sat at a table in front of the quayside café, reading the newspapers I had brought from France. A lorry full of Republican soldiers in their rather dirty uniforms stopped in front of me. They looked down at my newspaper with all their smiling flag-like faces like one face, and one soldier shouted: 'What do they say of our struggle over the frontier?' I smiled some reply, and the lorry roared away bearing its cargo of uplifted clenched fists.

Then firing practice began from headland to headland across the harbour, bullets flecking the sea to white foam. The whole town became agitated, with children shouting and dogs barking. An old man, running along the road, jogged past me with a senselessly elated smile on his face. 'Pom-pom-pom', he called out in blissful imitation of the firing.[2]

This prose account and the poem 'Port Bou' are locked inter-dependently together, twin downbeat records of the same experience. In poems like 'Port Bou' Spender becomes something more even than the Wilfred Owen of the Spanish Civil War (a claim often made of him) – rather he's its Edward Thomas.

But having written so unheroically and coolly in the interest of personal truth Spender nevertheless went on to write his

1. Stephen Spender, *Life and the Poet* (1942), p. 16.
2. Spender, *World Within World*, pp. 188–9.

heroizing Introduction to *Poems for Spain*. Just so, on the same evening as confiding to Harold Nicolson his concern for the young men who were still, early in 1938, joining the International Brigades, Spender debated against Nicolson at the Cambridge Union in favour of the motion that 'Art must be political'.[1] And – as has sometimes been pointed out – Spender couldn't yet bring himself to reveal the whole story of the International Writers' Congress when he reported on it for *New Writing*.[2] To his credit he did state that some of the Spanish writers 'felt about the propagandistic heroics of the war much as I did myself', and that André Chamson had outstripped most of the delegates in his apprehensions of the awfulness of war. But he did not expand, as he did later in *World Within World* and *The God that Failed*, on things he's content just to mention in *New Writing*: on *why* the visit to Minglanilla had been so memorably moving, or on the importance to the Congress of Gide – denigrated by many of the Communist delegates for his anti-Soviet book, just published, *Retour de l'U.R.S.S.* (1937). Spender could not yet bring himself to spill all the beans.[3] Nor, interestingly, has he actually ever tipped them all quite out of the bag.

Spender's 'three week' membership of the Communist Party is legendary,[4] as is his being allowed to express in the *Daily Worker* his reservations about joining the Party – an article which, according to *World Within World*, annoyed 'several influential comrades'. When one looks it up the article (in the *Daily Worker*, 19 February 1937) turns out to have been wholehearted enough to have annoyed no one: it was the editorial gloss stating that the Party was 'confident that in life and work with our Party, Comrade Spender will reach complete unity with the outlook of Communism' that gave the game away, and was perhaps even calculated to cause trouble for Spender. And those 'few weeks' of membership 'during the winter of 1936 to

1. Weintraub, *The Last Great Cause*, pp. 64–5.
2. *New Writing*, IV, Autumn 1937, pp. 245–51.
3. The *Spectator* article, 'Pictures in Spain' (30 July 1937, p. 199) was even more discreet about Spender's misgivings. Below, pp. 415–17.
4. See for example, David Caute, *The Fellow-Travellers* (1973), p. 5.

1937' (*The God that Failed*) must perhaps be stretched. At least one should notice Spender's much longer career as a *Daily Worker* contributor. His first review for the paper appeared on 29 October 1936, his last not until 28 July 1937. Active participation in the Party organ, then, lasted for longer than a mere 'three' or 'a few weeks'. (He was, though, definitely out by 28 February 1938, when there was a note on Group Theatre's production of his *Trial of a Judge*: 'Members of the Left Book Club will remember Spender as the author of *Forward from Liberalism*'. No mention, of course, of members of the Communist Party having anything to recall about their quondam comrade: once again the specialists had rewritten history much more thoroughly than Spender's lapses of memory could begin to do.[1]) And even Spender's considered rewriting of history – the rewriting of his poems – looks less singlemindedly revisionist than Auden's. Auden was rigorously suppressing a youthful self when he refused permission for poems like 'Spain' to appear in anything other than 'period' anthologies (Robin Skelton's *Poetry of the Thirties* he would condone, but not Philip Larkin's *Oxford Book of Twentieth-Century Verse*, with its claims for its contents to more enduring importance). Spender has frequently altered because he's still trying to get a 'malleable' idea right: if the poet 'feels he has failed to interpret' his idea 'in one version he can re-invent it', Spender claims in his Introduction to *Collected Poems 1928–53*, 'because he does not ever forget the complete intention behind the incomplete failure.' Many of the alterations that my collation of his texts reveals are simply fresh attempts to clarify a line that's not yet been quite hit-off. And some lines – Spender's never been a completely clear poet – even remain obscure after repeated attentions (like the 'In the high door'/ 'On the high door'/'In the high shelf' manoeuvrings in line 26 of 'Fall of a City'). But at least some of the Spanish War poems have been by revision very evidently purged of their original, distinctively personal note, in favour of a more generalized purport. An almost paradigm case of such afterthoughts is 'Thoughts During An Air Raid', a poem which raises the matter of the loss

1. Unsurprisingly, there's no mention of Spender in Mahon's *Harry Pollitt: A Biography*.

of individuality suffered by those who die among a mass of casualties. In the final version impersonal pronouns have ousted personal ones; 'my fingers' are generalized to 'the fingers', and so on. Unlike in the first version, there's little personality now left for the victim to lose. The most important point, though, about this kind of revision is that even the exponent of unheroic personal truth couldn't altogether resist the temptation to rejig his past, and tinker with the admirably personal presence he once sought to grant his poems.

The important lessons that Orwell and Spender absorbed from their war experiences, about putting personal truth above slogans, propaganda, and 'truths' that would serve immediate party ends, were absorbed by others. They had, in fact, a decisive impact on the direction in which 'thirties-poetry' and 'thirties-criticism' had been heading. Impersonality, 'objectivity', simple attitudes and language, widely available public writing: these had been the goals underlying the so-called 'socialist realism' movement in Britain. But Spain brought home to many writers that – in the crudely-made distinction of the time[1] – Freud had as big a role to play as Marx. That you were regretting being in Spain because, like Jimmy Younger, you had only gone out of homosexual pique, could be ignored no less than could the fear of being killed. Likewise, it were foolish to expect Spender to pretend that he could ignore the Communists' reluctance to let his friend return home, or Dos Passos to overlook the arrest and execution by the Communists of his friend José Robles.[2] And if personal feelings mattered in leftist politics they also mattered to poetry, even left-wing poetry.

Interestingly, in the last issue of *Kingdom Come* (III, No. 12, 1943), Alex Comfort – once quite renowned as a poet, but who subsequently went over, as it were, to psychology, or at least to sexology – claimed to have located the discovery of 'darkness' by modern English letters in the Spanish War:

The landmark which we can most easily identify as the first sign of the revelation of this darkness is the collapse of the school of socialist

1. See, for example, C. Day Lewis, 'Revolution in Writing', in *A Time to Dance* (1936).

2. Malcolm Cowley, *A Second Flowering* (New York [1956], 1973), p 85.

realism in England. The occasion of it was the Spanish War. Looking back at that period it seems clear that it was not the destruction of the socialist ideal in Spain, nor the certainty of European war which opened the eyes of poets, but the renewed contact with the work and discoveries of Lorca and Unamuno, brought back from Spain by writers who went overseas. It was at the time of defeat that the poets who had been inspired by Marxism were led by Lorca and Unamuno to look up and see the skull which was looking over their shoulder. They came to realize under the impact of actual death in the Spanish battles and imminent death in the suicide of Europe that death is real, and that all purpose is limited by the foreshadowings of personal extinction.

Whatever may be the exact timing and spiritual geography of this change there is no doubt of it: Spain spelled the end of English 'socialist realism'. It's impossible to speculate about what direction the Marxist writers who were killed – Donnelly, Cornford and, above all perhaps, because he had made a distinctive if more than occasionally 'crude' contribution to Marxist aesthetics, Christopher Caudwell – would have taken had they survived. But most of the writers who returned were driven to look inward. They soon abandoned the old clamour for simple, public poetry for the people. When in 1939 Auden and Isherwood left England, shockingly, for America the old movement was virtually all over.[1] So that when some committed remnants of the old gangs joined with the newer generation in trying to revive the passions of the early thirties their claims sounded hollowly and were evidently ineffectual. In 1940, for example, Mulk Raj Anand, Charlotte Haldane, Pat Sloan, Spender, John Sommerfield, Randall Swingler, Sylvia Townsend Warner and Alick West are all to be found signing a financial appeal for *Poetry and the People*: 'We have the opportunity of becoming the first real people's poetry magazine, read by ordinary people in every town and village in Great Britain.' But this tiniest of scrawny little magazines soon folded up. 'The poet is once more to be a mouth instead of a megaphone,' wrote Mac-

1. It was *certainly* all over when Rayner Heppenstall could write in *New Road* (1944), pp. 217–22 – a title almost tauntingly reminiscent of the thirties' *New Country*, *New Signatures*, *New Writing* and the other titular claimants to novelty – his (very amusing) piece 'I am not in favour of the working classes'.

Neice in *New Republic*,[1] 'and poetry, one hopes, is to develop organically from the organic premises of life – of life as it is lived, not of life when it is dried into algebra.' 'Poetry cannot take sides,' proclaimed Spender in *Life and the Poet* (1942): thus deftly overturning the old assurances he once gladly put his name to – not least in *Authors Take Sides*.

And it's not at all accidental that perhaps the most famous English poem to come out of Spain, apart from Auden's 'Spain', and arguably the best English poem of the war, is Cornford's untitled verses (the titles accreted later) beginning 'Heart of the heartless world'. Not only has it a very traditional form (and this from an author who had doubtless endorsed the period's cries for the invention of new, unbourgeois forms of art), but it is an entirely personal poem (and this from the keen revolutionary who once deplored the 'collapse into subjectivity of Eliot, Joyce, or Pound'[2]). War, the poem implies, even this revolutionary war, is terrible, for the poet readily confesses to fear of death, to fear, what's more, of fear itself, and above all to fear of not seeing his girl-friend Margot Heinemann again. It is of course a love poem; that it's written in a revolutionary war is merely incidental: there are no slogans, barely any politics at all, certainly little but the naming of Huesca to pin it to any particular time or place. As readers have, in fact, frequently observed, it could be the work of almost any soldier, to any woman, in any war, in any time.

The Spanish War, then, not only rescued English poets from the extraordinarily difficult, and guilt-laden, task of attempting to write in a 'public' mode, a public voice, it also pulled English poetry back from the brink of endorsing war as a good thing. Wilfred Owen and Siegfried Sassoon, among others, had effectively made it impossible for their generation to write dishonestly flag-waving poems that glorified wars – even wars intended, as was claimed for the Spanish Civil War as much as for the First World War, to 'save civilization' or to 'end war' –

1. Louis MacNeice, 'The Poet in England Today', *New Republic*, 102, No. 13 (25 March 1940).
2. 'Left?', *Cambridge Left* (Winter, 1933–4), in *John Cornford: A Memoir*, p. 125.

poems that ignored the horrors of modern warfare and extolled the opportunities battle supplied for men to become heroes. Under the promptings of Owen's and Sassoon's verse a generation had been schooled in pacifism. One of the commonest and most practical forms of activism for student leftists in the early thirties had been the university peace demonstration, the gesture against Armistice Day rhetoric, and the like. It was common form for public-schoolboy radicals to shun the O.T.C. But the Civil War inevitably raised the old pacifist Catch-22, graphically put by Orwell in his review of Koestler's *Spanish Testament* (1937): you are led 'to this conclusion: if someone drops a bomb on your mother, go and drop two bombs on his mother. The only apparent alternatives are to smash dwelling houses to powder, blow out human entrails and burn holes in children with lumps of thermite, or to be enslaved by people who are more ready to do these things than you are yourself; as yet no one has suggested a practicable way out.'[1]

In a bizarre about-turn, trained soldiers and veterans of the First World War suddenly became extremely valuable. The *Daily Worker* extolled Ludwig Renn as the 'famous German ex-officer and author' (24 November 1936). Possession of military skills and, above all, inurement to military discipline, the unlibertarian capacity to obey orders without question, became unquestionedly virtuous. Wintringham's account of the Spanish fighting in *English Captain* (whose very title lays significant claim to First World War experience) rescues the Great War from its position of disgrace in the register of socialist values. Verdun, Kitchener, the Somme, the Irish Guards: his repeated references conspire in effect to put back a sense of greatness into 'Great War'. The Europeans' distinctive contribution to the Spanish Republic, Wintringham suggests, has been their valuable experience in the conscript armies of 1914–18. Suddenly, youthful radicals were made to feel that they'd miserably backed the wrong horse: Esmond Romilly, a general's son and nephew of Winston Churchill, who had refused to join the school O.T.C. and then run away from Wellington to mount

1. *Time and Tide*, 5 February 1938; Penguin *Collected Essays*, I, pp. 329–30.

a campaign precisely against school militarism, felt driven to claim, when he joined the volunteers at the Marseilles recruiting office, in case he should be rejected as too ill-equipped, that he had been a member of the Wellington O.T.C.![1] In a revealingly symbolic manner Professor Cornford handed his son his First World War revolver when the lad set out for his second spell in Spain.[2] Orwell told Richard Rees that his generation 'must be marked forever by the humiliation of not having taken part' in the First World War.[3] And Philip Toynbee describes the Spanish War as providing an opportunity for liberation, in which the post-war generation might throw off its guilt at having missed the earlier struggle. The youthful anti-war campaigners, he suggests, had all along been half in love with the horrors they were deploring, envious of fathers and older brothers who had been called on to fight. 'In fact it seems to me now that our picture of war was as falsely romantic, in its different way, as anything which had stirred the minds of Edwardian boys, brought up on Henty and the heroics of minor imperial campaigns.'[4] And the pro-Republican rhetoric, the Left's insistent campaigning for funds, revived the tones, the atmosphere of 1914. And, what's more, you can hear some poets actually having doubts about the relevance to *this* war to save civilization and culture of the First World War writers' opposition to *that* war to do just the same. In his Introduction to *Poems for Spain* Spender tries to suggest that somehow a left-wing war can be nicer, because it's juster:

'All a poet can do to-day is to warn', the greatest of the English war poets, Wilfred Owen, wrote in 1918. That is true always of poetry written in the midst of a great social upheaval; but the poets of the International Brigade have a different warning to give from that of the best poets of the Great War. It is a warning that it is necessary for civilization to defend and renew itself . . . these poets and fighters are fighting not out of love for war, but because they are defending a life and culture which they see threatened.

1. Esmond Romilly, *Boadilla* (1937), p. 35.
2. Stansky and Abrahams, *Journey to the Frontier*, p. 360.
3. Stansky and Abrahams, *The Unknown Orwell*, p. 75.
4. Toynbee, *Friends Apart*, p. 91.

And some poets did put back the clock, reanimating the heroic postures and resuscitating the ringing accents of imperialist English poetry. It was perhaps a bit far-fetched of Orwell to suggest that there was little difference between Cornford's 'Full Moon at Tierz' and Henry Newbolt's 'There's a breathless hush in the close tonight', and that the socialist Cornford was merely built 'on the bones of a Blimp'.[1] But there's no doubt of the spirit of Newbolt breathing through Cecil Day Lewis's celebration in his 'The Nabara' of a brave naval encounter (one first described in Chapter 11 of G. L. Steer's *The Tree of Gernika* (1938)):

And now the gallant *Nabara* was left in the ring alone,
The sky hollow around her, the fawning sea at her side:
But the ear-ringed crew in their berets stood to the guns, and cried
A fresh defiance down
The ebb of the afternoon, the battle's darkening tide.

The poem's final stanza quite rightly reminded John Muste (and it's the one decent critical point made by his *Say that We Saw Spain Die: Literary Consequences of the Spanish Civil War* (Seattle, 1966)) of Housman's '1887', the opening poem of *A Shropshire Lad*. This was indeed an ironic consequence of the misguided notion that the reality of war might somehow be changed by its socialist content or context. Bombing in Liverpool *is* objectively as awful as bombing in Barcelona, and it's dotty of Edgell Rickword to pretend otherwise. Nevertheless he does so in his article 'Poetry and Two Wars':

The concrete experience, which must be the writer's starting-point, does not exist in isolation from the complex of social relationships. A hungry woman in a Barcelona food-queue during the war of intervention and a hungry woman in a Liverpool food-queue ... would at first glance appear to be objectively identical as subject matter for a poem or story. But their hunger (if we may be permitted to stretch the imagination so far in the case of the Liverpool woman) though due to the same ultimate cause, would have as immediate cause something quite different, one being a matter of the common interest, the other that

1. George Orwell, 'My Country Right or Left', (1940); Penguin *Collected Essays*, I, p. 592.

of individual interests. Each would have its particular emotional expression which it is the writer's job to clarify and represent in a vivid way. What brought out fortitude in Barcelona might provoke indignation in Liverpool. So, as it is not hunger 'in general' that provides the subject-matter for true poetry, so it is not war 'in general', but the particular war in which the writer is involved.[1]

Special pleading of this sort, which depended for its justification on the doctoring of the evidence (as we've seen in the case of Alec McDade's song about Jarama) and which, astoundingly but revealingly, shunted the socialist poet Day Lewis promptly into the arms of Henry Newbolt, didn't survive too many battles or even glimpses of battles. 'No wars are nice,' Cornford was quickly driven to conclude, 'and even a revolutionary war is ugly enough.'[2] Clive Branson jeered later on from India (whither he'd been drafted in the Second World War) at 'those insane fools who look upon war as a sport, good fun, etc.'[3] And that this kind of sanity did eventually prevail is evident in the re-actions of reporters (like Spender in his 'Heroes in Spain' article), medics (like Ewart Milne in his anti-heroic stories), and the soldiers (like T. A. R. Hyndman in his poem, and his later reflections in the gatherum of reflections edited by Philip Toynbee, *The Distant Drum* (1976), or William Teeley, who sent a poem to *Poetry and the People* in August 1938 (it was published in September 1938 in issue No. 3) saying: 'I have had twelve months of modern warfare. I have had the good fortune to understand exactly what I am fighting for, but that does not make war in the least desirable'). You can even catch again the tones and emphases of Wilfred Owen, subdued in poems like Tom Wintringham's 'The Splint', but loud and clear in the indignation of Spender's 'Two Armies' ('who can connect/The inexhaustible anger of the guns/With the dumb patience of those tormented animals?') or in the flat recording of horror in Corn-ford's 'A Letter from Aragon':

1. Edgell Rickword, 'Poetry and Two Wars', *Our Time*, I, No. 2 (April 1941) pp. 1-6.
2. *John Cornford: A Memoir*, p. 242. See below p. 116.
3. *British Soldier in India: The Letters of Clive Branson*, p. 9.

We buried Ruiz in a new pine coffin,
But the shroud was too small and his washed feet stuck out.
The stink of his corpse came through the clean pine boards
And some of the bearers wrapped handkerchiefs round their faces.

What poets had to learn was that even in a war for the justest
of causes, for democratic or socialist causes, being truthful
might drive poems to end up saying similar things to poems
written against a capitalist, imperialist war. It had to be grasped
again that modern, mechanized warfare is an evil thing and bad
for mankind in anybody's cause, anybody's poetry, anybody's
language.

*

The world of the 'thirties' poets is now emphatically the past.
Much of their work now seems to speak much less out of the
New Country of Michael Roberts's famous anthology of 1933
than out of (as one of Julian Symons's titles has it) quite *Another
Country*.[1] A country almost perversely dominated, in a fashion
difficult to imagine now (since no one currently commands – or
demands – that sort of respect), and even in the heat of the
hottest moments, by Auden and the echoes of the Audenesque
(less surprisingly, perhaps, in H. B. Mallalieu or Charles
Donnelly, but distinctively more so in 'Heart of the heartless
world' – a line, of course, that Cornford remembered from
Auden's Ode 'To Gabriel Carritt, Captain of Sedbergh School
XV, Spring 1927' in *The Orators*, as well as from Marx on the
'opium of the people'. Many of this far country's inhabitants are
largely forgotten men – Edgar Foxall, Bernard Gutteridge, H. B.
Mallalieu, even Richard Church. ' "H. B. Mallalieu",' Julian
Symons quotes a well-known poet as saying to him, ' "I
remember in my youth I used to be quite excited to see that
name in a magazine" ': but who reads him now? It's only the
occasional resurrection, like the gratifying appearance in 1975 of
Bernard Gutteridge's *Old Damson Face*, or the odd recollection
in Alan Ross's *London Magazine*, that keeps some of these
authors in mind. They wrote for now forgotten publishers, like

1. Julian Symons, *Notes from Another Country* (1972).

the man Caton who owned the Fortune Press, whose main line was books about adolescent boys, and who went in for sexy-sounding poets ('This fellow Ewart now, he's rather spicy, eh?'). Their work appeared in ephemeral, odd, and now forgotten little corners, the mosquito journals that rapidly came and went during long poetic summers, papers like *Kingdom Come* for instance, than which Julian Symons has doubted 'if any odder magazine has appeared since'.[1] And while some of their poetry remains and will remain intrinsically and not just historically unforgettable, some of it is, undeniably, quite forgettably bad. Some of it has been in fact forgotten even by the authors themselves. When I phoned him for permission to quote his youthful 'Guernica' A. S. Knowland had difficulty recalling writing it. J. C. Hall had 'no recollection whatever of my poem "Postscript for Spain"': 'How difficult to recapture the sentiments of a boy of 19! How far away it all seems!' he wrote to me, granting reluctant permission for its reprinting. Some of these poems were regretted later by their writers. A. L. Lloyd told me he didn't like his translations much ('I could do them better now'). Ewart Milne wanted it made clear that he had ceased to subscribe to his poems' opinions. Auden's reiterated repudiation of the sentiments of his 'Spain' is well known. But in the matter of forgettability, what of the volunteer soldiers and the Republican cause they fought for? 'We shall not forget you' was the moving claim La Pasionaria made to the International Brigaders at their last, stand-down parade in Barcelona on 15 November 1938. And the cause, and its literature, persist in remaining memorable: all the Stalinist lies, the politicking, the dodges and manoeuvres cannot dim the honour due to most of the volunteers. Sincerely and bravely they translated their faith into works: ready to endure death and, what is perhaps worse, having often to endure life afterwards – as refugees, or exiles, emotionally (perhaps) and physically (almost certainly) mutilated. One of the most moving letters in the British International Brigade Association archive is from a Ken White in Prague: one of the many British Brigaders who settled after the Second World War for what turned out to

1. ibid., pp. 59, 60, 68.

be the exigencies of exile in one of the People's Democracies of eastern Europe. A comrade had arranged to send him from London what he can't obtain in 'Praha': *stump socks*. But these special socks to go on the ends of his amputated legs hadn't, to his distress, arrived.

It was 'with a feeling as of world-end' that Jack Lindsay read in a newspaper of the final victory of Franco:

Stricken on a seat, I watched the unconcerned passers and tried to find words that would express my sense of horror and disaster. When, next day, I heard some girls laughing in the lane by our rambling house, I felt an anguish that seemed deeper than any pang I had ever known on my own behalf.

The forces of light – and they didn't all turn out to be, after all, the forces of darkness – had not prevailed. As Albert Camus put it when he wrote that the men of his generation had 'had Spain within their hearts . . . [and] carried it with them like an evil wound':

It was in Spain that men learned that one can be right and yet be beaten, that force can vanquish spirit, that there are times when courage is not its own recompense. It is this, doubtless, which explains why so many men, the world over, feel the Spanish drama as a personal tragedy.[1]

1. Quoted by Weintraub, *The Last Great Cause*, pp. 2f.

THE MAP OF PAIN

'As the sky is pierced with stars that look upon
The map of pain'

(From the original version of Stephen Spender's 'To a Spanish Poet')

Spain

Yesterday all the past. The language of size
Spreading to China along the trade-routes; the diffusion
    Of the counting-frame and the cromlech;
Yesterday the shadow-reckoning in the sunny climates.

Yesterday the assessment of insurance by cards,
The divination of water; yesterday the invention
7   Of cartwheels and clocks, the taming of
8 Horses. Yesterday the bustling world of the navigators.

9 Yesterday the abolition of fairies and giants,
The fortress like a motionless eagle eyeing the valley,
      The chapel built in the forest;
12 Yesterday the carving of angels and alarming gargoyles.

The trial of heretics among the columns of stone;
Yesterday the theological feuds in the taverns
      And the miraculous cure at the fountain;
16 Yesterday the Sabbath of witches; but to-day the struggle.

17 Yesterday the installation of dynamos and turbines,
The construction of railways in the colonial desert;
      Yesterday the classic lecture
On the origin of Mankind. But to-day the struggle.

21 Yesterday the belief in the absolute value of Greece,
The fall of the curtain upon the death of a hero;
23   Yesterday the prayer to the sunset
And the adoration of madmen. But to-day the struggle.

25 As the poet whispers, startled among the pines,
26 Or where the loose waterfall sings compact, or upright
      On the crag by the leaning tower:
'O my vision. O send me the luck of the sailor.'

And the investigator peers through his instruments
At the inhuman provinces, the virile bacillus
    Or enormous Jupiter finished:
32 'But the lives of my friends. I inquire. I inquire.'

33 And the poor in their fireless lodgings, dropping the sheets
34 Of the evening paper: 'Our day is our loss, O show us
    History the operator, the
36 Organiser, Time the refreshing river.'

And the nations combine each cry, invoking the life
That shapes the individual belly and orders
    The private nocturnal terror:
40 'Did you not found the city state of the sponge,

'Raise the vast military empires of the shark
And the tiger, establish the robin's plucky canton?
43   Intervene. O descend as a dove or
44 A furious papa or a mild engineer, but descend.'

And the life, if it answers at all, replies from the heart
And the eyes and the lungs, from the shops and squares of
    the city:
47   'O no, I am not the mover;
48 Not to-day; not to you. To you, I'm the

49 'Yes-man, the bar-companion, the easily-duped;
50 I am whatever you do. I am your vow to be
51   Good, your humorous story.
52 I am your business voice. I am your marriage.

53 'What's your proposal? To build the just city? I will.
I agree. Or is it the suicide pact, the romantic
    Death? Very well, I accept, for
56 I am your choice, your decision. Yes, I am Spain.'

Many have heard it on remote peninsulas,
58 On sleepy plains, in the aberrant fisherman's islands
59   Or the corrupt heart of the city,
Have heard and migrated like gulls or the seeds of a flower.

61 They clung like birds to the long expresses that lurch
Through the unjust lands, through the night, through the
  alpine tunnel;
They floated over the oceans;
64 They walked the passes. All presented their lives.

On that arid square, that fragment nipped off from hot
66 Africa, soldered so crudely to inventive Europe;
On that tableland scored by rivers,
68 Our thoughts have bodies; the menacing shapes of our
  fever

69 Are precise and alive. For the fears which made us respond
To the medicine ad. and the brochure of winter cruises
Have become invading battalions;
And our faces, the institute-face, the chain-store, the ruin

Are projecting their greed as the firing squad and the bomb.
Madrid is the heart. Our moments of tenderness blossom
As the ambulance and the sandbag;
76 Our hours of friendship into a people's army.

77 To-morrow, perhaps the future. The research on fatigue
And the movements of packers; the gradual exploring of
  all the
  Octaves of radiation;
To-morrow the enlarging of consciousness by diet and
  breathing.

81 To-morrow the rediscovery of romantic love,
The photographing of ravens; all the fun under
  Liberty's masterful shadow;
84 To-morrow the hour of the pageant-master and the
  musician,

85 The beautiful roar of the chorus under the dome;
To-morrow the exchanging of tips on the breeding of
  terriers,
The eager election of chairmen
88 By the sudden forest of hands. But to-day the struggle.

89   To-morrow for the young the poets exploding like bombs,
90   The walks by the lake, the weeks of perfect communion;
          To-morrow the bicycle races
92   Through the suburbs on summer evenings. But to-day the
          struggle.

93   To-day the deliberate increase in the chances of death,
94   The conscious acceptance of guilt in the necessary murder;
          To-day the expending of powers
          On the flat ephemeral pamphlet and the boring meeting.

97   To-day the makeshift consolations: the shared cigarette,
98   The cards in the candlelit barn, and the scraping concert,
          The masculine jokes; to-day the
          Fumbled and unsatisfactory embrace before hurting.

101   The stars are dead. The animals will not look.
102   We are left alone with our day, and the time is short, and
          History to the defeated
104   May say Alas but cannot help nor pardon.

                             W. H. AUDEN

Impressions of Valencia

The pigeons fly about the square in brilliant sunshine, warm as a fine English May. In the centre of the square, surrounded all day long by crowds and surmounted by a rifle and fixed bayonet, 15ft high, is an enormous map of the Civil War, rather prettily illustrated after the manner of railway posters urging one to visit Lovely Lakeland or Sunny Devon. Badajoz is depicted by a firing-party; a hanged man represents Huelva; a doll's train and lorry are heading for Madrid; at Seville Quiepo el Llano [sic] is frozen in an eternal broadcast. The General seems to be the Little Willie of the war; in a neighbouring shop window a strip of comic woodcuts shows his rake's progress from a perverse childhood to a miserable and well-merited end.

Altogether it is a great time for the poster artist and there are some very good ones. Cramped in a little grey boat the Burgos Junta, dapper Franco and his bald German adviser, a cardinal and two ferocious Moors are busy hanging Spain; a green Fascist centipede is caught in the fanged trap of Madrid; in photomontage a bombed baby lies couchant upon a field of aeroplanes.

Today a paragraph in the daily papers announces that since there have been incidents at the entrances to cabarets, these will in future be closed at nine p.m. Long streamers on the public buildings appeal for unity, determination and discipline. Three children, with large brown eyes like some kind of very rich sweet, are playing trains round the fountain. On one of the Ministries a huge black arrow draws attention to the fact that the front at Teruel is only 150 km. away. This is the Spain for which charming young English aviators have assured us that the best would be a military dictatorship backed by a foreign Power.

Since the Government moved here the hotels are crammed to bursting with officials, soldiers and journalists. There are porters at the station and a few horse-cabs, but no taxis, in order to save petrol. Food is plentiful, indeed an hotel lunch is heavier than one could wish. There is a bull-fight in aid of the hospitals; there is a variety show where an emaciated-looking tap-dancer does an extremely sinister dance of the machine-guns. The foreign correspondents come in for their dinner, conspicuous as actresses.

And everywhere there are the people. They are here in corduroy breeches with pistols on their hip, in uniform, in civilian suits and berets. They are here, sleeping in the hotels, eating in the restaurants, in the cafés drinking and having their shoes cleaned. They are here, driving fast cars on business, running the trains and the trams, keeping the streets clean, doing all those things that the gentry cannot believe will be properly done unless they are there to keep an eye on them. This is the bloodthirsty and unshaven Anarchy of the bourgeois cartoon, the end of civilization from which Hitler has sworn to deliver Europe.

For a revolution is really taking place, not an odd shuffle or two in cabinet appointments. In the last six months these people have been learning what it is to inherit their own country, and once a man has tasted freedom he will not lightly give it up; freedom to choose for himself and to organize his life, freedom not to depend for good fortune on a clever and outrageous piece of overcharging or a windfall of drunken charity. That is why, only eight hours away at the gates of Madrid where this wish to live has no possible alternative expression than the power to kill, General Franco has already lost two professional armies and is in the process of losing a third.

W. H. AUDEN

The Future is Near Us

    Those on the wooded highways, in the towers,
    Out on their islands caressed by the ignorant ocean,
    Those tongue-tied with the mad alphabet of flowers,
    Those deeply involved with love or with the sun:

5   Have caught the signal of the sentinel dead,
    Who had renounced the precious taste of words.
7   The signal was Spain. Over our grief it shed
    Its strict last-hour light, revealing the last birds
    To leave forever their magnificent trees.
10   The grey bomber has set limits to the air:
    Distance is death now and the carrier seas
    Hurl on these cliffs their message of despair.

13   Spain has changed the contours of the Earth;
    Imposed new frontiers though geography has grown:
    Light revealed in woodland unexpected dearth:
16   Towers have been cut off: and no seeds sown.

Rivers are crossed, the front line pushed back
18 Upon its base, but Spain continues our fight;
War is already flagrant in Europe and the black
20 Night of hatred sets boundaries to delight.
21 Love is too large in the short day before us,
The islands beyond our reach. Sight is sure.
23 Words shall have the discipline of the chorus:
Dreams leave us for a new pasture.

Reshuffle the alphabet and order words as guns
To discharge their shells into the doubtful ear.
Ours is not the unquestioning strength of stones,
But the future is near us and our line is clear.

H. B. MALLALIEU

The Landscape

The face of the landscape is a mask
Of bone and iron lines where time
Has ploughed its character.
I look and look to read a sign
Through errors of light and eyes of water
Beneath the land's will, of a fear
And the memory of a struggle,
As man beneath his mask still wears a child.

STEPHEN SPENDER

Heroic Heart

Ice of heroic heart seals plasmic soil
Where things ludicrously take root
To show in leaf kindnesses time had buried
And cry music under a storm of 'planes,
Making thrust head to slacken, muscle waver
And intent mouth recall old tender tricks.
Ice of heroic heart seals steel-bound brain.

There newer organs built for friendship's grappling
Waste down like wax. There only leafless plants
And earth retain disinterestedness.
Though magnetised to lie of the land, moves
Heartily over the map wrapped in its iron
Storm. Battering the toads, armoured columns
Break walls of stone or bone without receipt.
Jawbones find new way with meats, loins
Raking and blind, new way with women.

CHARLES DONNELLY

from *Calamiterror*

I

The English coast shivers and the American meadow faints;
The Rhone and the Rhine run mellowing with promised horror;
The Welsh mountain weeps and the Cumberland fell weeps;
London lies like a huge rot along the Thames, and Rome
Roars. O Spain, my golden red, she tears the rot out,
The Franco gangs that furrow in her heart. See how she stands,
Her Madrid middle growing vague with ravage,
Labouring to let out liberty, with the rat and the rot at her heart.

2

I remember again the three women weeping in Irun's ruins,
Whose tears will wash the Rhone and Rhine and whose grief
Thrust up like crystal towers the architecture of Time.
I see England
With the underground mines run bleeding along her like wounds,
I hear the great Lancastrian shafts delivering sounds
Of sorrow and appeal, or watch the factory stacks
Like hands for charity or fallen, clenched.

3

The centre of my heart like a red tree
Puts forth a hand and indicates the common red rose;
Which when I take lifts its petals like tongues
Articulating red; speaks of privations, poverty,
Duplicity, oppressions, camouflaged collusions;
And I observe that every move of its lips leaves blood.
What flower then shall the red tree in my heart wear
But the red tongues of the rose, which speak and bleed?

4

O Asturias Wyoming and Wales, I see the fuchsia
Remembering man has a crimson heart and I remember,
Hang out my fuchsia here. Your fuchsia, Asturias,
Spreading like sun over Spain shall be soon in bloom:
The dead is dead, but he gives and not takes his poppy,
His hammer his hand and his badge his blood.
It is already time to triumph, for tears and blood like time
Take tears and blood as time takes time to make good.

5

I see the swan's breast run like the pelican's red
To feed the crowded myriad her human,
I see the large parasites that dilate like leech
Torn, with war and agony, from my mother world's front.

But the whipporwill wends his way through the Wyoming woods
When the leopard, lying low, awaits, or the lion
Roars. And my mother world, with bomb holes in her bosom,
Goes gradually on, with the myriad of me at her breast.

GEORGE BARKER

The Moment Transfixes the
Space Which Divides

O the watch and the compasses!
At five the man fell under the trees
The watch flew off stopped at a moon
Of time staring from the dead wrist
Where no air breathes, hours creep no inches,
Shadows wag over transparent light
And the time and the place are death.

The watch and O the compasses!
He the dead centre, and I their arm
Thrown over mountains rivers and valleys,
When the clocks struck five and the wrist watch stopped
And nailed to his final loneliness
He lacked my assuaging glance of peace.
And the time and the place are death.

O the watch and O the compasses!
The hour at five, the corpse under the trees,
Distance over mountains rivers and valleys,
The leaden bullet which like a clock
Split open the moment dividing us,
And that space chained to my wrists for ever.
And the time and the place are death.

STEPHEN SPENDER

The Tolerance of Crows

Death comes in quantity from solved
Problems on maps, well-ordered dispositions,
Angles of elevation and direction;

Comes innocent from tools children might
Love, retaining under pillows,
Innocently impales on any flesh.

And with flesh falls apart the mind
That trails thought from the mind that cuts
Thought clearly for a waiting purpose.

Progress of poison in the nerves and
Discipline's collapse is halted.
Body awaits the tolerance of crows.

CHARLES DONNELLY

Spain and Time

World world O world,
Youth without promise in our long days,
A sun reflected in a muddy stream,
An eye duller than last night's dream.
The boys from the orphanage in files,
Walk beneath the practising wings
The hedge is full of rain and flies.

Time time O time,
Take into account what now ensues,
Collect the hours of peace and with the refuse,

The dead leaves, slivers of bark, the twigs,
Burn up the old, beautiful gods, the few
Which cannot live with our unusual burden,
And make them, if at all, quite new.

So so subdue
The mask, the malice, and the cheating sorrows,
The wrongs which hold their tallons [sic] over you
In your bright car and your blind escapade.
Subdue the road to the castle, to the stile,
Equal a thousand years with my faint smile
And bow. I bow to you
O crowd, O slanting cross; for in the field
Crows haunt your graves and sparrows dare the wind.

EDGAR FOXALL

Poem

Between rebellion as a private study and the public
Defiance, is simple action only on which will flickers
Catlike, for spring. Whether at nerve-roots is secret
Iron, there's no diviner can tell, only the moment can
show.
Simple and unclear moment, on a morning utterly
different
And under the circumstances different from what you'd
expected.

Your flag is public over granite. Gulls fly above it.
Whatever the issue of the battle is, your memory
Is public, for them to pull awry with crooked hands,
Moist eyes. And village reputations will be built on
Inaccurate accounts of your campaign. You're name for
orators,
Figure stone-struck beneath damp Dublin sky.

In a delaying action, perhaps, on hillside in remote parish,
Outposts correctly placed, retreat secured to wood, bridge
  mined
Against pursuit, sniper may sight you carelessly contoured.
Or death may follow years in strait confinement, where
  diet
Is uniform as ceremony, lacking only fruit.
Or on the barrack square before the sun casts shadow.

Name, subject of all-considered words, praise and blame
Irrelevant, the public talk which sounds the same on
  hollow
Tongue as true, you'll be with Parnell and with Pearse.
Name alderman will raise a cheer with, teachers make
  reference
Oblique in class, and boys and women spin gum of
  sentiment
On qualities attributed in error.

Man, dweller in mountain huts, possessor of coloured
  mice,
Skilful in minor manual turns, patron of obscure subjects,
  of
Gaelic swordsmanship and medieval armoury.
The technique of the public man, the masked servilities
  are
Not for you. Master of military trade, you give
Like Raleigh, Lawrence, Childers, your services but not
  yourself.

CHARLES DONNELLY

O Hero Akimbo on the Mountains of To-morrow

Star crossed on its own limbs I saw
Spain like a rose spreadeagled to a knife:
The mountain muscles and the Gibraltar jaw,
The French forehead and the fist of grief
Seized by a sadist for a Caesar's leaf
Big on the head: browbeaten I saw
The face of Spain struck to a badge of war
For a king's coat, but to a heart's grief.

O hero akimbo on the mountains of to-morrow,
Star crossed spreadeagled and browbeaten Spain –
I see your starved shape grow more strong from pain,
Leap finer and freer from the grave of sorrow.
I see you go gallivanting on the hills again –
O hero akimbo on the mountains of to-morrow:

GEORGE BARKER

Poem

Heart of the heartless world,
Dear heart, the thought of you
Is the pain at my side,
The shadow that chills my view.

The wind rises in the evening,
Reminds that autumn is near.
I am afraid to lose you,
I am afraid of my fear.

On the last mile to Huesca,
The last fence for our pride,

Think so kindly, dear, that I
Sense you at my side.

And if bad luck should lay my strength
Into the shallow grave,
Remember all the good you can;
Don't forget my love.

JOHN CORNFORD

Letters to Margot Heinemann
(*November–December 1936*)

Letter of 21st November.

It's a long time since I've written, but I simply haven't had
the chance, as the last ten days we've been at the front just by
Madrid, in the open all day. This is real war, not a military
holiday like the Catalan affair. We haven't done any fighting
yet: we are a group with a French machine-gun company which
has been in reserve most of the time. I'm writing in the sunlight
in a valley full of oaks, with one section leader twenty yards away
explaining the Lewis gun to a group of French. But though we
haven't yet fought, we've been having a sample of what's to
come this winter. Three times heavily and accurately bombarded
by artillery – and there are first-class German and Italian
gunners.

But the main trouble is the cold. It freezes every night, and
we sleep in the open sometimes without blankets. The trouble
is that the offensive on Madrid became so hot that we were
called out before our training was over, and without proper
equipment. But our International Brigade has done well. Continuous fighting, heavy losses, many of them simply due to
inexperience, but we've been on the whole successful.

The Fascist advance guard got very close to Madrid: but as
I've always said, their main trouble is shortage of men, and they
can't make a concerted advance: they push forward in alternate

sectors. And we've given the head of their advance a hell of a hammering.

I don't know what the press is saying over in England: but Madrid won't fall: if we get time to organize and to learn our guns, we shall do very well.

Now as to our personnel. Less good news. Our four best Lewis gunners were sent up with an infantry section. One is in hospital with two bullets in the guts. Steve Yates (ex-corporal in the British army, expelled and imprisoned for incitement to mutiny) is missing, believed 90 per cent certain dead. Worst of all, Maclaurin, picked up dead on his gun after covering a retreat. He did really well. Continuously cheerful, however uncomfortable, and here that matters a hell of a lot. Well, it's useless to say how sorry we are; nothing can bring him back now. But if you meet any of his pals, tell them (and I wouldn't say it if it weren't true) he did well here, and died bloody well.

Then worse still, our section leader, Fred Jones, he was a tough, bourgeois family, expelled from Dulwich, worked in South American Oil. Has been three years in the Guards, a hell of a good soldier, unemployed organizer, etc. Did magnificently here. Kept his head in a tough time after our captain got killed, and was promoted to section leader. Then on a night march got caught in some loose wire when a lorry passed, hurled over a bridge, and killed. We didn't see what happened: and to give some idea of the way we felt about him, after his death none dared to tell the English section for several hours. Well, we shall get along somehow. But that's a hell of a way to have your best man killed.

Bernard[1] has been doing fine. Worked terribly hard as liaison man and political delegate because of his knowledge of French: and he hasn't much reserve of physical strength. Two nights running he fainted from the cold, but hasn't made any complaints. There's a tough time ahead, and those that get through will be a hell of a lot older. But by Christ they'll learn a lot.

There's little enough else to say. Everyone here is very tired by the cold nights, often sleepless, a bit shaken and upset by our losses, depressed. And it's affected me a bit, though I'm

1. Bernard Knox.

getting a thick skin. If I'd written a few hours ago you'd have got a different kind of letter. For five weeks I scarcely missed you, everything was so new and different, and I couldn't write but formal letters. Now I'm beginning to wake up a bit, and I'm glad as I could be that the last few days I had with you were as good as they could be. I re-read your letter to me yesterday, and I was proud as hell. And as you say there, the worst won't be too hard to stand now. I don't know what's going to happen, but I do know we're in for a tough time. And I am glad that you are behind me, glad and proud. The losses here are heavy, but there's still a big chance of getting back alive, a big majority chance. And if I didn't, we can't help that. Be happy, darling. Things here aren't easy, but I never expected them to be. And we'll get through them somehow, and I'll see you again, bless you, darling.

John

I felt very depressed when I wrote this. Now I've eaten and am for the moment in a building. I feel fine. Warm. I'll get back to you, love, don't worry. God bless you.

Letter, 8.12.36.
Darling,
There is an English comrade going back, and this is my first chance of an uncensored letter. Remember that a good deal is not for publication. Excuse incoherence, because I'm in hospital with a slight wound and very weak. I'll tell you about that later.

I'll assume none of my letters have yet got through, as I've had no answers. First of all about myself. I'm with a small English group in the Machine Gun Company of the French Battalion of the First International Brigade. Luckily we are in the best company, the machine gunners; and in the best section of that, a Franco-Belgian section.

Now, as to the English blokes. Amongst the good blokes, Bernard, who is political delegate, replacing me because I did not speak enough French to get things done. He's been ill, and suffers terribly from the cold, but has borne up really well. John Summerfield [sic], tough and starting like me with no military training, has become a good soldier, and a good scrounger which is very important in a badly equipped army. David Mackenzie, a Scots student: age 19: first-class rifle shot and machine gunner: intellectual and writes good verse. A very good guy is Edward Burke of the *Daily Worker*. Ex-actor, looks like a sap, always loses everything, but has a queer gift for understanding machinery, became a good machine gunner in no time, was put *pro tem* on a trench gun, promoted to section leader he did well on a really nasty bit of the front line.

We had about a month's training at Albacete and La Rada. We English did badly, we were a national minority very hard to assimilate, mucked about between one station and another, starting work on one kind of gun and then having it taken away from us, taking part in manoeuvres which those that didn't speak French couldn't understand. When we at last got down to work with the machine gunners our training was interrupted almost before we started, and we were switched through to the front. That was early in November. We were put in general reserve in the University City, thought we could rest and take it easy. The first morning we were heavily shelled with 75's. I did quite well that day. The section leader, Fred Jones, was away, and so confident that all was quiet that he hadn't appointed a successor. I took charge on the moment, was able to get all the guns – we then had four – into position, and rescued one which the gunmen had deserted in a panic. But there was no attack after all.

Then in reserve in the Casa del Campo: a big wood, ex-royal forest, rather Sussexy to look at: but behind to the right a range of the Guadarama, a real good range with snow against a very blue sky. Then a piece of real bad luck. Maclaurin and three other Lewis gunners were sent up to the front. The French infantry company they were with was surprised by the Moors. The Lewis gunners stayed to cover the retreat. Mac was found dead at his gun, Steve Yates, one of our corporals, an ex-soldier and a good bloke, was killed too. Another, wounded in the guts. It's always the best seem to get the worst.

Then for the first time up to the front. We advanced into position at exactly the wrong time, at sunset, taking over some abandoned trenches. The Fascists had the range exact and shelled us accurately. Seven were killed in a few minutes. We had a nasty night in the trenches. Then back into reserve. The main trouble now was the intense cold: and we were sleeping out without blankets, which we had left behind in order to carry more machine-gun ammunition. Worse still to come; we had to make a night march back. There was a lorry load of wounded behind us. The lorry driver signalled, but wasn't noticed and got no answer. The four lines were so indeterminate that he thought we were a Fascist column and accelerated past us. Someone put up a wire to stop the car. The wire was swept aside, caught Fred Jones by the neck, hauled him over the parapet and killed him. Fred was a really good section leader: declassed bourgeois, ex-guardsman unemployed organizer, combination of adventurer and sincere Communist: but a really powerful person and could make his group work in a disciplined way in an army where there wasn't much discipline. That day the French redeemed their bad start by a really good bayonet attack which recaptured the philosophy building. We were in reserve for all this.

Then a spell of rest behind the lines. Back at the front in a really comfortable position in the philosophy and letters building. This was our best front line period. Comfortable, above all warm, and supplies regular. A great gutted building, with broken glass all over, and the fighting consisted of firing from behind barricades of philosophy books at the Fascists in a village below and in the Casa Velasques opposite. One day an anti-aircraft shell fell right into the room we were in. We were lucky as hell not to be wiped out completely: as it was there were only three slightly wounded, I gathering a small cut in the head. After the night in the rather inefficient but very nice Secours Rouge Hospital, where the amateur nurses wash your wounds like scrubbing the floor, I came back, feeling all right, but must have been a bit weak from loss of blood. Then came two heavy days work trench-digging in the frozen clay. The afternoon of the second day I think I killed a Fascist. Fifteen or sixteen of them were running from a bombardment. I and two Frenchmen were firing from our barricades with sights at 900: We got one, and both said it was I that hit him, though I couldn't be sure. If it is true, it's a fluke, and I'm not likely to do as good a shot as that again. Then back again into reserve. The first day we were there, David Mackenzie and I took a long walk towards the Guadarama. When I came back my wound began to hurt again: this morning I was very weak, a kind of retarded shock, I think, and am now in hospital for the time being.

Well, that's how far we've got. No wars are nice, and even a revolutionary war is ugly enough. But I'm becoming a good soldier, longish endurance and a capacity for living in the present and enjoying all that can be enjoyed. There's a tough time ahead but I've plenty of strength left for it.

Well, one day the war will end – I'd give it till June or July, and then if I'm alive I'm coming back to you. I think about you often, but there's nothing I can do but say again, be happy, darling, And I'll see you again one day.

Bless you,

John

JOHN CORNFORD

A Letter from Aragon

This is a quiet sector of a quiet front.

We buried Ruiz in a new pine coffin,
But the shroud was too small and his washed feet stuck out.
The stink of his corpse came through the clean pine boards
And some of the bearers wrapped handkerchiefs round their
   faces.
Death was not dignified.
We hacked a ragged grave in the unfriendly earth
And fired a ragged volley over the grave.

You could tell from our listlessness, no one much missed him.

This is a quiet sector of a quiet front.
There is no poison gas and no H.E.

But when they shelled the other end of the village
And the streets were choked with dust
Women came screaming out of the crumbling houses,
Clutched under one arm the naked rump of an infant.
I thought: how ugly fear is.

This is a quiet sector of a quiet front.
Our nerves are steady; we all sleep soundly.

In the clean hospital bed my eyes were so heavy
Sleep easily blotted out one ugly picture,
A wounded militiaman moaning on a stretcher,
Now out of danger, but still crying for water,
Strong against death, but unprepared for such pain.

This on a quiet front.

But when I shook hands to leave, an Anarchist worker
Said: 'Tell the workers of England
This was a war not of our own making,
We did not seek it.
But if ever the Fascists again rule Barcelona
It will be as a heap of ruins with us workers beneath it.'

JOHN CORNFORD

Diary Letter from Aragon
(Third Quarter of 1936)

Darling, I'll explain why in a minute, but just at the moment
I'm spending whole days at the front with nothing to do, and
so I am writing you an immense letter: if it wasn't so hot here
I'd try and get my ideas and impressions sorted out, but I can't,

so I'm writing everything down just as it comes out . . . First of all, a last will and testament. As you know there is a risk of being killed. Statistically not very great, but it exists all the same. First of all, why I am here? You know the political reasons. There's a subjective one as well. From the age of seventeen I was in a kind of way tied down, and envied my contemporaries a good deal their freedom to bum about. And it was partly because I felt myself for the first time independent that I came out here. But I promise this is the last time I shall leave you unnecessarily. Maybe that the Party will send me, but after this I will always be with you when I have the chance . . .

Well, all that's said. At the moment I am on top of a hill at the front in Aragon. A complete circle of rocky mountains, covered with green scrub, very barren, with a few fields in between. Two kilometres away a village held by the enemy. A grey stone affair with a big church. The enemy are quite invisible. An occasional rifle shot. One burst of machine-gun fire. One or two aeroplanes. The sound of our guns sometimes a long way off. And nothing else but a sun so hot that I am almost ill, can eat very little, and scarcely work at all. Nothing at all to do. We lie around all day. At night two hours on the watch – last night very fine with the lightning flickering behind Saragossa, miles away. Sleeping in the open with a single blanket on the stones – last night it rained, but just not quite enough to get through the blanket. How long we are to be here I don't know. And now comes the catch – I came up to the front and Richard was left behind. Enlisted here on the strength of my Party card. There was one little Italian comrade with some broken English. Now he's been sent off. So I'm here and the only communication I have is with the very broken French of a young Catalan volunteer. And so I am not only utterly lonely, but also feel a bit useless. Howeyer it couldn't have been expected that everything would go perfectly as it did to here. This loneliness, and this nervous anxiety from not knowing when or how to get back, and not yet having been under fire, means that inevitably I am pretty depressed. Even thought of using my press ticket to get home, but it would be too ridiculous to come out here to fight and go back because I was a bit lonely. So I am here provisionally until the fall of Saragossa whenever that is . . .

In the morning – it was a Sunday – before it was yet hot, the bells of the enemy village of Perdiguera sounded very slow and mournful across the distance. I don't know why, but that depressed me as much as anything ever has. However, I'm settling in now. Last night we began to make ourselves more comfortable – dug little trenches to sleep in and filled them with straw. So long as I am doing anything, however purpose-less, I feel fine. It's inactivity that just eats at my nerves. But the night before last I had a dream. One of the toughest people when I was small at school was the captain of rugger, an oaf called D—. I was in the same dormitory and terrified of him. I hadn't thought of him for years, but last night I dreamt extremely vividly about having a fight with him and holding my own, and I think that's a good omen. I don't know how long we stay on this hill, but I am beginning to settle down to it . . .

Now a bit about the political situation. That isn't easy to get straight, particularly as I haven't yet heard anyone explain the position of the Party (and the militia here I am with are P.O.U.M. – left sectarian semi-Trotskyists). But roughly this. The popular front tactics were worked magnificently to begin with. They won the elections. And under the slogan of defence of the Republic, they enabled us to arm the workers when the Fascist revolt started. Up till then the position is quite clear. But now in Catalonia things are like this. There is a left Repub-lican Government. But, in fact, the real power is with the workers. There are 50,000 or more armed workers in Catalonia – and in the Barcelona patrols they are organized in the following proportions: 325 C.N.T. (Anarchist), 185 E.R.C. (left Repub-lican), but this means simply the Civil Guard and the Guardia de Asalto, the police; 145 U.G.T. (Soc.-Com.); 45 P.O.U.M. Thus the Anarchists predominate. Seventy-five per cent of industry is already socialized – and mostly worked by the Anar-chists. In order to prevent a Fascist outbreak, every night splits, unpopular bosses, and known Fascists are taken for a ride. Assisted by the militia, there is a peasant war raging in the countryside and thousands of Kulaks and landlords have been killed. The Anarchists appear to be preparing to attack the Government after the fall of Saragossa. That would be disastrous. The only possible tactics for the Party are to place themselves at the head of the movement, get it under control, force recognition from the Government of the social gains of the revolution, and prevent at all costs an attack on the Government – unless the Government actually begin to sabotage the fight against Fascism. That may be what the Party is doing. But I have a fear that it is a little too mechanical in its application of People's Front tactics. It is still concentrating too much on trying to neutralize the petty bourgeoisie – when by far the most urgent task is to win the anarchist workers, which is a special technique and very different from broad Seventh Congress phrases. But I don't really know . . .

In Barcelona one can understand physically what the dictatorship of the proletariat means. All the Fascist press has been taken over. The real rule is in the hands of the militia committees. There is a real terror against the Fascists. But that doesn't alter the fact that the place is free – and conscious all the time of its freedom. Everywhere in the streets are armed workers and militiamen, and sitting in the cafés which used to belong to the bourgeoisie. The huge Hotel Colon overlooking the main square is occupied by the United Socialist Party of Catalonia. Further down, in a huge block opposite the Bank of Spain, is the Anarchist headquarters. The palace of a marquis in the Rambla is a C.P. headquarters. But one does not feel the tension. The mass of the people are oblivious of the Anarchist-Government trouble brewing, and simply are enjoying their freedom. The streets are crowded all day, and there are big crowds round the radio palaces. But there is nothing at all like tension or hysteria. It's as if in London the armed workers were dominating the streets – it's obvious that they wouldn't tolerate Mosley or people selling *Action* in the streets. And that wouldn't mean that the town wasn't free in the real sense. It is genuinely a dictatorship of the majority, supported by the overwhelming majority. Not yet in Soviet form – the elections to the committees aren't on the basis of localities or factories but representatives of organizations. That narrows the basis a bit, but not much, as a huge majority of the people are organized.

Going into action. Thank God for something to do at last. I shall fight like a Communist if not like a soldier. All my love. Salute.

John

Up till now this letter has been very miserable. For this reason. I came out with the intention of staying a few days firing a few shots, and then coming home. Sounded fine, but you just can't do things like that. You can't play at civil war, or fight with a reservation you don't mean to get killed. It didn't take long to realize that either I was here in earnest or else I'd better clear out. I tried to avoid the dilemma. Then I felt so lonely and bad I tried to get a pass back to Barcelona. But the question was decided for me. Having joined, I am in whether I like it or not. And I like it. Yesterday we went out to attack, and the prospect of action was terribly exhilarating – hence the message on the top of the page. But in the end we went back without doing anything. But I am settling down, picking up scraps of the language and beginning to feel happy. I think I'll make a good fighter, and I'm glad to be here. And since they won't let me go, it means that I don't feel useless or in the way, as if I were I'd be sent back. So I'll probably be here two months, and I will learn a hell of a lot. There is a 70 per cent chance of getting back uninjured and 90 per cent of getting back alive; which is, on the whole, worth while – and even if it wasn't, I'd have to stay . . .

Altogether I've passed the worst days of mental crisis, though all the physical hardship is to come. But I think I'll bear up. I've got a kind of feeling, rather difficult to explain, that my personality, I myself, was beginning to assert itself again. For days I've been shoved about from place to place, lost and anxious and frightened, and all that distinguished me personally from a unit in the mass obliterated – just a unit, alternately worried, home-sick, anxious, calm, hungry, sleepy, uncomfortable in turn – and all my own individuality, such strength as I have, such ability to analyse things, submerged. Now that's beginning to be different, I am beginning to adapt. Probably I'll be swept off my feet again when the first action starts. But now I, John Cornford, am beginning to emerge above the surface again and recognize myself and enjoy myself, and it feels good.

The army is a curious mixture of amateur and professional. There is practically no shouting and saluting. When somebody is told to do something, he gets up to do it all right, but not in a hurry. Officers are elected by acclamation, and obeyed. About half the troops are more or less in uniform, in blue or brown overalls and blue shirts. The rest are more or less nondescript. I myself am wearing a pair of heavy, black, corduroy trousers (expropriated from the bourgeoisie), a blue sports shirt, and that alpaca coat, rope-soled sandals, and an infinitely battered old sombrero. Luggage, a blanket, a cartridge case (held together with string) in which there is room for a spare shirt, a knife, toothbrush, bit of soap, and comb. Also a big tin mug stuck in my belt. But most are a good bit smarter than that.

What is new is the complete feeling of insecurity, new for me, but most workers have it from the day they leave school. Always in all my work before there has been the background of a secure and well-provided home, and friends that I could fall back upon in an emergency. Now that is no longer here, I stand completely on my own. And I find that rather difficult at first. But I shall manage. Just now, for instance, I have unlimited opportunity to write. And I have plenty of things which for years I've wanted to write. But I can't get them together in my head, things aren't straight enough: all I can put down are my immediate subjective impressions, and I can't think about Birmingham or anywhere else. Oh, for the objectivity of a Nehru. I'll learn: I am learning. But it's going to be something of a testing-time.

Yesterday I watched from the tiled roof of our hut the aerial bombardment of Perdiguera. The planes circling slowly and high above; then you would see a huge cloud of dust rising, beginning to float away, and then, seconds later, the sound of the crash. The comrades with me on the roof were shouting for delight as each bomb landed. I tried to think of the thing in terms of flesh and blood and the horror of that village, but I also was delighted. Now as I write three enemy planes have passed by and out of sight, but you can hear the thud of their bombs somewhere behind our lines.

Yesterday for the first time I was under fire. This is how it all happened, and it is one of the most curious experiences of my life. I found in the evening that we were due to make a surprise attack. That same evening there had arrived at Llecinena (Lerida) a new group of Italians. We lit a fire in the backyard, and I was given a chicken to pluck. Then the leader of the group, who for days now has let the house get into an indescribably filthy mess, suddenly set to work to straighten everything out and prepared a most extraordinary meal, the first we have had with clean cutlery and a clean table-cloth. After we had finished and smoked a cigarette – by now I am getting very used to listening to conversations of which I don't understand a word – we got our things together and marched out! We were kept waiting for an hour or two in the square, and I twice fell asleep on the pavement – for that morning I had decided that so little was happening and we were getting so much sleep at night, I wouldn't sleep any more during the day. Then after a bit we marched off. Halted on the road and again fell asleep. Even then the indiscipline of our troops struck me. Every one was whispering, and then every one would suddenly start shushing and altogether there was quite a noise. I was feeling quite good and cheerful then. After a bit we left the road, which was soft under foot and powdery with dust, and turned off into the mountains. We marched all night through the mountains, across the little, banked-up strips of field they have in Aragon, through stubble. For a while I slipped and floundered, then more or less fell into the rhythm. Then gradually it began to get light and I realized that this wasn't a night attack at all. Then far below us on the right we saw the lights of Saragossa. After that we halted for a bit, and a comrade pointed out to me Perdiguera miles below. I had no idea we had climbed so high. Then at last I understood the manoeuvre. By a night's march through the mountains we had got completely in the rear of the enemy. Sebastian, the fat Rumanian, who was more exhausted than anyone else by the climb, began to try and sing a song from the

Meistersingers, but I couldn't make out the tune. Then we went down. We were sorted out into groups, but almost immediately were dissolved again in the confusion. From on top of a hill – it was now about 5–6, and full day – we could see Perdiguera. Then we went down again and there was a ridge which hid it from view. Then the advance began. Our single column spread out like a fan over the parched earth of the fields, and we began to move quickly. I threw away the blanket I had carried all night for it was already hot. Then we came over the ridge in sight of the enemy, and at the same time heard an attack open up on the other side of the village. We moved forwards and were soon crouching in the vineyards a few hundred yards from the village, and for the first time heard shots whistling overhead. It was then our total lack of discipline made itself felt. The houses of the village came quite close on the left, but on the right were hidden by a ridge and only the church tower showed. But it seemed clear to me that we should attack to the right, because there was the enemy machine-gun which was holding up our counter-attack. But no such thing. A group of us crossed the fields in front of the vineyards and crouched with good cover below an olive field, the last stretch before reaching the village. Another group dashed off to attack the houses on the left and managed to get right up to them. All this time I hadn't the faintest idea who was winning or losing. Then I began to understand the planless nature of the attack. The group I was with was recalled back to the vines. There I began to collect the completely unripe grapes in my hands and suck the juice out of them. It didn't do much to relieve thirst, but it left a clean acid taste in the mouth. Then I saw the group which had taken the houses on the left come pouring back and take shelter. All this time I had not felt the least nervousness, but that may be because so far no one had been hit. I was surprised that the kick of my mauser was so slight – I hadn't had a chance of using it before – but all the same I couldn't get it under control. All this time I couldn't see any of the enemy, and so confined myself to shooting at doors and windows. Then quite suddenly we heard the noise of enemy planes. We crouched quite still among the vines: I was together with a long Italian, Milano, a member of my group, and did what he did. Apparently the planes didn't notice us. They confined themselves to bombing the other side of Perdiguera, where we were attacking. But after the bombardment our forces were completely dispersed – not out of cowardice, no one was in the least frightened, but simply through lack of leadership, no one had said where to go and all had taken cover in different directions. So Milano decided to retreat, and I followed him. A group of about fourteen collected, and we marched back. Presently we came to a well – a big, open, stone affair about six yards across. On top was floating a dead rat. We stopped for a drink, though Milano said we might be captured because of it. Then, as we were going back, we saw a group of men in the vines and marched back to them. But there weren't many there. I went to sleep for a few minutes in the vines, but was soon woken up and told we should retreat. We retreated to a big stone barn on a slope above the well. Resting in the barn a discussion was held. At last one comrade, a strong and intelligent-looking worker in overalls, took the initiative and introduced some kind of order. I couldn't understand the discussion, but I made out that a committee of three was being elected to take a decision on what to do. And in the end it was decided to retreat. On the way down I borrowed a mug off a comrade to go down to the well for a drink. I had a drink and several others followed. (We had been about twenty-five in all in the barn.) Then suddenly bullets began to whistle very close – zip – zip – zip. We crouched under the shadow of the stone rim of the well. Then eventually we sprinted up the fields in short bouts, bent double with the bullets all around us. After that we could retreat in peace. We marched back across the fields to the hills. My throat was utterly dry, so thirsty I could not swallow, and hungry and very weary. It was only by a desperate physical effort of the guts that I was able to move one foot after the other. The climb up the mountains was a serious affair because the heat of the sun was colossal. I placed myself behind Milano, who was a mountaineer, and followed as closely as I could the deliberate economy of his footsteps. We reached the top, and in spite of the fiasco I was beginning to feel better. At least I felt equal to the others, when, before, I had felt rather like a sham soldier. And this was exactly the kind of physical endurance my body was best capable of producing – certainly I was no more weary than the others and certainly made less fuss about water. The group split into two halves, one going off after water, the other with Milano keeping up high. Nearing the top the breeze was a real relief, and we came into a pinewood, the first proper vegetation for days. Then as we came out of the wood we saw some sheds below on the right. We went down to look for water. There was a well and a lame old man sitting by it. We hoisted the water in a leaky bucket. Just to show how thirsty I was, though the bucket was leaking rapidly I was able to fill and empty the cup ($\frac{2}{3}$ pint) five times before the bucket was empty. I noticed that the more experienced drank less. Then we went off to the barn and slept for three hours. Afterwards the old man put us on to a road, we moved slowly down, at his cripple's pace, through cypress woods, past those barren strips of climbing fields, past great slabs of marble sticking out of the hills, stopping at every well to drink. The worst was over. The rest was down hill. When we reached the first outpost we learned that five men had been killed in the frontal attack that day. Then home, past the big amphitheatre round the stagnant village pond with its green reeds, past the bare strip of earth which was a football ground, and back into Llecinena.

One thing that will come out of this. After having seen all the mistakes in organization, all the inefficiency, and yet the revolution is winning, I think I shall have far more confidence in my own organizing ability in such a situation. There are a whole lot of things I think I could do if I understood the language. And in spite of the fact that I understand so little, I think it will be possible to learn a good deal of military stuff – though the conditions here are so unique that there will probably be no opportunity of applying it – unless in Saragossa it is a question of street fighting.

The luckiest accident of the whole war was that which put me in touch with the German comrades. From this time on the days, which had dragged and stuck and jammed like a cart in a wet road, begin to rotate slowly and regularly like the wheels of a train just gathering steam. I think the days spent in the village alone were the hardest I have yet spent in my whole life. It was the same loneliness and isolation as the first term in a new school, without the language and without any kind of distraction of something to do. All the revolutionary enthusiasm was bled out of me. I simply counted the hours. But the Germans are a splendid lot – and incidentally have treated me with a quite extraordinary personal kindness; and at last I can live in the present, get outside of my own mind, and carry on until it is time to go back.

I was never more glad of anything in my life than the accident which threw me together with them. Four of them are ex-members of the party; one still a member. They have left because they genuinely believe the C.I. has deserted the revolution. Partly, perhaps, it is the uprootedness of emigrants. I do not know enough of the Spanish position to argue with them successfully. But I am beginning to find out how much the Party and the International have become flesh and blood of me. Even when I can put forward no rational argument, I feel that to cut adrift from the Party is the beginning of political suicide.

By far the greatest need is for something to read. In this heat, in spite of the fact that for two days we've been doing nothing in the shade of the monastery, it's very hard to sit down and study a language. I've forced myself to do about an hour and a half's German today, but only by an effort. About all one can do under these conditions is read. It isn't easy to write anything coherent or sensible.

To-day I found with interest but not surprise the distortions in the P.O.U.M. press. The fiasco of the attack on Perdiguera is presented as a punitive expedition which was a success.

Again into action for the attack on Huesca . . . So far there has been no fighting in this advance, and only under an inaccurate rifle fire for a few minutes. And I am now rested and fed, and feeling happy and content. All I want is some English cigarettes, some English tea, strong (insular, but can't be helped).

Since meeting the Germans I feel like myself again, no longer lost, and revolutionary again. Before I was too lost to feel anything but lost. Now I'll fight like hell and I think I'll enjoy it. They are the finest people in some ways I've ever met. In a way they have lost everything, have been through enough to break most people, and remain strong and cheerful and humorous. If anything is revolutionary it is these comrades.

JOHN CORNFORD

from *Poem in Spring*

Ten years ago was a Spring when we cleared our throats and spat the stale taste of narcotics from our mouths as the stuff by cartloads came in.

We fled from old haunts, ghost-ridden woods and in new and facile scenes found a new and facile language: found words whose accents tipped towards the future.

In the third decade we spoke again of man's love for man as motive and end.

Over pylon-straddled hills we set out for the marshes, compass in hand and the land thoroughly charted, to reclaim the dead acres, proclaiming a new plenty.

Our poetic purpose was to inspire towards action the calm beauty in the word's season of summer.

Over our plains tornado already circled. On the pavements of our precocious city the shadows fell.

The whisper of China blew sinister through the suburbs; the horror of Abyssinia was heard as an echo of the future.

The names of Harrar and Addis Abbaba became a new diction through which sorrow spoke of to-morrow.

Spain rose with menacing thunder of cloud, rumbling over Europe the names of Madrid, of Brunete, of GuadalaJara [sic] of Jarama: and from those guns broke the smoke and the shell of to-day.

Austria was down overnight, to our mortuary of names adding Vienna. Prague and Warsaw disappeared into the graveyard of Europe.

Ten years of sun and shadow. Ten years of the premonition of
love and the omens of death. Ten years of retreat for us who
for long thought we were advancing.

Our eyes burnt through to a vision of 1940 and saw, naming, the
flaming cities and the wounded caterpillars of refugees
winding hopelessly across Europe.

Again the names fall like wreaths on the grave of a continent.
We mourn for the unborn as we lament the dead.

H. B. MALLALIEU

Guadalajara

March-weather storms the house like shrapnel.
I hear the ice roar, and the guns.
And in the silent, sentry passes
the crazy dead stand to attention.

What did Napoleon see, who stared
at Moscow as I watch the fire?
Frost climbed the window-pane for him,
but for his men the snow piled higher.

And Hannibal in the Alps, did he
rage at the cold and blame his luck?
The elephants and soldiers did
not listen when they froze to muck.

Caesar with Spanish slingers shivered
in Gaul; but knew the beds at home
would yet be warm. The slingers died.
And Caesar – Caesar whored in Rome.

In Libya the shaken sword
aches in the sun. The conquering boor
sweats and grows hoarse. But here his men
20   cough death besides the dying Moors.

What shall the rigid soldier say
who knows the cheat, yet cannot turn?
The ice builds bayonets in his veins
and the rough frost like anger burns,

and pity plucks him by the sleeve
and whispers in his ear that kings
will still be snug when water runs
the courses of his blood in spring.

What is my pity worth? I fret
no frozen body, but my mind;
and if I tremble, all my rage
weighs nothing in the bite of wind.

Forgive me, men at posts, who stiffen
for furies such as kings' or mine;
and suffer me no more than speak
the words your lips will never form,

the hope that hangs there like a breath
that fate shall break your frozen line,
break kings and break fanatic men;
that March shall break the world with storm.

J. BRONOWSKI

Full Moon at Tierz: Before the Storming of Huesca

I

The past, a glacier, gripped the mountain wall,
And time was inches, dark was all.
But here it scales the end of the range,
The dialectic's point of change,
Crashes in light and minutes to its fall.

Time present is a cataract whose force
7 Breaks down the banks even at its source,
8 And history forming in our hands
9 Not plasticene but roaring sands,
Yet we must swing it to its final course.

The intersecting lines that cross both ways,
Time future, has no image in space,
Crooked as the road that we must tread,
Straight as our bullets fly ahead.
We are the future. The last fight let us face.

2

16 Where in the fields by Huesca the full moon
Throws shadows clear as daylight's, soon
The innocence of this quiet plain
Will fade in sweat and blood, in pain,
As our decisive hold is lost or won.

21 All round, the barren hills of Aragon
Announce our testing has begun.
Here what the Seventh Congress said,
If true, if false, is live or dead,
25 Speaks in the Oviedo mausers' tone.

Three years ago Dimitrov fought alone
And we stood taller when he won.
But now the Leipzig dragon's teeth
29 Sprout strong and handsome against death,
And here an army fights where there was one.

31 We studied well how to begin this fight.
Our Maurice Thorez held the light.
But now by Monte Aragon
We plunge into the dark alone,
Earth's newest planet wheeling through the night.

3

Though Communism was my waking time,
Always before the lights of home
Shone clear and steady and full in view –
Here, if you fall, there's help for you –
40 Now, with my party, I stand quite alone.

Then let my private battle with my nerves,
The fear of pain whose pain survives,
The love that tears me by the roots,
The loneliness that claws my guts,
Fuse in the welded front our fight preserves.

46 O be invincible as the strong sun,
Hard as the metal of my gun,
48 O let the mounting tempo of the train
Sweep where my footsteps slipped in vain,
October in the rhythm of its run.

4

Now the same night falls over Germany
And the impartial beauty of the stars
Lights from the unfeeling sky
Oranienburg and freedom's crooked scars.
We can do nothing to ease that pain
But prove the agony was not in vain.

England is silent under the same moon,
From Clydeside to the gutted pits of Wales.
The innocent mask conceals that soon
60 Here too our freedom's swaying in the scales.
61 O understand before too late
Freedom was never held without a fight.

Freedom is an easily spoken word
But facts are stubborn things. Here, too, in Spain

66
Our fight's not won till the workers of all the world
Stand by our guard on Huesca's plain,
Swear that our dead fought not in vain,
Raise the red flag triumphantly
For Communism and for liberty.

JOHN CORNFORD

Battle of Jarama 1937

The sun warmed the valley
But no birds sang
The sky was rent with shrapnel
And metallic clang

Death stalked the olive trees
Picking his men
His leaden finger beckoned
Again and again

Dust rose from the roadside
A stifling cloud
Ambulances tore past
Klaxoning loud

Men torn by shell-shards lay
Still on the ground
The living sought shelter
Not to be found

Holding their hot rifles
Flushed with the fight
Sweat-streaked survivors
Willed for the night

With the coming of darkness
Deep in the wood
A fox howled to heaven
Smelling the blood.

JOHN LEPPER

At Castellon

Backed to the brown walls of the square
2   The lightless lorry head lamps stare
With glinting reflectors through the night
At our gliding star of light.

Houses are tombs, tarpaulins cover
Mysterious trucks of the lorries over.
The town vacantly seems to wait
The explosion of a fate.

Our cigarettes and talking stir
10   Beneath the walls a small false ember.
A sentry stops us at his hut
12   Stamping with his rifle butt.

Beside him stands a working man
With cheeks where suns have run.
'Take this comrade to the next village,'
The lines ploughed with ravage

Lift to a smile, the eyes gleam
And then relapse into their dream.
Head bent, he shuffles forward
And in without a word.

The car moves on to suns and time.
22   Of safety for us and him.

134

But behind us on the road
The winged black roaring fates unload

Cargoes of iron and of fire
To delete with blood and ire
The will of those who dared to move
From the furrow, their life's groove.

STEPHEN SPENDER

Waiting at Cerbere

And on the hillside
That is the colour of peasant's bread
Is the rectangular
White village of the dead.

No one stirs in those streets.
Out of those dark doorways no one comes.
At the tavern of the Black Cross
Only the cicada strums.

And below, where the headland
Strips into rock, the white mane
Of foam like a quickened breath
Rises and falls again;

And above, the road
Zigzagging tier on tier
Above the terraced vineyards,
Goes on to the frontier.

SYLVIA TOWNSEND WARNER

Barcelona

When the soldiers came marching from the barracks of Mont-juich into the centre of Barcelona people supposed it was another parade. Parades had been frequent – sabre-rattling gestures supposed by the military authorities to have a sedative effect on the herves of the populace.

It was not till they opened fire, not till the women out marketing, the breakfasters in the cafés, the street vendors showing their wares, the gardeners tranquilly planting the flower-beds of the Plaza de Catalonia with scarlet salvia, looked up and saw people falling dead around them, that the sedative effect of this military parade was realized.

It was morning. The workers were already in their factories, safely out of the way. A large body of troops occupied the Hotel Colon, a block-wide building overlooking the Plaza de Catalonia and raking the long, straight boulevard of the Ramblas. Here they sent the guests to the ground floor, the servants to the top floor, and settled themselves and their machine-guns in the remainder of the building. Others continued down the Ramblas, small detachments entering the churches on their route.

What happened then is something which we in England must find almost unbelievable. The police ranged themselves with the people, fighting side by side with members of the middle class, with professors and journalists and intellectuals who left their coffee-cups and their newspapers to make history. The police carried arms already, the others ran to the gun-shops, taking what they could find, sporting guns and automatics, and hunting-knives when nothing better was left them.

Even stranger weapons were utilized. A tram, hastily blinded with some scraps of sheet-metal, was sent at full speed down the Ramblas, through a machine-gun barrage spraying from the heavy Baroque church which has subsequently become so famous and endeared as an exquisite work of art. Where the soldiers had gone in, the tram-cargoes of men with shot-guns and pistols followed, though they did not find so easy an access. However, they took the kingdom of heaven by storm, and put the machine-guns out of action. In the sturdily tranquil Barcelona which I saw two months later that tram was running as usual, distinguished, though, from trams of no past by the great wreath of flowers, renewed every morning, which it carried on its bows.

Wearing its proud wreath, it rumbles past the bullet-scarred walls, the trophies of flowers propped here and there against them to mark the death-site of some fighter in the July days, the street-vendors' stalls which line the broad asphalt walk under the trees. Mixed with the old wares, the flowers, the shaving-brushes, the canaries and love-birds, the watermelons, are new wares: militia caps, pistols (toy-pistols to our shame be it spoken), rings and badges and brooches carrying the initials of the anarchist F.A.I. and C.N.T., the Trotskyist P.O.U.M., the Communist P.S.U.C. and U.G.T., the inter-party clenched fist with its motto *No Pasarán* and the hammer and sickle. The bookstalls show new wares, too. Books on political theory, the classics of Marx and Bukharin, Proudhon and Ferrer, the novels of Zola and Rolland and Barbusse. Among them are many treatises – serious, not bawdy – on birth-control and sexual hygiene.

On such wares as these the empty sockets of the church windows stare down. They look very queer, these churches, Giant Popes abruptly changed to Giant Pagans: for with their gutted interiors, their unglazed windows, their broken, boarded-up doorways, they carry a sort of dissolute resemblance to Parthenon and Baalbec. Inside them accumulates that peculiar litter which arrives to every derelict building, however made derelict, whether by fire or flood or earthquake or war or the will of man: mortar and rubble, scraps of paper, scraps of clothing, pigeons' dung and pigeons' feathers.

The barrel-organs rattle out the 'Internationale', at intervals the loudspeakers confirm it. Technically, the broadcasts are pretty bad, the loudspeakers blare and rattle; but the quality of the music broadcast, both classical and popular, is good. It was a shock, even remembering what the B.B.C. is like, to return to the 'popular' programmes of the B.B.C.

It was interesting, too, to compare the commercial art posters still remaining on the walls with the new official posters. These are admirable, with a certain stringent and ascetic quality which exactly echoes the *No Pasarán* of a people who, drilling with broomsticks and fighting against the weight of Europe, drill and fight on. Turning from their sober colouring and grim line to the fading Cadum babies, the public statuary, is as much of a shock as returning to the B.B.C.

But to realize fully what sort of taste the new alliance of worker and artist has driven out one has to visit the *torres* – the suburban villas where the upper classes enjoyed pure air and a view over Barcelona.

If one is English one can undoubtedly swallow a good deal in the way of architectural delirium, if only because we live in a climate which makes any light-coloured building with a great deal of balcony and veranda and top-hamper seem invigoratingly light-hearted. At heart, too, nests the hereditary feeling that people on the Continent dwell naturally in casinos. But swallowing the minarets and the crenellations, the large bastard-Corbusier bathing-huts and the Fitzjohn's Avenue gothic, the toughest stomach quails before the interior decorations of these villas. They can be perfectly studied by those who have a mind to it since their owners left in a hurry, and the State, taking over, has preserved them intact. Or so I believed till at a local Comité I was shown sheet after sheet of typed lists of the valuables taken from these same dwellings: a dinner-service of 120 pieces, in gold; ten embossed wine-coolers, in gold; a chalice in platinum; a washhand set in silver; two grotesque figures, in gold; a coffee service in silver, jewelled.

'Most of them have been melted down. They were of no artistic interest.'

I could well believe it.

Out of the churches a great deal has been taken and placed in museums. Some of these preservations are interesting from other points of view than those of the artist and antiquarian.

One church was being burned out when a connoisseur who was present recollected that a certain exceedingly venerable tapestry had been overlooked in the preliminary sifting. He ran forward and beat out the flames which had already begun to consume it. As he did so pieces of charred paper were seen fluttering down. Further inspection showed that the back of the tapestry was wadded with bank-notes.

I heard other stories of non-sacred valuables stored in churches; and it seemed to me extraordinary that a cult sufficiently modern-minded to preserve machine-guns and ammunitions in its churches should not have a more accurate appreciation of the beauties of a bank-balance. I did not discredit the good faith of those who told me these stories, but I supposed that legend, always a quick breeder in a crisis, might have made fifty different versions of one incident.

When I had looked at the rich men's houses, when I had read the lists of the valuables taken therefrom, I revised my opinion. The Spanish aristocracy is in a primitive stage of capitalism, it preserves the medieval brag of possessions, it locks up its money in gold and jewels and keeps the gold and jewels for display.

An amusing example of this was the celebrated boarding-school for young ladies kept by the sisters of the Sacred Heart. No young lady was allowed to enter this establishment (officially sacred to the daughters of the nobility) without a trousseau in which every article of clothing was numbered by a dozen dozen. So valuable was the social prestige of this establishment that the un-enobled rich, equipping their daughters with the requisite 144 nightgowns, bust-bodices, etc., strained every nerve and every persuasion to get their daughters received there. So powerful was the tradition of the social prestige that the un-enobled daughters, even when they had been admitted, were not allowed to mingle with the blue-blooded.

The modesty of our English aristocracy, hanging its women-kind with Ciro pearls and synthetic emeralds while the genuine articles repose in the bank, is unknown to them. So strong is this tradition in Spain that the magnates of Barcelona, to seem aristocrats, did the same. That the tradition has its advantages is proved by the number of empty jewel-cases, bare ruined choirs where late the sweet dollars chinked, which they left behind in the villas. If the laity is thus medieval, no wonder that the church is medieval too, only with Christian humility burying its gold beneath the flagstones, lining its tapestries with bank-notes.

The works of ecclesiastical art are in the museums, the churches are bare and barred. Apologists in this country have tended to stress the first statement, but the second is the more significant. Those systematically gutted interiors are the more impressive when one contrasts them with the preservation of the villas. In the villas was as great, or greater, a demonstration of luxury, idleness, and superbity. In the villas were objects infinitely more desirable as loot than anything the churches could offer. Had the churches been sacked, as some say they were, by a greedy and envious mob, that mob would have sacked the villas with more greed and better satisfaction. But the villas are untouched, and the churches are gutted. They have been cleaned out exactly as sick-rooms are cleaned out after a pestilence. Everything that could preserve the contagion has been destroyed.

It is idle, too, to suggest that this work was the result of a policy imposed on the people by a Marxist leadership. One might well wish that it had been. It would be a feather in the Marxist cap. But actually, Barcelona is an anarchist town, and anarchism does not impose policies. It was the people themselves who, deliberately and systematically, put the churches out of action. So extensive, so thorough a campaign, could not have been carried out unless it were by the will of the people. And it was more than the expression of resentment at finding the churches used as arms-dumps and machine-gun nests. Not every church was so used, but the blameless on this count have not fared any better than the others. It was a longer, a more universal resentment which stripped the walls and burned the pulpits and confessionals, and barred up the doors, a realization that here, beyond the other strongholds of Fascism and capitalism, was the real stronghold of the oppressors.

I was lucky enough to see one belated example of this. It was reported that in the garden of a suburban villa a religious plaque which had escaped notice was being used as a private praying centre. The local Comité to whom this was reported sent two men with hammers. Seriously, without a vestige of either rage or contempt, they smashed it to bits. Their expressions were exactly those of two conscientious decontaminating officers dealing with a bag of infected linen which had been discovered in a house which was supposed to be free of infection.

A dozen people or so watched the ceremony, and when the plaque had been destroyed one of them drew the men's attention to a garden statue half concealed in bushes. The two men looked at it. 'It's not a saint,' they said, and went away.

Among those lookers-on was a servant girl who had been suspected of worshipping before the plaque. She had had a religious upbringing, she could neither read nor write. While the hammer-blows fell she watched with painful attention. Her face expressed profound animal fear. But it was not on the men that she fixed her terrified stare. It was the plaque itself which she watched with such bewildered and abject terror.

SYLVIA TOWNSEND WARNER

Barcelona Nerves

1   Neither fools nor children any longer:
    Those ways, traits, gone and away
3   That once made life a luck-game, death a stranger:
    We're going on.

    Dynamo-driven city waiting bombers,
    Roadways barricade-unpaved, fear
    In the torn minds: the mind remembers
8   What it's all for.

9   Death means the girl's corpse warm-alive when buried:
10 Death means the retching brothels where on black
    Death-tide, death-fear, an army of boys is carried
    To a pox-wreck.

And life's a matter of beating this, of breaking
By own hardness, and a held hand, out
From fury, frustration, fear, the waiting, the shouting,
The hate of fate.

17 Neither fools nor children we who are joining
    (Twenty years ago I knew war's face)
19 We make what can wreck others into our gaining,
    Into our choice.

TOM WINTRINGHAM

Today in Barcelona

I was in Barcelona from December 29th till January 9th. The most surprising things I saw were on January 9th – in Toulouse, where I landed by 'plane from Spain: food in the shops and on stalls in the streets, drink in the cafés, well-clad people, the street-lamps lit. It only takes one ten days to find these things surprising.

I had arrived in Barcelona after dark, the streets like limbo but crowded. A feeling of thousands of people circulating round one in the night. That is one thing there is plenty of here – human beings; two and a half millions now against one million before. These people's lives have become very much simplified and assimilated to one another; the topics of conversation are few and universal, money has lost its diversifying force, and everyone, one feels, is by necessity in the same boat. For this reason one feels very much at home in the dark streets of Barcelona. There may be bitter dissensions among the politicians, but the people in the streets, one feels, have become a family party – or, if you prefer it, are in on the same racket – united by material necessities, by hunger, by the fear of sudden death which enhances the values of life. I have never been anywhere where these values were so patent. It would be difficult to be a Hamlet in Barcelona.

The shops are ghosts of shops, only open in the morning, the counters and shelves bare, one object every two yards. The cafés are ghosts of cafés – no coffee, beer, spirits or wine, people making do with coloured water which is called lemonade or with terribly degraded vermouth (yet in one café there was a string quartet). They close at nine and the chairs are piled on the tables. But the people, though thin and often ill, are far from being ghosts of people. Facts in a city at war are necessarily uncertain; how can one know the truth about the Front or unravel the paradoxical knots of Spanish party politics or sort out truth from propaganda? One fact, however, is as clear – and as refreshing – as daylight: the extraordinary morale of these people – their courage, good-humour and generosity.

Their strength, of course, can also be their weakness. Optimism on the Government side has already meant several gains for Franco. Again, while a people must obviously adapt themselves to war conditions, it does not seem altogether desirable that war should become quite so much a habit as it has in Barcelona; one feels the people have almost forgotten about peace and might not know what to do with it if it came. Yet without this confidence and this adaptation to circumstances, Barcelona no doubt would have already given way to Goliath. Her people are essentially non-defeatist; no one this New Year admitted for a moment that Franco's present offensive might succeed. I saw a new *comedor* for children in an industrial district, which is being converted from a theatre and adjacent cinema.

In this, once the great city of cafés and taxis, you now have to get about by walking. And instead of cocktails and seven-course meals there are food-queues, rationing of acorns, a ladleful of lentils for dinner. By ordinary people food cannot be bought though it can be obtained by barter: soap, flints and tobacco are among the best currencies. (I am told that Arabs come into the port and sell soap at 250 pesetas a kilo.) In my hotel (where the bombing commissions stay) we had a privileged access to food – at fancy prices: a dish of chickpeas at 30 to 40 pesetas, horse and chopped swedes at 45, fried sprats (a very rare delicacy) at 60. (A superintendent of a *comedor* gets 400 pesetas a month salary.) People's rations at the moment (they are always decreasing) are as follows: – Bread: 150 grammes per day except on Sundays. Chickpeas (100 gr.) and peas (50) on one ticket, but you only get these once a week or maybe once a month. Oil: ¼ litre, but they have had none now for three months and then it was like machine oil. They have had no fish on ration tickets for two months, no meat for one month. Those who, instead of having ration-cards go to the *comedores*, seem to me to be better off, because at any rate they know what they will get. And the children are considered first; for all that their diet is causing a vast increase in rickets and in skin diseases such as scabies. I should add that the people who work in the *comedores* seem invariably good humoured, kindly and strictly conscientious.

In these extremities statistics are more important than impressions, but here are some snippets from my visit. *The crowing of cocks:* most characteristic sound in Barcelona (as if you were to hear cocks in Piccadilly). Lots of people keep hens or rabbits on their window balconies. *Lack of tobacco:* to give a man a cigarette is to give him the Kingdom of Heaven; I gave a Spaniard three cigarettes one night, and next day he sent me in return a hunk of dry bread wrapped in paper. *Refugee colonies:* often in converted convents, beds in the gloom under towering Gothic arches, old women with eye diseases making jokes about Mr Chamberlain, the children doing eurhythmics. *Schools:* shortage of teachers, but the children clean (though washed in cold water) and happy, the walls often decorated with figures from Walt Disney – the Big Bad Wolf representing Fascism – or with Popeye the Sailor knocking Mussolini for a loop. All the children seem to be natural artists; in some schools they still print their own poems and lino-cuts.

Air raids: The siren is like the voice of a lost soul, but the anti-aircraft defence is beautiful both to hear and to see – balls of cottonwool floating high in the blue day, or white flashes at night. The searchlights also are beautiful, and the red tracer bullets floating in chains gently, almost ineptly, upwards like decorations at a fair. After the raid on the centre on New Year's Eve the streets were heaped with powdered glass, and crowds collected to look at a spatter of black blood-spots fifteen feet high on a wall. During an alarm in Tarragona four girls romped down the square with their arms round each other's necks. *Ruins:* near the cathedral a house six stories high, its face and floors torn away; on the top story a plate-rack fixed to the wall with all its plates unbroken and a shelf with two unbroken bottles. The district to the side of the port, Barceloneta, has been evacuated; all the streets are rubble, and all the houses like skulls. *Irony:* the Banco de Vizcaya still announces stock market prices for July 17th, 1936, and the chemists sell cures for obesity. *Recreation:* every Friday afternoon a crack orchestral concert, well attended, in the enormous Teatro di Liceo; the theatres and cinemas all running; a newsreel showing a fashionable dog show in Moscow. And people still playing pelota. But the Zoo is macabre – a polar bear 99 per cent dead, a kangaroo eating dead leaves.

In the Barcelona air-port I met an American seaman, an ex-member of the International Brigade, short, square and tough, with a face like a gangster. On his lapel he wore the insignia of all the Government parties – to create good feeling, he said. He expressed the greatest admiration for the Spaniards – even, in spite of what some people say, as soldiers. I shared his admiration and, as I flew down from the Pyrenees to a country where money still goes, I felt that my descent into this respectable landscape was not only a descent in metres but also a step down in the world.

LOUIS MACNEICE

The Hour Glass (1)

Dryly across the street the late leaves fall Barcelona falls.
From the mind as from a wall the map of Spain stares squarely
And like the leaves in silence is not to be evaded.
How often and dumbly I revisit that city those provinces,

Salute again the outposts see again the mules meander up and
  slowly
Wind along the grey road to Cuenca to the parched plateau . . .
And your voice merging with memory is lost in the lost provinces
Where that army marched was cold and died and women from
  their empty shops came stumbling –
Ah now, I whisper, where now is the sanctuary! –
Then as your voice reassures me urgently then still
The olives broken by the sands and sea
Slope down and mean whatever they meant when I saw them
Bearing their wounds like a gain or a bud of reckoning.

Hearing your voice
Strange and urgent and as if through eddying
Nowhere tides of people stumbling, through the siege of cities,
I am conscious of that quality inescapable
In falling leaves of leaves in secret budding,
Clad O in all winter's harness
This glimpse comes brightening.

                                          EWART MILNE

The Hour Glass (2)

Why do you not take comfort then, my heart?
Now when the inoffensive and the trusting fall
Hearing not the volley's echo
Speak, O bleak heart, and by your silence forcibly
Say here as when through woody boles the sap
Persuades the wondering buds to swell
We too are beating and our beat is their beat

And never did we see the buds refuse
Nor thought their sure serenity of spears
Remits one moment in concerted urge
To oppose a people's bastion to the times;

Never did we think the sap had gone
Sunk downward and betrayed but once again
Faintly and less faintly it was storming and was flooding.

EWART MILNE

A Moment of War

It is night like a red rag
drawn across the eyes

the flesh is bitterly pinned
to desperate vigilance

the blood is stuttering with fear.

O praise the security of worms
7   *in cool crumbs of soil,*
flatter the hidden sap
and the lost unfertilized spawn of fish!

The hands melt with weakness
into the gun's hot iron

12   the body melts with pity,

the face is braced for wounds
the odour and the kiss of final pain.

O envy the peace of women
giving birth and love like toys
into the hands of men!

The mouth chatters with pale curses

the bowels struggle like a nest of rats

147

the feet wish they were grass
spaced quietly.

O Christ and Mother!

But darkness opens like a knife for you
and you are marked down by your pulsing brain

and isolated

and your breathing,

your breathing is the blast, the bullet,
and the final sky.

LAURIE LEE

Spanish Frontier, 1937

The Splint

Time stops when the bullet strikes,
Or moves to a new rhyme:
No longer measured by the eyes'
Leap, pulse-beat, thought-flow,
Minutes are told by the jerked wound,
By the pain's throb, fear of pain, sin
Of giving in,
And the unending hardness of the pillow.

Hours in the night creep at you like enemy
Patrols, quiet-footed: powers
And pretences that are yourself give way
As without sound the
Splint bites tighter; there are still
Four hours to dawn: why is it a sin
To moan, to give in?
There is no answer from the bitter pillow.

But there's an answer, back of your thoughts,
Can keep mind and mouth shut:
Can, if you'll hear it, release you. These men
Count you a man:
In and because of their friendship you can remember
One who's the world's width away: can think
To moan, to give in,
Would waken the curved girl who shares your pillow.

TOM WINTRINGHAM

British Medical Unit – Granien

1   Too many people are in love with Death
    And he walks thigh-proud, never sleeps alone;
3   Acknowledge him neighbour and enemy, both
    Hated and usual, best avoided when
    Best known.

6   'Weep, weep, weep!' say machine-gun bullets, stating
7   Mosquito-like a different note close by;
8   Hold steady the lamp, the black, the torn flesh lighting
9   And the glinting probe; carry the stretcher; wait,
    Eyes dry

    Our enemies can praise death and adore death;
12 For us endurance, the sun; and now in the night
13 This electric torch, feeble, waning, yet close-set,
14 Follows the surgeon's fingers. We are allied with
    This light.

TOM WINTRINGHAM

Barcelona, November 1936

Benicasim

Here for a little we pause.
The air is heavy with sun and salt and colour.
On palm and lemon-tree, on cactus and oleander
4   a dust of dust and salt and pollen lies.
And the bright villas
sit in a row like perched macaws,
and rigid and immediate yonder
the mountains rise.

And it seems to me we have come
into a bright-painted landscape of Acheron.
For along the strand
in bleached cotton pyjamas, on rope-soled tread,
wander the risen-from-the-dead,
14   the wounded, the maimed, the halt.
Or they lay bare their hazarded flesh to the salt
air, the recaptured sun,
or bathe in the tideless sea, or sit fingering the sand.

But narrow is this place, narrow is this space
of garlanded sun and leisure and colour, of return
to life and release from living. Turn
(Turn not!) sight inland:
there, rigid as death and unforgiving, stand
the mountains – and close at hand.

SYLVIA TOWNSEND WARNER

Note. At Benicasim on the east coast of Spain is the Rest Home for
the convalescent wounded of the Spanish People's Army, and the
Villa dedicated to Ralph Fox, supported by the Spanish Medical Aid.

Words Asleep

Now I am still and spent
and lie in a whited sepulchre
breathing dead

but there will be
no lifting of the damp swathes
no return of blood
no rolling away the stone

till the cocks carve sharp
gold scars in the morning
and carry the stirring sun
and the early dust to my ears.

LAURIE LEE

Andalucia, 1936

Poem

The Spanish hands are young and pitiful.
Captured by disciplined and certain men,
On their own farms
Dejectedly they stand. Manhood
Has not mastered yet their boy's material,
And in their forms
The land's hard-broken awkwardness is shown.

They will be shot. The guns point whiteless eyes
That blacken memories. Each weather of the earth
That had its manual sign
And earth's exactions made futility.

Those simple groups unchanged, the walls and trees
Of their habitual scene
Shall grant no recognition to their death.

The spade thrown down, utensils of the field
Daily familiar with their hands, discarded place;
And taken, implements
Of other kinds and for another use.
They rose against the nameless will of death,
Moving as winters will across their land,
Themselves to be the devastated yield
And ruined increment:
Knowing that in time's round
There would return for them no further season,
Balanced on arms and boughs, their lives' and summer's unison.

L. J. YATES

Till Death Completes Their Arc

Involved in my own entrails and a crust
Turning a pitted surface towards a space
I am a world that watches through a sky
And is deceived by mirrors
To regard its being as an external shell
One of a universe of stars and faces.

My life confronts my life with eyes, the world
The world with microscopes; and the self-image
Lifted in light against the lens
Stares back with my dumb wall of eyes:
The seen and seeing softly mutually strike
Their glass barrier that arrests the sight.

But the world's being hides in the volcanoes
And the foul history pressed into its core;

And to myself my being is my childhood
And passion and entrails and the roots of senses;
I'm pressed into the inside of a mask
At the back of love, the back of air, the back of light.

The other lives revolve around my sight
Scratching a distant eyelid like the stars;
My life, my world, scarcely believes they live;
They are the mirrors of the foreign masks
Stamped into shapes, obedient to their laws
Following a course till death completes their arc.

STEPHEN SPENDER

JUNKER ANGELS IN THE SKY

(From George Barker, 'Elegy on Spain')

Elegy on Spain

Dedication to the photograph of a child
killed in an air raid on Barcelona

O ecstatic is this head of five-year joy –
Captured its butterfly rapture on a paper:
And not the rupture of the right eye may
Make any less this prettier than a picture.
O now, my minor moon, dead as meat
Slapped on a negative plate, I hold
The crime of the bloody time in my hand.

Light, light with that lunar death our fate;
Make more dazzling with your agony's gold
The death that lays us all in the sand.
Gaze with that gutted eye on our endeavour
To be the human brute, not the brute human:
And if I feel your gaze upon me ever,
I'll wear the robe of blood that love illumines.

I

The hero's red rag is laid across his eyes,
Lies by the Madrid rock and baptizes sand
Grander than god with the blood of his best, and
Estramadura is blazing in his fallen hand.
All of a fallen man is what is heaven's;
Grievance is lowered to a half-mast of sorrow,
Tomorrow has no hand in the beat of his breath, and after
Laughter his heart is hollow.

For a star is against him, that fallen on his forehead,
Forward is blocked by the augury of our evil.
Sin is a star that has fallen on our own heads.
Sheds us a shower of chlorine, the devil's revel;
Evil lifts a hand and the heads of flowers fall –

The pall of the hero who by the Ebro bleeding
Feeds with his blood the stones that rise and call,
Tall as any man, 'No pasaran!'

Can the bird cry any other word on the branch
That blanches at the bomb's red wink and roar,
Or the tall daffodil, trodden under the wheel of war,
But spring up again in the Spring for will not stay under?
Thunder and Mussolini cannot forbid to sing and spring
The bird with a word of determination, or a blossom of
      hope.
Heard in a dream, or blooming down Time's slope.

But now for a moment which shall always be a monument
Draw like a murder the red rag across those eyes.
Skies in July not drier than they are,
Bare of a tear now that pain, like a crystal memorial,
Is their memorials scattered over the face of Spain.
Together this hero and the ghost of the Easter Irish,
Brother and sister, beaten by the fist of the beast,
Water tomorrow with the tears and blood of slaughter.

45

2

Go down, my red bull, proud as a hero,
Nero is done with, but the Hungerford Hundred,
The Tolpuddle Martyr, the human hero,
Rises and remains, not in loss sundered;
Plundered, is proud of his plenitude of prizes.
Now spiked with false friendship, bright with blood,
Stood did my bull in the pool of his passion,
Flashing his sickle horn as he sinks at the knees.

Peace is not angels blessing blood with a kiss; –
Is the axis pinning Spain through the breast
To the water-wheel that makes a nation a martyr
To the traitor who wheels the whips of gold and steel.
O bold bull in the ring, old ox at the wheel,

Sold for a song on the lips of a Hitler,
No halter shall hold you down to the bloodly altar
Longer than life takes to rise again from slaughter.

This flower Freedom needs blood at the roots,
Its shoots spring from your wounds, and the bomb
Booming among the ruins of your houses, arouses
Generation and generation from the grave
To slave at your side for future liberation.
Those who die with five stars in their hands
Hand on their ghosts to guard a yard of land
From the boot of the landlord and the band of war.

Drop, drop that heavy head, my less and more than dead,
Bled dry a moment, tomorrow will raise that hand
From the sad sand, less than death a defeat.
Beaten by friend, not enemy, betrayed, not beaten,
Laid let that head be, low, my bull, stunned,
Gunned from the royal box by a trigger pull.
Bigger no courage is than the blood it can spill.

Not in a wreath I write the death in a ring,
But sing a breath taken by heroes, a respite:
No fight is over when Satan still straddles a man;
Then the real battle begins which only ends
When friends shake hands over the break of evil.
O level out the outrageous crags of hate
To those great valleys where our love can slant
Like light at morning that restores the plant!

O Asturian with a burst breast like an aster,
Disaster sports blooms like that in many places;
Graces the grave of a nation with human pain.
Spain like a sleeping beauty finds her kiss
Is the lips of your wounds awakening her again
To claim her freedom from the enclosing chain.
Silence the blackbird, take away the tree,
He will not need them until he is free.

71

At evening is red the sky over us all.
Shall our fiery funeral not raise tomorrow also?
So shall the order of love from death's disorder
Broader than Russia arise and bring in the day.
Sleep gives us dreams that the morning dissolves,
But borne on death we reach the bourne of dreams.
Seems blood too bitter a bargain to pay for that day?
Too bitter a bargain, or too far a day?

Draw then the red sky over his eyes, and Sleep
Keep Orion silent above him, and no wind move
Love's leaves covering him at the French border.
The marauder snuffles among his guts for a night:
Right is capsized: but Spain shall not drown,
For grown to a giantess overnight arises,
Blazes like morning Venus on a bleeding sea,
She, he, shall stretch her limbs in liberty.

3

Madrid, like a live eye in the Iberian mask,
Asks help from heaven and receives a bomb:
Doom makes the night her eyelid, but at dawn
Drawn is the screen from the bull's-eye capital.
She gazes at the Junker angels in the sky
Passionately and pitifully. Die
The death of the dog, O Capital City, still
Sirius shall spring up from the kill.

Farewell for a day my phoenix who leaves ashes
Flashing on the Guernica tree and Guadalajara range.
Change is the ringing of all bells of evil,
Good is a constant that now lies in your keeping
Sleeping in the cemeteries of the fallen, who,
True as a circling star will soon return
Burning the dark with five tails of anger.

What is there not in the air any longer,
Stronger than songs or roses, and greater

Than those who create it, a nation
Manhandling god for its freedom? lost,
O my ghost, the first fall, but not lost
The will to liberty which shall have liberty
At the long last.

So close a moment that long open eye,
Fly the flag low, and fold over those hands
Cramped to a gun: gather the child's remains
Staining the wall and cluttering the drains;
Troop down the red to the black and the brown;
Go homeward with tears to water the ground.
All this builds a bigger plinth for glory,
Story on story, on which triumph shall be found.

GEORGE BARKER

Wings Overhead

Over Brunete came the sound
Of black wings crawling up the sky;
The soldier crouched against the ground
With straining limbs till they went by.
He heard the bombs sing down the air,
He felt them land, and everywhere
The earth in an advancing line
Rose up. The soldier said 'This time'.
This time he laughed at what he said,
And stretched his body to the heat;
The sun alone was overhead
And warmed the terror out of it.

Now, when the thin December gleam
Is driven off the sky by snow
And breath hangs in the air like steam,

161

The soldier on the plain below
Hears the familiar song of hate
And stoops behind the parapet.
When the black wings have passed beyond
He pulls his blanket closer round,
Grins at the younger man, who tries
To catch his courage from his eyes.
'We'll bring them all down bye and bye,
And then,' he says, 'they'll never come'.
The young man, looking at the sky,
Sees only white wings of the storm.

MILES TOMALIN

Joan Miró

Once there were peasant pots and a dry brown hare
Upon the olive table in that magic farm;
Once all the showmen were blown about the fair
And none of them took hurt or any harm;
Once a man set his fighting bull to graze
In the strict paths of the forgotten maze.

This was that man who knew the secret line
And the strange shapes that went
In dreams; his was the bewitched vine
And the crying dog in the sky's tent.

Once he had a country where the sun shone
Through the enchanted trees like lace,
But now it is troubled and happiness is gone
For the bombs fell in that fine place
And the magician found when he had woken
His people killed, his gay pots broken.

RUTHVEN TODD

The Bombed Happiness

Children, who extend their smile of crystal,
And their leaping gold embrace,
And wear their happiness as a frank jewel,
Are forced in the mould of the groaning bull
And engraved with lines on the face.

Their harlequin-striped flesh,
Their blood twisted in rivers of song,
Their flashing, trustful emptiness,
Are trampled by an outer heart that pressed
From the sky right through the coral breast
And kissed the heart and burst.

This timed, exploding heart that breaks
The loved and little hearts, is also one
Splintered through the lungs and wombs
And fragments of squares in the sun,
And crushing the floating, sleeping babe
Into a deeper sleep.

Its victoried drumming enters
Above the limbs of bombed laughter
The body of an expanding State
And throbs there and makes it great,
But nothing nothing can recall
Gaiety buried under these dead years,
Sweet jester and young playing fool
Whose toy was human happiness.

STEPHEN SPENDER

Madrid
To Ramon Sender

Sinister, this crack in the sierra and the horizon ringed with a
    storm of iron,
Sky without a smile left, not a single shard of azure there
Nor a bow to shoot a hope calling an arrow from the sun –
Tattered the trees stand up again wailing like violins unstrung,
A whole village asleep in death floats rudderless away
When the filter of silence is riddled by the machine-gun,
When the cataract of crashing explodes,
When the plaster-work of the heavens comes down
And in the city curved flames lick at the wounds of rents caulked
    over with night –
In the deserted little square where now the calm of terror sits
There is, yes, there is
On the torn and bloodied face of that child
A smile; like a pomegranate crushed under the tramp of a heel.

No more – the birds – or sweet bird-song on the hilltops,
The age of fire and steel is born, the season of apocalyptic locusts,
Comes the advance of tanks, the obstinate invasion of giant
    beetles,
And a man is walled in with his hate and with to-morrow's joy.
When he strides forth,
Death, hack me that down! That is Hans Beimler.
Death, threshing the cries and clamours of the plain,
Death's at his harvest.

Now with the snow the carious toothwork of the mountains
    stands forth,
Bullets in a swarm buzz over the carrion of the earth,
With fear in the deep of the shell-pits like a worm in a broken
    ulcer,
Evoking a season beyond belief, of honey in the orchards and a
    path beneath the branches,

Leaves ruffled and murmuring, the kind and tender laugh of a
    young woman,
Peace in the heavens and the secret of the waters.
Long oh long ago already she fell, Lina Odena,
In the olive-grove down there, in the South.

This is the region, this, that is threatened by fate,
This is the strand on which crashes from Atlas and Rhine
That surge composed of the brotherhood in crime
Bearing down on the driven faith of humanity.
But here too, despite the sacred-hearts broidered on Mahomet's
    standard,
The relics and scapularies,
Lucre-charm, totem of ignorance, murder-fetish,
The lie in all its vestments and the past in its dementia,
HERE dawn tears itself clean out of the tatters of night –
And from the humble, the anonymous blood of the peasant and
    worker
And the atrocious parturition
Comes to birth a world wherein the brow of man shall be freed
Of the sere brand of that sole equality which is called despair.

JACQUES ROUMAIN
(<i>Translated from the French by Nancy Cunard</i>)</div>

Bombing Casualties in Spain

Dolls' faces are rosier but these were children
their eyes not glass but gleaming gristle
dark lenses in whose quicksilvery glances
4   the sunlight quivered. These blench'd lips
were warm once and bright with blood
but blood
held in a moist bleb of flesh
8   not spilt and spatter'd in tousled hair.

In these shadowy tresses
red petals did not always
11   thus clot and blacken to a scar.
12   These are dead faces.
Wasps' nests are not so wanly waxen
wood embers not so greyly ashen.

They are laid out in ranks
like paper lanterns that have fallen
after a night of riot
extinct in the dry morning air.

HERBERT READ

Proud Motherhood (*Madrid, A.D. 1937*)

Jose's an imp of three,
Dolores' pride.
'One day', she dreamed, 'he'll be
Known far and wide.'

Kind Providence fulfils
Dolores' guess:
Her darling's portrait thrills
The foreign press.

Though that's no wreath of bay
About his hair:
That's just the curious way
Bomb-splinters tear.

F. L. LUCAS

Guernica

Irun – Badajóz – Málaga – and then Guernica

So that the swastika and the eagle
might spring from the blood-red soil,
bombs were sown into the earth at Guernica,
whose only harvest was a calculated slaughter.
Lest freedom should wave between the grasses
and the corn its proud emblem, or love
be allowed to tread its native fields,
Fascism was sent to destroy the innocent,
and, goose-stepping to the exaggerated waving
of the two-faced flag, to save Spain.

But though the soil be saturated with blood
as a very efficient fertilizer, the furrow
of the ghastly Fasces shall remain barren.
The planted swastika, the eagle grafted
on natural stock shall wither and remain sere;
for no uniformed force shall marshall the sap
thrilling to thrust buds into blossoms, or quicken
the dead ends of the blighted branches;
but the soil shall be set against an alien crop
and the seed be blasted in the planting.

But strength lies in the strength of the roots.
They shall not pass to ruin Spain!

A. S. KNOWLAND

From a Painting by Picasso

This woman by Picasso
De-scales me.
My whole self, with its ramifications,
Is loosened to a mild nobility,
A tender sense of beauty and abstracted power.
To me she is the far end of life,
And I worship her with awe.

What if this woman
(Who must exist)
Should be killed by shrapnel or gas,
Her precious body distorted and destroyed
And her quiet essence
Smothered in blood and smoke?

For myself and my friends,
All our impulsive strength
Is allowed to remain rude,
And is disciplined
Not for immediate ascent to the higher spheres of influence,
But for the disentangling of ourselves.
From what keeps us dirty and brutal.

For myself and my friends,
Shall we survive,
If we are tested and tortured to the final extreme –
If bits of our plebeian brains
Add to the litter of the bomb-pocked pavement
And lumps of our lumpy limbs hang sparely around –
If we are shot about and about
And collected, dead, indiscriminately,
Everywhere and for ever?

And, we not surviving, what of those others?
Think of those few,
Finer in faculty,
Farther in imagination –
Manipulators of words, materials, colours, sounds, motions
(Whose category all our descendants might join) –
Think of those women in history,
White peaks in hazy sunlight –
Think of that woman by Picasso –
How shall we see
These pure tints in the sky of life,
These firm notes in the symphony of matter,
Obliterated by a great void-black sudden daub of despair,
By the magnified yap of a little dragon,
Dying with such fire and threshing
And disproportionate slaughter?

ALBERT BROWN

To Eat To-Day

They come without siren-song or any ushering
Over the usual street of man's middle day,
Come unbelievably – abstract – beyond human vision –
Codicils, dashes along the great Maniac speech.
'Helmeted Nüremberg, *nothing*,' said the people of Barcelona,
The people of Spain – 'ya lo sabemos, we have suffered all.'

Gangrene of German cross, you sirs in the ether,
Sons of Romulus, Wotan – is the mark worth the bomb?
What was in it? salt and a half-pint of olive,
Nothing else but the woman, she treasured it terribly,
Oil, for the day folks would come, refugees from Levante,
Maybe with greens . . . one round meal – but you killed her,
Killed four children outside, with the house, and the pregnant
    cat.
Heil, hand of Rome, you passed – and that is all.

I wonder – do you eat before you do these things,
Is it a cocktail or is it a *pousse-café*?
Are you sitting at mess now, saying 'visibility medium . . .
We got the port, or near it, with half-a-dozen,' I wonder –
Or highing it yet, on the home-run to Mallorca,
Cold at 5,000 up, cursing a jammed release . . .
'Give it 'em, puta Madonna, here, over Arenys –
Per Bacco, it's nearly two – bloody sandwich it's made down
    there –
Aren't we going to eat to-day, teniente? *Te-niente*?'
Drive in the clouds fuming, fumbler unstrapping death.
You passed; hate traffics on; then the shadows fall.

On the simple earth
Five mouths less to feed to-night in Barcelona.
On the simple earth
Men tramping and raving on an edge of fear.
Another country arming, another and another behind it –
Europe's nerve strung like catapult, the cataclysm roaring and
    swelling . . .
But in Spain no Perhaps, and To-morrow – in Spain it is, Here.

NANCY CUNARD

Bombers

    Through the vague morning, the heart preoccupied,
    A deep in air buried grain of sound
    Starts and grows, as yet unwarning –
4   The tremor of baited deepsea line.

    Swells the seed, and now tight sound-buds
    Vibrate, upholding their paean flowers
    To the sun. There are bees in sky-bells droning,
    Flares of crimson at the heart unfold.

Children look up, and the elms spring-garlanded
Tossing their heads and marked for the axe.
Gallant or woebegone, alike unlucky –
Earth shakes beneath us: we imagine loss.

Black as vermin, crawling in echelon
Beneath the cloud-floor, the bombers come:
The heavy angels, carrying harm in
Their wombs that ache to be rid of death.

This is the seed that grows for ruin,
The iron embryo conceived in fear.
19 Soon or late its need must be answered
20 In fear delivered and screeching fire.

Choose between your child and this fatal embryo.
22 Shall your guilt bear arms, and the children you want
Be condemned to die by the powers you paid for
And haunt the houses you never built?

C. DAY LEWIS

Epitaph on a Tyrant

Perfection, of a kind, was what he was after,
And the poetry he invented was easy to understand;
He knew human folly like the back of his hand,
And was greatly interested in armies and fleets;
When he laughed, respectable senators burst with
    laughter,
6 And, when he cried, the little children died in the streets.

W. H. AUDEN

HE IS DEAD AND GONE

(Donagh MacDonagh, 'He is dead and gone, Lady . . .
For Charles Donnelly, R.I.P.')

He is Dead and Gone, Lady...
(For Charles Donnelly, R.I.P.)

Of what a quality is courage made
That he who gently walked our city streets
Talking of poetry or philosophy,
4   Spinoza, Keats.
Should lie like any martyred soldier
His brave and fertile brain dried quite away
And the limbs that carried him from cradle to death's
    outpost
Growing down into a foreign clay.

Gone from amongst us and his life not half begun
10   Who had followed Jack-o-Lantern truth and liberty
Where it led wavering from park-bed to prison cell
Into a strange land, dry misery,
And then into Spain's slaughter, sniper's aim
And his last shocked embrace of earth's lineaments.
Can I picture truly that swift end
16   Who see him dead with eye that still repents.

17   What end, what quietus, can I see for him
Who had the quality of life in every vein?
Life with its passion and poetry and its proud
Ignorance of eventual loss or gain.
This first fruit of our harvest, willing sacrifice
22   Upon the altar of his integrity
23   Lost to us; somewhere his death is charted –
24   Something has been gained by this mad missionary.

DONAGH MACDONAGH

Casualties

Who would think the Spanish war
Flared like new tenure of a star,
The way our rhymes and writings are?
That Hilliard spilled his boxer's blood
Through Albacete's snow and mud,
And smiled to comrade death, Salud.
That Charlie Donnelly, small, frail,
And flushed with youth, was rendered pale –
But not with fear: in what queer squalor
Was smashed up his so ordered valour,
That rhythm, that steely earnestness,
That peace of poetry, to bless
Discordant thoughts of divers men –
Blue gaze that burned up lie and stain,
Put out by death.
I keep my breath:
So many grow upon my stem,
I cannot take their sap from them.
But to right charity, with spurs,
Through spite's asperity infernal –
My verity of verse
Is nothing else
But rattle of light shells
With no kernel,
Since Dublin boys have striven, and are
Knit to that alien soil, where war
Burns like the inception of a star.

BLANAID SALKELD

Thinking of Artolas

Sirs and Senoras, let me tell you a story.
A story neither of long ago nor faraway
But close enough now and to you unhappily.
We will call it Going-Into-History
And you all know History is a cruel country
Where tiger terraces crouch drinking rivers waterless
And sheep immobilised by sombrero shepherds' piping . . .
It could be set in Estremadura or Cordova,
Time crawling like inches and napoleonic wars
Dogeared in textbooks seeming the latest in strategy –
At least until recently. Or as Shaw might have said
The life force gets going but man has his lag . . .
True. And to gain on his lag must man lose his leg,
And truncate himself, as in Estremadura?

Well, at Casada's we ate ortolans elsewhere we drank coffee.
In the Gran Via in the Colon we went into conference.
All day the starlings on the Ramblas whispered,
All day the dead air pacified the street,
Fat pigeons swaggered on the Plaza Catalunya.
It was easy enough to analyse an ortolan,
Conjure pigeon into pie: translate con leche . . .

But the starlings worried me, and their whispering,
I could never understand their whispering.
It weaved breathlessly up and up like the Coulin –
Or like that dissonance outsoaring ecstacy, heard
Near any roadside or beside any bed, disrupting the
Lovers enlaced, singing with no sound and saying
'O the world is bright and empty.'

At Madrid we dined with the newspaper bunch.
So-and-so shouted they all called him a Fascist –

There *had* been whispers – but he didn't care
He shouted for Empire. That was all right
Empire shouted for him – one supposes, somewhere.
All day I was a method of analysis . . . Did my heart, Tomas,
Or your depthless eyes tell me analysis was cowardly
While Los Madrilenos were barricading their old Madrid out?
. . . All day So-and-so the Fascist was blustering.
I analysed his quality as extreme
Scatology and efficiency walking backwards, with a shrug . . .
But sadly I knew the whispering starlings
Wintering would rise from the Plaza Catalunya
Before I returned.

With Jarama held they brought him in, the tankist.
From his Georgian hair the blood smiled through,
And smiled on the paving and from the verandah
Smiled as it dripped and adventured below . . .
In parks they dream of penny murder non-intervention –
He took the hammered blow and said Salud –
All day my heart with love was helpless, all day I knew
He had gone further than I towards finding a synthesis.
With Jarama held his wound wore on, the Georgian
Who held a dawnstar and not nettles as we do –
Whisper, starlings, whisper! Be incorruptible and saying
'O the world is bright and always living'.

Sirs and Senoras, let me end my story –
I show you earth, earth formally,
And Two on guard with the junipers.
Two, Gael and Jew side by side in a trench
Gripping antique guns to flick at the grasshoppers
That zoomed overhead and the moon was rocking.
Two who came from prisonment, Gael because of Tone,
Jew because of human love, the same for Jew as German –
Frail fragments both, chipped off and forgotten readily . . .

I set them together, Izzy Kupchik and Donnelly;
And of that date with death among the junipers

I say only, they kept it: and record the exploded
Spreadeagled mass when the moon was later
Watching the wine that baked earth was drinking.
Such my story, Sirs and Senoras. Whether you like it
Or pay a visit to your vomitorium, is all one . . .
Perhaps you'll like junipers and a moon steadied,
High baked earth and night's formalism,
Remembering that History is always a cruel country
And crueller man than April.

EWART MILNE

Requiem Mass
for the Englishmen fallen in the International Brigade

Call out the roll call of the dead, that we,
the living may answer, under the arch of peace
assembled where the lark's cry is the only shrapnel,
a dew of song, a sky wreath laid on earth
out of the blue silence of teeming light
in this spring-hour of truce prefiguring
the final triumph, call upon them proudly,
the men whose bones now lie in the earth of freedom.

Stand out on the crag of the morning to sound reveille.
Hark to the peal of silence, remembering.
This moment of honour claps our hearts with the future,
and already we taste, like wedlock in a first kiss,
the hour when the last barricade of estrangement
falls and the roaring night is warmly beaconed
with pledges of kinship, the peoples world-united,
world without end, the dawn on the earth of freedom.

Ask of the eagle that yelped overhead
where in the blaze of death the Spanish workers blocked
the Guadarrama passes with their dead.
Eagle of Spain, from your eyrie of the skies
answer, Where are they now, the young and the brave?

The brotherly dead pour out of the bugle-call.
Where are the faces we seek, the English faces?
Let the living answer the roll-call of the dead.

Where now is he, gay as the heart of spring
rich with the world's adventure, wandering from where the
   moon
hangs in a crooked willow of Samara
to where congested London clots with a toxin
England's aorta vein? In strength of pity,
as he had lived, he died, and the bullets whined
through boughs of winter over his broken face.
Where is Ralph Fox of Yorkshire?

Where now is he, the eager lad who beheld
England's fate whitening under Huesca's moon?
Where the shells splash enormous flowers of destruction,
flame-gawds of madness, fountain-plumes of terror,
there must freedom walk or the earth is surrendered
to these her ravishers, so I shall walk with freedom
and after the agony you will pluck fruits in the garden.
Where is John Cornford of Cambridge?

Where now is he, a voice among many voices,
who said: 'In poverty's jail are bolted the guiltless,
the thieves lock up their victims.' His voice protested.
Sentenced, he saw, through a stone wall, the truth.
Clearer that wall of privation than any arguments.
He struck his hand on the stone and swore he would break it
he took a rifle and smashed through that wall in Spain.
Where is Wilf Jobling of Chopwell?

Where now is he, who amid the grinding of plates
in the tramp steamer's fo'c'stle, listened. The waters
streamed through the hawsepipe, and the ship dipped shuddering.
He learned who was racketing, who had rigged orders to gain
the world's insurance money while drowning the crew.
Bearing an ambulance stretcher among the trenches of danger,

I have found my way home, he answered, before Madrid.
Where is Davidovitch of Bethnal Green?

Where now is he that came early to fighting?
In Sydney, while gulls screamed around Pinchgut, he learned
resisting evictions, that the people were all evicted
from the world of their making and stamped into hovels of
 hardship.
He came back, a stowaway, to Edinburgh –
but cried: 'I stand in the open bows of purpose
journeying to Spain where the people claim their birthright.'
Where is Jack Atkinson of Hull?

Over the faint blue streak of the sierras,
the bare scarps heaving ribbed and flattening-vague
where noon scoops out the shadows from the ravines,
rasped the Caproni planes. Is this a strange country,
you Scotsman? No. I have recognised it. See,
the village children clench their fists in welcome.
For we are they in whom love becomes justice.
Where is James Wark of Airdrie?

Where now is he, that leader of London busmen,
in ragged olive-groves on the Jarama sector,
a company commander? Wiping grit from his eye,
he laughed, and swung his machine-gun at the ledge
of toppling fascists, then to the higher ground
ordered his men. The fiery rocks split flailing
and the barrage shogged battering up the hill.
Where is Bill Briskey of Dalston?

Where now is he, that comrade quick with laughter?
Behind the sandbags he crawled with bleeding knees,
sweat blurred the pounding distance, still he fired,
the claws of heat were fastened in his arm
that scraped along the stone. A wallowing roar
fire-drenching billowed. As he was borne away,
dying, he sang the International.
Where is Alan Craig of Maryhill?

Tanks lurched up over the rise, and men from their hands and
    knees
flung forward on the gust of attack staggering
head-down. Our rifle fire's long crackle was drowned,
the booming racked and rocked the earth, but wavering
the crumpled line stumbled on grass-tussocks,
clumsily pitching. Out of the trench we rushed,
the tanks heeled crunching, but where is he that led us?
Where is Robert Symes of Hampshire?

Where now is he, that tramping on means-test marches,
knew that the road he had taken against oppression
led to the front in Spain? For he was marching
in country lined with harlot-hoardings of menace,
England seared into slums by the poison-bombs of greed.
That road of anger and love must lead to Spain,
the shouts in Trafalgar Square to No Pasaran.
Where is Tommy Dolan of Sunderland?

Where now is he that sold the 'Daily Worker'?
The poster waved from his hand was a red flag
hoisted on the barricades of choice.
I have seen the world dividing at the voice of truth,
so there is nothing strange in the clang of this war.
I have seen its first skirmishes when the police drew batons
and charged my friends, and so I shall go to Spain.
Where is Jock Tadden of Dundee?

This war has roots everywhere, in the soil of squalor.
He watched on the tarnished slates the glistening moon,
a milky drip of light mocking the mouth of hunger,
a promise of cleansing beauty, a pennon of freedom.
and midnight, yawning, creaked with the ghosts of old pain,
till resolution regathered like the moonlight flowing
in through the cast iron bars at the end of the bed.
Where is T. J. Carter of West Hartlepool?

As summer is plighted in the little red cones of larch,
so will the fullness of freedom unfold from these,

our comrades, in its hour. For unless the onset
of spring was here in the spears of the daffodil
and eyes of stickleback emerald in water-darkness,
no summer breath would gloss the plum or ruffle
the hill's gold harvestfur. And so we cry:
Where is Syd Avner of Stoke Newington?

These men as types of the English dead in Spain
we summon here in the nested hush of the Spring,
rising amid grey clouds of travellers-joy,
with marshgold smouldering in the hollows of sunset,
and sweetness plaited in the hazel catkins.
Here in this green hawthorn moment of England,
we conjure them, brief as an azure drift of windflowers
and lasting as the earth of unity.

1938

JACK LINDSAY

To a Spanish Poet
(To Manuel Altolaguirre)

  You stared out of the window on the emptiness
2 Of a world exploding;
  Stones and rubble thrown upwards in a fountain
4 Blown to one side by the wind.
5 Every sensation except being alone
6 Drained out of your mind.
7 There was no fixed object for the eye to fix on.
8 You became a child again
9 Who sees for the first time how the worst things happen.

10 Then, stupidly, the stucco pigeon
11 On the gable roof that was your ceiling,
12 Parabolized before your window
13 Uttering (you told me later!) a loud coo.

183

14   Alone to your listening self, you told the joke.
15   Everything in the room broke.
16   But you remained whole,
17   Your own image unbroken in your glass soul.

18   Having heard this all from you, I see you now
19   – White astonishment haloing irises
20   Which still retain in their centres
21   Black laughter of black eyes.
22   Laughter reverberant through stories
23   Of an aristocrat lost in the hills near Malaga
24   Where he had got out of his carriage
25   And, for a whole week, followed, on foot, a partridge.
26   Stories of that general, broken-hearted
27   Because he'd failed to breed a green-eyed bull.

28   But reading the news, my imagination breeds
      The penny-dreadful fear that you are dead.

30   Well, what of this journalistic dread?

31   Perhaps it is we – the living – who are dead
32   We of a world that revolves and dissolves
33   While we set the steadfast corpse under the earth's lid.
34   The eyes push irises above the grave
      Reaching to the stars, which draw down nearer,
      Staring through a rectangle of night like black glass,
37   Beyond these daylight comedies of falling plaster.

38   Your heart looks through the breaking ribs –
39   Oiled axle through revolving spokes.
40   Unbroken blood of the swift wheel,
      You stare through centrifugal bones
42   Of the revolving and dissolving world.

STEPHEN SPENDER

The Heart Conscripted

The shock of silver tassels
the sledded breath . . .
I who have fought my battles
keep these in a sheath.

5   The ulcer of exact remorse
from which the Lake poet perished,
the owl's indifferent hood –
these have vanished.

9   I hear only the sobbing fall
of various water-clocks
and the swift inveterate wail
of the destructive axe.

Lorca was killed, singing,
and Fox who was my friend.
The rhythm returns: the song
which has no end.

HERBERT READ

For R. J. C. (Summer, 1936)

No, not the sort of boy for whom one does
Find easily nicknames, Tommy and Bill,
Not a pleasant bass in the friendly buzz
Of voices we know well,
But not much changing where he goes
Divides talk coldly with the edge of will.

185

When he began, he talked too fast
To be heard well, and he knew too much.
He never had, though learned a little at last,
The sure, sincere and easy touch
On an audience: and his handsome head
Charmed no acquiescence: he convinced and led.

Any movement, going north or south,
Can find a place for charm and open shirts,
The sun-bright hair, the lovely mouth,
But needs as much the force that hurts
And rules our sapphire dreams.
For seeing visions on the evening sky
I can do tolerably well; but I
Can read no blue prints and erect no schemes.

They fear the meddling intellect,
Cold, gritty, loveless, cynical, pedantic –
Rightly, had he no work but to dissect
Romance and prove it unromantic,
Breaking the scenery with his conscious hands.
But we are working towards a richer season,
And mean to plough our lands
With this unfruitful reason.

Thought, which our masters cannot use,
Walks on the slag heaps, wags on broken wires
At the old pit head, hears no news.
Thought rakes the fires
That keep our furnaces at even heat.
Capricious as a starving flame
Frail inspiration flickered till he came
To give the fire a world to eat.

MARGOT HEINEMANN

Grieve in a New Way for New Losses

And after the first sense 'He will not come again'
Fearing still the images of corruption,
To think he lies out there, and changes
In the process of the earth from what I knew,
Decays and even there in the grave, shut close
In the dark, away from me, speechless and cold,
Is in no way left the same that I have known.

All this is not more than we can deal with.

The horror of the nightmare is that it evades
Your steady look, steals past the corner of the eye,
Lurks in the sides of pictures. Death
Is fearful for the fifth part of a second,
A fear that shakes the heart: and that fear lost
As soon, yet leaves a sickness and a chill,
Heavy hands and the weight of another day.

All this is not more than we can deal with.

If we have said we'd face the dungeon dark
And gallows grim, and have not meant to face
The thin time, meals alone, in every eye
The comfortless kindness of a stranger – then
We have expected a privileged treatment,
And were out of luck. Death has many ways
To get at us: in every loving heart
In which a comrade dies he strikes his dart.

All this is not more than we can deal with.

In our long nights the honest tormentor speaks
And in our casual conversations:

'He was so live and young – need he have died,
Who had the wisest head, who worked so hard,
Led by his own sheer strength: whom I so loved?'
Yes, you'd like an army all of Sidney Cartons,
The best world made conveniently by wasters, second rates,
Someone that we could spare,
And not the way it has to be made,
By the loss of our best and bravest everywhere.

All this is not more than we can deal with.

MARGOT HEINEMANN

Lament for a Lover

The world curled in the bud,
The world unfolds its flower,
The canker is gnawing in the bud,
And my love I'll see no more.

The world unfolding in the bud,
The canker in the flower,
The canker will be drowned by the sap rising,
But my love I'll see no more.

He has departed on a ship,
He departed on a train,
The hazel ripens in the wood
But my love lies dead in Spain.

Despair goes stepping sombrely
Across the haze of the hills,
Despair sprouts up in the solitudes
Of the hemlock hollows.

It echoes across the tenements
Where men walk in their haunts,

Pressed by enormous shadows
Men walk in their haunts.

My love rose up in the sound of bugles,
He rose and came to me,
The sirens sounded in the morning
My love vanished away.

He rose and spoke in the sound of bugles,
Across the tenement air,
'Oh, do you not hear a new murmur
That denies despair?'

'For I shall sprout in the bluebells,
And I shall sprout in the bud,
For men are rising, rising, rising,
Rising to avenge my blood.'

He rose and spoke in the sound of bugles,
He rose and spoke to me,
'I live in the sinews of every man
That fights for liberty.'

The world curled in the bud,
The world unfolds its flower,
I rise in millions by your side,
In this zero hour.

MAURICE CARPENTER

Poem
(For M.S., killed in Spain)

1   Great cities, where disaster fell
     In one small night on every house and man,
3   Knew how to rub the flesh from fable:
     One crying O, his mouth a marble fountain;
5   In all preserving lava her thigh bones
     At compass points, the west and east of love.

7   The necks bent looking for the geese,
8   Or over blocks gazing into freedom;
9   The heads were all alike, short noses, brows
     Folded above, the skin a leather brown;
11   The wrists were thick, the finger-pads worn down,
     Oppression built itself in towering stone.

     Now uncovered is the hero,
     A tablet marks him where his life leaked out
     Through grimy wounds and vapoured into air.
     A rusty socket shows where in the night
     He crammed his torch and kept by flame at bay
     Dark, prowling wolves of thought that frightened him.

     The poor outlasted rope and crucifix,
20 We break the bones that blenched through mastic gold.
21 We excavate our story, give a twist
     To former endings in deliberate metre,
     Whose subtle beat our fathers could not count,
     Having their agile thumbs too far from fingers.

          I fear the plucking hand
          That from our equal season
27   Sent you towards the spring
          But left me suavely wound

In the cocoon of reason
That preluded your wings.

As the more supple fin
Found use in crawling, so
Some new and rapid nerve
Brought close your flesh to brain,
Transformed utopia
To death for human love.

And my existence must
Finish through your trauma
The speechless brute divorce
Of heart from sculptured bust:
Turn after five acts' drama
A placid crumpled face.

I see my friend rising from the tomb,
His simple head swathed in a turban of white cloth.
The vault is spotted with a brownish moss,
One corner broken, fallen to the floor,
Whereon I read *Spain* as he advances like
An invalid, changed terribly with pain.

A quiet room holds him, half raised from the bed,
Eyes big and bright, a waxwork and the blood
Of waxworks running down his cheek. Two candles
Rock their light. The bed is moving, tilting,
And slips him rigidly to take a new position
The elbow sharp, the skin a yellow leaf.

The third time he stands against a summer country,
The chestnuts almost black in thunderous air,
The silver-green of willows lining dykes
Choked with flesh. He moves along the furrows
With gestured fingers, spreading death against
The imperishable elements of earth.

47
50
53
57
59

What is the meaning of these images?
62   The wish to leave natural objects richer,
To quicken the chemistry of earth, to be
Immortal in our children. Such desires
Are bodies in a pit, the rotting and bloody
Backwash of a tidal pestilence.

67   Take it out, out of my back!
68   The scalpel in my dream
Has extended in a scythe,
Is passing through the quick,
Forcing like strychnine
My body to its curve.

73   Eyes open is not waking
Nor the name and number
Of distorted figures, and knowledge
Of pain. It is the breaking
Before we slumber
Of the shaping image.

So from the nightmare, from
The death, the war of ghosts,
Those chosen to go unharmed
May join the tall city, the swan
Of changing thoughts
Set sailing by the doomed.

ROY FULLER

To a Fallen Comrade

With those that bled, with those that gave their lives,
Who had no thought for individual gain,
But rather, as a man, like one who strives
For fellow men, he joined the fight in Spain.

He fought to aid a people, strong and great,
Forged in steel, by common struggle one;
Fought to see a world that knew not hate –
That all might take a place beneath the sun.

He will not see the people that shall rise
In the new-born world for which he gave his life;
Yet o'er his grave, a sound that never dies –
A happier, joyous sound, unmarred by strife.

BILL HARRINGTON

Jarama Front

I tried not to see,
But heard his voice.
How brown the earth
And green the trees.
One tree was his.
He could not move.
Wounded all over,
He lay there moaning.

I hardly knew:
I tore his coat
It was easy –
Shrapnel had helped.

But he was dying
And the blanket sagged.
'God bless you, comrades,
He will thank you.'
That was all.
No slogan,
No clenched fist
Except in pain.

15

T. A. R. HYNDMAN

Jarama

Unrisen dawns had dazzled in your eyes,
Your hearts were hungry for the not yet born.
In agony of thwarted love and wasted life,
Through all long misery, from countries torn
With savage hands, you did not shrink or bend,
But marched on straighter, prouder to the end.

Not blindly, fighting in another's war,
Lured by cheap promises and drugged with drums,
Striking down brothers in the name of lies,
Slaves of the blackest with all senses numbed –
But clear-eyed, bravely, counting all the cost,
Knowing what might be won, what might be lost.

The rifles you will never hold again
In other hands still speak against the night.
Brothers have filled your places in the ranks
Who will remember how you died for right
The day you took those rifles up, defied
The power of ages, and victorious died.

Comrades, sleep now. For all you loved shall be.
You did not seek for death, but finding it –
And such a death – better than shameful life,
Rest now content. A flame of hope is lit.
The flag of freedom floats again unfurled
And all you loved lives richlier in the world.

A. M. ELLIOTT

In Remembrance of a Son of Wales
(Who Fell in Spain)

Amid the roar of guns that split the air,
 Faint moaning reached him from a tortured field;
He followed to a city passing fair,
 His soul aflame, his flesh a living shield.
There death-charged missiles blazed a trail of woe,
 Leaving each shattered hearth a vain defence
While flocks of iron eagles, swooping low,
 Clawed out the life of cradled innocence.
Far from the hills he loved, he faced the night,
 Bearing, for freedom's sake, an alien yoke;
He fell exalting brotherhood and right,
 His bleeding visage scorched by fire and smoke;
E'en as the sweetest note is born of pain,
So shall the song of songs be born in Spain.

       T. E. NICHOLAS

For the Fallen

Brave sons of liberty, fallen in battle,
Fallen that we, their successors, might live,
Bravely they faced the machine-gunner's rattle,
Giving so bravely all they'd to give.

Hurriedly, carelessly, rudely, we buried them,
Buried them quickly, beneath the brown soil.
Hurriedly, quickly, we gave them our blessing,
Then we returned to our heart-breaking toil.

Theirs was no splendour, the fallen in action;
Theirs was no pomp, neither glory nor show,

They were the cream of the Communist fraction,
We are the reapers, but they went to sow.

Shall we forget them who never forgot us,
Defending the workers, while fighting in Spain?
Shall we stay passive while Fascism threatens us?
Shall their great effort be made all in vain?

Never forget them, the lesson they taught us,
Think of their travail, their suffering, pain!
Raise the Red Standard and help us support us,
Lest we see in England what happened in Spain.

W. B. KEAL

In No Man's Land

Only the world changes, and time its tense
Against the creeping inches of whose moons
He launches his rigid continual present.

The grass will grow its summer beard and beams
Of sunlight melt the iron slumber
Where soldiers lie locked in their final dreams.

His corpse be covered with the white December
And roots push through his skin as through a drum
When the years and fields forget, but the bones remember.

STEPHEN SPENDER

To the Mothers of the Dead Militia

They have not died!
they stand upright in the midst of the gunpowder,
they live, burning as brands there.

In the copper-coloured prairie
their pure shadows have come together
like a curtain of armoured wind,
a barrier colour of fury
like that same invisible breast of sky.

Mothers, they are standing amidst the corn
as tall as the profundity of noon
that possesses the giant plains.

They are a peal of sombre voices
calling for victory through the shapes of murdered steel.

Sisters as close as
the dust fallen,
hearts that have been broken
keep faith in your dead –
they are not roots only
beneath stones dyed in blood,
not only poor fallen bones
at work now in the finality of earth,
for their mouths are shaping the dry powder ready for action,
they attack in waves of iron,
in their clenched fists lies death's own contradiction.

See, from so many bodies an invincible life rises!
mothers, sons, banners,
in one single being as living as life;

one face made of all the slain eyes is guard in the darkness
with a sword that is strengthened and tempered with human
   hope.

Cast aside your mourning veils, join all of your tears
till they transmute into metal –
so that we may strike day and night,
so that we may hammer day and night,
so that we may spit forth day and night,
till the portals of hatred be overthrown.

I have not forgotten your tragedies
and your sons, they are known to me,
and if I have pride in their deaths
in their lives, too, I have pride.
Their smiles
are like flashes in the murk of the workshops,
and in the underground
every day their feet ring by mine.
I have seen
.amongst the oranges of Levante
and the fishing-nets of the south,
in the ink of the printshops
and the masonry of the buildings,
I have seen
the flame of their hearts fashioned out of fire and valour.

And, as in your hearts, mothers,
in mine there is so much of death and mourning
that it seems like a forest flooded
with the blood that quenched their smiles;
to it come the furious snows of sleeplessness,
the wrenching solitude of the days.

But, beyond your curse on the hyenas
out of Africa, blood-parched, baying their foul cries,
beyond wrath and contempt, beyond tears,
Oh mothers, transpierced by anguish and death,

look into the heart of the new day that is dawning
and know that your dead smile up at you from the earth,
raising their clenched fists above the corn, there, look, they are
   standing!

PABLO NERUDA
(Translated from the Spanish by Nancy Cunard)

The Word Dead and the Music Mad

The word on the hill
The music in the water –
The music reflects
The word on the guitar.

When the guns spoke
The fat poet fled
Till he came to Lerida,
Name peaceful as the dead.

The black spies watched
Trellised by balconies:
The poet hid in a cellar:
They reported to the police.

The police took down his name
And the words from his mouth
They found in his pockets
A letter from the South.

While the police read the letter
The poet stood silent
Staring at a dream
Of his childhood's violence.

He saw light flood a pillar
Stating summer's total sum:

A wolf leapt from behind it
And devoured a white lamb.

The ink on the paper
Seemed the wolf that tore
The white flesh of inocence
In a barbarous claw.

The black police seized his wrists
And tied them in fetters
They said 'A socialist,
Wrote you this letter.'

They drew their revolvers
And they shot him there
On a midsummer day
In peaceful Lerida.

The balconies clanged
Their bars like guitars
Where the spies and lies shone
Through a night of stars.

The police dissected
The tongues of peasants
To cut out the words
The poet had made pleasant.

A musician, friend
Of the poet, rose
His mind struck through
With one song to compose.

The musician stared
At the stillness of one word
The splitting moment
Of the single chord

SPENDER

When space divides
And the bullet flies
And, spun into terror,
Like worlds, float eyes.

The word was 'death'
And his mind froze
Fixed in the madness
Of terrible snows.

The word on the hill
The music in the water –
The music reflects
The word on the guitar.

STEPHEN SPENDER

THE CRIME WAS IN GRANADA

('The Crime Was In Granada, His Granada. "I saw García
Lorca being assassinated . . ."' Front page article in the
Socialist daily of Valencia, *Adelante*, 15 September 1937)

The Crime Took Place in Granáda

To Federico García Lorca

I

The Crime

He was seen, walking among the guns
down a long road
that gave upon the country-side cold
in the dawn, yet beneath the stars.
They killed Federico
as the first light pricked.
The murderous band
dared not look on his face.
They all closed their eyes;
they prayed: . . . Even God shall not save thee . . .
Federico fell dead
– blood on his face, lead in his bowels –
. . . There in Granáda the crime took place.
You know – . . . poor Granáda . . . – his Granáda.

II

The Poet and Death

He was seen walking alone with Death
fearless before her scythe.
– Even now the sun from tower to tower
hammers on the anvil,
anvil on anvil in the forges.
Federico spake,
jocund with Death. She gave ear.
'Because yesterday in my verse, companion mine,
crackled the brittle sound of thy palms,

the gleam to my song thou gavest, and to my tragedy
the sharpness of thy silver scythe,
I will sing thy fleshless bones,
thy eyeless holes,
thy windblown hair,
thy rosy lips that were kissed . . .
to-day even as yesterday,
gitane, death of mine,
such friends, alone together, thou and I,
the life-breath of Granáda? . . . my Granáda.'

III

He was seen to fade in air . . .
                        Cut, friends,
in stone and dreams, in Alhambra,
a tomb for the poet,
over a fountain where the water weeps
and eternally cries:
the crime took place in Granáda . . . his Granáda.

ANTONIO MACHADO
(*Translated from the Spanish by D. Trevor and ? . . Neumann*)

Lorca

The Fascists have only one answer for a poet –
Their stuttering lead syllables prevent repartee
Putting an end to his stanzas and fancy speech.

And the poet dies easily, his human flesh
Parts easily as a babe's for the bullets to enter
And all his words are done and there's an end to him.

And for Lorca the civil guard had a special hatred
A personal spite: there were certain deeds in the past
Had been pilloried, had been whistled through Spain in a ballad.

So they smelt him out and marched through the town, to the
  trees,
He walking straight as a tree, and knowing to what end:
While others behind piled his books on the Plaza del Carmen.

They halted to take their stance: Lorca alone
Continued away from Granada. How many steps
Would they let him take towards freedom? A flutter of capes

Raising of rifles. They would let him take all but the last one,
Hoping that he would run for it, hoping for fear.
But the bullfighter's friend was not afraid of their hate.

And he stopped and turned and faced them, standing still;
He stared at their aiming eyes, his imminent murder;
He was one with the people of Spain and he stood as they stand.

What is the power of words against flight of bullets?
A puff of articulate air, no deflector of death;
But they dared not listen, they burst the bubble of speech.

And a volley was heard in Granada. Lorca fell.
His books, a billow of smoke, rose over the Plaza.
The civil guard marched back, and there was an end of him.

A poet dies easily, easily as a babe.
So Lorca merges with Spain, and over the city
In ashes his writings disperse, disappear like a shell burst.

And they in the city drink to that easy death,
The generals and colonels who feared to be put in a ballad:
The foul-mouthed general in Seville announces an end to him.

But this side of the line, and secretly that side
His friends, the people, the peasants, remember his songs
And chant them through Spain. And to them there will be no
  end.

GEOFFREY PARSONS

The Death of Garcia Lorca

Step after step into the darkened landscape
we mourners walk with you: until the guns speak.
Speak to the muffled dead for the loss
of the gipsy's glory and the matador's.
Walking, did you see the cape and the dancers
flutter and fall still, the falling lances?
The picador is Don Quixote,
the gipsy begs, and the poet's
mouth is bloody. Blood reddens
the windmill arms of Armageddon.
O this is your end, your end, your end;
the sails say it. Call to your friend
or the gunman, but neither is with those
you loved: the spendthrift, the mumming, the toreros.
None walked so far the roads of the tramps
and the singers to the gipsy camps,
and joked with the sharpers and dancers and whores
and the trick-riders and picadors.
You joked with the dead: did you not hear
their voices lower year by year?
their dumb trumpets? and the word Doom
when the gun's echo answered the drum?
You walked with ghosts, and their time is done.
Call to your friends, but we are one
with the gunmen then. Ours is the cause
of the grinding mill and the crowded house
and the men who walk between mill and home.
Our future is not easy come.
Step by step into the darkened country
we walk with you there; but the light gentry
walks no more, not the gipsy kings.
And out of that dark the poet sings.

J. BRONOWSKI

PRISONER

On Being Questioned after Capture. Alcaniz

I stood before my questioner who asked
'Why leave home?
Why have you come?
Why?' He must have guessed
'Because he is a Communist'.

I thought of all the answers I could give
whether death is correct or whether save
life for a rainy day
and told a lie to cheat his bullet with a word
to use a bullet afterward

On him the bigger lie – a conscript
'volunteer' to rape Spain where she slept
to save his own skin
he had come when he sought 'The Leader' on his hands and
    knees
To crush a thousand years in half an hour
To make Guernica
a wilderness.

I could wait and so could lie
for adjournment to another court
meanwhile to live on my bended knee
to make occasion for another start.
I could imitate the victor, cringe
till I and the world beyond
take our revenge.

CLIVE BRANSON

1939

Death Sentence Commuted to Thirty Years

When this sunrise put the question 'why
should birds sing?' Even the machine-gun
kills in rhythm. For the ordinary eye
enjoys the redness in blood, the purple of wine,
Death's proud carnation
a murdered man twists at the corner of his mouth.

While we sat down by the river barbed wire
was stretched between us and a circling cloud
to emphasise our horizon, perpetual window,
wall's edge, the beat of a guard on duty.
Caged in, to see a star, to think the world,
to live life's compass in a flat gravel yard,

The homeward rail imagination ran
outdistanced time with modern mockery.
Slow passed each day, compiled a week,
our patient waiting streamed by the prison bars
till we grew tired of counting; only knew
Death is no sudden, but reiterated speed.

CLIVE BRANSON

The Nightingale

You spent your voice upon the midnight air
Here, when we were newcomers, you were alone.
No one listened. Your music died to share
Each tedious darkness with the deaf mute moon.

A sleepless captive swears to hear you sing
Whom his sorrow renders still. We too cower
Awake under the dead blanket thinking
Of that illusive freedom you echo each hour

And even through the shouting of the guard
Their chain of noise, we hear you secret bird,
Their strength, their arrogance, though bayonet proud
Can't still the voice humanity has heard.

Your silence is articulate when you
Must be obedient, sing when ordered to.

CLIVE BRANSON

San Pedro, 1938

Prisoners

Like stones on stones
peeling potatoes
prisoners were
seated in a circle
seeing each other
looking at potatoes
young and old ones.

CLIVE BRANSON

San Pedro, 1938

The Aeroplane

This winged machine that cancels distance out.
New steel Icarus senseless to the sun.
Would have Da Vinci end what he'd begun
knowing his dream materialised? – the rout

of innocents from field and home – the shout
of joy to spot an aeroplane. Tis done
The metal bird now sings and man has won
Power to touch the stars or turn about.

Small looks the pilot below the wings spread.
Ailerons quiver. The propeller roars.
This time-derisive bird, perfect to plan,
Takes off. Trees become weed size. Earth withdraws
It wheels to find his course. Then straight ahead
Springs to achieve the destiny of man.

CLIVE BRANSON

San Pedro, 1938

San Pedro

A foreign darkness fills the air to-night.
The moon betrays this unfamiliar scene.
Strange creatures, shadow-ghosts of what had been
Live with no aim than groping through half light,
Talk dreamily, walk wandering, delight
In trivial acts that formerly would mean
Nothing. A livid memory, this lean
Ill-clad rabble of a lost dreaded might.

Look longer, deeper, the accustomed eyes
Know more than quick appearances can tell.
These fools, this shoddy crowd, this dirt, are lies
Their idiot captors wantonly compel.
These men are giants chained down from the skies
To congregate an old and empty hell.

CLIVE BRANSON

To the German Anti-Fascists in San Pedro

1   The evening went beyond the bars, passed by us
2   His face at the window
His voice in a frame
He 'who ought to be shot' and will be
5   when the Nazis get him home.
He was singing
this German prisoner, self exiled workman,
common songs of the beer-garden in his home town.
Singing to memories of friends
who could not hear.
And others, some half dozen, sang too.

I have lain in my blanket at night
kept awake by lice and a dry itching skin
looked at the blue window panes broken
15   with a star up in one corner.
Outside a night-bird intensely sings
17   unseen and to no-one.
18   Only to memories of friends did he sing?
Only to the deaf ears of these ghosts?
Was there meaning in his song, or meaningless
21   Like that of the nightingale?
Mere repetition of a few notes through centuries
with no gain
Just a song of the beer-garden?

In the strains of music
In the discipline of song
27   This prisoner, the captive voice
sang of the freedom in trees, of cloud and wind
the movement of men on bicycles, hiking,
of animals not afraid of leaving their cages
who do not need the safety of their cell
the security of a gaol.

33	He sang the promise of a dream
34	sometime come true, of free men
	whose homes are not prisons,
36	beds not graves, play not in murder
	work for creation.

This German sang to us of home
Our heritage in one-another
Comrade, Brother – no foreigner.

CLIVE BRANSON

San Pedro De Gardena, 1938

In the Camp

The storm has cleared the air
but not barbed wire.
Here we can bask in the sun,
should our eyes have forgotten,
pointed at by the guard's bayonet.

We're like young trees set
on a wide landscape and mountain
in a picture for ever certain.
Clouds pass and fine weather
and with them the liberty we long for.

CLIVE BRANSON

Palencia, 1938

By the Canal Castilla

It is difficult to think
of the noise of guns while men die
while we sit and in the hot sun lie
beside the lazy still water of the canal.

Get up, dive and shatter illusion!

The guard's bayonet splinters the sun.
A gilded Iris shrivels up.
A Poppy's crimson cup
breaks petal by petal to the wind
That carries memories
of other trees, stretches of water, wings

An unseen shadow sings
Everything waits what the next journey brings
Even the authorities.

CLIVE BRANSON

Palencia, 1938

The Prisoner's Outlook

Sun swayed, huge flower, from morning to night
Our neck hurt watching the pendulous flight.
The chords of the heart were strained to repeat
Wide beat, beat, throb of the day-great pulse beat.
As we lay in the grass looking up sky wide
Dangled the senseless sword from side to side.
The moon's recurrence, stars persistence,
Speed kills, but speed so vast is slow suspense,

217

Torments the quicker springs, wearies the brain,
Stretches quick light back to its end again
After eternity of search and travel
Millions of times died in an eye's pupil
Mutinous water, tides, tropic rain, attend
Monotonous as clouds and wind with no end.
A long white road bending back against itself –
War not to end wars. Sentence for life
No chance to repeat, no hope for reprieve.

CLIVE BRANSON

Palencia, 1938

Sunset

Like a new cut on a young girl's shoulder
the sun left a crimson scar.
Through barbed wire
we can feel the day's passing
and evening
warns us of night, the complete end.

CLIVE BRANSON

Palencia, 1938

A Sunday Afternoon

A delicate breeze sufficient to stir
Light dust, a little leaf, by an insect's wing

Dance music on the wireless; between prisoner
And a girl dressed like a rose, a smile.

A leaf, a frog, a shadow, a piece of paper
A trickle of water, reading, writing

218

These things on a stillness deeper than all
Took a whole afternoon to drift with the canal.

CLIVE BRANSON

Palencia, 1938

On Dreaming of Home

Silver wings travel like sunlight across the field.
The wind creates waves over long grass and sea.
Snow and cloud crest mountains. Still eternity!

Not even sunlight can rise like the aeroplanes
Surge over the edge of the moon, oceans and field,
Ride the motion of time, thinking, thought free
Waves of the fixed mind, span distances, outstrip
The evening star, the course of the lagging moon,
And the recurrent sun, completed the millionth lap.

Yes, we can take off, easily leave and circle
Into the course of our desires. But where?
Where to land? Where is the lettering of your name,
That spells the safe hangar, aerodrome, and home?

No good the map of the will alone, not enough
The sure imagination, swiftest dream,
Most certain and accurate chart of the mind's eye.
These are most necessary, but waiting between
Are storm clouds no sane pilot dare to enter
Are moods of weather and daylight shutting in
And white mists, the shrouds of certain death
And the variable wind, uncertain friend.

More, there is the gap from mind to mind
Which has not yet revealed its winged machine;
No-one has crossed. Though thought has left its hangar
Risen with ease and powerful at the start,

Soared over barbed wire, walls, made the near world
Seem distant or forgotten, soon has followed
A quick return or inevitable crash.

Daring friends are keen with good advice:–
'Don't dream, don't let the brain tick over, don't
pour fuel into the engine of the mind, don't
test the ailerons, or think of one direction.
Stay in the club-house and have another drink.'

But we are pioneers, we who dream and think.
Dream of wide spaces that sever man from man.
Think out the journey and in detailed plan
Of the end. Even though we crash soon and near
Our thought's beginning is our dream's conqueror.

CLIVE BRANSON

Palencia, 1938

On the Statue of Christ, Palencia (1)

Still symmetry! Is this our human aim?
Knowing conceit! Should child of woman born
live perfect death to reach a deathless fame?
Her child still-born! Spain's body mangled, torn.

Historic judgement no confusion mars.
Perhaps this statue climbs upon the hill
better to win the plentitude of stars:
Ride with the sun beyond earth's window sill.

Perhaps it cheats the sight its splendour bars,
Its high pretence to life lives on to kill.

CLIVE BRANSON

Palencia, 1938

On the Statue of Christ, Palencia (2)

When I first saw this venerable stone
Statue standing up against the sun-rise
I learnt how vast it was to be alone
To pause in solitude before men's eyes,

Not to move while the day's wide motion threw
The sun above all else, whose blazing heat
Parched tongues to flame, white-powdered roads; and drew
the cool of evening past the statue's feet.

At night dogs howl, the firmament spins round,
Dark is the noise of unseen insects wings,
And yet I know you are on your high mound
Straight, upright, fixed, immune to living things,

Dead as a rock memento of the past
Life's immortality in death held fast.

CLIVE BRANSON

Palencia, 1938

Lines written in a book of drawings done by the order of the Commandant of the Italian Camp

These drawings needed a little freedom,
The eye and hand of man enjoying life.
Great Art demands fulfilment of a dream
Of human peace and friendship, no more strife.

CLIVE BRANSON

On being ordered to copy a large signature of MUSSOLINI under a slogan written on the camp wall

For years I've trained, burnt out my sight, not spared
my health, my strength, my life's too tender flame.
I strove to heights no former vision dared –
to scrawl in black this Fascist's bloody name.

CLIVE BRANSON

BALLADS OF HEROES

(Ballad of Heroes, Opus 14, by Benjamin Britten, text by Randall Swingler and W. H. Auden. First performed 5 April 1939, Festival of 'Music for the People', Festival Hall, London)

The Hero

I could tell you of a young man
Blown with heroism into Spain.
He had a knapsack of philosophy,
And as he went he scattered the small grain
Of his few songs under the dangerous sky.

A girl, grown fond, thought him too young to die.
She put the memory of their secret joy
8   Behind her heart, and turned to public deeds,
Neglecting the earth he trod, and his scattered seeds.

10   But soon she was brought to child-bed, with a boy
Smiling up at her as his father had smiled.
And thankfully she saw that his plump back
Carried no philosophic haversack.
14   She saw, too, that his lips displayed no zest
For song, but only for his mother's breast.
That being so, she found she could forgive
The man who died so that a dream might live,
And faith with prudence remain unreconciled.

RICHARD CHURCH

May Day

We marched in London, May Day of last year,
   We shouted and sang, I had never marched before
But thought it pretty good, I liked to hear
   Us letting them know what we were marching for.
We were ready to start
   When somebody put a flag pole into my hand:

225

The girl who unrolled and held the other end
Was the neatest thing I had seen for years, I thought.
Once we got to the Park, I didn't waste time,
   I told her this was the parting of the ways
   For I was off to Spain in a couple of days.
Thank god that girl's ideas were the same as mine.
I wrote her letters, she wrote me a lot,
   She has sent a box of cigarettes or two,
Saying, she still remembers, have I forgot?
   Taking it as she means it, I don't know
Whether I have or not.
I say to myself, crouching in this trench,
   What memory of her have I? Very small,
And now she's further than a banner's length.
There's more fish in the sea, the fellows say,
   But she fitted in so neat – no, damn it all,
I don't forget that day.

MILES TOMALIN

Self-Destroyers

Load upon load of bomb and shell
Shakes down the brick and stone and dust,
But what does all this ruin spell
When only brick and stone are crushed?
Beneath your storm of steel the town
Shivers, and sinks slowly down,
And you believe that hearts lie deep
With homes under the rubble heap!
Your loss is greater than your gain;
Men whose homes are here no longer
Spread the fever of their anger
Through the length and breadth of Spain.
A million hearts you have made stronger,
You have armed a million men.

226

What you destroy, shatter burn,
Are not the things that in their turn
Will strike you and your cannons dumb,
Is not the spirit in whose name
We built an army, and defied
Your steel, your thunder and your flame:
These cannot die till we have died.
You understand so little. You
Have more than walls to batter through –
Men
Such as your brutish heroes never knew
The way to overcome.

MILES TOMALIN

Christmas Eve 1937

The soldier, standing guard,
Thinks, 'Back at home the party's on by now,
And most of them enjoying it, what's more.
This year they'll all get solemn half way through
And toast the unlucky chap that's at the war.
It aint that hard,
I don't miss coloured lights and Christmas trees
Provided I'm where company is good,
To be among a bunch of men like these
Makes up for what you miss in drink and food'.
The soldier winks at half a moon, his feet
Shuffle an outline to the tune he's humming,
He thinks, 'The day we get these fellows beat,
There's going to be a merry Christmas coming'.

MILES TOMALIN

Last Letters of a Hero

Extract from a letter, 9 December 1936

I expect it will be a surprise to you, but I am leaving for Spain the day after tomorrow. You know how I feel about the whole mad business of war, but you know also how I feel about the importance of democratic freedom.

The Spanish People's Army needs help badly; their struggle, if they fail, will certainly be ours tomorrow and, believing as I do, it seems clear where my duty lies . . I am going out as a driver in a convoy of lorries and we shall make the journey by road through France.

Postcard from Perpignan, 17 December

Just arrived at the frontier. Convoy had engine trouble all through France. Spain tomorrow. *Salud!*

Extract from a letter, 30 December

Just a line to let you know that we delivered the lorries safely at [*name censored*] and have now been drafted into the British Unit of the International Brigade. At the moment, we are at a training-centre, but do not expect to stay here long.

My letters will be very sketchy from now on, and do not be surprised if you do not hear from me at all for a fairly long time.

Extract from a letter, 7 January, written to the brother of a fallen comrade in the International Brigade

I am writing to you because I have only just heard the news of your brother's death – though I gather that it must have been known to you soon after it happened.

I want to pass on the sympathy with your mother and you that all the English-speaking battalion here feels; and above all I

228

want to tell you of the tremendous pride and admiration the whole International Brigade feels for those few English comrades, including your brother, who were with the Thaelmann Battalion of the Brigade from the very start.

In [*name censored*] I met the German under whose command your brother served soon after the casualties had occurred, and although he was a reserved kind of man, he was so moved by them that he was going up to every Englishman to explain in his broken English what admiration the whole Battalion felt for them. [*Name censored*] asked the same man why the casualty rate among the English portion of his unit was so high, and he answered, 'Because every one of them was a hero.'

I think you can understand what that means, coming from the commander of the Battalion which played such a vital part in the early days of the Madrid fighting.

Extract from a letter, 14 January, from Albacete

Our training is almost over now. It has been extraordinarily interesting; the International Brigade in its composition and organisation is so entirely different from any ordinary army.

Our commandant is thoroughly at home in this Spanish fighting, which is about as different as possible from that of the Great War; a very extended front, continual flanking movements and a very mobile type of fighting.

At Madrid, of course, there is a certain amount of digging-in. A feature of this war is the tremendous use of machine-guns – far eclipsing the last war, so I am told. In this connection we are 5 handicapped by shortage of ammunition due to the Arms ban. We are also short of artillery and aeroplanes.

English recruits are coming out fairly well now and we are already forming an English Battalion. Of course, we are tremendously outnumbered in the Brigade by the Germans and the French and the Italian sections.

Extract from a letter, 30 January, from Albacete

We expect to move off very soon.

We've been here so long now, waiting for new drafts to arrive to bring us up to battalion strength – that I am almost beginning to feel an old soldier, and already act as machine-gun instructor to our group.

England seems centuries away, and we are yearning to get to the Front. No rifles yet – the arms shortage is acute here – but we should get them very soon now and will then move off.

Extract from a letter, 7 February, from Albacete

This is only a short note, written in haste. I may not find time to write again for some time. You will understand why. So until I write again, all the very best to you both.

CHRISTOPHER CAUDWELL

Five days after writing that letter he was killed in action outside Madrid. One of his comrades, himself wounded, wrote this letter describing how he died:

On the first day Chris' [*sic*] section was holding a position on a hill crest. They got it rather badly from all ways, first artillery, then machine-gunned by aeroplanes, and then by ground machine-guns. The Moors then attacked the hill in large numbers and as there were only a few of our fellows left, including Chris, who had been doing great work with his M.G., the company commander – the Dalston busman – gave the order to retire.

Later, I got into touch with one of the section who had been wounded whilst retiring, and he told me that the last they saw of Chris was that he was covering their retreat with the advancing Moors less than 30 yards away. He never left that hill alive, and if any man ever sacrificed his life that his comrades might live that man was Chris.

When I come out of hospital I will try to obtain further details for you, but I am afraid it may prove a little difficult, as out of the 600 men of his battalion who went into that engagement less than 200 are now left.

Caption to photo at head of News Chronicle page:

(Christopher St John Sprigg was killed on February 12 while fighting with the International Brigade among the olive groves of Madrid. Though only 29 when he died, he had a remarkable record of literary achievement. Under the name of Christopher Caudwell he had published seven novels and several aviation text books. His last book, 'Illusion and Reality', was published posthumously. Here the *News Chronicle* prints extracts from his last letters.)

Plaza de España

If there is peace among these branches
Hanging here without a sound,
The wind brings other tales of trenches,
Tales of war on Spanish ground.

Don Quixote, why at rest?
Centuries have turned the wheel
Since your fathers died and left
Their arms of honour and of steel.

Is your heart not fierce and burning
Underneath your old cuirass
To hear your enemies returning?
Don Quixote, shall they pass?

Drop your shield and shirt of iron,
Drop your cumbrous sword and lance,
Swing out of your saddle, down
From Rosinante's crazy flanks!

Take a gun and shrapnel hat,
The day of swords is dead and gone;
Arm as a soldier, not a knight,
And ride the Spanish camion.

Men are standing, wet and cold,
Underneath the parapet;
Here's the way we change the world,
Stand with us – we'll change it yet!

Stoop, or they'll get you in the head,
Their line is fifty yards from here
And six-foot men are soonest dead.
Have caution where you have not fear!

This is no windmill in a field,
This is the fighting force of shame;
We face them, strength for strength, and yield
To death it must be – not to them!

ZOFIA SCHLEYEN

The Madrid Defenders

In the broken house of man
Show where the pictures hung,
And the soot in the flue.
An era has gone,
Its death-knell has rung;
We have come with a plan,
We will build something new.

Is the Cross in the way;
The mysterious soul;
Individual love?
Then they fetter, betray;

232

They are ruins to move,
They baulk us, they stay
Our path to the goal.

Our love is another,
Much greater than one
For husband, for mother,
For wife or for son.
No longer human,
Compelled by our need,
Neither child, man nor woman;
An Act, not a Creed;
The People, the One!

RICHARD CHURCH

Harvest in 1937

The road from Valencia to Madrid descends in a series of dramatic hairpin bends to the gorge of the Rio Gabriel; and rises again as dramatically. In those swooping few miles one changes country, leaves behind the orange groves and the olives, the oleanders growing wild along the dried winterbournes, the roses edging the dusty road; and comes into a vast austere table-land that rolls onward towards distant Madrid, and grows corn. Here, as we drove on our way to attend the Madrid sessions of the Second Congress of the Writers in Defence of Culture, the harvest was being reaped, reaped with a sickle.

It is a beautiful gesture, if one cares for the picturesque. As the reaper stoops, grasping the locks of corn, and swings the sickle with a movement made elegant by centuries of hereditary use, and casts the swathe behind him, and stoops and grasps and swings the sickle again, it is as though one watched a series of caresses. And along with him his shadow, small under the mid-day sun, repeats the movement in a contracted perspective.

Women reap among the men. Looking closely, one sees how

these groups acknowledge war Women of all ages, old men, children, make up the greater part of these bands. The babies sit along the edge of the corn-strips, sometimes there is a dog with them, or a tethered mule or donkey, chewing at the harsh stubble.

The reapers are too sunburned to look hot. Faces and bared arms are dark, shining with sweat they look like oiled wood. The men wear broad-brimmed straw hats, the women muffle their heads in thick kerchiefs, sometimes they have a white cloth bound over the mouth. This prevents the rasping straw dust from irritating the throat. The dust settles on faces and bared arms, the flies buzz.

Mile after mile the beautiful reaping gesture persists, tireless, identical. And one begins to remember the feel of corn, to remember that those locks of corn which seem so yielding as the reaper gathers them are in truth harsh and spiky; that to tread on corn-stubble is like treading on metal filings; that along with the sweet scent of corn flies the teasing, tickling corn dust. Among the corn are the sharp, low-growing thistles, the small aggressive weeds of a dry soil, clawing and scratching the feet of those who tread them.

There are many weeds among the corn. By our English standards it is a poor crop, short in straw, light in the ear. Scanty as is the corn, the reapers are scantier yet. As the road goes on over the interminable plain one begins to wonder if the corn will ever be reaped, the landscape is so large, the little groups of reapers so widely spaced.

At intervals along the enormous horizon mountains appear. The plain is a general sunburned tawny colour, the rock of the mountains is painted by distance to a lovely colour like lavender. But in spite of the tender colour given to them by depth of air, these mountains have an inimical aspect, they seem to have the watchfulness of tyrants, not of guardians, as they overlook this landscape of poor corn and scattered reapers.

And where do they live, these reapers? Bound to the soil, it is as though they rose out of it to serve the corn, and, the harvest gathered sank into the ground again. The villages lie leagues apart, sometimes there are not even villages, only long barrack-like farmsteads, what old Scotch husbandry called 'a town', the bailiff's house, and the barns and stables and granges, and the field-workers' quarters all enclosed within one wall. No lesser roads, no lanes, branch off the main road, only a few tracks and footpaths. A signpost is an eye's wonder on this journey.

It is the harvest of 1937, the first harvest these peasants have ever reaped for themselves. When the great landowners fled these melancholy miles of corn-land were allotted among the workers. This year, like every other year, the harvest goes on, the harvesters repeat their gesture, the babies, docile with heat, sit patiently along the edges of the corn-strips. The harvest goes on, the sickle swings forward. And as though it were a ground-bass in a piece of counterpoint the rhythm of harvest after harvest becomes apparent, is a recurring gesture like the movement of the reaper, stooping to grasp the locks of corn, swinging the sickle, casting the swathe behind him. Subdued to this rhythm, working on under the heavy sun, the corn-dust flying, the flies buzzing, the beat of the swollen vein, the ache in the loins ... to those who reap it can this harvest of 1937 seem so very different from the harvests of other years?

There is a heavy sound on the road behind us, an imperious klaxon. Our car draws to one side, and one of the new Government lorries tears past. The reapers lift themselves from the corn, with stiff, awkward movements they straighten themselves, the sweat pouring off their faces with the effort of wrenching themselves so suddenly upright. They hold up their clenched fists in the salute, they cheer and shout greetings, and the soldiers salute and shout in answer. The lorry passes, the reapers stoop to the corn again. All along the road the groups of reapers, one after the other, straighten themselves out of the corn to salute and cheer as the lorry sweeps on towards Madrid.

SYLVIA TOWNSEND WARNER

The Nabara[1]

They preferred, because of the rudeness of their heart, to die rather than to surrender.

Phase One

Freedom is more than a word, more than the base coinage
Of statesmen, the tyrant's dishonoured cheque, or the dreamer's
   mad
Inflated currency. She is mortal, we know, and made
In the image of simple men who have no taste for carnage
But sooner kill and are killed than see that image betrayed.
Mortal she is, yet rising always refreshed from her ashes:
She is bound to earth, yet she flies as high as a passage bird
To home wherever man's heart with seasonal warmth is stirred:
Innocent is her touch as the dawn's, but still it unleashes
The ravisher shades of envy. Freedom is more than a word.

I see man's heart two-edged, keen both for death and creation.
As a sculptor rejoices, stabbing and mutilating the stone
Into a shapelier life, and the two joys make one –
So man is wrought in his hour of agony and elation
To efface the flesh to reveal the crying need of his bone.
Burning the issue was beyond their mild forecasting
For those I tell of – men used to the tolerable joy and hurt
Of simple lives: they coveted never an epic part;
But history's hand was upon them and hewed an everlasting
Image of freedom out of their rude and stubborn heart.

The year, Nineteen-thirty-seven: month, March: the men,
   descendants
Of those Iberian fathers, the inquiring ones who would go
Wherever the sea-ways led: a pacific people, slow

---

1. The episode upon which this poem is based is related in G. L. Steer's
The Tree of Gernika.

To feel ambition, loving their laws and their independence –
Men of the Basque country, the Mar Cantabrico.
Fishermen, with no guile outside their craft, they had weathered
Often the sierra-ranked Biscayan surges, the wet
Fog of the Newfoundland Banks: they were fond of *pelota*: they
   met
No game beyond their skill as they swept the sea together,
Until the morning they found the leviathan in their net.

Government trawlers *Nabara, Guipuzkoa, Bizkaya,*
Donostia, escorting across blockaded seas
Galdames with her cargo of nickel and refugees
From Bayonne to Bilbao, while the crest of war curled higher
Inland over the glacial valleys, the ancient ease.
On the morning of March the fifth, a chill North-Wester fanned
   them,
Fogging the glassy waves: what uncharted doom lay low
There in the fog athwart their course, they could not know:
Stout were the armed trawlers, redoubtable those who manned
   them –
Men of the Basque country, the Mar Cantabrico.

Slowly they nosed ahead, while under the chill North-Wester
Nervous the sea crawled and twitched like the skin of a beast
That dreams of the chase, the kill, the blood-beslavered feast:
They too, the light-hearted sailors, dreamed of a fine fiesta,
Flags and their children waving, when they won home from the
   east.
Vague as images seen in a misted glass or the vision
Of crystal-gazer, the ships huddled, receded, neared,
Threading the weird fog-maze that coiled their funnels and
   bleared
Day's eye. They were glad of the fog till *Galdames* lost position
– Their convoy, precious in life and metal – and disappeared.

But still they held their course, the confident ear-ringed captains,
Unerring towards the landfall, nor guessed how the land lay,
How the guardian fog was a guide to lead them all astray.

For now, at a wink, the mist rolled up like the film that curtains
A saurian's eye; and into the glare of an evil day
Bizkaya, Guipuzkoa, Nabara, and the little
Donostia stepped at intervals; and sighted, alas,
Blocking the sea and sky a mountain they might not pass,
An isle thrown up volcanic and smoking, a giant in metal
Astride their path – the rebel cruiser, *Canarias.*

A ship of ten thousand tons she was, a heavyweight fighter
To the cocky bantam trawlers: and under her armament
Of eight- and four-inch guns there followed obedient
Towards Pasajes a prize just seized, an Estonian freighter
Laden with arms the exporters of death to Spain had sent.
A hush, the first qualm of conflict, falls on the cruiser's burnished
Turrets, the trawlers' grimy decks: fiercer the lime-
Light falls, and out of the solemn ring the late mists climb,
And ship to ship the antagonists gaze at each other astonished
Across the quaking gulf of the sea for a moment's time.

The trawlers' men had no chance or wish to elude the fated
Encounter. Freedom to these was natural pride that runs
Hot as the blood, their climate and heritage, dearer than sons.
Bizkaya, Guipuzkoa, knowing themselves outweighted,
Drew closer to draw first blood with their pairs of four-inch
    guns.
Aboard *Canarias* the German gun-layers stationed
Brisk at their intricate batteries – guns and men both trained
To a hair in accuracy, aimed at a pitiless end –
Fired, and the smoke rolled forth over the unimpassioned
Face of a day where nothing certain but death remained.

Phase Two

The sound of the first salvo skimmed the ocean and thumped
Cape Machichaco's granite ribs: it rebounded where
The salt-sprayed trees grow tough from wrestling the wind: it
    jumped
From isle to rocky isle: it was heard by women while
They walked to shrine or market, a warning they must fear.

238

But, beyond their alarm, as
Though that sound were also a signal for fate to strip
Luck's last green shoot from the falling stock of the Basques,
    Galdames
Emerged out of the mist that lingered to the west
Under the reeking muzzles of the rebel battleship:

Which instantly threw five shells over her funnel, and threw
Her hundred women and children into a slaughter-yard panic
On the deck they imagined smoking with worse than the foggy
    dew,
So that *Galdames* rolled as they slipped, clawed, trampled,
    reeled
Away from the gape of the cruiser's guns. A spasm galvanic,
Fear's chemistry, shocked the women's bodies, a moment
    before
Huddled like sheep in a mist, inert as bales of rag,
A mere deck-cargo; but more
Than furies now, for they stormed *Galdames'* bridge and
    swarmed
Over her captain and forced him to run up the white flag

Signalling the Estonian, 'Heave-to', *Canarias* steamed
Leisurely over to make sure of this other prize:
Over-leisurely was her reckoning – she never dreamed
The Estonian in that pause could be snatched from her shark-
    shape jaws
By ships of minnow size.
Meanwhile *Nabara* and *Guipuzkoa*, not reluctant
For closer grips while their guns and crews were still entire,
Thrust forward: twice *Guipuzkoa* with a deadly jolt was rocked,
    and
The sea spat up in geysers of boiling foam, as the cruiser's
Heavier guns boxed them in a torrid zone of fire.

And now the little *Donostia* who lay with her 75's
Dumb in the offing – her weapons against that leviathan
Impotent as pen-knives –

Witnessed a bold manoeuvre, a move of genius, never
In naval history told. She saw *Bizkaya* run
Ahead of her consorts, a berserk atom of steel, audacious,
Her signal-flags soon to flutter like banderillas, straight
Towards the Estonian speeding, a young bull over the spacious
And foam-distraught arena, till the sides of the freight-ship
   screen her
From *Canarias* that will see the point of her charge too late.

'Who are you and where are you going?' the flags of *Bizkaya*
   questioned.
'Carrying arms and forced to go to Pasajes,' replied
The Estonian. 'Follow me to harbour.' 'Cannot, am threatened.'
Bizkaya's last word – 'Turn at once!' – and she points her
peremptory guns
Against the freighter's mountainous flanks that blankly hide
This fluttering language and flaunt of signal insolence
From the eyes of *Canarias*. At last the rebels can see
That the two ships' talk meant a practical joke at their expense:
They see the Estonian veering away, to Bermeo steering,
Bizkaya under her lee.

(To the Basques that ship was a tonic, for she carried some
   million rounds
Of ammunition: to hearts grown sick with hope deferred
And the drain of their country's wounds
She brought what most they needed in face of the aid evaded
And the cold delay of those to whom freedom was only a word.)[1]
Owlish upon the water sat the *Canarias*
Mobbed by those darting trawlers, and her signals blinked in vain

1. Cf. Byron's comments upon 'Non-Intervention' in *The Age of Bronze*:

> Lone, lost, abandoned in their utmost need
> By Christians, unto whom they gave their creed,
> The desolated lands, the ravaged isle,
> The fostered feud encouraged to beguile,
> The aid evaded, and the cold delay
> Prolonged but in the hope to make a prey: –
> These, these shall tell the tale, and Greece can show
> The false friend worse than the infuriate foe.

After the freighter, that still she believed too large to pass
Into Bermeo's port – a prize she fondly thought,
When she'd blown the trawlers out of the water, she'd take
    again.

Brisk at their intricate batteries the German gun-layers go
About death's business, knowing their longer reach must foil
The impetus, break the heart of the government ships: each
    blow
Deliberately they aim, and tiger-striped with flame
Is the jungle mirk of the smoke as their guns leap and recoil.
The Newfoundland trawlers feel
A hail and hurricane the like they have never known
In all their deep-sea life: they wince at the squalls of steel
That burst on their open decks, rake them and leave them
    wrecks,
But still they fight on long into the sunless afternoon.

– Fought on, four guns against the best of the rebel navy,
Until *Guipuzkoa*'s crew could stanch the fires no more
That gushed from her gashes and seeped nearer the magazine.
    Heavy
At heart they turned away for the Nervion that day:
Their ship, *Guipuzkoa*, wore
Flame's rose on her heart like a decoration of highest honour
As listing she reeled into Las Arenas; and in a row
On her deck there lay, smoke-palled, that oriflamme's crackling
    banner
Above them, her dead – a quarter of the fishermen who had
    fought her –
Men of the Basque country, the Mar Cantabrico.

Phase Three

And now the gallant *Nabara* was left in the ring alone,
The sky hollow around her, the fawning sea at her side:
But the ear-ringed crew in their berets stood to the guns, and
    cried
A fresh defiance down

The ebb of the afternoon, the battle's darkening tide.
Honour was satisfied long since; they had held and harried
A ship ten times their size; they well could have called it a day.
But they hoped, if a little longer they kept the cruiser in play,
Galdames with the wealth of life and metal she carried
Might make her getaway.

Canarias, though easily she outpaced and out-gunned her,
Finding this midge could sting
Edged off, and beneath a wedge of smoke steamed in a ring
On the rim of the trawler's range, a circular storm of thunder.
But always *Nabara* turned her broadside, manoeuvring
To keep both guns on the target, scorning safety devices.
Slower now battle's tempo, irregular the beat
Of gunfire in the heart
Of the afternoon, the distempered sky sank to the crisis,
Shell-shocked the sea tossed and hissed in delirious heat.

The battle's tempo slowed, for the cruiser could take her time,
And the guns of *Nabara* grew
Red-hot, and of fifty-two Basque seamen had been her crew
Many were dead already, the rest filthy with grime
And their comrades' blood, weary with wounds all but a few.
Between two fires they fought, for the sparks that flashing spoke
From the cruiser's thunder-bulk were answered on their own
    craft
By traitor flames that crawled out of every cranny and rift
Blinding them all with smoke.
At half-past four *Nabara* was burning fore and aft.

What buoyancy of will
Was theirs to keep her afloat, no vessel now but a sieve –
So jarred and scarred, the rivets starting, no inch of her safe
From the guns of the foe that wrapped her in a cyclone of
    shrieking steel!
Southward the sheltering havens showed clear, the cliffs and the
    surf
Familiar to them from childhood, the shapes of a life still dear:

But dearer still to see
Those shores insured for life from the shadow of tyranny.
Freedom was not on their lips; it was what made them endure,
A steel spring in the yielding flesh, a thirst to be free.

And now from the little *Donostia* that lay with her 75's
Dumb in the offing, they saw *Nabara* painfully lower
A boat, which crawled like a shattered crab slower and slower
Towards them. They cheered the survivors, thankful to save these lives
At least. They saw each rower,
As the boat dragged alongside, was wounded – the oars they held
Dripping with blood, a bloody skein reeled out in their wake:
And they swarmed down the rope-ladders to rescue these men so weak
From wounds they must be hauled
Aboard like babies. And then they saw they had made a mistake.

For, standing up in the boat,
A man of that grimy boat's-crew hailed them: 'Our officer asks
You give us your bandages and all your water-casks,
Then run for Bermeo. We're going to finish this game of *pelota*.'
Donostia's captain begged them with tears to escape: but the Basques
Would play their game to the end.
They took the bandages, and cursing at his delay
They took the casks that might keep the fires on their ship at bay;
And they rowed back to *Nabara*, trailing their blood behind
Over the water, the sunset and crimson ebb of their day.

For two hours more they fought, while *Nabara* beneath their feet
Was turned to a heap of smouldering scrap-iron. Once again
The flames they had checked a while broke out. When the forward gun
Was hit, they turned about
Bringing the after gun to bear. They fought in pain
And the instant knowledge of death: but the waters filling their riven

243

Ship could not quench the love that fired them. As each man fell
To the deck, his body took fire as if death made visible
That burning spirit. For two more hours they fought, and at
    seven
They fired their last shell.

Of her officers all but one were dead. Of her engineers
All but one were dead. Of the fifty-two that had sailed
In her, all were dead but fourteen – and each of these half killed
With wounds. And the night-dew fell in a hush of ashen tears,
And *Nabara*'s tongue was stilled.
Southward the sheltering havens grew dark, the cliffs and the
    green
Shallows they knew; where their friends had watched them as
    evening wore
To a glowing end, who swore
Nabara must show a white flag now, but saw instead the fourteen
Climb into their matchwood boat and fainting pull for the shore.

Canarias lowered a launch that swept in a greyhound's curve
Pitiless to pursue
And cut them off. But that bloodless and all-but-phantom crew
Still gave no soft concessions to fate: they strung their nerve
For one last fling of defiance, they shipped their oars and threw
Hand-grenades at the launch as it circled about to board them.
But the strength of the hands that had carved them a hold on
    history
Failed them at last: the grenades fell short of the enemy,
Who grappled and overpowered them,
While *Nabara* sank by the stern in the hushed Cantabrian sea.

*

They bore not a charmed life. They went into battle foreseeing
Probable loss, and they lost. The tides of Biscay flow
Over the obstinate bones of many, the winds are sighing
Round prison walls where the rest are doomed like their ship to
    rust –
Men of the Basque country, the Mar Cantabrico.

Simple men who asked of their life no mythical splendour,
They loved its familiar ways so well that they preferred
In the rudeness of their heart to die rather than to surrender ...
Mortal these words and the deed they remember, but cast a seed
Shall flower for an age when freedom is man's creative word.

Freedom was more than a word, more than the base coinage
Of politicians who hiding behind the skirts of peace
They had defiled, gave up that country to rack and carnage:
For whom, indelibly stamped with history's contempt,
Remains but to haunt the blackened shell of their policies.
For these I have told of, freedom was flesh and blood – a mortal
Body, the gun-breech hot to its touch: yet the battle's height
Raised it to love's meridian and held it awhile immortal;
And its light through time still flashes like a star's that has
    turned to ashes,
Long after *Nabara*'s passion was quenched in the sea's heart.

C. DAY LEWIS

This New Offensive (Ebro, 1938)

This new offensive drugs our old despair,
Though, distant from the battle-line,
We miss that grave indifference to fear
That has so often now saved Spain.

Let fools and children dream that victory
Drifts lightly on the waves of chance,
And all that riveted and smooth-tooled army
Should melt before this proud advance.

Not this war's weathercock, brave when things go well,
Afraid to think of a retreat,
By turns all singing and all sorrowful:
We've not to watch, but win this fight.

Offensives must be paid for like defeats,
And cost as dear before they end.
Already the first counter-raids
Take no positions but they kill our friends.

A miracle is not what we can hope for
To end this war we vainly hate.
We shan't just read it in the evening paper
And have a drink to celebrate.

For two long years now when you sighed for peace
To slip from heaven as an angel drops,
You were confronted with your own sad face,
And once again time holds the mirror up.

It was not a few fields they fought to gain,
But months and maybe years of war.
Time's on their side: by time we mean
The heirs of time they thought worth dying for.

This narrow ridge of time their valour won,
Time for us to unite, time to discover
This new offensive is your life and mine,
One nation cannot save the world for ever.

MARGOT HEINEMANN

The Gunner

The gunner on his crest
Watched the battalions waiting to assault
And saw his friend, relaxed there as if dead
Among the rest.
He'll go at the first shout, the gunner said,
Meantime the waiting makes his mind stand still
As a watch when it's wound up sometimes will
Until you shake it.

He'll go – I know that fellow well enough,
I shouldn't wonder if the going's tough.
Oh God, the gunner said, I hope he'll make it!
There's that dammed [*sic*] fascist rattler going again.
Give me another five, Chief, or they'll start
Before we've got it. Give me another five –
I want to see that man come out alive.

MILES TOMALIN

Asturias

High in your mountain fastness still you fight,
Lacking in arms out-numbered by the foe.
Rather than bondage, to die for what is right
And with your ebbing strength deal blow for blow.

Proudly you give your all in freedom's cause,
A bright example to oppressed mankind,
Cut off from aid, yet fighting without pause,
Steel horde ahead, wild barren rock behind.

From belching cannon's mouth and from the skies,
The steely death rains on you day and night,
Traitorous diplomats ignore your children's cries,
Deaf to your agony, blind to your plight.

Yet when the history of this war is writ
And all this bloody massacre exposed,
We your brothers will then in judgement sit
And deal out justice to our mutual foes.

Then you shall be avenged, Asturias,
For every drop of blood you gladly gave,
To make our fight for Liberty victorious
From fascism and war the world to save.

H. G. SUTCLIFFE

A Song for the Spanish Anarchists

The golden lemon is not made
  but grows on a green tree:
A strong man and his crystal eyes
  is a man born free.

The oxen pass under the yoke
  and the blind are led at will:
But a man born free has a path of his own
  and a house on the hill.

And man are men who till the land
  and women are women who weave:
Fifty men own the lemon grove
  and no man is a slave.

HERBERT READ

Spain's Air Chief in a Mechanic's Blue Dungarees

Two organizations have played a decisive part in checking the advance of the rebels in the Spanish War; one is the International Brigade; the other, the Spanish People's Air Force. In November, Madrid experienced a two-fold salvation: by land, when the first columns of the Brigade resisted the rebel attack; and by air, when the Republican aeroplanes first brought down some of the aeroplanes which day after day had bombed the centre of Madrid with impunity.

In the early stages of the war, the Air Force had a large proportion of foreign volunteer pilots; today, just as the role of International Brigade is being changed because the Spanish

People's Army grows larger, better trained and accustomed to the conditions of war, so there is an increasing number of trained Spanish pilots. In fact, the transformation of the Air Force is more spectacular even than that of the Army, since only a limited number of pilots is required and therefore the foreign volunteer pilots have mostly been sent home.

At the moment, 90 per cent of the pilots in the Government Air Force are Spanish, and an almost equal proportion are Communist Party members. In all its activities, the Air Force has the pride of anonymity; the name of its lieader [*sic*], Cisneros, is hardly ever mentioned in the Spanish Press: however brave an action, no pilot is ever singled out for special praise; one reads in the Spanish papers of 'our heroic aviation', but never of heroes.

The clue to the extraordinary achievement of the Government in training pilots so rapidly and building up an Air Force lies largely in the character of Colonel Hidalgo Cisneros, who is one of the most remarkable Spaniards I have met. Although he has greying hair, he is young-looking, lean and athletic, with an angular face of great seriousness and honesty.

Whenever I met Cisneros he was dressed in a mechanic's blue dungarees, with only the two metal stripes pinned on to show his rank. I have rarely felt so much at ease with a man of action, for there is nothing affected or even preoccupied about his camaraderie, whether he is talking with his fellow pilots about flying or with me about the poetry of his friend, Rafael Alberti.

But we did not only talk about Spanish poetry. He told me that the Government Air Force is already more efficient than the Italo-German rebel Air Force against which it is fighting. Indeed, except that it is limited in numbers, it is one of the most efficient Air Forces in Europe; and the rest of Europe has to reckon with the fact that when the Government has gained the war, the Spanish Republic, with a nationalized armaments industry and aeroplane factories in Barcelona will be one of the great air Powers of the world, a powerful ally of democracy.

The amazing success of the Government Air Force is not a propagandist story. When I went through the trenches at Morata, soldiers of the International Brigade told me again and again the same story: the enemy bombers would come over their lines and they would experience the most terrifying sensation which even modern war can provide – an air raid on men lying in an open place with no kind of defence. Then suddenly the Government chasers would appear; and always these planes are so fast that they can not only make circles round the bombers but are much faster even than the enemy chasers.

An aerial battle of this kind is so astonishing and exciting that it is the one occasion on which the entrenched sides will stop fighting in order to watch the spectacle. Nothing has done more to encourage the morale of the Government side than the victories of their Air Force; when the chasers have beaten off the enemy it is almost impossible to prevent our men from jumping out of the trenches with elation.

In many ways the Spanish Civil War is not a final test of modern mechanized war – there is almost no very heavy artillery, for example, and the conditions of a war in which all the 'advances' on horror since the last war can be staged, do not exist.

However, the battle of Guadalajara showed more decisively than any action until today the terrible efficacy of aerial bombardment on a massed army. The Government bombers swooped down, and the Italians were trapped. The result of this bombardment was complete panic, followed by an Italian defeat as overwhelming (according to the military authorities who sympathize with the Fascists) as that of Caporetto in the Great War.

Before the war, Cisneros was for some years military attaché in Rome. Smilingly he showed me photographs of himself watching military manoeuvres with Mussolini. Like many other people high in the Spanish Army or in the Government, he respects the Germans as an enemy, but has nothing but contempt for the Italians. The whole of Fascist Italy, from Mussolini downwards, is one enormous bluff, and the battle of Guadalajara was the first occasion on which that bluff was called.

Like many other Spaniards, he pressed me very seriously to explain British policy, which truly puzzles the Spanish Government. To Spaniards it seems obvious that England is in a better position than any other Power to call Italy's bluff, and that she is in an excellent position to do so. If she does not do so, her position in the Mediterranean is threatened.

I have written at some length here of Cisneros, partly because I am convinced that after the war he will have a considerable role to play in Spanish history, so that his is a name for readers of the *Daily Worker* to remember; partly because, to everyone who has come in contact with him, he symbolizes the type of man who is typical of what is best in the new Republican Spain. For it is important to realize that there has already taken place a complete change in the psychology of the Spaniards of the younger generation. The Germans and Italians seem to imagine that they have to deal with a country of picturesque, but surly peasants and decadent aristocrats, who are united by a certain racial pride. They were wrong.

The fact is that a fundamental change has taken place in the mentality of the Spanish people. No one can talk with older peasants and workers in Spain, and the young, politically-minded people of the Republic, without realizing that a gulf of centuries divides the two generations living in Spain at this moment. Military defeats of the Spanish people there may be, but a conquest of their minds is now impossible, and since that is so, they will eventually win. As Cisneros remarked to me whilst we were looking at a large wall-map of Spain, 'They will never defeat us.' And the extraordinary achievements of the Spanish People's Air Force go far to show that Franco will never win the war.

STEPHEN SPENDER

On a Lost Battle in the Spanish War

This is defeat of a sort.
Whoever wins now, these have lost.
These have seen faces of bad dreams
Look at them down a levelled gun,
And nothing has broken the dream nor woken.

Those who died at Badajoz
Will be dead when men who shot
Their brothers, Fascists, foreign tools
Are nothing; when across the world
The people stand on victory.

These saw the cities race with flame,
The friendly streets run blood,
The walls fall, the ignorant
Murder the honest, and whatever happens
They will not see the rest.

They have no immortality
But what their dying works in us.
Blood does not cry to heaven, nor take
Its own revenge when they are dead.
By their agony the living learn to fight.

MARGOT HEINEMANN

Passionaria

You are the great figurehead
At the prow of the ship: Spain
Forging forward

You are stalwart, strong;
Long generations of sturdy miners
Have forged you – iron is in your blood.

You are good. You have stood
Always in the vanguard, leading,
Hands held out to uphold
Children and women above this sea
Of hatred and of blood.

You are wise. In your eyes
That smiled at me so lovingly
I saw and understood
Also the buried tears.
Crystallised toil and struggle,
Years of hardship, privation, sorrow, –

But never for yourself alone,
Never to moan in solitude,
But ever surrounded and uplifted by your comrades,
The valour of your people,
The honourable, proud, and noble unknown
Of whom you were one, and are still

The indomitable will. Now a leader among them
Great carved woman at the prow
Who knows sorrow; suffers hate; feels love:
Whose eyes and hands and voice have moved
Thousands into battle-line:

In you I salute, Comrade Dolores,
Spain, forging a new world for us too!

CHARLOTTE HALDANE

On Guard for Spain!
A Poem for Mass Recitation

What you shall hear is the tale of the Spanish people.
It is also your own life.
  On guard, we cry!
It is the pattern of the world to-day . . .

I speak for the Spanish people,
I speak for the Spanish people to the workers of the world.
Men and women, come out of the numbered cells
of harsh privation, mockingly called your homes,

break through the deadening screen with your clenched fists,
unrope the bells that jangle in the steeple of the sky,
make the least gap of silence in the wall of day
and you will hear the guns in Spain.

Face here the map of your own fate, and say:
This suffering shall not be in vain.

Thus we plead with you our need.
Cannot you hear the guns in Spain? . . .

Have you ever come out of the tangled undergrowth
into the clearing of history?
Then you have lived in Spain,
Spain of these years of pang and aspiration,
Spain the arena where a weaponless man
takes the charge of a bull of havoc,
Spain where the workers, going to battle,
go as to a fiesta,
Spain.
    Salute to Spain!

After the February elections
the people sang in the streets of work.
The echoes of time were notes of guitars
and the moons smelt of oranges
amid the jasmine-stars.
Bodies that had been jailed by fear
turned to the slopes of light once more.
The sun tied ribbons in all the trees
when we led the prisoners out of the jails,
thousands of comrades came singing out
while the waves of the sea clicked castanets
from shore to dancing shore.
The locks of the prisons of poverty
were broken by the hammers of unity,
and brushing the cobwebs of old night away
we came out into the factories of day.

We cried, and cried again:
On guard, people of Spain.
Franco the Butcher lurks in the Canary Islands.
Queipo de Llano in Seville mutters threats in his drunken sleep.
Batet sneers in Barcelona.
Sanjurjo waits in Lisbon for the gong of murder to sound.
Mola, masked with a grin, chats with death at Burgos.
On guard, people of Spain!

Gil Robles whispers in the jungle of darkness.
There is a chinkle of bribes, a smell of powder
in draped sacristies, and bombs beside the pyx.
The crucifix is held up by a stack of rifles.
The muddy light drowning in cathedral-aisles
favours conspirators, or their leathery faces sweat
where Juan March and bankers have a word
behind the frosted windowpane of importance,
their heads scarfed with cigar-smoke
as they smile and bend closer.

Remember, Spanish people,
the humble marchers shot down out of side-streets,
the shattered men splashed on the shattered walls of the Asturias,
the cobbles slippery with blood,
the girl screaming in the midnight of her rape,
the scythe of machine-gun volleys,
women and children mown down on red earth,
the cells of torture,
the long night of starvation,
the thugs of the Falange
sniping from taxis, hiding
round corners of the night.
Remember what was suffered in 1934.
Cry out, and cry again,
On guard, people of Spain!

But amid the guitars of laughter,
amid the orange-suns
in Liberty's newly-opened orchard,

a light of plenty
shining its promise into the crannies of slums,
and children playing
amid the carnation-glow
of the shadows of Granada,
who was there to hearken?

Why should they take our hope away?
Surely no cloud of greed can tarnish our bright day.
In spring we shall dance on the terraces by the sea,
our sweat shall make the summer gold with corn,
autumn shall ooze from the olive-presses,
and we shall pluck from our flesh sharp winter's thorn.

Then came the blow
A mailed fist of thunder struck down that sun of hope,
and in the deliberate darkness the murderers moved.
Out of the barracks of conspiracy
were led the hoodwinked soldiers.
Gold was silently spilt
to grease the wheels of counter-revolution.
Those dumps of reaction, the arsenal churches,
bared their armouries of oppression.
The fascist monster, slimed from the night,
roared out over Spain.

On guard, Spain, on guard!

Now was the testing time of the people,
now with the terrible trumpets of the dawn
crying out over the grey-green olive-slopes
that ran down to the shimmering sea,
crying out over the plains of peasant-toil,
crying out over sierras of buffeted limestone,
crying out over Madrid and Barcelona,
the moment of choice appeared.
Seize, it, Spanish people,
or lose it for evermore.

Are they right, the fascists,
calling the people swine,
mud to be trodden, mud that has no purpose
except to breed
the flowers of leisure for the few?

The people answered.

That dawn of crystal suddenness,
that lightning of choice,
shuddered across Spain
from the rosy heights of the Pyrenees
to the wide grey combers of the Atlantic,
from the striped valleys of Andalusia
to the tumbled crags of the Asturias.

Through hammerclang we heard it,
through clatter of looms, through chop of the machines,
down in the burning darkness of the mines,
on the red plains of dust,
along the sheeptracks on the heights of loneliness,
among the rocks of heat,
along the tinkling waterways,
where we were threshing corn in the cracked barn,
standing up in the dry shadow of the corktrees,
digging beside the silver shoals of olive-leaves,
coming off work at the junction,
wiping our oiled hands with some cotton-waste –
all over Spain we heard it.

We came from field and town, from clay-huts on the hills
and tenements of dirt. We poured out on the Ramblas,
asking for news, pulling the railings up.
Shots pitted the morning-hush.
We sought the heart of that alarm, tracking
the spoor of danger. We were freedom's foresters
on that wild morning. We trod with grace like dancers
the stage of our apprehension, with gritted teeth,
waiting for what would come out of the shadowy eaves.

Then we saw
the soldiers in the square, we smelt
the stink of the beast, and knew what we must do.

With wrath, with unshakeable determination
the people uprose.
On guard, people of Spain!
With some old pistols and our bare hands
we charged
we charged
we charged the soldiers there.

Now at last had the enemy shown his face
unmasked. No longer now
behind the veil of incense and the words of solemnity,
no longer behind the legalised titles of theft,
the enemy hid. Our brightening hopes
had forced them out undisguised to avow
their need to feed on the meat of broken lives,
to snuff the steam of simmering slums,
to alloy their gold with the blood of the poor.
Power ran openly amok in the barracks,
Greed took the glove from its leprous fingers in the square.
Two worlds stood face to face.

Now you behold the people, fascists; what do you say to us?
Now you have heard the people, fascists; why are you silent?

Rise up, morning of July the Twentieth,
burn up into the sky of history.
Rise up, old sun, never to be forgotten,
and let the people speak.

Tear down the oppressors.
Tear down the forts of stone with our bare hands.
Smash with our bare hands
the iron door of greed.
Open the sluice-gates of time
and let the irrigating waters flow.

We found an odd gun,
we brought it up on a truck from a beer-factory.
We rushed the Montana barracks
with some old pistols and our bare hands
through the swivelling machine-gun fire.
I was there.
   I saw the officers cowering,
their faces chalked with fear.

I rose from the bed of my wife's young body
at the call of Liberty.
O feed with my blood our flag's red flame.
Comrades, remember me.

The fascists shot my children first,
they made me stand and see.
O dip the flag in my heart's blood.
Comrades, remember me.

Spain rose up in the morning,
roused by the bluster of bullets.

Unbreakfasted, the people
put the fascists to rout.
Spain rose up in the morning,
Spain rose up in the morning,
Spain rose up in the morning,
and drove the fascists out.

Therefore they came with Moors deceived and bribed,
therefore they came with Foreign Legion scum.
The fascist war-plot opened, with aeroplane-whirr,
It pockmarked Spain with spouting craters of bombs.
Mussolini the gangster rapped out his murder-instructions.
Hitler the gambler rattled his loaded dice,
to crush the people of Spain.

Therefore they shot the workers at Badajoz,
gouged and scourged and maimed and lamed and murdered,
blew up with grenades the wounded in hospital-wards,

mangled and hanged and flogged and smashed and
    ravished,
a fist of force slogging at every heartbeat
over the people of the invaded districts.
The rotary-presses of the world's frightened masters
champed day and night with the stereotyped lies of hate,
to crush the people of Spain.

But the workers, going to battle,
went as to a fiesta.

Now is no time for tenderness
when the heart grows most tender.
Now when the whole love of a life
brims into the farewell-kiss.
We kiss with closed eyes as the train-whistle jags us.
Darling, darling, your tear-wet lashes
brush my cheeks, and then the gust of war
wrenches us apart like a leaf torn
from its tree of safety and blown headlong
into autumn. A cold wind slides
along the grinding rail-tracks of departure.
Time and the carriage-door slam between us.
The train foreshortens, concertinas into distance,
into the lifted hills of menace,
Samosierra Front,
the screech of bullets in the splayed bush of heat,
like cigarras in remembered olive-groves of home,
the phenic-acid gas in murmuring tent glooms
where Juan's breast-wound bubbles,
and the sun's great hammer clanging
in the sickle of the skies,
and the shadow of the wings of death
flickering over Spain.
Toledo in the splintering rain of destruction,
in a twisted skein of tempest-light,
with time a tower of toppling stone.
Irun a town pulled down on the heads of heroes
to give them a fitting grave.

The scarred flanks of Oviedo
where miners blast their way through death's thicket.
The ruined homestead where through the window
the dying man still fires.
The cornered peasants who fight to the end,
shooting from whited holes in the cemetery-walls.

And then the flails of the chilly wind
the spikes of pain in the stark midnight watch.
We lie in coffin-grooves of rock and shoot,
while winter flaps and howls
and rides us with cruel spurs.
Yet we cry louder than the winds of darkness,
louder than all the fields of frenzy
gashed with the flame-flowers of grenades.
Hammer of industry, strike down those who would steal from us.
Sickle of plenty, cut down those who would starve us.

Forward, the sudden command jerks.
Extend in skirmishing order,
into the storm of death, the filth of pain,
into the stunning cyclone barbed with beaks of metal,
recalling only
tear-wet lashes that brushed my cheeks
and the voice that cried out over Spain:
They shall not pass!

That cry broke round the world; its tides of power
foamed upon every shore of man. The workers
answered; the International Brigade
swung through the streets of torn Madrid.
Shoulder to shoulder stood
the workers of all lands.

Therefore, dropped from a throbbing sky,
with venom of flame the snakes of death leaped jagged
among the women and children of Madrid.
Therefore the fascists gathered in greater numbers,
Hitler the gambler tosses for his world-war.

On every front of thought,
in every street dark with the stench of hunger,
in every house throughout the world
where the loudspeakers of capitalism blare,
the fascists fight this war
to crush the people of Spain.

For the war in Spain is war for the human future.
All that crawls evil out of the holes of the past,
and all that rises with love for the lucid warmth of the day,
meet in this grapple. In it meet
the evil and the good that swarm
in your inherited blood.
Yes, yours, and yours, and yours.

Listen, comrades,
if you would know our pride.
Have you ever faced your deepest despair?
Then what you see in the agony of Spain
is your own body crucified.

Listen, comrades,
if you would know our pride.
Can you dare to know your deepest joy,
all that is possible in you?
Then what you see in Spain's heroic ardour
is your own noblest self come true.

Then, workers of the world, we cry:
We who have forged our unity on the anvil of battle,
we upon whom is concentrated
the shock, the breath of flame
belched from the hell of greed,
we who are pivot of all things since we give
to-day the ground of courage and devotion,
the fulcrum of power to shift the harried world
into the meadows of the future's plenty,
we who have claimed our birthright, O hear our call.

Workers of the world, unite for us
that bear the burden of all.
You shall not hear us complain
that the wolves of death are ravening in our streets
if you but understand, if your bodies flow
into this steel of resistance, this welded mass,
making you one with us, and making us
unconquerable. Workers,
drive off the fascist vultures gathering
to pick the bones of Spanish cities,
to leave the Spanish fields
dunged with peasant dead
that greed may reap the fattened crops.
Fuse your unity in the furnace of our pain.
Enter this compact of steel,
and then we shall not complain.

On guard for the human future!
On guard for the people of Spain!

JACK LINDSAY

The Will to Live

A Review of *John Cornford : A Memoir*, ed. Pat Sloan, 1938

Men and women are so deeply influenced by the circumstances which surround them through their adolescence, that during times of rapid change, like the present, generations divided by completely different views of life succeed to each other in less than ten years, instead of thirty. The attitude of young men at the Universities is a good test of this. Since the war, the Universities have seen three different generations. The post-war generation of young men whose adolescence was spent in preparation for fighting in the war, and who were then miraculously released to a life which, having expected death, they did not know what to do with. The 'boom' generation, who were adolescent during the optimistic 'twenties of trade expansion, the League of Nations and the Weimar Republic. Last of all there comes the 'crisis' generation of young men, adolescent since 1929 and brought up in an intensely political, revolutionary and counter-revolutionary atmosphere.

John Cornford was a leader of this youngest generation. Like several of the most promising of his contemporaries, he went to Spain to fight in the International Brigade. He was killed on the day after his twenty-first birthday.

This clear and factual collection of examples of his own writing and essays by those who knew him gives a portrait of a character so single-minded, so de-personalized, that one thinks of him, as perhaps he would wish to be thought of, as a pattern of the human cause for which he lived, rather than as an individual, impressive and strong as his individuality was. His brother says: 'Trying to know him was like standing on a railway embankment and trying to grab an express train.' In Victor Kiernan's account of him at Cambridge, even in Professor Cornford's careful and informative recollections of his childhood, one has the same impression of a person who was driving himself like powerful machine.

The steam in the engine which Christopher Cornford saw as his brother was Communism, to which he became converted in 1932, the time of the depression, when, it will be remembered, the brothers Esmond and Giles Romilly, both of whom have fought in Spain, were conducting another campaign at another public school. Before he left school, Communism had become his whole life. A group of his contemporaries have contributed simply an account of Cambridge Socialism to this book, instead of any reminiscences, because John Cornford was so completely identified with this movement.

The few years of Cornford's active life as a Communist were an exercise in orthodoxy, both in theory and practice. Until shortly before he died, he had ambitions as a poet; but poetry took second place to political action, or rather, had to grow out of it; when it ceased to do so, the Muse went overboard, like love affairs, *The Waste Land* and everything else.

> All we've brought are our party cards
> Which are no bloody good for your bloody charades.

The last poems he wrote are interesting for the determination with which he was trying to force political lessons into rhyme and imagery:

> Time present is a cataract whose force
> Breaks down the banks even at its source
> And history forming in our hands
> Not plasticine but roaring sands,
> Yet we must swing it to its final source [*sic*].

These poems are violent and insensitive, yet it is these very defects which make them effective and give them a defiant metallic clang, which does not lack a certain richness, because it is single and strong.

Cornford's own essays are extremely able arrangements of intractable material into a dynamic, if preconceived, pattern. They show the energy of a strong intellectual will and a great intelligence; what is most convincing in them is the single-mindedness of the writer which identifies itself with an objective cause.

How far his disinterestedness could go, is shown by Cornford's death. If he had chosen, he could no doubt have played a leading part in the Socialist movement in this country. All the essays show that he had the rare quality of leadership, great intellectual gifts and a power of organizing both himself and others. But he went to Spain, first of all, as he explains in a moving letter to Margot Heinemann, 'with the intention of staying a few days, firing a few shots, and then coming home'. However, he soon discovered that 'you can't do things like that. You can't play at civil war, or fight with a reservation you don't mean to get killed. It didn't take long to realize that either I was here in earnest or else I'd better clear out ... Having joined, I am in whether I like it or not. And I like it.'

John Cornford was a leader rather than just an original person, because his remarkableness lay in his having qualities that others share, only in a pattern of greater abundance, strength and clarity.

Reading this book, one is discovering the potentialities of a generation. Cornford lived for a form of society for which he was also willing to die. When democracy in Spain was threatened, it was natural for him to fight, and in fighting he felt that he was both defending something real and helping to create something new. His spirit was not a resurrection of 1914.

Cornford is immensely significant not merely because he was young and brave, but because he lived and died with the courage of a purpose which reaches far beyond himself and which effectively challenges the barbarism and defeatism of the age we live in. One may feel, as I do, that the pattern of this young hero is over-simplified; his vision of life is impatient and violent, it leaves too many questions unanswered, he burns out too quickly, rushing headlong to his death; but nevertheless it is a pattern which in other lives may take on a greater richness without losing Cornford's power and determination. The spirit of Cornford and some of his comrades rises like a phoenix from the ashes of Spain, which are the ashes of Europe.

STEPHEN SPENDER

ROMANCEROS

Spanish Folk Song of the War

Frontiers that divide the people,
Soon we'll tear apart.
The masses speak a thousand tongues –
But have one heart.

For the workers no boasting Fatherlands,
Only freedom and peace,
So that through peace and freedom
All may find release.

The men sing as they work.
The women sing at their tasks.
All the World is singing
When the people are free at last.

But silent now the guitar
And the jota aragones.
First comes the International,
Then the Marseillaise.

Red with the people's blood
From the bombs of the enemy's raids,
Our flags are blooming like flowers
On freedom's barricades.

Girl of the People's Army,
Do not be jealous of me
If to my heart I take
Both you and liberty.

ANON
(Translated from the Spanish by Langston Hughes)

A Spectre is Haunting Europe

... and the ancient families seal their windows,
bolt their doors,
under cover of darkness the priests run to the banks,
and the pulse of the Stock Exchange weakens,
and one dreams in the night of bonfires,
of burning granges
that instead of wheat yield flames,
instead of grain sparks, coffers,
iron coffers full of glowing embers.

Where are you?
Where are you?

They are pursuing us with guns.
Oh!
peasants march by, stepping
in the puddles of our blood.

Who is that?

Let us close,
let us quickly close our frontiers.
See how he comes borne on the East wind
from the red steppes of hunger.

may the workers not hear his voice,
may his whisper not penetrate into the factories,
may the men of the fields be unable to divine
the sickle that he raises in the sky!
Hold him! Hold him!
For he leaps the seas,
spreading over the whole geography.
He hides in the holds of vessels
and speaks with the stokers,

and sooty as they are he draws them under cover,
arousing hatred and misery in them,
stirring up tribulations.

Open!
Open all the windows!
His voice strikes against the walls.

Who is there?

But we, we follow him,
we make him come down from the East wind that brings him,
we question him concerning the red steppes of peace and
     triumph,
we set him down at the lean table of the peasant,
we present him to the owner of the factory,
we make him preside over our strikes and our demonstrations,
we see him speak with soldiers and seamen,
he appears in the offices to the astonishment of clerks,
and raises his clenched fist in parliaments of gold and blood.
A spectre is haunting Europe, the whole world,
and we,
we call that spectre 'Comrade'.

RAFAEL ALBERTI
(*Translated from the Spanish by A. L. Lloyd*)

The Tower of El Carpio

Bird beloved tower, fled are your doves,
Your swallows swift and your martens;
The crows have crowded them out,
And the vultures awaiting carcasses,
Your desecrated nests of peace
Are turned into nests of murder;
Machine-gun beaks spit lead and flame
Into the windows of workers' homes.

In the tower the curate's soft hands,
And the jowls of the fat caciques,
Give the orders, and sprinkle death
Over the workers in the streets.
No one dares come near this church
Which sings with a choir of machine-guns
Whose incense is gunpowder, the church
Which the clergy have turned to an arsenal,
Its bell tower into gun turrets.

Empty is the square; the shunned streets
Leading to the square are empty.
The tower has made a desert.
But the siege goes on. Our militia
Do not flinch; the town will not be
A prey to the perch of vultures.
See, underneath the olive trees
Men swarming, clenched fists raised, –
Fists to the sky that the tower blackens.

Eight men leave the crowd, step forth;
Their hearts are deep in willing death;
Their pockets deep with dynamite,
Eight miners make an offering
Before this church, an offering of their lives
For the humanity this church betrays.

They climb into an open truck.
'Faster,' cry these hurriers to their doom;
'Faster,' echo back the hollow streets.
The housefronts and the paving stones
Have taken on the hue of shrouds.
Pallid are the eight faces; pallid
The walls beside, as if blanched with awe.
Has there been seen in the world
Sacrifice so stainless, heroism so pure,
Such a proud pacing into death,
As these miners in the open truck
Riding the mortal streets.

The bullets come, and one by one
The miners topple; one by one
Their names stand up, and stand forever
Risen to height of immortality.

The truck arrives
With three alive.
They stand at the root of the tower
That they will soon uproot;
They gaze down the impossible street
That they have passed, and think
Of the impossible return; but not long.

They dig the ground and pierce the walls
Preparing their own sepulchre.
Then peals the thunder from their hands.
And when, among the olive trees,
Triumphant thunder echoes back,
The tower crashes to the earth.

Dull heap of stones and shapeless hill,
Soon as the wonder settles, like the dust,
Becomes a glorious monument.
Dynamite sticks for funeral tapers –
Never was heroes' burial so sublime, –
Never such a funeral salute!

Dull heap of stones and hill of ruin,
Where three brave hearts now lie entombed,
Is far more eloquent
Than any splendid Alcazar.

The tower toppled to the earth
Has strengthened our foundations,
Cemented there with heroes' blood.
Our strength renewed, our ardor fired, –
Millions heed the valorous example.

Thus was El Carpio stormed.
Long live the armed people!

MANUEL ALTOLAGUIRRE

(Freely translated from the Spanish
by Isidor Schneider and Stephen Williams)

My Brother Luis

(Translated from the Spanish of Manuel Altolaguirre)

My brother Luis
used to kiss me doubting
on the platforms of the stations.
He always waited for me
or accompanied me to say goodbye
and now
when he left me to go I know not where
I did not arrive in time,
there was no one ...
Not even the most remote echo
not even a shadow,
nor my reflection on the white clouds.
This sky is too immense.
Where are the sons of my brother?
Why are they not here?
I would go with them
amongst real things.
Perhaps they would give me his portrait.
I don't want them to be in a room
with black clothes.
It would be better if they ran by the river,
if they ran among flowers without looking at them,
like flowers also,
like boys,
who never stop,
as I have stopped,
too much at the edge of the sea and of death.

STEPHEN SPENDER

Madrid

(Translated from the Spanish of Manuel Altolaguirre)

Horizon of war, whose lights,
whose unexpected sunrises, so brief,
whose fleeting dawns, promises, fires,
multiply the interminable death.
Here in Madrid, by night, solitary, sad,
the front and my frown are both synonymous
and above my gaze like a lament
the heroes crash, they fall submerged
in the green abyss of my face.
I know that I am deserted, that I am alone
that the front parallel with my frown,
disdains my grief and me accompanies.
Before the glorious circle of fire
I can evoke nothing, nor anything from anyone.
There is no memory, pleasure, lived before,
which I can call back from my past.
There is no absence, no legend, no hope
to calm my agony with its illusion.
Here in Madrid, facing death
my narrow heart keeps hidden
a love which grieves me which I cannot
even reveal to this night
before this immense field of heroism.

STEPHEN SPENDER

I Demand the Ultimate Death
(Translated from the Spanish of Manuel Altolaguirre)

I demand the ultimate death of this war
because to look at myself in the current
like a grievous body mortified
I wish, as the tree they rob of its fruits,
tearing out its branches
and profiting from its trunk made a log . . .

And if I cannot see myself
if only my roots remain;
if the birds seek vainly
the place of their nests
in the sad absences of my arms,
then, from the depths,
with the silence of the Spring,
will pour forth from the earth like lament
insinuations of verdure and life.
I shall be that multitude of adolescents,
that crown of laurel which binds
the trunk struck down by the axe.
Multiplied life from death.
Multiple are the rays of dawn.

STEPHEN SPENDER

Ballad of Lina Odena

Past the gates of Granada
Runs a trickle of blood
From whose margins the evening
Drinks of ochre and brown:

Tragedy's livid stain
Burns with the corpse of shadow,
The corpse of a frozen shadow
That falls on the olive trees.

Enemies wait in ambush
Hidden among the branches;
Weeping comes to the eyes,
Harvests go up in flames,
And hysterical Death
Over the puddles of blood
Howls and dances in rage,
Leaps and fastens on flesh.

Lina Odena, a dewy rose,
Like a flower in her green array,
Penetrated the hostile camp,
Showing no fear that she might be slain.
Owls of ill-omen, shadowy black,
Hovered over the country-side,
Danger lurked in the olive-trees,
Dark Death snatched at her green array.

Lina Odena, trapped in the pines.
Twenty Moors were hunting her down,
Twenty Moors, and a cutlass each,
Death in their eyes, and plague in their blood,
Trying hard to take her alive,
Make her sport for their lewd delight.
Lina, courage is not enough,
Run, and be safe from so foul a foe!

Lina Odena, a dewy rose,
Like a flower in her green array,
Figures the windage out, and fires.
Hark! The wild sound rebounds again,
Rolls and echoes from height to height,
Over the valleys beyond the plain,

And the rebellious Moors go down
Stricken like badly wounded bulls.

Now there are seven. Now there are eight,
Now a round dozen hunks of meat,
Lumped on the ground in the afternoon,
Fallen never to rise again.
'Run, and be safe from so foul a foe,
Maybe the shadows can save you yet!'
Again and again the wailing air,
Cries a warning, but cries in vain.

For Lina, never moving,
Motionless in the dusk,
Broken, with eyes still burning,
Cries out her final challenge:
'I am a girl of courage,
Who'd rather die with honour,
Than live and be a coward.
You'll never get me living!'

At the gun's chilling sound
Her slender body falls.
Move no more, ye pines!
Winds, be quiet and still.
Endeavour to yield no more,
Blossom; pause in your flight,
Birds of the air, be still;
Roses, bloom no more.

Lina Odena, our dewy rose,
No one will ever forget you now:
Guadix to Granada, all the way,
Men will remember your green array.

PLA Y BELTRAN
(*Adapted from the original Spanish by
Rolfe Humphries*)

Revolutionary Madrid

Revolutionary Madrid!
You have proved your worth today,
In a day that will be remembered
With the glorious Second of May!
Long live the Revolution
Of all the working-class,
The men of Oviedo,
The men of Asturias,
And the workers of Madrid –
Who like one man have taken
Up arms, and stand on guard!

We, the men of the fields,
Shout out like a word of command
Our slogan: They shall not pass!
Not while a soldier stands
To fight for the people's bread,
To fight for the people's land.
Our land, that is above all:
Queipo and Mola may snatch at it,
But we will make their names
A byword for future times.

We, the men of the fields,
Today are all in arms;
And our shout rings overhead.
Long live the People's Army
That fights for the people's bread,
And for better times to come!
And it is for this reason
We march to the beat of the drum.

4

Long life to our Captain Lister!
Long life to our Captain Carlos!
Long life to the People's Front
That stands for the working-class,
That will not rest or falter
Till the victory is ours!

And now I take my leave
Of all soldiers and friends,
And if my song is amiss
Remember a countryman made it.
And if you would know my name,
Francis Fuentes I am.

FRANCIS FUENTES
(Translated from the Spanish by Sylvia Townsend Warner)

Single Front

Anarchist and brother, wasn't there a time
when argument on argument parted you from me?
Don't you agree?
Sure, you agree!
We had each our ways to heaven, not at all the same:
Marx said, Bakunin said . . . Hell, but we were dumb!
Your sweat and my sweat
made the same earth wet;
your girl went barefoot, famished;
always ill, my little son;
and the old folks of both of us,
those who taught us everything,
from the cradle onwards
always stretching, always searching
for shade and rest and shelter, shelter from the sun –
and you and I arguing
whether Marx or Bakunin . . .

Hell, but we were dumb!
Now in field of fighting
our companions
pierced by the same shrapnel
their broken bodies mingling
cry out in their death-rattle
the crime of our disputes.
Anarchist and brother: we know their cry is true.
When the enemy pours out
his barrage on our parapet
shoulder close to shoulder,
courage beside courage too,
we grip hands with nothing said.
And Marx and Bakunin . . . hug each other warmly
as brothers swearing loyalty
there where lie our dead.

PEDRO GARFIAS
(*Translated from the Spanish by Tom Wintringham*)

La Peña

Dark was the night
when I went on guard,
and took my station
behind a rock.

A silence of death
was in the hills;
then in a whisper
the rock spoke:

Keep quiet watch,
soldier, tonight.
No traitor bullet
shall pierce your flesh.

So much and no more
said the rock to me.
Was it a dream? –
I ask. But no!
I did not slumber,
no dream was there.

But the rock, may be,
fellowed my feeling,
and after its fashion
fought for the people.

JULIO D. GUILLÉN
(Translated from the Spanish by Sylvia Townsend Warner)

Hear This Voice

Nations of the earth, fatherlands of the sea, brothers
of the world and of nothing:
inhabitants lost and more distant
from the sight than from the heart.

Here I have a voice impassioned,
here I have a life challenged and indignant,
here I have a message, here I have a life.

Look, I am opened, like a wound.
Look, I am drowned, drowned
in the midst of my people and its ills.
Wounded I go, wounded and badly wounded,
bleeding through the trenches and hospitals.

Men, worlds, nations,
pay heed, listen to my cry pouring out blood,
gather together the pulses of my breaking heart
into your spacious hearts,
because I clutch the soul when I sing.

Singing I defend myself
and I defend my people when the barbarians of crime
imprint on my people their hooves
of powder and desolation.

This is their work, this:
passing, they destroy like the whirlwind,
and before their funeral choler
the horizons are arms and the roads are death.

The lament pouring through valleys and balconies,
deluges the stones and works in the stones,
and there is no room for so much death
and there is no wood for so many coffins.

Caravans of beaten-down bodies.
All is bandages, pain and handkerchiefs:
all is stretchers on which the wounded
have broken their strength and their wings.

Blood, blood through the trees and the soil,
blood in the waters and on the walls,
and a fear that Spain will collapse
from the weight of the blood which soaks through her meshes
right to the bread which is eaten.

Gather together this gale,
nations, men, worlds,
which proceeds from the mouths of impassioned breath
and from hospitals of the dying.

Apply your ears
to my clamour of a violated people,
to the 'ay' of so many mothers, to the groans
of many a lucid being whom grief devoured.

The breasts which drove and wounded the mountains
see them languish without milk or beauty,

and see the white sweethearts and the black eyelashes
fallen and submissive in an obscure siesta.

Apply the passion of your entrails
to this people which dies with an invincible gesture
scattered by the lips and the brow,
beneath the implacable aeroplanes
which snatch terribly,
terribly ignominiously, every day,
sons from the hands of their mothers.

58   Cities of work and of innocence,
youths who blossom from the oak,
trunks of bronze, bodies of potency,
lie precipitated into ruin.

A future of dust advances,
a fate advances
in which nothing will remain:
no stone on stone nor bone on bone.

Spain is not Spain, it is an immense trench,
a vast cemetery red and bombarded:
the barbarians have willed it thus.

The earth will be a dense heart, desolated,
if you, nations, men, worlds,
with the whole of my people,
and yours as well on their side,
do not break the ferocious fangs.

MIGUEL HERNÁNDEZ
(*Translated from the Spanish by Inez and Stephen Spender*)

The Winds of the People

The winds of the people sustain me,
spreading within my heart.
The winds of the people impel me,
and roar in my very throat.
Oxen may bow their heads
gentle and impotent
before their punishment;
but lions lift their heads
and with their strident claws
they punish in return.
I come not from a people of oxen,
my people are they who enthuse
over the lion's leap,
the eagle's rigid swoop,
and the strong charge of the bull
whose pride is in his horns.
Oxen were never bred
On the bleak uplands of Spain.
Who speaks of setting a yoke
on the shoulders of such a race?
Who has set yoke or shackle
on the rigorous hurricane,
or held the thunderbolt
a prisoner in a cage?

You Basques of armoured stone,
you brave Asturians,
lively Valencianos
and tempered Castillians,
worked-over like the soil
yet as airy as wings,
Andalusians like lightning,
born amidst guitars

285

and forged in torrential
smithies of tears,
rye-field Estremadurans,
Galicians of calm rain,
dour trustful Catalans,
pure-born of Aragon,
dynamiting Murcians
so fruitful in your race,
men of Navarre and Leon, masters
of hunger, sweat, and the axe,
kings of the mineral kingdom
and lords of the work of tillage,
you who amidst the roots,
like noble roots yourselves,
go from life to death,
go from nothing to nothing:
you men of the scant grasslands,
they would set on you a yoke,
a yoke that you must shatter
in two across *their* backs!
The twilight of the oxen
heralds a sparkling dawn.
The oxen are dying, clad
in the humble smell of the barn.
But the eagles and the lions,
and behind them the sky,
and the arrogant bulls
are calm, will not die.
The agony of oxen
is of little countenance.
That of the virile animal
travels the universe.
If I must die, then may I
with my head high at least.
Dead and twenty times dead,
my mouth in the coarse grass.
My teeth shall remain clenched
and my beard bristling.

Singing, I wait for death,
for there are nightingales that sing
above the rifles' voice
and in the battles' midst.

MIGUEL HERNÁNDEZ
(*Translated from the Spanish by A. L. Lloyd*)

Yo estar un rojo!

Morning at Peguerinos,
with the Escorial beneath.
The machine-gun splutters.
Men climb the slope
like trunks midst the other trunks:
Spaniards and Moors.
And there below, Saint-Rafaël
protects them. They climb, terrible,
the 'regulares' of Larache,
that they have sent against us,
all these criminals of generals
who claim to be Catholics.
Busta ben Ali Mohammed,
blackbearded and blackeyed,
– all black –, from his advance post
detaches himself cautiously.
And drawing himself through the grass,
he speaks, all at once erect,
his fist in the air, and very calm,
alone, bared, before the guns,
'I am a red, comrades,
Don't shoot, *yo estar un rojo!*'

ANTONIO GARCÍA LUQUE
(*Translated from the Spanish by D. Trevor and ?. Neumann*)

The Moorish Deserter

Early one pitch-black morning,
A worked-out mine in the background.
Machine-guns rattle and stammer.
Men, like stumps among others,
Climbing, Spaniards and Moors;
And below them, St Raphael,
Patron, protector. They climb,
Larache's desperate outfit,
Whom they have sent against us,
All of those criminal leaders
Claiming to be devout.
Horrible, they come on.

Busta ben Ali Mohammed,
Beard as black as his eyes,
Black all over, discreetly
Creeps away from his station,
Crawling among the grass,
Then says, suddenly rising,
Fist in the air, alone,
Calm in front of the rifles,
'Comrades, I am a Red;
Don't shoot, I am a Red!'

ANTONIO GARCÍA LUQUE

*(Translated by Rolfe Humphries
from the French version of Roland-Simon)*

Encarnacion Jimenez

Her name confessed the Word
made Flesh: fate fleshed in her –
curt payment for her virtues –
five times a rifle-fire.

The Council sat and judged:
her crime was clear and plain –
a crime which those who interpret Christ
religiously arraign:
for she had washed the linen
of wounded militia-men.

In words of holy writ
the Evangelists have told
how Mary of Heaven and Nazareth
washed the clouts of the Child:

so they believe who judged her,
so they believe who gave
sentence on the brook's evidence –
death, and a handy grave.

Good laundress Incarnation,
out of the foaming suds
what love-tokens of clean linen
you fetched for your brave lads!
How many times the aches
through your old bones have gone
like labour-pangs, washing for many
as for one wounded son!

Old and guileless – we greet you
we bare our heads in your honour,

and greet on your tattered carcass
each springing gillyflower,
each gout of blood blossoming
under the metal shower.

And from your gillyflowers left us
we will raise others, and prouder,
five times more flowering,
that bloom at the barrel's point
with a fine scent of powder.

FELIX PAREDES
(*Translated from the Spanish by Sylvia Townsend Warner*)

Against the Cold in the Mountains

Oh, peaks of Malagosta,
You must be calm.
Reventon, so lonely,
Let the earth grow warm.

Mountains in the icy wind,
Become green gardens,
So the soldiers of the people
May not be frozen.

Passes shining in the frost,
Rid yourselves of snow,
Autumn, full of clouds,
And the sad September weather,
Leave the militia men alone,
Who sleep at the front this winter.

To the North, may they fly to the North,
The cold, the snow and the frost,
From whence the Fascists are marching
Behind their black cross.

Unleash the mountain winds,
Make their teeth chatter!
Tear off their heavy capes,
Their caps, their overcoats.
To *them* the cold must bring
Death during the winter nights!

By Marichive and Mingeta,
O winds come down from the ranges!
Cut them like a knife,
Or like a whip's lashes
Whistle about their donkey's ears,
Their muzzles so bloodstained,
Their hypocrite's shifty eyes
And their souls of serpents.

Sad winds of September
Leave the militia men alone.
For Spain fights on their side,
Who are the best in all Spain!

JOSÉ HERRERA PETERE
(*Translated from the Spanish by A. L. Lloyd*)

El dia que no vendra

Day of metal, day of masses,
Day of cannon, day of churchbells,
Day of shrines and day of bullets,
Strewn with fresh blood and with blossoms –
Such the day the Fascists looked for
On that morrow of that nightfall
When they took Madrid.

Day of metal and of masses –
All the Fascist drums foretold it,
All the parrot voices hailed it.

Not tomorrow? Well, the next day,
Wednesday perhaps, or Thursday
(All are one to Radio Burgos).
Then the morning's light would lighten
Under the triumphal archway
Franco stepping from his chariot;
Then the Moors would swing their sabres
And the Spanish heads go rolling;
Then the Archbishop of Burgos
Would bestow an ample blessing
On the Arabs and the Bedouins,
On the Nazis and the Ethiops,
On the frizzled and the smooth-haired
Saviours of Spain.

Day of metal, day of masses,
Day of rose-coloured illusions,
Dog-day dream of raving traitors,
When, oh when, shall we behold it?
When is the triumphal entry?
When shall we behold the mule-team
Dragging Hitler and his baggage
To our city gates?

It was not Saint James's feast-day
Nor the tenth day of October,
And the slow days of November
All are hidden in the vapour
Of time gone and days departed.
Christmas came, and New Year's Day,
Candlemas and Lady Day,
And the calendar sighed onward
But the day long-looked-for came not.
Where is Franco? Where is Mola?
When will those bedizened warriors,
Fat and spruce like horseshow stallions,
Prance into Madrid?

Day of metal, day of masses,
Day of bloodshed, day of terror,
Day of days the Fascist sewer
Clamours for with all its voices –
From Madrid we toss this greeting:
Day, remain in endless darkness
Of the black hearts that desired you.
Never shall you dawn.

JOSÉ HERRERA PETERE
(*Translated from the Spanish by Sylvia Townsend Warner*)

Salud

'Salud . . . comrade!'
Brotherly the voice I hear
Speaking the brotherly word.
'Salud,' I answer, my joyous heart
Timing the syllables.

I too have answered the alarm,
I too, at the front, stood under the war flags.
Quiver my nerves and sinews
Like strings of a played guitar.

An old man doesn't grow younger,
Nature gives no exemptions, they say;
But in these days you push Time aside.
I do not listen when they say:
'Old man, soon death will be your crony.
Soon your shoulders will sag, your eyes
Be dim with the sixty-fifth shadow.'

Yes, all things have their time.
But I can bear the year's burden.
The battle for freedom gives strength.
The song of liberty is ever young.

293

My heart consoles me. 'Salud!'
Three score and five? To be
Three score and five in a young world?
That is not bad. You and I are young
Fighting for all on this earth
That is healthy and young.

So no matter how many years
Our lives count up to, we're young
Singing our battle songs
Our free songs that made the enemy
Age, in a day, with fear.

If I won't be able to stand in a trench
To wear the weight of my rifle,
I will not then, or ever, feel finished
While I can answer the front with a song
Meet every new day with a song;
I will live in our dawn.

Salud to you all in the stormy distance!
Hail, sons of free Spain!
Health, fighters of Navalperal!
Greetings Madrid, heart of the country!

Salud to you, women and children;
Salud to her whom the voice strengthens to name,
Who is dearest to us of all earth.
To whom the singer his breath gives
And the soldier his blood,
Salud to you, oh, my Spain!

You will conquer, make still nobler your name,
Raise your banners reddening with blood.
The darker the night, the brighter the flame!
Salud, Spain, Salud!

LUIS DE TAPIA
(Freely translated from the Spanish by Isidor Schneider)

Long Live the Revolution

The bullfighters are monarchists,
The monks are preachers of fascism.
And the miners of the Asturias?
Long live the revolution!

My grandfather came from Mieres,
His wife from Pola de Siero.
The capital city of my blood
Must surely be called Oviedo!

The Moors are outside Oviedo.
Oviedo they'll never take
Though they kill all the Spaniards and threaten
Their wives with murder and rape!

The Regulars are bathing
In the Covadonga flood.
The lords swim at Majorca,
While the miners swim in blood.

In October there are no fiestas
Except those of the season.
But October only means to us
'LONG LIVE THE REVOLUTION!'

GONZÁLEZ TUÑÓN
(Translated from the Spanish by A. L. Lloyd)

Poem

There is no rest or peace in all this land,
Along this bitter, this hard-trodden road,
And in these hearts.
Listen, road-menders, shepherds,
Workers of Paris, London and the world;
There is no rest or peace in all this land!

Men, workers like yourselves, they too
With bullocks yoked to plough just like your own,
With lathes like yours,
Or dusty flocks smelling of rosemary,
Under the same sky, in the same factories,
Trudging and working, and never resting.

Men, workers like yourselves, they too
With children just as lovely
And sheets as poor on beds just like your own,
And with fresh bread that smells as good as yours,
Fight on and triumph under olive trees
And in the yellow cornfields,
And on the eternal snow that sleeps beneath the pines.

Under a manly sky, men among men,
Strong and glad as you are strong and glad,
Leave in forgetfulness
Their blazing houses and their old folk crippled.
There is no rest or peace in all this land
Which shall forever bear the name of Spain! –
Because we are and shall be the only masters of the day,
Masters of all our cities, and the real masters of our fields.

The men from the mines,
The herdsmen and the men from up the hills,

The men who make the bread and those who grow the wheat,
The poets, blacksmiths, woodworkers,
Defending here a people's name and life
On the baked soil out with advance posts,
And in the factories.

There is no rest or peace in all this land!
But only flowers growing in earthen pots.
Letters the Artillery finished.
And men who do not rest,
Are ever watchful, like our chestnut trees,
And stand on guard, waiting for victory's fruits.

LORENZO VARELA
(*Translated from the Spanish by A. M. Elliott*)

Madrid Front

Dark falls the afternoon,
Dark amid rain and mud,
Tramcars, militiamen . . .
Huddled along the streets
Carts without horses,
Asses bearing the wretched
Villager's all.
Colourless faces flee
From Toledo's fields,
Children and old men,
Women who once were fair,
Flower of their village then,
Flower among rags now.
No one speaks, all of them,
All of us going
To the war, for the war,
Flying or drifting
By thousands like the leaves
In golden autumn.

297

The war-lorries go by,
Lines of militiamen
Between zones of silence,
The rain and the mud.
Red pass the banners by,
Madly outstreaming
Heralds of victory
On the prows of cars.
While the women stand in queues
For milk and peas and coal
Lentils and bread.
The ground is littered
With glass, the houses now
Have no bright eyes, but stare
With frozen cavities,
with tragic gaps of space.

Here are tramway rails
Rearing like horns;
Streets ringed about by bands
Plumed with the crest of smoke.
And barricades of stone
Where once we sat to gaze
On the clear sky of this
Madrid, serene and free,
Open to all the winds,
And kindly thoughts of men.

Bewildered like a fish
In its watery bowl, I tread
Lost in the streets I knew.
I climb, retrace my steps,
To the Tube stations where
Like sacks the homeless sleep.
A reek like cattle-sheds;
The air is foul to breathe.

I mount and leave, return
To the clouded afternoon.

VILLA

I feel myself shut in,
In Madrid, an island tomb,
Alone, in an asphalt sky
Where plane the crows in search
Of the children and the old.

Dark is the afternoon,
With rain, with rain,
Tramcars, militiamen . . .

JOSÉ MORENO VILLA
(*Translated from the Spanish by Stanley Richardson*)

THE INTERNATIONALS

(Nancy Cunard, 'Sonnet in Five Languages:
The Internationals')

Sonnet in Five Languages:
The Internationals

1   Adesso è altra sosta, ma dove su Dante?
2   If the fire burn low, it is the same, I see;
3   Por mudo que vas tiras por adelante,
4   Et tout ce qui fut avant peut renaître ici.
5   Noch gibt es einigen Moorsoldaten die
6   Are ready to spring to their appointed place,
7   E quantí altri, vicini e lontani ...
8   Se no se dice, consabido és.
9   So mischt man Sprächen mit Hoffnung wohin man geht,
10 I treni misti vanno molto lontano;
11 May our suns and moons coincide in the rising spate,
12 Per quien me dirá la fecha de este ano?
13 Courage persiste si le coeur conserve ses as ...
14 Y cuando te toca el turno, ah! Cuanto cosecharás!

NANCY CUNARD

The International

We'd left our training base
And by the time night fell
Stood facing the Universe
Singing the 'International'.

I remember it so well
Waiting in the station yard
The darkness stood around still
And the stars, masses, stared.

That's when I first understood
One is never alone in this fight.

303

I'd thought the 'good-bye' was for good
And left *all* behind that night.

But everything new that I meet,
No matter how strange and uncertain,
Holds something familiar that
Proves the fight is still on.

17 How often I marched, and marching
I sang of an England unseen,
Watched the great crowds gathering
And the tramp of their feet beat in tune.

Even in the grip of prison
I joined in the singing of millions
As they wait at their wayside station
24 That leads to the battle lines.

I'm singing in every country
26 Where I tread through the streets of Time
27 One man, one woman, humanity
The 'International' our theme.

CLIVE BRANSON

January 1940

Monument

When from the deep sky
And digging in the harsh earth,
When by words hard as bullets,
Thoughts simple as death,
You have won victory,
People of Spain,
You will remember the free men who fought beside you,
    enduring and dying with you, the strangers
Whose breath was your breath.

You will pile into the deep sky
A tower of dried earth,
Rough as the walls where bullets
Splashed men to death
Before you won victory,
Before you freed Spain
From the eating gangrene of wealth, the grey pus of pride,
   the black scab of those strangers
Who were choking your breath.

Bring together, under the deep sky
Metal and earth;
Metal from which you made bullets
And weapons against death,
And earth in which, for victory,
Across all Spain,
Your blood and ours was mingled, Huesca to Malaga;
   earth to which your sons and strangers
Gave up the same breath.

Bring to the tower, to its building,
From New Castille,
From Madrid, the indomitable breast-work,
Earth of a flower-bed in the Casa del Campo,
Shell-splinters from University City,
Shell-casing from the Telephonica.
Bring from Old Castille, Santander, Segovia,
Sandbags of earth dug out of our parapets
And a false coin stamped in Burgos by a traitor.

Carry from Leon, from the province of Salamanca,
Where the bulls are brave and the retired generals
   cowards,
From near the Capital of treason and defeat, bring now
Clean earth, new and untouched, from the cold hills,
And iron from the gate, that shall now be always open
Of Spain's oldest school, where there shall be young
   wisdom.

40 From Extramadura, earth from the bullring
 Where they shot the prisoners in Badajoz;
 And lovely Zafra shall give one of its silver crosses;
 Galicia, sea-sand and ship-rivets. From Asturias
 Spoil from the pits that taught our dynamiters
45 To face and destroy the rearing tanks, and a pit-haft
46 That has cut coal and trenches, and is still fit for work.
 From the Basque country, Bilbao, Guernica,
 City of agony, villages of fire,
 Take charred earth, so burnt and tortured no one
 Knows if small children's bones are mingled in it;
 Take iron ore from the mines those strangers envied;
 And wash your hands, remembering a world that did so.

 Navarre shall give a ploughshare and a rock;
 Aragon, soil from the trench by the walnut-tree
 Where Thaelmann's first group fought towards Huesca,
 And steel from a wrecked car lying by a roadside;
 Lukacsz rode in that car.
 Catalonia, Spain and not Spain, and our gateway
 (For myself a gateway to Spain and courage and love)
 Shall bring a crankshaft from the Hispano factory
 And earth from Durrutti's grave;
 Valencia, black soft silt of the rice fields, mingled
 With soil from an orange-grove – also
 Telephone-wire, and a crane's chain.
 Murcia, a surgeon's scalpel and red earth;
 Andalucia, the vast south, shall pay
 The barrel of a very old rifle found in the hills
 Beside a skeleton; earth
 That the olives grow from.
 And Albacete, where we built our brigades:
71 Knife-steel and road-dust.

 Take then these metals, under the deep sky
 Melt them together; take these pieces of earth
 And mix them; add your bullets,
 And memories of death:

You have won victory,
People of Spain,
And the tower into which your earth is built, and
    Your blood and ours, shall state Spain's
    Unity, happiness, strength; it shall face the breath
81   Of the east, of the dawn, of the future, when there will be
    no more strangers . . .

TOM WINTRINGHAM

August 1937

Comrades of Jarama

The name of Jarama means, to most of us who came back from
Spain, the long and dreary weeks of trench warfare among the
stripped olive trees of that valley, where the British Battalion
spent three months in the line without relief. And to some it
means the unsuccessful attacks carried out, during the earlier
months of this trench warfare, the attempts to take Pingarron
Hill.

Those months of fighting made the word Jarama mean something to us that is embodied in the words of our song: It is the
valley in which 'we wait patiently'. And those months were
considered as a military job of work, almost as important as
anything else that the Battalion did. The Spanish army was
learning how to be dangerous in attack, and we made some of
the experiments.

But the first days of the Jarama Battle included the severest
fighting and had a greater political and military importance than
has been realized by many people. If we had failed in those first
days to hold our ground, under conditions more difficult and
dangerous than any the Battalion met until the counter-attack at
Brunete, the last road into Madrid would have been cut and the
great city would have been surrounded.

That would have meant the loss of Madrid two years before
its eventual surrender. And such a loss of Madrid might have

meant the present world war would have reached us perhaps two years earlier.

But when we piled out of our lorries at the farm cook-house on the Chinchon road, early on the morning of 12 February 1937, we knew little of all this; the main thing we knew was that the British Battalion was going into action for the first time. And when we had begun moving up and a 'dog-fight' of planes swung over us, many of us were changed suddenly from spectators, or men marching as they had marched in demonstrations and in peace, to soldiers, men marching with weapons and a purpose more commanding than that of any peace-time march.

Whoever remembers Jarama is likely to remember the moment they crossed for the first time the sunken road, that later was our rallying point; coming out on the crest of the hill, they saw in front of them the grass valley and the slopes that most of us called 'Suicide Hill'. Some, like myself, may have seen beyond those slopes the first parties of the Moors spreading out for their attack.

Many of the men who held Suicide Hill through almost all that grilling day did not realize why it was necessary for them to stay there, with their twenty-year-old, almost useless colts and 'Shoshers', without adequate support, and with cross fire striking them from both flanks. The reason was that we were the left of the whole line; beyond us on our left there was a gap of three miles through which Franco's troops could have poured if we had failed to hold the hill – a gap not filled until the next day. And it was a very considerable feat of arms for a battalion put together within a few weeks, out of men the majority of whom had no training, to hold its position without artillery or machine-gun support against a whole brigade of trained and experienced troops.

Many other days of desperate fighting followed that first day, but it stands in my memory as the symbol of our effort in Spain and our achievement.

And I think also of the cost of that achievement, and of three men, company commanders, who can be representative of those who died in the first fight on the Jarama in order that Madrid, the symbol of freedom and true democracy, should live. These three are:

HARRY FRY of Edinburgh, at one time of His Majesty's Brigade of Guards;

KIT CONWAY of Dublin, at one time of the Irish Republican Army;

WILLIAM BRISKEY of London, at one time of the Busman's Rank and File Movement.

They were known by the man who commanded them and by the men they commanded to be equals, in courage and comradeship, to the fighting men of the past, whose names wake pride in the British people.

TOM WINTRINGHAM

'The Italian soldier shook my hand'

The Italian soldier shook my hand
Beside the guard-room table;
The strong hand and the subtle hand
Whose palms are only able

To meet within the sound of guns,
But oh! what peace I knew then
In gazing on his battered face
Purer than any woman's!

For the fly-blown words that make me spew
Still in his ears were holy,
And he was born knowing what I had learned
Out of books and slowly.

The treacherous guns had told their tale
And we both had bought it,
But my gold brick was made of gold –
Oh! who ever would have thought it?

309

Good luck go with you, Italian soldier!
But luck is not for the brave;
What would the world give back to you?
Always less than you gave.

Between the shadow and the ghost,
Between the white and the red,
Between the bullet and the lie,
Where would you hide your head?

For where is Manuel Gonzalez,
And where is Pedro Aguilar,
And where is Ramon Fenellosa?
The earthworms know where they are.

Your name and your deeds were forgotten
Before your bones were dry,
And the lie that slew you is buried
Under a deeper lie;

But the thing that I saw in your face
No power can disinherit:
No bomb that ever burst
Shatters the crystal spirit.

GEORGE ORWELL

An English War-Poet

In another respect the Spanish War
– Fought on the Republican side
Not by doped conscripts, foreign mercenaries, professional
  soldiers,
And Moors and worse than Moors,
But by men who passionately believed
In the cause for which they fought, –

Has stamped all the men I know,
The members of the International Brigade,
With a different bearing altogether
Than even the best, the most anti-militarist, gained
Of those who fought against Germany in the first Great War.
There in a man like Siegfried Sassoon, for example,
Despite the undeniable honesty, the little literary gift,
What is 'Sherston's Progress' but an exposure
Of the eternal Englishman
Incapable of rising above himself,
And traditional values winning out
Over an attempted independence of mind?

Second-Lieutenant George Sherston went on strike against the
    war.
But his pacifism led him, not before a court-martial,
But into a hospital for the 'shell-shocked'.
There a psychiatrist, as clever as calm,
Coupled with plenty of good food and golf,
Restores Sherston to sanity.
He decided finally to return to the front,
Did so, found the job not too awfully awful, don't you know.
Was wounded, and ended up
In a rather nobler type of hospital
Where members of the royal family stopped by his bed
To offer forty-five seconds of polite sympathy.
And there the narrative ends, with Sherston as muddled as ever,
And given to rather vague – and glib – interrogations
That may be taken to express
His partial dissatisfaction with the universe.

As a transcript of a young man's actual emotions in war
The book is convincing enough. You must, however, regard
The young man as extremely average,
With no real self-knowledge
And no fixed scale of values.
He is anybody who has seen the blood and horror of war,

Which is a great deal less than we are supposed
To take Sherston to have been. Furthermore,
Seeing that almost twenty years lie
Between Sherston's experiences
And the writing of them down,
One looks for a sense of perspective,
A revision of values, a growth of understanding,
One nowhere encounters.
This is what happened to Sherston,
And so far as the book is concerned
Nothing ever happened afterwards.

There is possibly an argument in favour
Of presenting things simply as they were,
Of leaving them inclosed
Within their own time and place,
Without hindsight, without revaluation;
Though it is not easy to put it forward here,
Since the Sherston of today constantly and pointedly
Keeps interjecting himself into the picture.
But what is really wrong with the book
Is the portrait of Sherston as he then was:
A man so quickly able to accommodate himself,
After one flare of defiance,
To prevailing sentiment.

It is not that Sherston was either
A weak or a cowardly person.
It is rather that his rebelliousness was only
Superimposed on his profoundly English nature.
It would be unfair to say that, after coming out
Against war and all it signified,
He traduced his principles. Rather he changed his mind,
Regained the national disease of 'seeing things through',
Saw them through, and ended up, pleased
That the royal family should stand by his hospital bed
And confer its verbal largesse. In other words
Sherston rebelled under stress of feeling,

Then conformed again under stress of feeling;
Throughout the ordeal he was altogether
The victim of his emotions.

This is not the stuff the members
Of the International Brigade were made of.
This is not enough to create, for me,
A provocative book.
Set against any of the better narratives of the war
By Continental writers, *Sherston's Progress* seems
Not only confused, but confused
In an immature and childish way.
In Mr Sassoon's book there is simply no evidence
Of a thinking mind; there is neither
Psychological nor philosophical substance.
There is only a young man who lets himself in
For a bad quarter of an hour and then,
Not because he lacks courage,
But because he lacks conviction,
Falls back into the ranks.
His real interests are golf,
Chasing the fox, reading poetry;
Is it too cynical to think at times
That his real objection to the war
Is its interfering with these pleasures?

But the members of the International Brigade
Were made of different stuff,
And will never fall back into the ranks.
And the war in Spain – and everywhere else –
Will never end till they win it,
Since they fight for Spain and not
        Just for castles in Spain.

HUGH MACDIARMID

The Volunteer

Tell them in England, if they ask
What brought us to these wars,
To this plateau beneath the night's
Grave manifold of stars –

It was not fraud or foolishness,
Glory, revenge, or pay:
We came because our open eyes
Could see no other way.

There was no other way to keep
Man's flickering truth alight:
These stars will witness that our course
Burned briefer, not less bright.

Beyond the wasted olive-groves,
The furthest lift of land,
There calls a country that was ours
And here shall be regained.

Shine to us, memoried and real,
Green-water-silken meads:
Rivers of home, refresh our path
Whom here your influence leads.

Here in a parched and stranger place
We fight for England free,
The good our fathers won for her,
The land they hoped to see.

C. DAY LEWIS

It's a Bohunk

The dark green plane went away without dropping anything, and we got out of the irrigation ditch. The path to the river curved down by the dead mule and the Dimmies' kitchen. The river was a disappointment, almost dry.

'Walk up a bit.' At the bend a pool shone among the hot stones; part of it was dark with the shadow of the railway bridge. A naked man was sloshing in the water. He could not swim; there was not enough water.

'Haya, pal,' said Hank and pulled his shirt off. The naked man bubbled something and waved his foot. Then he burst out laughing and gave an unorthodox version of our army's salute, using his right arm and his left leg: as he lay on his back in the water he clenched his fist and shoved it up and at the same time raised a square-toed foot and gnarled the toes together, as if to make a second saluting fist.

This amused him a good deal; he shook with laughter and the water splashed round. Touching dry stones the water sizzled. Spain in August is hotter than Hell (and less safe: Hell's underground).

'*Salud*, eh?' said Hank tolerantly. He was of the Lincoln battalion and saluted officers only when he forgot himself. But he let others salute if they liked.

I was sitting down to get my *alpargatas* off. I returned the salute with one of these rope-soled canvas shoes in my hand, thinking: that fellow has sharp eyes to spot the three little gold bars over my shirt pocket.

The naked man got out of the water. That was necessary because there was only room for two to lie full length in the pool. When he sat down in the shade, away from the blink of sun on water, I saw that he was short, broad, wide, square. And hairy; but patches of hair had been shaved off and scars showed every two or three inches from forehead to shins. They were grey-blue-green and red scars: some of them crossed as if he had been tattooed with chicken-wire.

'Who's your pal?' I asked Hank. He answered: 'Him? It's a Bohunk.' Hank was in a hurry to get in the deeper end of the pool ahead of me.

One of the 'Dimmies', then. Americans called most of the Dimitroff battalion Bohunks. I could not talk any of that battalion's five languages, so I tried the 'Spanish' of the International Brigades: '*Bombas*?' I asked, nodding at his chest. '*Si, bomba aviacion acqui.*' He pointed to a point ten feet away from him: yes, a bomb from a plane had fallen there. He looked at the scars: '*trenta-seiz heridas . . .*' And then, after those thirty-six wounds, hand-grenades had given him seven more.

Hank shook his straggle of wet red beard. 'Yeh, 's a boy. One of Chip-chop's or the Division's scouts. Came over with us at Pingarron and got all those splinters in him. Then he held the bomb-hole – big deep hole it was – for a couple of days while we could sap forward to it. Way up the slope it was. He wouldn't let anyone else in it; said it was his bomb.'

'Two days? You took your time getting the sap forward.'

Hank answered: 'Warn't enough of us to hold our trenches, far less dig new ones.' And we both thought of Pingarron Hill, that looks down towards the Jarama river on one side and Madrid's last main road on the other. Too many boys from Britain and the States lie on its slopes and in the valleys that flank it.

'First night,' Hank went on, 'the Moors came out and dropped a couple of grenades almost on this Bohunk. He heard the pineapples rolling down into his bomb-hole and lit out quick: that's the scars on his back. Second night he lay outside the hole as soon as it was dark and gave them the works while they were still creely-crawlin' towards him. 'S a boy.'

I lay in the tepid water and did not care if he was a boy or not. Tomorrow we were going to take Quinto, one of the keys to Aragon. There had been no transport, but the Brigade was hijacking its way into position, stopping every lorry it saw. There had been new machine-guns – why did we always get machine-guns of a type entirely unknown to us two days before a push? But we had tested them all and instructed most of our gunners on them. That had been my job: for twenty hours I had done it. It was done. I lay in the trickle of water and wondered if I was tired.

Half an hour before I had been wondering if I was too sleepy to eat or too hungry to sleep. Hank's invitation to 'swim' had caught me in this indecision: now I knew that I would soon go back to the tall rows of maize where my kit lay and sleep till evening. Brigade staff would move in the night . . .

Hank kept on babbling about Bohunks, Polacks and Wops. I paid no attention. My head and shoulders were in the shadow of the railway bridge; the sun could not catch much of the rest of me, though I could feel it through the couple of inches of water that covered me. The little pause of peace that comes before real fighting was on me. Nothing on earth, I thought, could disturb me now.

The one thing that could disturb me came, not on the earth but in the sky.

A poet has described the beginning of that sound, the feel of it in the air before it is a sound. The loaded bombers crawling across the sky reach the senses in a faint trembling of not-yet-noise, like the trembling of a baited deep-sea line.

Then the trembling grows to an actual sound, and the sound climbs in the mind to dominate it. Behaviour begins to replace ordinary living. The conditioned thing, the way of action trained into you, replaces all normal thinking and deciding. Hank half sat up, then turned on his face swearing softly to himself. The Bohunk flattened his squareness down. I pulled my knees up to my chin, my back to the bombers. My eyes blinked at the steep river bank a hundred feet away. Too far, far, far – the word wrapped itself into the engine's rising drone. The shadow of the bridge made me sweat.

They were over us. The sound drilled at the backs of our necks. We could feel them above us bigger than all the arch-angels of heaven, all-seeing, all-powerful. God, why were they so slow? The seconds stretched out on the rack of the sound of the engines. None of us looked up.

We had been taught not to look up. From cover and open

317

country, the green or brown or rock-grey of Spain, faces show, can be seen from the air. Men who lie quiet, face down, or stoop or crouch in stillness, are not easy for pilots to see.

Some of us had fought a year of war under the wings of enemy bombers. We did not feel the need to look at them.

We were doing as we had been trained to do. In fact it would have made little difference if we had looked up: perhaps we might have been more difficult to see. Our bodies, pink-brown, and our burnt faces, would not show very clearly against the grey-white stones in the river-bed. Perhaps the Bohunk's black hair would show more than his brown face. But we had been taught to keep our faces down and stay still . . .

Bombs scream. When you first hear them you are surprised, sometimes lifted to your feet, by the warning note in that scream. It is louder, and lasts longer, is more terrifying, than the scream of a shell; gunners' gifts often reach you before you hear them, but bombs take a mile of air and wrench it apart to tell you they are coming. Louder than any klaxon, steep up the scale as the bomb drops faster, the racking yelp makes the sky into a spinning blue circular saw shearing through the bones that cover your head. The bombs screamed: for a pulse-beat we were not alive: one bomb was coming near.

Two fell very near us. The sound of a bomb exploding some distance away, once you are used to it, is a relief – that one has missed. But you cannot get used to a bomb falling really near: the shock, blast, air-wave from its explosion wrenches at your throat, you choke; your eyes are blacked out; the noise of the explosion is not a noise but the defeat of your ears – there will never be any noises again.

The three planes were swinging up the sky to turn, their engines stating arrogant jeering imperious power. Stones lifted by the explosions fell with a tap-clatter (so hearing was possible, after all!). A pebble had tapped my knee; a little blue-hot sliver of metal fell onto my shoulder and the burn stabbed me; my fingers jerked to brush it off and were stabbed.

While the dust and fume was still in the air Hank jumped from the water and grabbed his shoes. 'Stop,' I said. My ears were ringing and I felt I said it very weakly indeed. Hank was furious: the curse-words jammed in his mouth. He was only getting his shoes, to be ready to run if those — got out of eye-shot . . .

Running to the river-bank? Not he! As he flopped back into the pool the Bohunk dropped at the edge of it between us. He had been a little higher than we were. A new white weal showed where a flying stone had caught him. And along his left arm a thin line of dark red came very slowly, as blood comes from a razor-cut. 'Hullo, *herido*?' I said.

Yes, he answered: a wound, a very slight one. The other, he said as if regretfully, was not a wound, only a stone-graze. He did not know the Spanish word for stone and picked one up to show us his meaning. Then, as if reproving himself for that amount of movement, he put the stone back very carefully.

The planes, turning, came to my eyes and were for a moment the graceful fascinating things I have always loved to watch. Then I put my head down, guiltily. They were the enemies' eyes.

'*Volver*?' said the Bohunk. Yes, they were turning. We must again be logs or corpses, to their eyes. They had got within twenty feet of the bridge, first shot; they would try again.

They had finished turning, were drumming straight up the road. 'Jeez!' groaned Hank, 'are they trying to kill us, or what?' Again the bomb-scream tore through my head and back and seemed to reach, white-hot, to my guts. A man afraid curls himself round his guts to protect them: poor protection, our knotted muscles and tubed bones, but under bombing or shell-fire most men try to cover somehow eyes, with their hands, stomach and sex with their legs. Hank's knees, like mine, were almost up to his chin. But the Bohunk lay between us flat, straight, square on his solid belly.

Six bombs this time, none quite so near to us, but one struck high up on the earth approach to the bridge and burst our way. A great lump of earth knocked me on the back and winded me; I gulped air, whining. Hank got his share of the dirt. But the Bohunk's legs and backside were ripped by flying metal that had passed just beyond our curled-up toes. The back of one thigh was mashed spouting redness. I saw it just at my elbow as I fought for breath, fought to stop sobbing and free my eyes from the tears and the shooting stars.

The cloud of earth and dust was settling round us as my breath came back. The Bohunk clutched his thigh, twisting round to look at the wounds. Hank reached for my shirt and tore it in half. And the loosed engines of the three planes climbing and turning threw down their intolerable clangour at us.

If I had not been winded I might have run. It would have been wrong: our whole army corps was there, round Hijar and up to the Ebro, and the enemy did not know it yet. Everywhere round me men were hiding, dead-still in the fly-stirring heat, because the enemy's eyes were over us. It would not have mattered if his plane had seen three men near the bridge: but if it had seen three men near the bridge and six on the road and two in this village and seven on a hill-side – then those winged eyes would have reported: movement. And movement reported there, near that unexpected almost peaceful bit of front, might mean that we failed to surprise them tomorrow; which would be suicide.

This I knew. Yet I might have run for cover, away from the bridge. Fear is a strong master. I was not able to run while the dust-cloud hid me. Hank, who was afraid also, had not run. He helped the Bohunk wrap half my shirt round his leg and back-side. The wounds were not deep; the blood that was staining the pool was not coming with the bright jetting flow that means a severed artery. '*No es mucho*,' said the Bohunk. And again the planes swung round the sky to a point where I could see them. They were lower. Were they coming back?

'How many wounds?' asked the Bohunk. 'Six,' I said. He added six to the forty-three he already possessed, and shook his head. 'Fifty would be a better number,' he said. Hank put his head down on his arms and laughed. Then swore.

The noise of the engines had lessened. Were they going away? Or had they throttled down to come lower? I waited, calling to help me a man killed in my first day's fighting and a woman who had held me back from dying, by her own live strength and unwavering twenty-four-hour awakeness, through weeks of typhoid. And I summoned to keep me there, naked on that grey altar of small stones, memory of the fact that the man I thought of as my leader had once been fool enough to call me a coward. We waited.

The engines could be heard plainly, but they were not loud. The planes were not coming round in a tight circle as they had done before; that was clear. I did not know how close I was to panic until the Bohunk suddenly gripped my right hand with his left. He jerked out a word that was a statement, not an appeal or a curse. What the word meant I did not know: but I knew that it meant the fear was shadowing us again. Yet I was already released from fear; stronger than the courage of the dead or of my woman was the physical grip of his square hand, the friendship of men who know how to die and live. I heard the 'whick, whick' of propellors turning slowly and knew that one of the planes was only a couple of hundred feet above us . . .

No bomb dropped. The plane's engines took up their masterful tune, and it climbed back to its companions. Twenty seconds more, and they were thin-pencilled wings a mile away. 'Say when it's O.K., captain,' came in a subdued voice from Hank.

I sat up and watched them lift away from us. 'O.K., brothers.' We busied ourselves with shoes and picked up our clothes, not putting them on. We wrapped the second half of my shirt round the Bohunk's thigh, knotting the ramshackle bandage in place with a belt. He put his right arm round Hank's neck and walked. I offered to help on the other side, but he said, 'O.K.' and grinned and used his left hand to hold the bandage in place.

We got to the river bank. 'Take him to the German doctor, Hank.' 'Sure,' said Hank. But long-legged Willy the doctor was already coming down the path to see . . . As usual he was sardonic and absurd, in precise impossible German-English. 'I forget my education. The vague painters call a scene so attractive "The Three Graces". But I will be more particular: this your companion youth who exhibits so blond and proud a nakedness is Venus; you, my dear Staff-instructor-captain, must Minerva of the wisdoms be; but what is my patient?' As he said these things he was stripping off the shirt-bandage and doing a rough and painful first examination. The Bohunk grinned and grumbled, saying *eeya*! occasionally – which is much more sensible than proudly biting your lip and not letting a squeak out.

I growled at the doctor, as I pulled my trousers on. Then his curious determination to seem civilized captured me, as it always had done. 'Your patient, doctor? It's a Bohunk – seems a sufficient rank. But if you insist on being classical, wasn't the third of them Juno – a close acquaintance of Mars and Vulcan?'

The doctor nodded. 'It is to be regretted if so much beauty is scattered, I think. I will keep him here for you.' 'Thank you and damn your eyes!'

But his threat worked to schedule. In a few days – Quinto taken and my shoulder splinted – the Bohunk came to see me in hospital. He brought an American who talked his language and gave me a hatful of 'crackers'. The Bohunk was in great glee: in counting his wounds we had forgotten the first long slash in the arm that a fragment had given him under the bridge. With this reckoned in, the total was fifty. Was not that a nice figure?

I agreed.

Before they left my bed I asked the American: what are Bohunks, anyway? 'Oh, they come from Father Christmas' country ...'

And it was much later, when I had left Spain and that war, I realized that the people Americans called Bohunks come from Prague way and are really called Czechs.

TOM WINTRINGHAM

Thaelmann Battalion

This is our moment.
You can hear us singing
Where the earth is brittle under the southern sun
Watch us marching in serried ranks to the death that is our
    homage
To the unbroken spirit of our dishonoured country.

For here we are showing the world our country's other face,
And the voice that for three years in Germany has been silenced
Utters its songs of freedom under an alien sun.

We were in Barcelona with the masses that stormed the Colon;
We left with the first militia for the Eastern Front;
Then we went to Madrid;
We were at Casa del Campo,
Guadalajara, Brunete, Belchite and Teruel,
Putting to rout the Italians in the name of Thaelmann.

Here we have shown to the world our country's other face;
And not the face of the hangman with the sprouting forelock
But the face of the young men who march together singing
Through southern plains where the clay is brittle under the sun.

AILEEN PALMER

To the Heroes of
the International Brigade in Spain

They tramped across the earth –
    they sailed the intervening sea
When the call went out like a fierce shout
    from the throat of Liberty.
From plough and bench to battle trench
    the steady march was made:
To save the land came a fighting band
    of men who were unafraid.

They curbed the beasts of the crooked cross
    and the thugs of Rome:
They helped disperse the winged curse
    that was smashing the Spaniard's home:
Calm and sane through the leaden rain
    that drowned each battle's length,
From every side the brigade replied
    with miracles of strength.

Their blood was spilt on barricades,
    yet still their banners flew,
As with dauntless eyes to the shining skies
    they forced each flight anew,
And weary men struck back again:
    but after each attack
There were always found, on sodden ground,
    those who would never go back.

Ye peoples of the world salute
    the brothers of the free!
Honour the toil of the brave and loyal
    who shield our destiny!
Pause for the dead, whose faith is bred
    out of a nation's pain:
Remember the youth that died for the truth
    on the battered fronts of Spain.

L. KENDALL

The Battalion Goes Forward

From Chinchón across the Tajuña
Six hundred men set out,
Knowing the odds against them
But harbouring never a doubt,
Towards San Martin went marching,
Crossing the sunken road,
Topping the hills and gazing
Down where the Jarama flowed.

With our Franco–Belgian comrades
We lads took up our posts;
With the Dimitrov, Thaelmann and Spanish
Awaiting the fascist hosts;

Thirty thousand opposing
A handful of untried men ...
What was the chance of holding
The road to Valencia then?

And yet, since we knew the reasons
That had brought us to Spain to fight,
We halted the Moorish legions,
The Italian and German might.
With our second company captured,
With half now for ever still,
The fascists ne'er saw the Tajuña
The other side of the hill.

Then, who vanquished the Spanish people?
Who beat off each fierce attack?
Fascists there are without labels,
And THEY stabbed Spain in the back.
So now we trust not the fair words
Of Daladier and Chamberlain,
When they cry: 'Freedom is in peril!'
We answer: 'Who murdered Spain?'

So this February we remember
Our comrades dead on the ridge,
And swear in our new positions
To hold the Arganda bridge;
With the knowledge that Spain has taught us
To keep open freedom's ways,
And to hold all fascist battalions
As in the Jarama days.

ERIC EDNEY

Salud, Brigade–Salud!

In days unborn, when tales are told
Of Freedom's vanguard, strong and bold,
When o'er the world a hush is spread,
And we pay homage to our dead,
A cry will ring in every heart:
      Salud! Brigade, Salud!

They, in our hearts, will never die,
Who carried Freedom's banner high,
And fighting died, and gave their all
To break the strangling Fascist thrall.
That cry must live for ever:
      Salud! Brigade, Salud!

We, who are young, must all unite,
A deeper fire yet we'll light,
To show the path that we must tread,
If we with honour face our dead.
They will answer in response:
      Salud! Comrades, Salud!

ANON.

Salud!

Men of all lands from field and factory sped,
United in purpose, but of that purpose dumb
To one another till Spain welcomed them,
And, understanding, each man thither come
First heard the word: Salud!

A nation's mighty purpose in one word
That moment showed; and each one felt his heart
Uplifted, and his will and arms more strong,
And in the struggle played a worthier part
For hearing that: Salud!

A machine-gun suddenly a whistling chain
Projects, and Death hurtles perilously by;
We raised clenched fists high in the riven air,
Taunting defiant, and ironic cry
The single word: Salud!

Black figures looming beneath the olive trees
Dig shallow graves for the heroic dead;
Plant two crossed laths of ammunition-box,
Bearing no eulogy, above their head,
But just one word: Salud!

This is no mystery, and needs no priest
To guarantee us victory over Death.
That word itself bears witness, time to come
Men 'neath whatever heaven drawing breath
Shall cry to life: Salud!

ERIC EDNEY

But No Bugles

No sounding trumpets to stir these men.
No marching feet on a sunlit road.
No cheering crowds, nor the rapt praise
Mouthed by sheep-skinned patriots.
But in the first quiet of mass indifference
A thousand left their homes and more.
Each knew the price and a pledge was made
No bugles for this, no shining parade!

And history's hand stretched forth anew,
To write a glorious thing.
Of English workers at the gate of Spain.
Freedom is no longer a name!
They shall not pass! They shall not pass!
We who are left may rise in honour,
For these buy back our heritage.
Rejoice then, there are such as these,
Who once knew this rain-swept isle,
Left those loved to die in Spain.
And clear from each silent grave,
From olive grove and war-torn peak
A proud history shall hear their name,
Take this, our all.

W. B. KEAL

International Brigade

No bands played Colonel Bogey at their departing.
No ribboned generals mouthed speeches about honour.
Troop-train threading the night toward the death-line
Carried no exaltation of remembered pride and weeping.

No headlines raved about the manner of their dying.
No flower-petals fell from slim, fair fingers
On the few who came back limping, torn or blinded.
No cathedral praised them with sad chanting.

They had no country but the hope of a new country.
They answered the secret radio in their hearts.
From the factories, fields and workshops of all nations
From the millions shackled by greed, made less than human.

So they fought and died for their grave, proud duty,
Without the fawning praise of kings and prelates –
Were digged into the red footings of the future,
And will be remembered in the songs of a new freedom.

R. GARDNER

Volunteers for Liberty

Your country does not matter.

You have forgotten the name
of the city that shielded your childhood.
But the songs of your cradle
remain to return in your voices
and quieten the corn
now dark with the kiss of flaming suns.

The factories you left,
and the fields with their richness, the places
impelled into life
by your rough and vigorous hands.
Your home you have left and your bed
that daily called you to rest.

Your country does not matter
now that one fatherland answers for all.

Your language does not matter.

Those words are forgotten
which whispered the names
of your loved ones, the tender caress
of the anguished mother.
Forgotten the tremulous word
that troubled the ear of the lover.

·   ·   ·

329

Your language does not matter,
for free men speak one language alone.

That language alone now matters.

Here you have spoken
in thirty-eight different tongues,
but each vibrated with one impulse,
with only one passionate voice,
clamourous and pure,
That is the voice of the blood that sings.

LUIS PEREZ INFANTE
*(Translated from the Spanish by Hans Kahle and
Leslie Phillips)*

UNHEROIC NOTES

Two Armies

1   Deep in the winter plain, two armies
2   Dig their machinery, to destroy each other.
    Men freeze and hunger. No one is given leave
    On either side, except the dead and wounded.
5   These have their leave; while new battalions wait
    On time at last to bring them violent peace.

    All have become so nervous and so cold
    That each man hates the cause and distant words
9   That brought him here, more terribly than bullets.
10 Once a boy hummed a popular marching song,
11 Once a novice hand flapped their salute;
12 The voice was choked, the lifted hand fell,
    Shot through the wrist by those of his own side.

14 From their numb harvest, all would flee, except
    For discipline drilled once in an iron school
16 Which holds them at the point of the revolver.
    Yet when they sleep, the images of home
    Ride wishing horses of escape
    Which herd the plain in a mass unspoken poem.

20 Finally, they cease to hate: for although hate
21 Bursts from the air and whips the earth with hail
22 Or shoots it up in fountains to marvel at,
    And although hundreds fall, who can connect
    The inexhaustible anger of the guns
25 With the dumb patience of those tormented animals?

26 Clean silence drops at night, when a little walk
    Divides the sleeping armies, each
    Huddled in linen woven by remote hands.

When the machines are stilled, a common suffering
Whitens the air with breath and makes both one
As though these enemies slept in each other's arms.

Only the lucid friend to aerial raiders
The brilliant pilot moon, stares down
34 Upon this plain she makes a shining bone
35 Cut by the shadows of many thousand bones.
36 Where amber clouds scatter on No-Man's-Land
She regards death and time throw up
38 The furious words and minerals which destroy.

STEPHEN SPENDER

Heroes in Spain

G—, a driver in the convoy of the Unit to which I managed to attach myself from Barcelona to Valencia, was formerly a cellist in a Corner House orchestra. Fat, frank, spectacled and intelligent, he had learned to drive a lorry on the day of his arrival in Barcelona: he drove with too much concentration, leaning over the wheel to fix his attention short-sightedly on the road. In a moment of emotion, when we were driving along the moonlit coastal road between Tarragona and Tortosa, he told me that he had only wept three times in his life: once at the Wembley Tattoo when the whole crowd was hysterical with imperialist fervour, and looking round he had a sudden vision of what it all meant and was leading to; once, when after playing musical trash for months in the restaurant, he went to Sadler's Wells, and hearing *Figaro* performed, realized what music might be and what the standards were by which he earned his living; once, that very morning in Barcelona, when he realized, as he put it, that 'the people in this town know they are free'.

All the time I was in Spain I remembered these three occasions on which G— had wept; they seem to me a monument of personal honesty, of the spirit in which the best men have joined the International Brigade. I believe that at certain moments in history a few people – usually unknown ones – are able to live not for themselves but for a principle. One man goes out to Spain because his dislike of the Corner House orchestra and his love of Mozart suddenly becomes a rule of action with which his own life is identified. A young girl, who happens to be an Anglo-Catholic, and who is politically ignorant, goes out to nurse the wounded because she wishes to alleviate human suffering. Her patients, as soon as they are convalescent, bully her for her lack of 'ideology', and she suffers far more than they are able to imagine.

The unity which exists today in Governmental Spain is the unity of a people whose lives are identified with a principle. This unity is real, though it is something far more difficult to put one's finger on than the obvious differences of the political parties. Talk to people and they are best able to express their differences of opinion, and these differences soon produce various degrees of feeling. Read the editorials of the newspapers in Valencia and the differences which are labelled under such initials as U.G.T., F.A.I., C.N.T., P.O.U.M., soon appear very alarming indeed, especially when 'unity' is being discussed. As one newspaper correspondent said: 'The more they speak of unity, the more they seem to quarrel.'

Yet the unity which was G—'s and my own first impression of Barcelona is a reality which is probably moulding Spanish democracy more quickly than those who deal in journalism and political controversy realize. The attitude of the Spanish people to members of the International Brigade is a good test of their fundamental agreement. In the first place, propaganda about the Brigade has perhaps not been handled as tactfully as it might have been. For example, the battle of Morata was a turning point in the war because the Spanish troops rallied instead of fleeing at a critical moment. When I went along the lines at Morata, in March, I found that the Spanish Lister battalion was entrenched in positions nearer the enemy lines than any trenches of the Brigade. Yet almost all the credit for Morata has gone to the Brigade. Again, quite apart from the decisive action of the Republican Air Force, which is now 90 per cent Spanish,

Spanish troops fought courageously at Guadalajara, yet all the glory went to the Italian Garibaldi battalion.

Tactless propaganda about the International Brigade might appear humiliating to the Spanish people, so it is sometimes suggested that the Brigade is rather resented in Spain. Yet during my six weeks of travelling in Spain I was almost invariably mistaken for a member of the Brigade and treated with extraordinary generosity on that account. Again, it is suggested that the Anarchists are afraid of what the Brigade may do after the war is won. But in practice, Anarchists and members of the Brigade work and fight side by side and the boundaries between political movements are broken down at the front.

I went to Barcelona, Valencia, Madrid, Morata, Alabacete and Tortosa (where the entire population had camped out on the hills at night for fear of an air raid); and I travelled a good deal between these places, going in trains, lorries and private cars. My first and last impressions were not the struggle for power amongst the heads of committees in the large towns, nor inefficiency and bureaucracy, common as they are during a revolution which is also a war; but the courage of the people in Madrid, the enthusiasm of eighty per cent of the people everywhere for the social revolution, the generosity of the workers wherever I met them, in the streets, in trains, in lorries; the marked difference between the awakening younger generation of Spanish workers and the stupefied older ones. Every observer who stays in Republican Spain comes back again and again to a realization that it is the people of Spain who count.

At first the war strengthened and unified the social revolution, but in the long run war demands its own measures which threaten to engulf the whole social system. I set beside the story of G—, the lorry driver, the story of H—, a member of the International Brigade, who first came out as correspondent for one of the most reactionary English newspapers. H— fought in the battle of Morata, where there were four hundred casualties in three days out of a battalion of six hundred men. The worst part of this battle was fought without trenches or other protection, except olive trees, in hilly country amongst the fields and olive groves. On the first day of the battle a friend of H— died of a stomach wound, bleeding to death. H—stayed by him, under fire, until he died. That night H— disturbed his comrades, who were trying to sleep, by walking along the lines shouting out that he was thirsty and must have water ... The next morning he happened to be fighting next to a friend of mine in the olive grove. He said repeatedly to my friend: 'You see that wall over there? How far do you think it is?' My friend answered, 'One hundred yards.' 'Well, you take a range of 120 and I'll try one of 100,' etc. ... That evening he appeared in the lines holding a bundle of telegraph wires which he waved above his head. He said 'Look, I've cut Franco's communications.' He had gone mad.

I tell this story in order to counteract the propaganda about heroes in wars. The final horror of war is the complete isolation of a man dying alone in a world whose reality is violence. The dead in wars are not heroes: they are freezing or rotting lumps of isolated insanity.

People try to escape from a realization of the violence to which abstract ideas and high ideals have led them by saying either that individuals do not matter or else that the dead are heroes. It may be true that at certain times the lives of individuals are unimportant in relation to the whole of future history – although the violent death of many individuals may modify the consciousness of a whole generation as much as a work of art or a philosophical treatise. But to say that those who happen to be killed are heroes is a wicked attempt to identify the dead with the abstract ideas which have brought them to the front, thus adding prestige to those ideas, which are used to lead the living on to similar 'heroic' deaths.

Perhaps soldiers suspect this, for they do not like heroic propaganda. When I was at the Morata Front several men complained of the heroics in left-wing papers. Some praised very highly the report of the battle of Morata, written by Philip Jordan, which appeared in the *News Chronicle*: but they complained that even that, restrained as it was, was too heroic. I had the impression that soldiers in a war have an almost pathetic longing to know the truth.

I returned from Spain feeling more strongly than I have ever felt before that I support the Spanish social revolution. Since the war must be won if the revolution is to be retained, there is nothing to do but accept it as a terrible necessity. Shortly before he died, the poet Garcia Lorca is reported to have said that he would write in time of war the poetry of those who hate war; and when the Indian writer Mulk Raj Anand asked the soldiers fighting in the trenches at Madrid what message they would send to the Indian peasants and workers, they answered: 'Tell our Indian comrades that we hope that when the time comes, they will not have to fight for their freedom as we are doing.' I like the Spanish people because it seems to me that they are emotionally honester than any other people. There are few heroics, no White Feathers, and genuine hatred for the necessity of the war, in Spain. A war such as the present one may be necessary: but it seems to me that the left-wing movement in this country can never afford to forget how terrible war is; and that not the least of its crimes is the propaganda which turns men into heroes.

STEPHEN SPENDER

The Coward

Under the olive trees, from the ground
Grows this flower, which is a wound.
3   This is wiser to ignore
4   Than the heroes' sunset fire
   Raging with flags on the world's shore.
6   These blood-dark petals have no name
7   Except the coward's nameless shame.
8   Here one died, not like a soldier
9   Of lead, but of lead rings of terror.
10   His final moment was the birth
11   Of naked revelatory truth:
12   He saw the flagship at the quay,
13   His mother's care, his lover's kiss,
14   The white accompaniment of spray,

15 Lead to the bullet and to this.
16 Flesh, bone, muscle, eyes,
17 Built in their noble tower of lies,
18 Scattered on the icy breeze
19 Him their false promises betrayed.
20 All the bright visions in one instant
21 Changed to this fixed continual present
22 Under the grey olive trees.

23 There's no excuse here for excuse.
  Nothing can count but love, to pour
25 Out its useless comfort here.
26 To populate his loneliness
27 And to bring his ghost release
28 Love and pity dare not cease
29 For a lifetime, at the least.

STEPHEN SPENDER

Sierran Vigil

Where the lazy wall is down
where the lemon leaf is poisoned
where the road is holed: where gloom of
cloud and sky is blessing: we

Speaking no good word for war
for heroics, for the kingly dust,
exalting not the self-evident murder,
turn: not assuming hope: turn, offering hands.

Where blue is war zone's leading light
where blue lights plead for morning: where
doorways wince the darkness out:
12 we there, ill-starred too, offer hands.

Guitarists who with Yi Yi Yi
haunted melody with reflection
heed now the rifle's acid action
and find through fingering a new notation.

The boy with the goats takes over, takes power.
The boy with the goats, green Gabriel still,
dyes the terraced hillsides with his Never . . .
20   and in his river.

Here where the lazy wall is down
here where the lemon leaf is poisoned
where the road is holed, is trustless,
we, remembering love, kill cruelly . . .

Kill cruelty. Hi and you nestle in gunfire, poet!
Hi and you mow down the forests briefly!
Hi and you gain the cunning touch
that low on Andalusian evenings strikes your match.

For this is the act, the chorus argument.
This is the work we have said is to do.
This is the thing now trust and fear both fail
we have resorted to:

Though no man here is hero, and we
34   line up defending the unheroic unalterably!
35   Who taught us war? This time
those who did not begin will finish it . . .

37   For chico's sake, for chica's pride . . .

And where the lazy wall is down
where the lemon leaf is poisoned
where the road is holed, is trustless,
here shall we grow the olive, and the orange blithely.

EWART MILNE

Ultima Ratio Regum

The guns spell money's ultimate reason
2   In letters of lead on the Spring hillside.
But the boy lying dead under the olive trees
Was too young and too silly
To have been notable to their important eye.
He was a better target for a kiss.

7   When he lived, tall factory hooters never summoned him
8   Nor did restaurant plate-glass doors revolve to wave him in
His name never appeared in the papers.
The world maintained its traditional wall
11   Round the dead with their gold sunk deep as a well,
12   Whilst his life, intangible as a Stock Exchange rumour, drifted outside.

13   O too lightly he threw down his cap
One day when the breeze threw petals from the trees.
15   The unflowering wall sprouted with guns,
16   Machine-gun anger quickly scythed the grasses;
Flags and leaves fell from hands and branches;
The tweed cap rotted in the nettles.

Consider his life which was valueless
In terms of employment, hotel ledgers, news files.
21   Consider. One bullet in ten thousand kills a man.
22   Ask. Was so much expenditure justified
23   On the death of one so young, and so silly
24   Lying under the olive trees, O world, O death?

STEPHEN SPENDER

Escape

The train stopped with a jerk and a rattling. It had stopped
with a jerk and a rattling a hundred times already, so for a while
nobody took much notice. There was a subdued barrage of
voices from the carriages. Dimly under the dim blue lights of
the war-zone platform uniformed or cloaked figures stood
motionless or drifted among the station olives whose leaves
seemed actually two dimensional with the half light slanting up
and among their grey green foliage. Sleepy dark Spanish eyes
stared out from closed windows at sleepy dark Spanish eyes
staring in. The shadowy figures massing on the platform moved
about with a great air of indifference and of waiting for something they didn't terribly care for that never came. But as the
train went on being stopped, gradually as the minutes dripped
by, the hundreds of feet crammed together in the carriages began
to shuffle until it seemed as if the whole train shuffled in a slow,
measured dance, and gradually the barrage of voices became less
and less subdued until the roar growing louder and louder
drowned the derisive thin high whistle of escaping steam from
the engine. The roar was like the roar of the dragon of China
awakened, it sounded meaningless, but individually some quite
sensible conversation was going on, sapped not at all of energy
and gesture by the sweltering humidity of the dusk. Most of the
carriage windows were closed, but through such as remained
unaccountably open a faint tang of eucalyptus and oranges and
something acrid seeped and spread. There were eucalyptus and
orange trees growing on either side of the railway, on the left
looking northerly toward Barcelona orange groves lined up
inland to the foothills of the Sierras, while on the right they
tapered down to shingly beaches with the Mediterranean
gleaming beyond, soft and deeply still . . .

The name of the stopping place, Villagorbo, was painted on a
white signboard in bold blue lettering which hung beneath a
tiny blue bulb on the tressellated woodwork of the Estation

hacienda. Close by were three other haciendas surrounded by what looked like a rubber tree and a few orange trees and creepers, while slightly to one side, but unpleasantly close to the train was a divided hut marked Lavabos, and in smaller lettering, 'Senoras', then the division, then 'Caballeros'. They had seen huts lettered and marked similarly at a hundred way-side Estations since leaving Albacete, and a hundred times Michael had wondered how it came about the lettering had not been changed and brought up to date. Surely Caballeros should have been painted out and a nice fresh Camaradas painted instead? But perhaps difficulty had arisen through the Senoras also having become Camaradas, and while no doubt under certain circumstances a plain blunt 'Camaradas' splashed right across the huts might have to serve, Michael felt no inclination to draw attention to the matter, having already had occasion to feel grateful for the distance, however slight, afforded to the sexes by the oversight, bewilderment, carelessness, or whatever it might be on authority's part that had left the markings un-altered. At any rate, once aware of the hut's existence it became obvious at once what the acrid odour mingling with eucalyptus and orange was, though even then Michael wondered whether it was that his nose was merely reacting to what his eyes saw, and for a moment he speculated on where precisely seeing ended and smelling began. But only for a moment, the hot earth soon left no doubt, and finally his carriage companions with horse snortings and holdings of noses and laughter verified and clinched it.

One there was, however, a wounded and sick man, whom Michael was watching over until they got to Barcelona, who neither joked nor laughed. He was English, little more than a boy, and he was being sent to Barcelona for special treatment. He had suffered a head wound while fighting in the International Brigade, and looked haunted by pain. But when asked whether he suffered he would shake his head and slump down further into his seat, smoking the precious cigarettes that either Michael or one of the others in the carriage handed him, ravenously, devouring the smoke madly with closed eyes, inhaling half asleep. But every now and again his eyes would open with the sideway roll of a terrified hack bolting from something imaginary at its heels, and at such times either Michael or one of the others, the American or the Chilean, would speak to him soothingly until he took another cigarette and slumped back in his seat. It was their English soothed him, as Michael had been told it would soothe him, for whenever the two Spanish militiamen who made up their carriage complement began to talk other than in whispers he would start upright as if shot, and it would take a lot of soothing and shushing to quiet him. The lean American was proving the best hand at the soothing and shushing.

'What's matter with your comrade?' he had asked Michael when they were leaving Albacete, and Michael replying had thought how queerly the words came out of the American's mouth, particularly the 'comrade', despite that he had no American accent to speak of, but was just lean and shirted and had a shaved head and sunburnt body that gave off heat like a radiator, and spoke in a wellbred voice that might have come from anywhere, apart from the peculiar intonation.

'Shock and wounds, I believe,' he'd replied. 'I've been asked to see him safely to a specialist in Barcelona, and I don't mind telling you I'm not in love with the job. His wounds are healed, they tell me, but he was left for months only half attended, among Spaniards, going dottier every day. He doesn't speak the language, they told me –'

'Ah,' said the lean American. Then, 'What are you doing out here? Newspaperman?'

Michael had nodded. 'Sort of. My name's Sernis, and I was born in Ireland. There are times when that means a lot to me, even if only curses. But d'you know, I was annoyed when they asked me at Albacete to look after this poor boy. I felt the people concerned were palming him off on me, because, just because they wanted to be shut of him! I told them I wasn't a doctor or a nurse; I said I'd be helpless if he threw a fit or had a heart attack, and that anyway I'd no time to be trotting round Barcelona ... which is perfectly true; I'm supposed to be back in London tomorrow. Not that it matters, but ... perhaps I'm nervous ... they said he'd be quite normal with anyone he'd understand, English-speaking, but look at him! If that's normality . . .!'

The American had been amused watching how in spite of his grumbling Michael went to great lengths making the young volunteer as comfortable as he knew how, fussing around like a hen and stuffing the lad's pockets with more than half his own cigarette supply, which either he forgot to smoke for the rest of their journey, or else was determined to keep stowed away for a rainy season. At all events he continued to smoke what the American or the Chilean offered until Michael felt quite unhappy and almost doubted his own gift . . .

'He is sick, that's all,' said the Chilean. 'You believe me it's not so hot to be sick when you are lost and don't know what the people are saying about you! I'm telling you! Me, I was sick for many months when I have come to New York from Chile, then I could speak Mexican and some Spanish, but not Americano –'

'Your Americano's O.K. now, anyway, Manuel,' said the American, grinning, and the swarthy good-natured fat Manuel laughed and shrugged, then, seeing that the two pleasant militiamen were whiling time away by comparing their revolvers he took hold of one of the guns and began to discuss its merits and demerits with them. The American joined in and all four became involved in a discussion on the comparative effectiveness of different makes of revolvers. The wounded man seemed to sleep, a cigarette dangling from his fingers. The train continued blandly where it stood, blowing derisive steam. Many of the carriages were empty, their occupants presumably were wandering about the crowded platform, but ever the uproar increased. Michael stared at the haciendas and dark trees, trying to fix his mind on a line or curve of thought which would enable him to forget discomfort until such time as the train chose to get restarted. It seemed a good idea to drug oneself somehow on Spanish journeys, where, calling to his mind a little Donegal railway and the dead years, trains are more stopped than starting, and engine-drivers very philosophic indeed. His mind went wandering along a kaleidoscopic blur of things, of images and half formed unsifted thoughts like colours dividing up, like disconnected notes of music made tangible on the air from a half heard concert played by the elves of the undersoil. But whether his wounded charge acted as a brake and fixation for that part of him wishful to remain keenly conscious of all that was going on, at any rate he found it impossible, useless to try and forget for a moment the insoaking heat, the stifling carriage, the perspiration, the lavabos smells seeping in stronger and more permeating than the eucalyptus. Moreover, it was certainly the wounded man, with his look of a soul already dead, who made it impossible to forget altogether in the heat, the packed carriages, the colourful blue night, the smells, that behind lurked the war agony they were leaving behind (at the train's pleasure) which was precisely that which he wished and craved to forget, almost without realizing it. Even when children, chicas and chicos added to the throng, ran underneath the dark orange trees and picked up the fallen oranges to bring them laughing to the yelling carriages and throw them up, he was more conscious of the barely perceptible brightening across the wounded, sunken face than of the black-eyed urchins, the brightening of that one face meant more to him than the pageant of dark Goya children outside, as if only when the wounded man smiled was he himself free to smile too.

'Guess he's got his packet, your convalescent,' suddenly said the American, while the soldier tried to smile at the children, making signs for them to throw him up oranges. 'Well, he knew what he was doing, I suppose. Anyway he seems to like the kids, the poor guy, whatever his not so private opinion of their mammas and pappas may be –'

'I don't know what he's thinking,' broke out Michael, 'or whether he's in pain, or anything about him. I want to get under his skin to help him, but he's so dumb, I feel helpless –'

The American nodded, vaguely. 'What we want,' he began, following some trend of his own, 'Is a soviet of the senses. Maybe if we could realize every shade and prism colour of emotion in each other, and feel them in each other, we might find brotherliness thata·way? Eh? Gosh, there's some I know of back home, grand people with real intelligence, but all the same they're dead from the mouth down, they're fine and charming, but in a way as dead and distant as the moon –'

'And the moon is a leper,' said Michael, smiling a limping smile. 'How does that poem of your John Dos Passos begin, you know the one, "Lines to a Lady"?' The American looked pleased:

> 'Do you remember the little princess in Hans Andersen
> whose brothers were enchanted into wild swans?
> She sat in the graveyard among weirdwomen
> and witches and twelve nights
> gathered nettles under the moon.
> O wild swan I have gathered nettles . . .'

he quoted promptly.

'That's it,' said Michael. 'Great stuff. Of course we knew it in Ireland a long time before Dos Passos! But talking of feelings, it seems to me they are not to be trusted either, I distrust people's feelings –'

Just then the train hooted, blandly, with a lofty warning note, and immediately from the passengers came answering loud lofty hoots and yells of laughter. Those walking the darkened platform clambered lazily aboard, some even lingering until the train began clanking and slowly gathering speed out of the station before they ran and jumped the high steps and swung themselves up like monkeys. Adios, Villagorbo! Adios! Rattle shuffle went the wheels, To What Loyalty, To What Loyalty, To What Loyalty! Rattle shuffle faster faster I Shall Be Late, I Shall Be Late, I Shall Be Late, faster faster, like the White Rabbit in Alice I Shall be Late . . .

Michael glanced to see whether his convalescent was all right. In the dimness of the swaying, jolting carriage the wounded man was staring straight at him with eyes that seemed bolting from his head, seeing nothing, or else a horror. They were tawny, yellow, oval eyes, like the eyes of his friend, Ted Mallard, whom he had last seen at Chinchon, and at Colmenar during the worst of the Jarama attack. But how unalike in expression! But who could tell, perhaps Mallard's eyes would have got that

347

'bolting' look by now, if he had gone through all that this man had? Or perhaps not. It was difficult to think of Ted except as he had looked when they'd said goodbye at Colmenar front lines, the village eerily silent and deserted except for troops and the artillery rumbling beyond on the night hills. Ted's eyes when he had asked whether he wasn't returning shortly to Valencia! 'No,' Ted had said, 'There's work to be done here . . .' and his young tawny eyes tortured by war and the sights of bloodiness. Tortured, yes, but somehow he had known Ted Mallard had the proper sharp edge to his soul, the perceptive edge that is perhaps undefeatable! And Ted still in the thick of it, while he himself . . .

Rattle shuffle went the wheels, To What Loyalty, To What Loyalty. Darkness over the humid earth, and a giggling moon skipped along with the train, leering on the Sierras. Jolting about on their seats the two militiamen and the American and Chilean slept, exuding waves of heat from their bodies. His wounded charge rose to his feet, and, muttering something indistinct about toilet, went into the ill-lit corridor. Michael followed behind him, feeling intuitively anxious and nervous. The man walked the length of the corridor, but instead of going into the lavatory he opened the end door, and glaring back at Michael with eyes from which all sense had fled, stepped out. Michael shouted and ran, and behind him the American jumped alertly awake, pulling the communication cord. People were trouping, shouting, from the train, which had stopped at a high rocky point overlooking the sea, the Mediterranean sheerly beneath and boulders leading steeply down to it. There was not a sign of Michael's escaped convalescent. Many people began climbing and slithering down the rocks, Michael among them, soon they could see the whole length of the snaky outline of the train above their heads, bluely in the moonlight.

'Well,' said the American's voice beside him as they scrabbled gingerly downward, 'I hope we're not delayed long enough for the planes to find us, I don't want any apples dropped on my head. Say, if I hear a plane I'm making for the engine-driver pronto and get him moving. It's harder to hit a moving object, they say!' . . .

There was a shout below them, and then many people talking at once, their voices drifting into nothingness where the sea was. It seemed they had found the body, the man was dead; they were bringing him up the slopes, heaving him up in turn on willing shoulders. A few moments and all had reached the train again and those carrying the body laid it out on the carriage seat, and as the American covered the eyes Michael thought the eyes were now more unalike to Ted Mallard's than they had been in life, although they had lost their look of being haunted by some terror now, and only stared.

'Seems silly to have to come to Spain to commit suicide,' said the American thoughtfully. 'Why, any guy could do that at home! Not that I hold with doing away with yourself. Anyway the poor guy won't have to go under any more operations, he's escaped that much at least –'

'It is a crime this suicide,' said the Chilean. 'But this one he was sick, he is mad with pain. May the good God be merciful to him! His sickness, his wounds are no disgrace, I'm telling you ...'

The body jigged slightly up and down on the carriage seat as the train jerked forward again. They had strapped the body so that the jerking of the train could not possibly unseat it. Michael stared out of the window and the moon swimming alongside the carriages seemed to leer at him, leering and skipping over the dark harsh rhythm of the Sierras. Rattle Shuffle went the wheels. To What Loyalty, To What Loyalty, To What Loyalty! It was all very fine for the American to say 'the poor guy' had escaped operations and pain in future, but what sort of escape had he made! He had gone down into death terrified and insane, his soul had gone into death in that fashion! That could not be called escape! The way of escape was the way of courage, always. Whatever your beliefs, with courage you escaped from yourself into something greater than yourself. No, it was Ted Mallard who had stayed at Colmenar who had escaped. At the very least, Mallard had escaped all that he himself was returning to! The lifeless Sundays, the intolerable Mondays ...

EWART MILNE

349

Thoughts During an Air Raid

1   Of course, the entire effort is to put oneself
      Outside the ordinary range
      Of what are called statistics. A hundred are killed
4   In the outer suburbs. Well, well, one carries on.
5   So long as this thing 'I' is propped up on
6   The girdered bed which seems so like a hearse,
7   In the hotel bedroom with the wall-paper
8   Blowing smoke-wreaths of roses, one can ignore
9   The pressure of those names under the fingers
10   Indented by lead type on newsprint,
11   In the bar, the marginal wailing wireless.
      Yet supposing that a bomb should dive
13   Its nose right through this bed, with one upon it?
14   The thought's obscene. Still, there are many
15   For whom one's loss would illustrate
16   The 'impersonal' use indeed. The essential is
17   That every 'one' should remain separate
18   Propped up under roses, and no one suffer
      For his neighbour. Then horror is postponed
20   Piecemeal for each, until it settles on him
21   That wreath of incommunicable grief
      Which is all mystery or nothing.

STEPHEN SPENDER

Fall of a City

1 All the posters on the walls,
2 All the leaflets in the streets
3 Are mutilated, destroyed, or run in rain,
4 Their words blotted out with tears,
5 Skins peeling from their bodies
6 In the victorious hurricane.

7 All the names of heroes in the hall
8 Where the feet thundered and the bronze throats roared
9 FOX and LORCA claimed as history on the walls,
10 Are now furiously deleted
11 Or to dust surrender their gold
12 From praise excluded.

13 All the badges and salutes
14 Torn from lapels and from hands,
15 Are thrown away with human sacks they wore,
16 Or in the deepest bed of mind
17 They are washed over with a smile
18 Which launches the victors where they win.

All the lessons learned, unlearnt;
The young, who learned to read, now blind
Their eyes with an archaic film;
22 The peasant relapses to a stumbling tune
23 Following the donkey's bray;
24 These only remember to forget.

But somewhere some word presses
26 In the high door of a skull, and in some corner
27 Of an irrefrangible eye
28 Some old man's memory jumps to a child
29 – Spark from the days of liberty.
30 And the child hoards it like a bitter toy.

STEPHEN SPENDER

Spain

Pity and love are no more adequate:
2 They have not saved ten thousand who are dead,
Nor brought relief to peasants who in dread
Gaze at that sky which held their hope of late:
5 They have not stifled horror nor killed hate.
Europe is not impatient of her guilt,
But those on whom her tyranny is built,
8 By love deserted have grown desperate.

9 Tears are no use. Those who mourn grown mad.
10 May sanity have strength and men unite
Who in their individual lives are glad
That what remains of peace may yet prove strong.
13 We have the will, then let us show the might,
Who have foreborne and pitied far too long.

H. B. MALLALIEU

A Stopwatch and an Ordnance Map
(To Samuel Barber)

A stopwatch and an ordnance map.
At five a man fell to the ground
And the watch flew off his wrist
Like a moon struck from the earth
Marking a blank time that stares
On the tides of change beneath.
7 *All under the olive trees.*

A stopwatch and an ordnance map.
He stayed faithfully in that place

352

From his living comrade split
By dividers of the bullet
12 Opening wide the distances
Of his final loneliness.
14 *All under the olive trees.*

A stopwatch and an ordnance map.
And the bones are fixed at five
Under the moon's timelessness;
But another who lives on
Wears within his heart for ever
20 Space split open by the bullet.
21 *All under the olive trees.*

STEPHEN SPENDER

The Room above the Square

The light in the window seemed perpetual
2 When you stayed in the high room for me;
3 It glowed above the trees through leaves
Like my certainty.

The light is fallen and you are hidden
In sunbright peninsulas of the sword:
Torn like leaves through Europe is the peace
8 That through us flowed.

9 Now I climb alone to the high room
10 Above the darkened square
11 Where among stones and roots, the other
12 Unshattered lovers are.

STEPHEN SPENDER

Port Bou

As a child holds a pet
Arms clutching but with hands that do not join
And the coiled animal looks through the gap
To outer freedom animal air,
5   So the earth-and-rock arms of this small harbour
6   Embrace but do not encircle the sea
7   Which, through a gap, vibrates into the ocean,
8   Where dolphins swim and liners throb.
9   In the bright winter sunlight I sit on the parapet
10 Of a bridge; my circling arms rest on a newspaper
11 And my mind is empty as the glittering stone
12 While I search for an image
13 (The one written above) and the words (written above)
14 To set down the childish headlands of Port Bou.
A lorry halts beside me with creaking brakes
16 And I look up at warm downwards-looking faces
17 Of militia men staring at my (French) newspaper.
18 'How do they write of our struggle over the frontier?'
19 I hold out the paper, but they cannot read it,
20 They want speech and to offer cigarettes.
21 In their waving flag-like faces the war finds peace. The
     famished mouths
22 Of rusted carbines lean against their knees,
23 Like leaning, rust-coloured, fragile reeds.
24 Wrapped in cloth – old granny in a shawl –
25 The stuttering machine-gun rests.
26 They shout – salute back as the truck jerks forward
Over the vigorous hill, beyond the headland.
28 An old man passes, his mouth dribbling,
29 From three rusted teeth, he shoots out: 'pom-pom-pom'.
30 The children run after; and, more slowly, the women;
31 Clutching their skirts, trail over the horizon.
32 Now Port Bou is empty, for the firing practice.

33 I am left alone on the parapet at the exact centre
34 Above the river trickling through the gulley, like that old
man's saliva.
35 The exact centre, solitary as the bull's eye in a target.
36 Nothing moves against the background of stage-scenery
houses
37 Save the skirring mongrels. The firing now begins
38 Across the harbour mouth, from headland to headland,
39 White flecks of foam whipped by lead from the sea.
40 An echo spreads its cat-o'-nine tails
41 Thrashing the flanks of neighbour hills.
My circling arms rest on the newspaper,
43 My mind is paper on which dust and words sift,
44 I assure myself the shooting is only for practice
45 But I am the coward of cowards. The machine-gun
stitches
46 My intestines with a needle, back and forth;
47 The solitary, spasmodic, white puffs from the carbines
48 Draw fear in white threads back and forth through my
body.

STEPHEN SPENDER

The Statue

To be sure it was Sunday. But I had stayed over in Barcelona
on many other occasions, and on those other occasions Sunday
hadn't seemed to matter. I mean Sunday in our sabbath sense,
church sense. Sunday with people decked out in their finery as
we know it in England and France, the streets half empty and
those that have the misfortune to be loitering out too fed up
even to listen long to one Sunday orator, but merely drifting
from orator to orator in the hopeless effort to get away from
themselves, listening to the oracles of the parks and pews and
pubs, until it grows dark and they can make love for a while and
then sleep.

To be sure it was Sunday. But those other Barcelona Sundays had been the same as week-days, the Ramblas and the Plaza Cataluna had been blue with folk in overalls and other uniforms jammed together sardine-tin tight, with the U.G.T. radio from the Colon bellowing and the air vibrating the greetings of Salud! Salud! Salud! There had always been sardine-tin groups packed round the sellers of militia caps, sardine-tin groups watching the myriad pigeon wings ascending and descending at the fountains of the Square, sardine-tin groups standing gaping up at the twenty-foot statue of the militiaman, a gigantic piece of work, which fairly convinced me that the sculptor must have paid a visit to England and there seen Genesis and while under the influence carved out the militiaman bayonet and all in a frenzy of adoration, which is not quite the correct order because the lady Genesis being apparently about to give birth nobody but our militiaman could have done it, so by rights he should have been sculpted first . . .

'He was a darling,' said Vita regretfully, 'I don't know why they took him down.'

'It seems a pity, yes,' I said. 'He certainly was a beauty. But where are they all, where are the crowds?' There were, it is true, a few drifters wandering along Gracia, a few red, snorting buses, a tram or so tinkling and groaning past the Colon . . .

'Well, you see, on Sundays the Catalans used to go picnicking and its become popular again since the May revolution – I mean revolt –' said Vita. 'What they do is they begin early in the morning to pack their food and about twelve o'clock they've finished packing then they set off for the mountainside above the city and there they lay out the food and start eating and when you come back from your hike at seven o'clock that evening they've not quite finished, but they're feeling better because usually they've reached Flamenco singing and the scraps left over by then, they used to leave all the bottles and paper uneaten though, only now the Government tells them off about it, so now Mamma calls loudly: Be careful, children, or you'll hurt yourselves with those bottles and come home at once you've had enough, there's dears . . .'

'Definitely,' I said, feeling that with this word I gave her oration its properly back-dated date. 'And, Oh, for the sands of Blackpool, and where are the bourgeois tonight, tonight!'

'Oh, no, they're not bourgeois,' Vita protested. 'They're workers and Catalans, but when you know the language it's disappointing to find they talk the same and enjoy the same gastronomic and horseplay pleasures as a labour outing on May-day, though I don't know why it is disappointing, but I could bring you on the hillside and show you, only you've just come from Valencia and are tired, so we'll go to the flat and make tea instead, because, anyway, I want to talk to you, rather . . .'

She seemed to have been talking to me rather, but I was quite content she should go on, indefinitely if she pleased, provided I could drink tea and gaze out of the flat windows over the semi-African barbaric structure of Barcelona's architecture. Moreover, I liked Vita's greeny eyes and hair and graceful movement, all the hidden positivity of her, so to speak, of which her conversation was only one, and that negligible, facet.

'I want to tell you about an English boy who's in jail here.' she began promptly, as we sipped the tea with lemon. 'I went to visit this boy, and he says he was one of the first Englishmen out, he came out in August, 1936, and later did flying and brought down many Italian planes – planes of Italian make, he said. He says he was one of the first aviators for the Government and now they've jailed him – at least actually he's in hospital now, that was where I saw him, in hospital, they put him there because he went on hunger-strike because he couldn't eat the food in jail and screamed at the guards. He told me he had left Spain and gone into France on some job for the authorities, and then had come back all the way from Marseilles to Barcelona in a rowing boat, but when he landed they had arrested him and kept him in prison. And there he's been for months. I think it's terrible; his mind is in an awful state, he can't speak Spanish let alone Catalan, and he says he's going mad. You should have seen him when I brought some cakes and cigarettes, he could hardly believe an English girl really had come to visit him. But when I told others like you passing through Barcelona, they mostly advised me not to go near him again . . .'

We were sitting elegantly with the sun pouring in on us and

into us with a long, even warmth, that soaked through into our veins and beyond, deeper, and that was what we wanted; we didn't shut our inner bodies against the sun, as people who go sunbathing usually do, so that they only succeed in getting burnt like sausages for breakfast fried too hurriedly on the outside only.

'They were probably quite justified,' I said. 'Your boy's story smells fishy to me. But why this sudden insistence on the word English, Vita?' I felt if it had been any other race she wouldn't be bothering so much, and I felt very cold towards her, suddenly.

'But you don't understand,' Vita cried. 'He's only a boy twenty-two or twenty-three at the outside, and he's ill, he can't eat and they're holding him until his papers turn up or they find charges against him, or prove something, something . . .'

'Under the circumstances very sensible of them!' I commented. 'Did he tell you much else?'

'He told me he's been to Germany and that he'd taken some passports in with him belonging to men who'd been killed, German men from the Thaelmann Brigade, and with the passports brought about the release of other German boys from the concentration camps . . .'

I looked at her. 'Yes,' she cried. 'I know it sounds utter rubbish, but you should see him and listen to him. I'm sure something should be done. I'm so sorry for him.'

I wasn't so sorry or sure something should be done. I sat and played with the sun in my veins and remembered the cold Spanish winter, and how cold Albacete had been, the dry, desolate cold of that endless dusty-white road to Albacete across the yellow plateau two months ago. And I thought of a night when I'd tried to find someone I'd known in London, a night I'd searched all over Albacete in the company of two Scotchmen who, the later it got and darker under the palms than curfew, and the more cafés we looked into unavailingly, became after each drink more and more enthusiastic for our search. We talked to French, Slavs, Greeks, Germans, Dutch, Swedes, Finns, and even to one of the Emperor of Abyssinia's ex-generals, who had been very mournful over his wine because the Italians had killed his brother, so that, he said mournfully, all he wanted was to fight and die for the Spanish people who were fighting Mussolini. Probably we talked to other nationalities that I forgot, Albacete being a military camp and a second Tower of Babel, but at last Andy and Jock had decided my friend must be at the Salamanca barracks. Salamanca is the detention barracks for the International Column. Andy and Jock said if we went to Salamanca and the guards let us in they certainly wouldn't let us out again. However, for my sake they said they would go. I said it didn't matter, but they insisted.

At the barracks, once a big private residence, two guards stood with crossed rifles, arguing with camaradas who wanted to get in, and also with camaradas who wanted to get out. The two Jocks pulled me forward brusquely and began to explain me and my wants to the guards. The guards were French, but when Andy called one of them a lousy bastard he hit Andy very hard. When he showed signs of recovering his senses again the guards got tired of us and shoved us in all three. Inside was a long spacious hall with a mighty unlit chandelier and a spiral staircase at the far end, softened for feet by a thick, rich, red carpet. The search proved fruitless (as they say), so next had come the job of getting out. I suggested that we arm ourselves with salvo conductos, with passes from the 'responsible', who had not known where my friend was staying, but Andy and Jock said why should we get passes, this was the army of the proletariat. A bit later we waved our passes at the guards, but even then it was difficult to get the crossed rifles unglued, and we had to charge through, galloping like a rugby match. When we stood on the pavements grey Jock and I were grinning, but Andy ground his teeth and turned and shook his fist at the guards, who were arguing with camaradas who wanted to get in, and also with camaradas who wanted to get out . . .

'Oh, God, if only I had a bomb!' he shrieked. I have seldom seen a man's face more twisted by hate, bewilderment, despair, fear, shame . . .

It's true that the bewilderment and shame had predominated, but still I remembered Andy with some distaste, talking to Vita. Bewilderment and ignorance causing fear had warped Andy all too quickly, and although, on the other hand, he might have been a dangerous customer, it seemed feasible the 'English Boy' of Vita's tale was possibly in a similar plight. Of course Vita thought the customer was always right! Oh, nation of shop-keepers! . . .

'Try, do, for me, do something about him,' she urged, like a monologue. 'You're going back home. Tell them about him, tell . . .'

I cut her short. 'I'll tell them,' I said steadily. 'Of my friends who were killed at Madrid, of bombings of civilians and children, of the work of English nurses.' I emphasized the adjective.

'But I don't see all that, nothing happens in Barcelona,' cried Vita. 'It's newspaper talk. I read it before I left to come to Spain. This boy is real, he exists . . .'

'So did my friends, Vita,' I answered. But I could no longer feel they had existed (though I could believe it), unless perhaps one, because I had read and memorized his poetry, so that he was part of me.

'The only experience I've had,' Vita went on, more dis-gruntled as she talked, 'was the revolt. For three days we were shut up; I sat right here where I'm sitting watching them firing across the rooftops and down into the street at armoured cars. The police and the Catalan Government troops and the Com-munists there opposite in Carlos Marx building were firing at the others, the anarchists and others who had brought about the rising. There were over a thousand killed –'

'Newspaper talk!' I said, smiling at her. 'And so you saw the streets littered with dead – which, without any doubt, might be said to have belonged to them, then. At least didn't La Batalla say in flaring letterpress: 'People of Barcelona, for three days the streets of Barcelona were yours' – and, of course, there was nobody on the streets – only the dead and the dogs and the sound of rifles. Correct me if I'm wrong, but I'm sure out in the Sierras the Monarchist general staff took note of it all, very hopefully . . .'

'The police climbed up from the flat to the roof,' Vita said, as if I hadn't spoken, 'and I listened to the rifles' crackle and, after a while, I went up and sat beside them, they didn't say a word, they didn't tell me to clear off, as I thought they would. After an hour or so I handed the bullets to them when they took off their bandoliers to make themselves more comfortable where they crouched, and they only nodded at me. I stayed with them the live-long day, there wasn't anything else to do, but I didn't begin to understand what it was all about. Of course I've only been living in Spain a couple of months. But you see that's why I feel so sorry for that English boy, because he doesn't understand either, I'm sure he doesn't, things move so fast in Spain, I don't understand why boys who have come out to help and are airmen get themselves into jail –'

'But you understand how other boys who have come out to help get themselves into graves?' I asked. 'I'm afraid I'm a cynical babe about your Englishman, Vita!'

We were silent and the city was. We looked downward from the flat window along the wide bracing sweep of Diagonal, with its sideshows of palms, that every now and then shuddered with a hoarse, dry sound, as a small wind moved among them quietly, on along towards where the tall phallic monolith or monument that marks the cross-section of Gracia and Diagonal stood tautly against the deep skies; the palms shuddered one by one and yet in unison and then were stiller than before. I thought:

I am going to write a story and I am going to call it A Pair of Ragged Claws. It will be a story of a crab who lived when the earth was a jagged lumpy rock before the corners were smoothed and rounded by the dark erosive column of Time going over it in a sea inescapable and unceasing, of a crab who lived when the wild rock of the earth went grinding sickingly along, of a crab who was fashioned delicately with no shell, but with a beautiful sheen on his streamlined body, and who one day preened himself somewhat and went out to meet his love. And his love walked to meet him on her little snow white feet and long arching legs, but when she came close his heart sank, because he thought she looked derisive about him and boastful about herself. And that was right, too, because when she *did* get close enough she pinched his beautiful streamlined body viciously in a most carefree mocking manner. Then she walked away arching her long legs on her little snow white feet and the crab sobbed: 'Ow, I'm going to get me protection from this sort of thing!' AT FIRST HE THOUGHT OF HIRING A GANGSTER TO DO THE DIRTY ON HER! but then he considered that that was a disgraceful kind of revenge anyway, so he brooded and had a brainstorm, or he thought it was a brainstorm. HE WOULD GROW A SHELL! He would grow a shell and hide in the winds and be wistful and then she, his love, would come along arching her long legs on little snow white feet and looking derisive about him and boastful about herself, but when she reached out daintily to pinch him he would laugh and laugh and laugh . . .

'It's nearly time for your broadcast,' said Vita. 'What's the matter? You look distraught or ill or something?'

'Nothing,' I mumbled. But I knew my hands were shaking and I fancied my face was white.

'It's nothing,' I mumbled a second time. 'Only the unshored fragments of many nightmares tinkling somewhere – like stories we think are new until we think again and find they've got long, white whiskers . . .'

But Vita wasn't listening. She was leaning over the balcony looking excitedly along down Diagonal.

'Gosh,' she said, loudly. 'If it isn't our militiaman! Where in hell are they taking him now?'

The huge figure had been placed standing bolt upright on a drag cart, which was being pulled along by ropes in a procession like a carnival with seas of flower garlands and multifarious uniforms. Even viewed from the balcony the statue loomed enormous, towering, dwarfing the tiny men and women, so that in perspective they seemed even tinier than they were. It was for all the world a stone Gulliver in Lilliput, only that this Gulliver had broken free of his chains and ropes, and, finding that those who had chained him were waving flowers in his face and smiling at him and airing pretty speeches, had risen blind and wordless in his rough, uncouth clothes to act as their sombre, giant, and pathetic sentry, their last lookout over their Spanish Lilliputian earth, and over all the Lilliputian earth.

'Well,' said Vita, 'here's Moloch if you like! I wonder where

362

they'll put him now? Perhaps they'll take him out to the front at Aragón, to be a mascot in the Sierras! Oh my, oh my, oh my, what a lovely target, though! I'd simply hate to think of a shell getting him!'

The procession moved on neither fast nor slow down Diagonal, the inevitable band busy with renderings of Bandera Roja, the procession and even the statue appearing to dwindle as they receded, the strains of band music growing fainter in the same ratio, until there was left only the shuddering among the palm fronds, and the hoot of a taxi speeding hastily after the procession.

'It wouldn't matter if a shell did get him,' I said. 'He's always dying or being killed, he's used to it. He died when an anarchist, Durutti, died, and when an Englishman, Ralph Fox, died, and when millions of peasants died, and an Irishman, Connolly, died, to mention but few. But there he is again, you see, always popping up like a daisy, that democratic flower –'

'Don't I wish he could talk though!' said Vita, jesting plaintively. 'I'm sure he'd talk like García Lorca, tender and expressive and sensual for all his bigness and bayonet and village blacksmith arms . . .'

I laughed. Politically, Vita seemed to be coming on. But it was time for me to go to the broadcasting station. Having just returned from Madrid and Valencia, it had been arranged that I should speak for a few minutes during the English broadcast.

'Did you ever meet a village blacksmith?' I asked her. 'He'd educate you. But let's go – I've got to hurry!'

I did one broadcast and then at midnight a second. I knew I was tired, but I knew in a few minutes it would be over and I could go. Vita had gone long since back to her flat, and I was saying words into the microphone. This was the official Barcelona station broadcast to the world, on a wave length that I forgot as soon as the announcer had announced it and with it me. My voice seemed to be coming from some cavern within me but unconnected with me, without volition: I felt that I I was quite detached from it, and that I had a queer dislike and distaste of what it was repeating, and yet that I was determined

to go on, volitionless. I knew that what I was saying like a lesson
I was teaching myself could be heard in a great many countries,
but that comparatively few people would listen in, and that even
of those who did very many would yawn widely in utter boredom.
I thought, in a dreamlike, unhappy way, of the silent statue of
the militiaman, the giant mate for Genesis, the monstrosity that
seemed to thud with life in its stonehard grimness; I thought of
Vita and her Englishman and the uneaten scraps of Catalan
picnics; I thought of Andy warped; I thought of someone long
ago, who had come walking coldly, blithely towards me, and for
whose sake I had been, as it were, a Pair of Ragged Claws; and
all the time my voice went on evenly:

> so that Saturday I returned from Madrid . . .
> People who go to Madrid and return always
> speak of the heroic spirit of the
> defenders of the city. It is one thing
> to be heroic when one's belly is full
> and quite another when one's belly is
> empty. It is one thing to be heroic
> at the front, and another to lie awake
> night after night, listening for the
> double explosion, for the deadly apples
> of the triple engined planes. The women
> of Madrid lie awake, the women
> of Madrid . . .

EWART MILNE

After Brunete

It seems to me, in this quiet place, dawns are like evening
And days condensed to hours from that ceaseless work.
With you, rooks loll on the lazy air,
The fields are fantasies of yellow feather flowers,
The day not buttoned up under a storm of hate.

TOMALIN

In the confused callous flurry of war, over
Fantastic horror-haunted ground I ran with others
This and that way like an aimless dream, but
This night is long, I may never reach
Your reassuring breakfast cups.

Comrades, what outline of yourselves is true?
Why are you laughing? Last hour
You crouched with tightened nerves
Teeth white, forecasting skeleton jaws, waiting
For the whine to scream, the scream to roar.
Every mind knows more comes, long months more:
Is laughter like thirsty water, material need?
One says, you got to let off steam,
It isn't all so grim, another says.

I have beaten my fear dry,
The sensitive surface has hardened
Against the shrapnel's second throw.
But I stood at the end of thirty four years facing loss,
I had already in custody the close and vital organs
That crave what the child craved, feeling
The long hurt of war.

I saw both roads spread upwards from the ford
Taking their dead.
They could not push me away, I stood as close to the dead
As to my own child.
Like children they were, aping the life of men
With their disused bodies in grotesque games.
I saw a driver scrambled about his wheel
And the wax hands of little Will, no gentler
Alive than dead.
Never call heroes men of glory
Who rake in bloody dung and climb stinking out:
They'll tell you heroism breeds in the pitted scars
Where life is rotten.

365

Hold up your flags, young followers,
With resolution, not joy,
For the air is thick with other smells than spring.

If the space between us never folds
And I am sucked into death,
Remember me with understanding, Nicholas,
Though for all my hopes of a world of homes
I never built my own.
This is the time when labour and sweat shape up men's minds:
Now in my own, dusty with discredited hopes,
I have found a gateway, I have taken a course
Which, however hateful, is whole.
Reality makes adults of us all,
There is no other fortune-teller.

MILES TOMALIN

Nicholas

My son is very young, while he plays
He remembers me. I am not there.
My son is very young, he fears to ask
Who sent me away.
Night after night, breaking in dream from war,
I find him
Laughing, soothed, running after me terrified
Because I walked away.

In the night, the cause I fight for
Draws a mist of horror up, damps me with blood,
My ignorant senses angrily demand
Truth, truth!
In sleep I tell it,
Night after night fingers away the slight curtain.

366

TOMALIN

My son is very young, he alone
Never doubts, never examines me.
When I dream and think of him
I want to live.

MILES TOMALIN

INSENSIBLE AT SUCH A TIME

'That we should be insensible at such a time
makes deafness kill and peace the bloodier crime'
(Clive Branson, 'Spain. December 1936')

Spain. December 1936

You, English!
Can't you hear the barrage creeping
that levels the Pyrenees?

Is time tangible
that bears so audible
and visible a thing?

Can't you hear the men scream
where the fascist bomb
makes the people's home
a tomb for you and me?

Can't you see the gashes in the street
where our people stumble
when the city trembles?
Can't you smell the rose held in their teeth
tighter than death?

They who lie so still
with no Cross,
only this, their courage, their faith
manures the barren earth
for new trees
to spring up the hill-side to the very sky.

That we should be insensible at such a time
makes deafness kill and peace the bloodier crime.

CLIVE BRANSON

London 1939

Instructions from England
1936

Note nothing of why or how, enquire
no deeper than you need
into what set these veins on fire,
note simply that they bleed.

Spain fought before and fights again,
better no question why;
note churches burned and popes in pain
but not the men who die.

VALENTINE ACKLAND

To England from the English Dead

We, who were English once had eyes and saw
The savage greed of those who made this war
Tear up from earth, like a hog loose in flowers
So many lives as young and strong as ours,
You, England, stood apart from Spain's affair,
You said you were secure in sea and cliff
While others sank in filthy war, as if
You kept some old virginity in there.
While the black armies marched and the dead fell,
You toldeo [sic] your English people all was well,
And shutting eyes to war was finding peace.
You told them once, all slavery must cease.
Dishonourable England! We in Spain
Who died, died proudly, but not in your name;
Our friends will keep the love we felt for you
Among your maist [sic] green landscapes and smooth hills,
Talk of it over honest window sills
And teach our children we were not untrue.

Not for those others, more like alien men
Who, quick to please our slayers, let them pass,
Not for them
We English lie beneath the Spanish grass.

MILES TOMALIN

To the Wife of Any
Non-Intervention Statesman

Permit me, madam, to invade,
Briefly, your boudoir's pleasant shade:
Invasion, though, is rather strong,
I volunteered, and came along.
So please don't yell, or make a scene,
Or ring for James to – intervene.
I'm here entirely for the good
Of you and yours, it's understood.
No ballyhoo, what I've to say
May stand you in good stead one day.

I have to broach a matter that
Less downright folk might boggle at,
But none need blush because we try
To analyse the marriage tie.

The voice that breathed o'er Eden laid
Some precepts down to be obeyed:
To seek in marriage mutual trust
Much more than sentiment or lust:
To base our passion on esteem
And build a home for love's young dream.
With this in mind, I'll state a case
Of interest to the human race.

23   Suppose a husband yarns in bed,
Of plans that fill his lofty head,

373

Think what should be a wife's reaction
If he turned out the tool of faction,
Who put across the crooked schemes
Of statesmen sunk in backward dreams;
Whose suave compliance sealed the fate
Of thousands left to Franco's hate –
(Those very Basques whose fathers drowned
To keep our food-ships safe and sound,
Sweeping for mines in furious seas).
Our Fleet stood by, but ill at ease:
Restive, our sailors watched the shore
Whilst hundreds drowned who'd starved before,
Victims of Franco's sham blockade –
Though in the way of honest trade
Potato Jones and his brave lass
Had proved this husband knave or ass.

Suppose he argues: Though I swerved
From honour's course, yet peace is served?

Euzkadi's mines supply the ore
To feed the Nazi dogs of war:
Guernika's thermite rain transpires
In doom on Oxford's dreaming spires:
In Hitler's frantic mental haze
Already Hull and Cardiff blaze,
And Paul's grey dome rocks to the blast
Of air-torpedoes screaming past.
From small beginnings mighty ends,
From calling rebel generals friends,
From being taught at public schools
To think the common people fools,
Spain bleeds, and England wildly gambles
To bribe the butcher in the shambles.

Traitor and fool's a combination
To lower wifely estimation,
Although there's not an Act in force
Making it grounds for a divorce:

32

374

But canon law forbids at least
Co-habitation with a beast.

The grim crescendo rises still
At the Black International's will.
65 Mad with the loss of Teruel,
The bestial Duce looses hell;
On Barcelona slums he rains
German bombs from Fiat planes.
Five hundred dead in ninety seconds
Is the world record so far reckoned;
A hundred children in one street,
Their little hands and guts and feet,
Like offal round a butcher's stall,
Scattered where they'd been playing ball –
Because our ruling clique's pretences
76 Robbed loyal Spain of her defences,
The chaser planes and A-A guns
From which the prudent Fascist runs.

So time reveals the true intent
Behind the Gentlemen's Agreement,
And lest a final crime condones
Fresh massacres with British loans,
83 Would she not have its sponsor outlawed
From power, position, bed and board?
Would not a thinking wife contemn
The sneaking hand that held the pen
And with a flourish signed the deed
Whence all these hearts and bodies bleed?
Would not those fingers freeze the breast
Where the young life should feed and rest?
Would not his breath reek of the tomb
And with cold horror seal her womb?
Could a true woman bear his brat?
The millions wouldn't.
                              Thanks, my hat.

                              EDGELL RICKWORD

The Non-Interveners

In England the handsome Minister with the second
and a half chin and his heart-shaped mind
hanging on his thin watch-chain, the Minister
with gout who shaves low on his holly-stem neck.

In Spain still the brown and gilt and the twisted
pillar, still the olives, and in the mountains
the chocolate trunks of cork trees bare from
the knee, the little smoke from the sides
of the charcoal-burner's grey tump, the ebony sea-
hedgehogs in the clear water, the cuttle speared
at night; and also the black slime under
the bullet-pocked wall, also the arterial blood
squirting into the curious future, also
the greasy cloud streaked with red in yellow: and,

In England, the ominous grey paper, with its
indifferent headline, its news from our own
correspondent away from the fighting,
and in England the crack-willows, their
wet leaves reversed by the wind; and
the swallows sitting different ways like
notes of music between the black poles on
the five telephone wires.

GEOFFREY GRIGSON

Dulce et Decorum Est . . .

('The Foreign Office . . . have for some time past received letters from anxious mothers whose sons have gone to Spain . . . In view of this . . . and the fact that volunteering is illegal, the Government . . . have decided to put a stop to it.' *The Times*, 12 January)

Though sweet and glorious for the Motherland
To die, as patriots in the highest sense,
To die in foreign quarrels must be banned –
A criminal offence.

When Britain summons to a hero's grave
Her sons die gladly to defend her laws,
But now for British mothers to be brave,
There is no cause.

There is no cause which Englishmen should hear,
Thinking to die that liberty may live,
Nor the misguided lives they volunteer
Their own to give.

Not theirs to stand, a few against a flood,
With French, Poles, Slavs and Swiss, by passion led,
With zealots' gore their democratic blood
Must not be shed.

Spontaneously, spectacularly first,
Great Britain shows the world how not to strike,
While all Spain's interveners, uncoerced,
Do as they like.

But, using like a mouse our giant's might,
We stand from history's judgement not exempt;
Above suspicion, and above the fight,
Above suspicion and beneath contempt.

SAGITTARIUS

For Those with Investments in Spain

I ask your patience, half of them cannot read,
Your forbearance if, for a while, they cannot pay,
Forgive them, it is disgusting to watch them bleed,
I beg you to excuse, they have no time to pray.
Here is a people, you know it as well as he does,
Franco, you can see it as plain as they do,
Who are forced to fight, for the simplest rights, foes
Richer, stupider, stronger than you, or I, or they, too.
So, while the German bombs burst in their wombs,
And poor Moors are loosed on the unhappy,
And Italian bayonets go through their towns like combs,
Spare a thought, a thought for all these Spanish tombs,
And for a people in danger, grieving in breaking rooms,
For a people in danger, shooting from falling homes.

BRIAN HOWARD

They Don't Know

The ordinary Japanese don't know
Why they must pick on China so,
Although by propaganda they
Convincingly revile and slay.

The Spanish fascist bloods don't know
Truly why they must overthrow
By sarcasm and bombs their kin
And let those foreign microbes in.

Our democratic friends don't know
Why their own governments must show

Such shilly-shally in the face
Of fascist strutters with no case.

Those who are not concerned don't know
The complications that must flow
If private-owners anywhere
Falter, and folks like me get there.

ALBERT BROWN

Almeria

A dish for the Bishop, a dish that's well-kneaded and
   bitter,
A dish made of iron-ends, ashes, a dishful of tears,
A dish overflowing with sobbing and walls that have
   fallen,
A dish for the Bishop, a platter of blood – Almeria.

A dish for the Banker, a dish that's contrived from the
   cheeks
Of the happy South's children, a bowl of
Explosions, crazed waters, of ruins and terror,
A dish of smashed axles, a dish of heads trampled on,
A black dish, a tray of blood for him – Almeria.

Each noon, each turbid morning of your lives
Pungent it glows and faces you on table,
Push it away a touch with *soigne* hands,
The sight offends, digestion is not able . . .
Let it stand awhile between the bread and the grapes
   there!
This dish of silent blood that
Will be there every morning, each, every
Morning.

379

19   A dish for the Colonel, a dish for the *frau* of the Colonel,
At the fete in the barracks, a dish at every banquet
    there,
Nobler than oaths or spittle, under that light of
    morning
Sharp as wine and cold over the world, behold it, you,
    trembling.

Yes, a dish for the lot of you, the rich of the whole
    earth,
Ambassadors, ministers, guests in abominable assembly,
Aristocrats, landowners, writers labelled *neutrality*,
Ladies of tea-room and of divan ease –
A dish of destruction, befouled with the blood of the
    poor,
Every noon, every week, for ever and ever from now on,
Before you, a dishful of blood – Almeria – for ever.

PABLO NERUDA
(*Translated from the Spanish by Nancy Cunard*)

They Got What They Wanted

'This great meeting ... expresses its earnest hope ... that the
Nationalist cause will gain an early triumph for unity, order, liberty
and religious freedom.' – Friends of National Spain, Queen's Hall,
23 March 1938.

The friends of Nationalist Spain
Who prayed for Franco's settlement
Regardless of material gain,
With Spain's well-being well content,
At last may publicly rejoice
Her good old order is restored;
Her people have declared their choice –
And friendship is its own reward.

Though Nazi Party enterprise
Will British interests displace,
Though legionaries mobilise
In bristling camp and beetling base,
Though Franco dam the stream of trade
His friends still give their glad accord –
Armed intervention must be paid
But friendship is its own reward.

The extirpation of the Red
The victor of all blame acquits
Who saved the day for Christ instead
With Heinkels, Fiats and Messerschmidts.
Where liberty and faith return
Mere business claims may be ignored
So British friends of Franco learn
That friendship is its own reward.

SAGITTARIUS

To a Certain Priest

'I have no time for you,' this preacher said,
And turned his pen to propagating lies.
About war's victims, and the martyred dead
He wrote with gusto vile; and closed his eyes
On Guernica and bloody Badajoz,
On you, Madrid, Life's glorious capital:
He wrote for tyranny, ignoring truth,
And praised to Heaven Franco's Fascist Hell.

God, in that day when every proof is read,
Show all thy charity to this poor priest
Who basely wore the livery of thy Son:
Thy mercy on the traitor's tonsured head,
Who heaped his cruel message on thy least,
And served the rich, and knew it, and sinned on.

STANLEY RICHARDSON

Analogy in Madrid

Christ brings a sword, the Archbishop said.
The wide jaws of the newly dead
And their appearance of surprise
Testify this. From innocent skies

Out of wind's mouth or sun's breath
Came the most high, the triple death
And with its omnipresent purr
Drew out the thirsty listener.

Thirsty still, under jungle law
The deer dies under the striped death's paw;
And who can be sure of the ways of the Lord?
Both Christ and Franco carry a sword.

ELISABETH CLUER

Ship for Spain

'I had a ship,' the captain said,
'A ship that sailed for Spain,
And if I had that ship right now
I'd sail there once again.

'I'd take a story with me then
And let the people know
In Barcelona why their bread
Is fathoms deep below.

'With my own lips I'd to them say:
The English people true

Want you to hold against the foe,
But it's more than the Government do.

'Any fool with eyes could see
When the planes swept over low
They didn't give a damn for the Union Jack
Spread out across the bow.

'And why don't they care for the English flag
And the rules of the bloody game?
Because they know that Chamberlain
Has traded the English name.

'Has traded the name to the Japanese,
Licked Mussolini's boots,
Let Hitler get hold of the Austrian lands
For you doesn't care two hoots.

'We sent a wire when we got to land,
And in Parliament next day,
Franco's lackey got up and said
We just went there for our pay.

'These are the taunts we have to bear
From the traitors we've got at home,
From the traitors who sullied the English name
And played second fiddle to Rome.

'I had a ship,' the captain said,
'A ship that sailed for Spain,
And when I get another ship
I'll sail there once again.'

HERBERT L. PEACOCK

Down the Road

My letter reached the girl on holiday,
She read it walking down a seaside lane
And felt, instead of me being far away
She walked with me in Spain.

Next walk I took, I fancied she was there,
'You don't hear birds,' I said. 'You may hear shells.
The one that misses us hits someone else,
And now and then it hits him fair and square.

'There's one beside the highway further on,
I saw it happen, and got a cursing, too,
Because I told his pal the man was through.

'There wasn't anything he could have done.
Why, the man's blood was thickening on the ground,
The grey had reached his face, and when he spoke
There wasn't any sound.

'Death on an English country road seems huge,
One sight would spoil your holiday,' I said.
'But here one doesn't let one's feelings loose
Even when a man one knew and liked is dead.

'One murder, and all England makes a fuss;
God knows, one cigarette means more to us.
War's crude, oh sure.
But you can tell the smug ones over there
Another hair's breadth, it'll be the same
To walk in England as to walk in Spain.'

MILES TOMALIN

(*Written in Spain, 1938*)

384

The Victors

They that with torches
Ravening the skies
Delineate the darkness
And intensify the night with cries

They whose breath parches
The growth of pity
Whose rootless, ruthless dust
Chokes with death the sewers of the city

Whose triumphal marches
Echo desolate
In empty market places
And widows' hearts. What is their fate?

Where famine forges
Their lurid friendless fame,
Their monument is hatred
And anger still perpetuates their name.

REDMAYNE FITZGERALD

Ballyseedy Befriends Badajoz [1]

O'Duffy's dupes are killing as their Fascist masters bid.
Gas bombs are falling on the Mothers of Madrid.
(The birds at Ballyseedy picked flesh from off the stones
And Spanish suns at Badajoz are bleaching baby bones.)
God, they claim, is Fascist – The voice that Pilate feared
Is spitting streams of hellish hate from a Moorish soldier's
  beard!

They use the Cross of Calvary to veil their foul designs.
'Vivat Hispania' the voice of Hitler whines.
Vivat Hispania, but not as they would ask:
'Defend our Young Republic' cries out the sturdy Basque.
'Tis the Crescent not the Sickle is looming over Spain,
But the servants of Mohammed will sate their lust in vain.
The hireling hordes of Italy that come with ev'ry tide
Will conquer proud Iberia when all her sons have died.
O'Duffy calls his 'godly band' and leads them to the fray.
(They murdered Liam Mellows upon *Our Lady's Day*.)

God help you! Spanish 'Connollys', if Lombard–Murphy's
    crew
Should blood their drunken hellhounds and send them after
    you!
Our lanes are marked with wayside cross to trace their bloody
    trail,
While other lie in quicklime pit in ev'ry Irish gaol.
They cant of Salamanca, our Irish Pharisees;
'Tis the flag of black reaction they flaunt upon the breeze.
They hope to lure out Irish youth to learn their murder trade
And bring them back to Ireland as a Fascist Shock Brigade.
They talk of Hearth and Altar as the things that they defend.
(Which means in Fascist lingo the sweater's dividend.)
O'Duffy crowned Dictator 'midst the rolling of the drums
And the fools that listened to him are rotting in the Slums!

SOMHAIRLE MACALASTAIR

1. Press reports state that the advance guard of General O'Duffy's
Blueshirt column has sailed to fight for the Spanish rebel, General Franco.
Ballyseedy, in Kerry, was the scene of a savage massacre of Republicans
by Free State soldiers.

Arms in Spain

So that men might remain slaves, and that the little good
they hoped for might be turned all bad and the iron lie
stamped and clamped on growing tender and vigorous
    truth
4   these machine guns were despatched from Italy.

So that the drunken General and the Christian millionaire
might continue blindly to rule in complete darkness,
that on rape and ruin order might be founded firm,
these guns were sent to save civilisation.

Lest the hand should be held at last more valuable than
    paper,
lest man's body and mind should be counted more than
    gold,
lest love should blossom, not shells, and break in the land
12   these machine guns came from Christian Italy.

And to root out reason, lest hope be held in it,
to turn love inward into corroding hate,
lest men should be men, for the bank-notes and the
    mystery
 these guns, these tanks, these gentlemanly words.

REX WARNER

Battle Song of 'Irish Christian Front' :
'Off to Salamanca'

My name is Owen O'Duffy,
And I'm rather vain and huffy.
The side of every Bolshie I'm a thorn in.

But before the break of day,
I'll be marching right away,
For I'm off to Salamanca in the morning.

Chorus:
With the gold supplied by Vickers,
I can buy Blue Shirt and knickers,
Let the Barcelona Bolshies take a warning.
For I lately took the notion,
To cross the briny ocean
And I start for Salamanca in the morning.

There's a boy called Paddy Belton,
With a heart that's soft and meltin',
Yet the first to face the foemen, danger scorning,
Tho' his feet are full of bunions,
Yet he knows his Spanish onions,
And he's off to Salamanca in the morning.

Now the 'Irish Christian Front',
Is a Lombard-Murphy stunt.
(Hark! the ghostly voice of Connolly gives warning)
And Professor Hogan's pals,
Can don their fal-de-lals
And start for Salamanca in the morning.

When they get kicked out of Spain,
And they travel home again,
Let them hearken in good time to this, our warning.
If they try their Fascist game,
They'll be sorry that they came
Back from Salamanca in the morning.

SOMHAIRLE MACALASTAIR

THAT FIGHTING WAS A LONG WAY OFF

(From Bernard Spencer, 'A Thousand Killed')

A Thousand Killed

I read of a thousand killed.
And am glad because the scrounging imperial paw
Was there so bitten:
As a man at elections is thrilled
When the results pour in, and the North goes with him
And the West breaks in the thaw.

(That fighting was a long way off.)

Forgetting therefore an election
Being fought with votes and lies and catch-cries
And orators' frowns and flowers and posters' noise,
Is paid for with cheques and toys:
Wars the most glorious
Victory-winged and steeple-uproarious
. . . With the lives, burned-off,
Of young men and boys.

BERNARD SPENCER

Grief's Reflection

In the Cretan winding of the brain,
Finding my way by the dropped thread
From the present world driven insane
To the sanity of the dead,
I grew callous toward the slain,
The millions mutilated,
The maimed children of China and Spain,
Fugitive, stricken dumb,
And the generation to come
Warped in the womb.

I turned from this reality
And looked in Ariadne's loom,
Map of the labyrinth, the grey
Corridors of time and thought
Where the past looks like the Bull.

And what I saw was beautiful;
An old death, a brother dying,
His music at that moment wrought
And frozen, and falling silently,
Snowy sound, and the storm done,
Covering a vanished day,
For a white eternity
Settled there, for ever lying.

What might this be, I wondered,
Since no man might condone
My craven flight into the past,
The responsibility pondered
And dropped, the retreat alone,
The seeking of a private grief
In the brain's labyrinthine path,
Snatching therefrom some relief
From today's universal wrath?

But there's no answer! No, none!
The gentle loss, the musician dying,
Holding a brother's hand, my hand,
Sweet life resigning with a sigh;
All this, forgotten for so long
Or recalled like an old song,
Is now a stabbing agony!
And in response I have lost sight
Of our immediate grief, the lost
Millions in this European night
Of tyranny and holocaust.

RICHARD CHURCH

The Tourist Looks at Spain

Is it anything like sea, Spain, above your body?
   Are limbs and eyes distorted,
hair plucked, and features magnified by water
and flood of war? Is what is real drowned?

All cupolas, all storks, all holy virgins,
   curious uniforms, oranges,
what every tourist knows, both the flowers and the dancing,
pompous processions are dim as seen through gauze.

And is that the face and image of our living,
   what is cosy, queer, or lovely?
Was the walk wonderful? Was the stolen kiss perfection?
Was what we saw the thing, or do we see it now?

All those of us who loved, who read the classics,
   who were pleased when with friends,
who enjoyed nature or drinking, had views on life,
followers of football, holding up the mirror;

and those who believed in miracles or in understanding,
   who had dignity in some profession,
who read the daily papers, whose eyes were honest,
who deplored disaster, holding up the mirror,

holding the mirror see what we did not think,
   see sierras indistinct,
see something like sea over the comfortable scene,
hear hiss of water and find the whole view moving.

What we saw dead was all the time alive,
   and what we see is living.
It is over our own eyes that the mist holds.
Say clearly: Spain has torn the veil of Europe.

Truth stared the untrained mind in the face. Courage
    came through the drawn veil.
The emotional, the stolid, the frank, the suspicious,
hear what the people say who speak in deeds.

Hear what they say who came from farm and factory,
    the few-weeks soldiers slain
or kept in the cruel wire, for fear and fury,
the tragic joke or abject surrender of the cracked nerve:

'The comfortable doctrine is now open war.
    Christ is crowned with bombs.
The most saintly have become noted for their lies.
They have wept and handed out the guns for slaughter.

'It is against mankind those guns are loaded.
    Slowly and subtly the defenders
of saint and artist king and religious leader
changed, and in our time have become the aggressors.

'What was their truth became our poison. Their love
    is aimed at man's destruction.
But our hate is love, and even our inaccuracies
are nearer truth than their finest syllogisms.

'Late and at last we knew hope, heard like the wind
    that blows the dust and grasses
the same words spoken by many different voices:
"There is a world to win: we know the oppressors."

'Not the long hands that fingered the fearful mystery,
    not the bland and soothing voices
can bring us peace, nor the roar and rant of bullies
declare decision or disguise the ferret's temper.

'It is we who feel future flowing in our veins,
    the past and the pressing present:
what was stifled stirs: what was hoped is in our hands:
what betrayed in the dark is now the desperate visible foe.

'What we have of the frayed nerve, hate, and the poor abandon,
    stupidity, vanity, cunning,
taking fire, fusing, fixing to the correct end
have become more estimable than our foes' best manners.

'It is the aim that is right and the end is freedom.
    In Spain the veil is torn.
In Spain is Europe. England also is in Spain.
There the sea recedes and there the mirror is no longer blurred.'

9 Listen. Look. There is nothing at all like sea
    on Spain's real face.
It is rather around us that the mist is clinging,
and our oldest landmarks that have become a veil.

See in the mirror rather our most holy buildings,
    our smoothest kindest words,
our most successful pageantry, our parades
as trash and blots and blurs on the moving truth.

Behind the solemn sentence, and behind the grin
    of the dressed peace-maker.
behind the eyes that are pasted to what is venerable
the rat-mask waits and odour of what has long gone sour.

War without heralds is waged now and in our boundaries.
    It is peace that is pretended.
Chiefly on Spain light falls, but in the ambient dark
already are creeping the same aggressors from their misty
        towers.

Not for many years now will love be guiltless,
    or boating or autumn leaves.
The tense communion of sympathy with panic,
and indignation will replace the promenade.

See Spain and see the world. Freedom extends
    or contracts in all hearts.
Near Bilbao are buried the vanguard of our army.
It is us too they defended who defended Madrid.

                                              REX WARNER

Looking at a Map of Spain
on the Devon Coast (*August, 1937*)

The waves that break and rumble on the sands
gleaming outside my window, break on Spain.
Southward I look and only the quick waves stretch
between my eyes and ravaged Santander moaning
with many winds of death, great blackening blasts
of devastation and little alley-whispers
where forgotten children die.

The map of Spain
bleeds under my fingers, cracked with rivers
of unceasing tears, and scraped with desolation,
and valleyed with these moaning winds of death.
Aragon I touch, Castilla, and Asturias.
The printed words black on the small white page
wavers like mountains on the expanse of day.
They ring me round, sierras of history
granite above time's stream with human meanings
that make the stars a tinsel and the thundering
waves on the rattled beach a trivial echo
     of their tremendous wars.
I lean towards Spain over the sundering waters.

The brittle mask has broken, the money-mask
that hid the jackal-jaws, the mask of fear
that twisted the tender face of love; and eyes
now look on naked eyes. The map of Spain
seethes with the truth of things, no longer closed
in greed's geography, an abstract space
of imports, exports, capitalist statistics,
the jargon record of a tyrannous bargain.
The scroll of injustice, the sheet of paper is torn,
and behind the demolished surface of the lie

the Spanish people are seen with resolute faces.
They break the dark grilles
on custom's stuccoed wall
and come into the open.

In the city-square the rags of bodies lie
like refuse after death's careless fiesta.
Sandbags are piled across
the tramlines of routine,
A bullet has gone through the townhall clock,
the hands of official time are stopped.
New clocks for the Spanish people:
New springs and cogwheels for the Time of Freedom.
The garotting machines are snatched
out of the chests of old darkness
and strung between lamp-post and balcony
in the streets of sunlight in Barcelona.
My friend is holding the cartridge-belt, the gun
is trained on the corner, the turn in the dark street,
round which the Fascists will come.
The noticeboard of the People's University
is nailed above the church's door of stone
over the face of the Virgin in the shrine.
New clocks for the Spanish people:
New springs and cogwheels for the Time of Freedom.

These images slip through the mesh. They flush
the superficial map with hints
of what the tumult means.
You girls in overalls with young breasts of pride
bearing the great banner down the street
your pulse accords with the day's terrific cymbals.
You militiaman leaning
beside the soup-cauldrons on the ridge of stones
and bushes flickering with heat, your hands
speak of the sickle and hammer, and the rifle
you hold in such a way

breaks to a cornsheaf in your dreaming hour
deep-rooted in Spanish earth, because you love
that girl with flower-eyes and breasts of milk
lifted with promise on the day of work
like olive-trees tousled silver under the wind.
The old man choking among the thistles
by the peaked windmill with the lattice-wings
has spoken a curse. The child blindly crying
down lanes of terror in the endless night
of bursting faces, and the mother riddled
with rape on the dungheap, and the friend
who smiled at you yesterday
now crucified on the garden-wall,
litter these names. Oh, watch the map of Spain
and you can see the sodden earth of pain,
the least blood-trickle on the broken face,
and hear the clutter of the trucks that bring
the moorish firing-squad along the village street,
and through the frantic storm of shattering guns
the child's small wail. You hear it in your heart,
louder than all the roaring. An accusation
that shall be answered.

And louder too than all the hell of war
clanging over the tiles or the hilltops-hoarse
with raiding planes, there sounds the pulse of work,
the hum of factories in communal day.
The girl with the cap of liberty at the loom
weaves the fate of Spain,
the web of brotherhood on the warp of courage.
The factory-windows crimson with the sunset
flash signals to the fields of toil;
the slow echelon of sickles
advance upon the wheat. Now in the battle
the Spanish workers ride
the horses of the year, wild mountain-horses,
tamed to draw the plough of man.
Hear the confederate engines throb

the belts whirr and the hammers of power leap thudding,
to bring about at last the generous hour
when man and nature mate in plenty's bed.

Oh, Map of Spain creviced with countless graves,
even now, even now, the storm of murder comes.
The burning face of day is blind with tears.
I stand at the atlantic edge and look
southwards and raise my hand to Spain. Salute.

JACK LINDSAY

A Cold Night

Thick wool is muslin tonight, and the wire
Wind scorches stone-cold colder. Boys
Tremble at counters of shops. The world
Gets lopped at the radius of my fire.

Only for a moment I think of those
Whom the weather leans on under the sky;
Newsmen with placards by the river's skirt,
Stamping, or with their crouching pose,

The whores; the soldiery who lie
Round wounded Madrid; those of less hurt
Who cross that bridge I crossed today
Where the waves snap white as broken plates

And the criss-cross girders hammer a grill
Through which, instead of flames, wind hates.

I turn back to my fire. Which I must.
I am not God or a crazed woman.
And one needs time too to sit in peace
Opposite one's girl, with food, fire, light,

And do the work one's own blood heats,
Or talk, and forget about the winter
– This season, this century – and not be always
Opening one's doors on the pitiful streets

Of Europe, not always think of winter, winter, like a hammering
    rhyme
For then everything is drowned by the rising wind, everything is
    done against Time.

BERNARD SPENCER

Cold in England

It's bitterly cold in England today
And I crouch over a heaped-up fire and still
Can't get warm.

Over there in that front line held by a miracle
An army shaped by a people's will,
Crucible-tested,
Faces, with stern but hungry jaws,
Well-fed, well-clothed barbarians,
And shivers – with cold, not fear . . .
Somebody opens a door and the icy wind
Cuts through the room and the razor-thrusts my back,
Can't get warm.

Over there they will jump out of bed tonight
– They are hungry, had no supper before they lay down –
They will put on those summer frocks and hide underground
They will be cold with the gnawing cold of ill-clad hunger,
Before they are cold with the peaceful cold of sudden death
Sent from the sky by the well-fed barbarians.

Shall I ever get warm again?
Can I ever be warm again?

400

Not till my comrades and I
Have sent that foodship,
Sent those clothes,
To carry warmth,
Warmth of body,
And the rich warmth of comradeship,
Warmth.

It's bitterly cold in England today,
And I crouch over a heaped-up fire and still
Can't get warm.

H. M. KING

Fata Morgana

While those were on the march to their desires
Through painful brilliance of Iberian day
These arguing remained by their homefires
Still living in the old, unhealthy way.

I

I have experienced little in the past
That can entitle me to reconcile
The haven of a rentier indolence
With theories that I have endured the worst.

Books, idle books, and hours, unfruitful hours,
Weigh on my genius and lay waste my will,
While heavenly wings are without power to raise
Me from beneath the stone with which they kill.

The younger ones do better on the whole,
They still are free, they lie with whom they please,
There is no good in living on my dole
And leaving freedom, with its price, to these.

Stupidity, preservative of honour,
And idleness, the crowning joy of home,
Incompetence, a woman's highest favour,
I know that they will try to suck me down.

But I, who have no words, nor heart, nor name,
Can still suppose how it would feel to march
Guided by stars along the roads of Spain
Because of what I learn, but cannot teach.

Can words invent gorillas, sweats, and murders?
Can breaths of local breezes set us free?
Or the great tempest of invading soldiers
Redeem us from our own captivity?

II

Is it a rape, when God begets in virgin
A pure allhallowed embryo, himself?
Is it forbidden tree for us to sin?
Sin! with the tempter at the source of life?

And can a woman still be heaven's chosen?
Impartial planets bear the godly names;
And I, unstable as the changeless ocean
Cannot resist the places and the times.

I have had beauty, children, home and friends,
Culture and snobbery and food and wine,
And all are wasted in pursuit of ends
That others urged, but were no ends of mine.

But even now reproaching stars can sound
From death's horizon into which they dive
And the hated northern seas resound
Upon the pebbly shore, provincial grief.

Oh was it I who found the earth still green?
And was it I in natural rapture went

A child that saw and yet was never seen
Through days with privacy and wisdom spent?

Now far away from there, music, in vain
Travels the railway journey to my brain.
The sleepers are so numerous and so old
I do not try to count them from the train.

Oh railway journey to the holy wells,
O train, where somewhere I will find my love,
Oh many doors, partitions, stops and cells,
Give way for me, and make me force to move.

III

Last night as I was marching on the road
That leads my unknown comrades to the wars
I was more free and happy as I trod
White dust between the dark and shadeless trees.

There was a village with no people left
It was like England, but it was in Spain,
The awnings were in ribbons on their posts,
We paused to look, and then marched on again.

The villagers had learned to know defeat,
We were not sure that vengeance could prevail.
The enemy was safe in his retreat,
And our advance was pretty sure to fail.

Did I then hope to reason with the guns?
Or did I hope to pass the bullets by?
And did I pity the old men whose sons
Upon the white plains are about to die?

No, I had fear enough to keep me silent
And hope that soon the face of things might change.
It was an ordinary and dull event
To shorten mile by mile the rifle's range.

I am no longer, alas, a charmed life,
One whom the gods will favour, ill can spare,
But target for the bullet and the knife
Like any other soldier, wolf, or hare.

Yet it was brave to keep our secrets close
That we had once had egoism to lose.
We swallowed back our pride, obeying orders
From leaders that in wiser days we chose.

It is remarkable to dream so much
And yet wake up to spend another day
With all the people I can only touch
With tales of long ago and far away.

KATHLEEN RAINE

The News

A jazz-band fades; and stops.
Silence – until
A voice, with measured, calm indifference
Proclaims today's events: –
'Madrid . . .
'Nothing unusual to report . . .
'The self-same contradictions . . .
'The rebels claim . . .
'The Government . . .'
Switch off! There's nothing in the news tonight.
God! Life is dull!

A worker in the night
Cold, wet and hunger-grey,
Clutching his rifle,
Peers through the rain
With only one dull thought –

To hold the Fascist dogs
At bay.

Five hundred yards away
Another such as he,
Clasping his rifle with numbed hands,
Damns the grim enemy in front;
And sees behind – a grey wall,
And the rifles raised.

What if these two
Should lay their fears aside?
And creep across the night
And grip each other's hand?
There would be neither rain,
Nor cold, nor anything that mattered then,
In all the land.

Just, NEWS –
A jazz-band stuttering, stopped –
An anxious lull –
Then, calm and strong and clear,
A worker's voice
Sweet in your ear – 'Comrades . . .'
Would you still sit, and poke the fire,
And mutter that the world was dull?

HANS HAFLIN

Poem

He awoke from dreams of the fortunate isles,
waters heavy with unaccustomed fish,
olive and cyprus down the exciting bank
and phallic sneers in harbour lights;
it was day already, the morning roll
fresh on the plate, the paper folded.

Where are those isles? Oh, the war in Spain,
and torrents waiting to fall from the sky;
the pressed trousers and the perfect part
in the thin hair of the a.m nuisance.
All the blonde typists with hot legs
and minds like turkeys, birds with mean eyes.

Lower the sky to spire, the church to rot,
let the bell ring the fat to warm bath,
draped bone and muscular impotence reborn
in the Monday world without end. O white
gangrene of certainty like the dead park,
all the embittered foliage of peace.

EDGAR FOXALL

In September

Coming, in September, through the thin streets,
I thought back to another year I knew,
Autumn, lifting potatoes and stacking peats
On Mull, while the Atlantic's murky blue
Swung sluggishly in past Jura, and the hills
Were brown lions, crouched to meet the autumn gales.

In the hard rain and the rip of thunder,
I remembered the haze coming in from the sea
And the clatter of Gaelic voices by the breakwater
Or in the fields as the reapers took their tea;
I remembered the cast foal lying where it died,
Which we buried, one evening, above high-tide;

And the three rams that smashed the fank-gate,
Running loose for five days on the moor
Before we could catch them – far too late
To prevent an early lambing the next year.

But these seemed out of place beside the chip-shop
And the cockney voices grumbling in the pub.

In September, I saw the drab newsposters
Telling of wars, in Spain and in the East,
And wished I'd stayed on Mull, their gestures
Frightened me and made me feel the unwanted guest.
The burden on the house who having taken salt
Could never be ejected, however grave his fault.

In September, we lit the fire and talked together,
Discussing the trivialities of a spent day
And what we would eat. I forgot the weather
And the dull streets and the sun on Islay,
And all my fear. I lost my carefully-kept count
Of the ticks to death, and, in September, was content.

RUTHVEN TODD

Poem (For C.C.)

Here, in this quiet spot, apart
From the turmoil of Europe,
The flurried engine's noisy start
And the bomb smashing hope;
I sit still and think now of you,
Measuring river's pearl against sea's blue;

Think of the sun's glare
And twisted cactus plant
Against this grey and heavy air
And a mast's indolent slant;
Wish I were where you are, or you here,
To stop these minutes tapping at my ear.

THAT FIGHTING WAS A LONG WAY OFF

I wait the morning paper –
How many killed in Spain?
Yet now, before the deeper
Knowledge of pain,
I give you the minutes of this hour;
All that I have, so treasure them, my dear.

RUTHVEN TODD

PHOTOGENIC WAR

('A complacent ass who was, temporarily, Propaganda
Minister of Catalonia, said to me: "This is the most
photogenic war anyone ever has seen".' Claud Cockburn,
In Time of Trouble: An Autobiography (1956), p. 252.)

Newsreel

Enter the dream-house, brothers and sisters, leaving
Your debts asleep, your history at the door:
This is the home for heroes, and this loving
4   Darkness a fur you can afford.

Fish in their tank electrically heated
Nose without envy the glass wall: for them
Clerk, spy, nurse, killer, prince, the great and the defeated,
Move in a mute day-dream.

9   Bathed in this common source, you gape incurious
At what your active hours have willed –
Sleep-walking on that silver wall, the furious
Sick shapes and pregnant fancies of your world.

There is the mayor opening the oyster season:
A society wedding: the autumn hats look swell:
An old crocks' race, and a politician
In fishing-waders to prove that all is well.

Oh, look at the warplanes! Screaming hysteric treble
In the long power-dive, like gannets they fall steep.
But what are they to trouble –
These silver shadows to trouble your watery, womb-deep
    sleep?

See the big guns, rising, groping, erected
To plant death in your world's soft womb.
Fire-bud, smoke-blossom, iron seed projected –
Are these exotics? They will grow nearer home:

Grow nearer home – and out of the dream-house stumbling
One night into a strangling air and the flung
Rags of children and thunder of stone niagaras tumbling,
You'll know you slept too long.

C. DAY LEWIS

'Spanish Earth'

Now we can walk into the picture easily
To be the unknown hero and the death;
We who have watched these things as stunts
And held our startled breath.

In Hampshire or in Yorkshire these same moving arms
Like pendulums across the marching fours
Are lifted, work; they will not wait;
Death does not make them pause.

Eyes are another signature of Spanish death.
This evening in the cinema will kill
This man we watch direct his troops;
A man whose eyes are still

Searching the landscape for his dying countrymen
In buildings burning fast as celluloid,
Impotent here in the empty city
Italian bombs destroyed.

Over the mud I have watched the broken wild duck
Chucked down from the railing wind. Now I climb
Memory as from Norfolk swamps
And wars and wars fill time –

Destroying all the countries, all the incidents
Clasped in my childhood's wishes like my toys
And present past and future seem
These marching, dying boys.

Perhaps we shall be killed: there is no life secure.
Yet they want so little, water for crops,
Schools for the children, hospitals.
The shooting never stops.

BERNARD GUTTERIDGE

War Photograph

1 I have an appointment with a bullet
At seventeen hours less a split second
3 – And I shall not be late.

Where the sun strikes the rock and
The rock plants its shadowed foot
6 And the breeze distracts the grass and fern frond.

There, in the frond, the instant lurks
With its metal fang planned for my heart
When the finger tugs and the clock strikes.

I am that numeral which the sun regards,
The flat and severed second on which time looks,
My corpse a photograph taken by fate;

Where inch and instant cross, I shall remain
As faithful to the vanished moment's violence
As love fixed to one day in vain.

16 Only the world changes and time its tense
17 Against the creeping inches of whose moon,
I launch my wooden continual present.

The grass will grow its summer beard and beams
Of light melt down the waxen slumber
Where soldiers lie dead in an iron dream;

22 My corpse be covered with the snow's December
And roots push through skin's silent drum
When the years and fields forget, but the whitened bones
  remember.

STEPHEN SPENDER

In September 1939

The last war was my favourite picture story.
2   *Illustrated London News* bound in the study;
3   The German bayonet we believed still bloody

But was just rusty. Privacy of death.
My uncle's uniform meant more than glory;
Surprise that grief should be so transitory . . .

All the predictions of adolescence had
8   Disposed of glory in their realist path:
9   There'd be no need to duck and hold your breath.

10   Now, looking as useless and as beautiful
As dragonflies, the plump silver balloons
12   Hang over London also like zany moons.

13   Yet from the blacked-out window death still seems
Private, not an affair that's shared by all
The distant people, the flats, the Town Hall.

But some remember Spain and the black spots
They shouted 'Bombers' at. That memory screams
That we know as a film or in bad dreams.

Fear will alight on each like a dunce's cap
Or an unguessed disease unless death drops
Quicker than the sirens or the traffic stops.

BERNARD GUTTERIDGE

Pictures in Spain

Before we left Minglanilla – a village between Valencia and Madrid, where we were banqueted and, after the banquet, danced to by the children whilst the women without their men stood round weeping – a woman took me to her house, showed me photographs of her two sons, both on the Madrid front, and insisted on giving me half a dozen sausages, about half of all she had, because she felt certain that I would be hungry before we reached Madrid. Then we of the International Writers' Congress got into our cars, and, as my car waited for the 'caravan' to start, one old beggar woman pressed forward from the crowd to ask me for some money. I was about to give her a few coppers when a boy leapt forward and exclaimed, with a passionate gesture, 'No, no, give her nothing. The Spanish people do not accept charity.'

This little incident lives in my mind with several others which go to impress on me what I can only call the seriousness of the people's movement in Spain. Another is my surprise when I saw for myself that the University City – with the Government buildings only separated from those taken by the rebels by yards – is still used as a place of learning, for in half-ruined class rooms, their walls perforated with bullets, the soldiers attend classes.

The welcome given to the International Writers' Congress, by the people of small villages, by soldiers in the trenches, by a deputation of tramway workers in Madrid, by the common people in the streets, in *cafés*, in barber shops, in bars, if they happened to realize that one was a member of the Congress, were all signs that the Spanish people have acquired that passion for education and popular culture which goes with a fundamental revolutionary change in a nation's life. It was our good fortune to symbolize popular culture for them, and this explains the great welcome which we received.

To me, perhaps the strangest of my impressions of Madrid was that of the interior of a great and massively built church on the outskirts of the city – looking over, I think, that part of the front which is called the Caso del Campo – where a vast collection of treasures from the palaces and churches of Madrid has been collected. The domed, gloomy, vast interior of the church, with its congregation of royal coaches, rood screens, crucifixes, candelabras, tapestries, ceramics, was like a meeting of all the centuries in a solemn fancy-dress ball, not of people but of objects. Our little party from the Congress walked round, feeling as out of place as a member of the audience on a stage set. We made M. Julien Benda sit in a royal coach, which suited him well, M. Egon Kisch looked handsome in an eighteenth-century wig, but apart from these courageous isolated attempts we did not succeed in adapting ourselves to our surroundings. Myself, I made no attempt to take the plunge back into the past. On the contrary, I thought in terms of making films of these stage properties, particularly one propaganda film, to show that the Republic cares for Spain's art treasures.

In this church all the lesser works of art from the palaces and churches of Madrid have been collected. Along the passages, in vaults and in chapels, there were placed thousands of canvases, a varied and unequal collection of ceramics, ivory crucifixes, antique watches, jewelry, fans, and in one vault so many images of saints that we could only make our way through them along the narrow gangway which they had discreetly left. Our guide explained that this vault had been the home of what Franco refers to as the 'Quinta Columna' of his allies in Madrid. But some of the French writers lifted their fists in vigorous response to one Saint Anthony, whose clenched hand was raised in an eternal '*Salud*'. There are traitors in both camps.

Everything in this collection was catalogued, giving the name of the palace or church from which it was taken, as well as its number in the depositary. Among the pictures catalogued here and in the cellars of Madrid, taken from private collections, are 27 Grecos, 8 Rubens, 13 Zurbaranes, 51 Goyas, 9 Titians, 6 Tintorettos, 6 Tiepolos, &c. Many pictures and many valuable first editions and manuscripts have now been brought to light for the first time.

Other pictures and treasures are in bomb-proof and damp-proof cellars of Madrid. The pictures from the Prado are in the vaults and cellars of Valencia, each of them packed so as to protect it from the damp. I was assured by members of the Government that nothing from these collections has been destroyed or (as has been said) given to the Russian Government in exchange for aeroplanes. The only pictures going abroad are those lent to Paris for the Exhibition of Spanish Art. I saw some of the pictures that are soon to be shown in Paris in the chapel of a seminary at Valencia. The chapel itself was strongly built, but the main arches under which the pictures lay in packing cases had been further strengthened by piles of sandbags placed above pillars of reinforced concrete.

It is true that at the beginning of the Civil War anarchists burned churches and buildings in Spain which they saw not as things of beauty but as symbols of tyranny and superstition. Yet even in these early days, they removed and collected the treasures of art from the churches, which have been saved. Maria Therésa Lèon, the wife of the great poet Rafael Alberti, told me that when the Government made an appeal that art treasures should be saved, they were embarrassed by the quantity of stuff, some of it good, some trash, which was brought to them. Naïvely and eagerly the people look on the art treasures of Spain as their own heritage. The spirit in which, during a terrible siege, under bombardments, in a time of penury and hunger, the Junta del Tesoro Artístico in Madrid collected and arranged and catalogued meticulously the objects which we saw in that great church shows the same seriousness as that of the boy who passionately forbade me to give money to a beggar, as that of the women in Minganilla who received us with tears and asked one of us to speak to them in Spanish, just to show that we understood their fate (*suerte*). A people who speak in the language of war and armaments are looking ahead a month, perhaps a year, to victory. But a people who educate the soldiers in the trenches, who collect the art treasures of the nation because they have become the concern of the whole democracy, are looking forward not a month or a year, but to a future in which whole generations are liberated not by guns, but by the great tradition of Spanish painting and literature.

STEPHEN SPENDER

Picasso : for Guernica

Frozen in the fright of light chilled skull and spine
Drip bone-shriek-splinters sharper than the Bren:
Starve franco stroke and stave the hooves of bulls.
I am the arm thrust candle through the wall.

Up cities crack firelaughter, the furious
Minutes and bark a ruin at man in
His sealoneliness; hair rearing finrays.
I am the spinning coil distilled eyes' iron.

Neigh horse terror through steel teeth and a thicket
Of bricks! Beam an eyebomb, cellar, and stride
Nerve, peeled pupil's enamel, rhomboid head!
I am the tiled blind hand plunged bulb in socket.

Splint for the shriven shin, I foster mantrump out
Of festered history; sprout pointed fingers
Where an afterbirth is dung-and-rubble-teat.
I am the eyeball blown world! Axis of anger!

J. F. HENDRY

Guernica

Picasso's *Guernica*, at the New Burlington Gallery

André Gide writes in *Verve* that *Guernica* fails because it is *excentric*, it breaks away from its centre, or has no centre. Other critics complain that it is neither expressionist nor abstract, but falls between two stools; that it is terrifying without producing any sensation of pity; and so on. All these criticisms are attempts to answer the question whether or not this picture is a great masterpiece. Otherwise, they would not be criticisms at all, but just descriptions, which so far from being *against* it, might well be an account of its merits.

Guernica affects one as an explosion, partly no doubt because it is a picture of an explosion. If one attempts to criticize it, one attempts to relate it to the past. So long as a work of art has this explosive quality of newness it is impossible to relate it to the past. People who say that it is *excentric*, or that it falls between two stools, or that it is too horrible, and so on, are only making the gasping noises they might make if they were blown off their feet by a high-explosive bomb. All I can try to do is to report as faithfully as possible the effect that this very large and very dynamic picture makes on me.

In the first place, it is certainly not realistic in the sense that Goya's etchings of another tragedy in Spain are realistic. *Guernica* is in no sense reportage; it is not a picture of some horror which Picasso has seen and been through himself. It is the picture of a horror reported in the newspapers, of which he has read accounts and perhaps seen photographs.

This kind of second-hand experience, from the newspapers, the news-reel, the wireless, is one of the dominating realities of our time. The many people who are not in direct contact with the disasters falling on civilization live in a waking nightmare of second-hand experiences which in a way are more terrible than real experiences because the person overtaken by a disaster has at least a more limited vision than the camera's wide, cold, recording eye, and at least has no opportunity to imagine horrors worse than what he is seeing and experiencing. The flickering black, white and grey lights of Picasso's picture suggest a moving picture stretched across an elongated screen; the flatness of the shapes again suggests the photographic image, even the reported paper words. The centre of this picture is like a painting of a *collage* in which strips of newspaper have been pasted across the canvas.

The actual figures on the canvas, the balloon-like floating head of a screaming woman; the figure throwing arms up in despair; the woman running forwards, and leaving behind one reluctant, painful, enormous, clumsy leg; the terror of a horse with open mouth and skin drawn back over the teeth; the hand clutching a lamp and the electric lamp glowing so that it shows the wires, as though at any moment the precious light may go out; the groaning bull, the woman clutching her child, a complex of clustered fingers like over-ripe fruit; all this builds up a picture of horror, but to me there is grandeur in the severed arm of a hero lying in the foreground, clutching the noble, broken, ineffective sword with which he has tried to ward off the horrors of mechanical destruction; and there is pity in the leaves of the little plant growing just above this hand.

Picasso uses every device of expressionism, abstractionism and effects learnt from *collage*, to build up the horror of Guernica. Diagonal lines of light and shade in the background, suggest searchlights and confusion, and the violent contrasts of the faces revealed in a very white light suggest the despair of light and darkness in air raids; despair of the darkness because it is too complete and you are lost; despair of the light because it is too complete and you are revealed to the enemy raiders.

The impression made on me by this picture is one that I might equally get from a great masterpiece, or some very vivid experience. That, of course, does not mean that it *is* a masterpiece. I shall be content to wait some years before knowing that. But it is certainly worth seeing. And if you don't like, or resist, or are overwhelmed by explosions, there are the sixty-seven studies for Guernica, some of them quite unlike anything in the picture itself, which are certainly amongst the most beautiful and profound drawings Picasso has ever made.

STEPHEN SPENDER

TALKING BRONCO

A Letter from the San Mateo Front

Against the Bogus prophets of the Day
Chained to Corruption, Failure, and Decay,
What can I do but take the trampled sand,
Diestro by the Rightness of my hand,
Whose opening Palm, of Victory the Sign,
Branched from the mesa with the Bread and Wine,
By the same toil engendered as the grain
With many a million more, the Might of Spain,
With palms of triumph foresting the day
To wave the golden harvest on its way,
Of which strong millions, strictly contraband,
I introduce this sample to a Land
Where all the sweet emoluments are thrown
To that snug, sinister, and bungling drone,
The fist-shut Left, so dextrous with the dirk,
The striker, less in battle than from work:
The weed of Life that grows where air is hot
With 'Meetings' for its aspidistra-plot:
That leaves its labour to the hammering tongue
And grows, a cactus, out of hot-house dung:
A manual head-ache, fastened in a fist,
And fed with fumes of foul carbonic mist:
A vegetable cramp: a bolted clam
Whose grudging doors on life and daylight slam:
The 'No'-to-life translated as 'I Am,'
A Life-constricting tetanus of fingers
Under whose sign an outworn Age malingers,
While from its back the nails eat slowly through,
For communists out-fakir the Hindu,
And hanker for stagnation thrice as vast
Where all must starve beneath the lowest Caste;
The fungus that, by still decaying, grows;
Sleep's Aegis, save when dealing dirty blows;

Like the raised claw-bunch of an ancient stork,
With cork-screwed fingers, as a crumpled fork,
In a rheumatic ecstasy of hate
Clenched at the world, for being born too late;
This weary fist infests the world entire
As common in the palace as the byre,
As limply fungoid in the idle rich
As when it grimly toadstools from a ditch,
Or, friend to every cause that rots or fails,[1]
Presides in Bloomsbury with tinted nails;
As doomed anachronisms, Sire and Son,
Capitalist and communist make one,
The scrawny offspring and the bloated sire
Sentenced by nature to the same hot fire;
So in red Bloomsbury the two are tied
Like gangsters to be taken for a ride –
Smug rebels to Society, the tame
Charaders in a dreary parlour game,
Where breaking crockery gives a lawless thrill
And Buffaloes each smug suburban Bill,
Where the Left Fist will pelt you from the fence,
But when you lift a hand in self-defence,
Although it scorns the bourgeois law and state,
Off to the lawyers takes the broken pate,
And at the first sign of lifted quirt
Will cling his Mother Grundy by the skirt.
From every communist you can unsheath
The snug fat 'bourgeois' creeping underneath,
And every Babbit is a foxes' hole
From which a scrawny 'comrade' snarls for dole!
So in Red Spain they're fighting side by side
By common desperation both allied,
Both indispensable and no more strange
Than the unhealthy hide is to the mange –
But on our side such itches cannot grow
Since, with us, the whole Donkey had to go!

1. 'All we have succeeded in producing is totalitarian State Capitalism instead of Communism.' Lenin.

For though with lies your hearing they belabour
Theirs is the Capital as ours the Labour –
As fat Prieto boasted with a grin
'The Rights are penniless, and cannot win.'[1]
But nature's elements, except for gold,
Will shun the Communist's convulsive hold,
And it's an axiom that mere eyesight yields –
Grass hates to grow on communistic fields!
The plains and valleys fought upon our side
And rivers to our Victory were allied
That (loosed to whelm us and to flood the land)
Were parted like Red Seas on either hand:
Our comrades' blood, still conscious in their veins,
Headed the waves away with curling manes,[2]
And, swerving on both sides to let us free,
Galloped them foaming headlong to the sea –
In death still present, hand upon the reins,
Such friendship links us riders of the plains.
Nor can a clenched left fist create or fight
With the calm patience of the open Right,
Nor help a needy comrade, as we see
Each time they leave their wounded, when they flee,
When to remove their numbers to the rear
Might sow the grey, demoralizing fear.
Yet see this smuggled Right hand that I bring
The lightest feather moulted from the wing
Of our great Victory, spread from star to star,
With thunder-hackled mountains in her car,
Which all the way from Portugal to France
She inspans in her thundering advance,

1. Minister of Defence, Indalecio Prieto. 'We have by far the greater
half of the fleet, all the industrial areas, and superior armaments. But
what is even more to our advantage, the rebels are penniless and we have
Napoleon's three requisites for victory, 'Money, money, and more money.' "
The Russians took this money, the property of the Spanish people, and
the biggest gold deposit in the world; and Russia became second gold-
exporter in the world market.
2. The Reds opened the dam of the Alberche river which flooded the
Tagus valley.

Changing their fiery teams at every stage,
For new ones filled with ever-towering rage,
And loosing these in turn to drink and graze
The peace-calm waters and the flowery ways,
Till, last and most superb, the Pyrenees,
Snorting a fiery steam around their knees,
Shall trail her spoor of villages set free
Through waving cornfields to the Midland Sea.
By this light hand, this feather of her wing,
Had you but cared to watch the careless thing –
Just by the mere direction it was blown
This war was long predicted and foreshown –
Directness, Rightness, has that airy power,
Anticipating victory to the hour:
While Leftness fails in all, as it befell
When Strachey prophesied at Teruel.
Through its brown palm as through the map of Spain
The Lucky line runs free of worldly gain
Like Tagus through the brown Castilian plain;
Inept the gadgets of the Mode to peddle,
But while a working stirrup is my treadle,
A serviceable implement enough
To rope a Calf or Red-Neck[1] by the scruff
And treat them kindly though they cut up rough;
Whose knot of nerves, by common labour spliced,
The rope and rein for manicure sufficed,
It scorns the scarlet nail-dye of the Left
And only in dexterity is deft,
Too business-like, unladylike a fist
To tantalize a British Communist,
As found the Tomboys of the Summer Schools
At San Mateo rounded up like mules,
As if they came not here to fight and kill
But to some nudist camp of Swedish drill
With semaphores no soldier understands
First clenching fists then throwing up their hands,

1. Rooinek, S. African for Limey, Pommie, Rubio, etc.

And when they're wearied of their jamboree,
Ask to be bathed and taken home to Tea!

But firstly, to fulfil the boastful promise,
In my last Book, of SAYING IT WITH POMMIES,[1]
To show I was in earnest when I spoke
And did not Dedicate them as a joke,
And though I could not say just where or when
Was certain they would flounder to my pen
Which never yet in prophecy has failed
And had them counted years before they sailed
And over lands and seas were puffed and floated
To within half a mile of where I wrote it –
Equestrian Muse of our Castilian trails,
Accept this offering (as of votive quails)
Of these three hundred Red-Necks, thrilled and caught
By Prophecy, on the live wires of thought,
Brought here to learn why communists 'feel small'[2]
And we so perpendicular and tall
(Like a Cathedral over Comrades' Hall)
For whom I sent the gay whip-cracking words
To round them up in flabbergasted herds,
And stretched the wire of rhyme, and switched the shock
That numbed the birdsclaws of their noisy flock –
Those scrawny fists, late screwed into a knot,
But now their manual tetanus forgot,
As with the grapenuts reddening in their crops,
In Roman fashion, they salute the Wops –
Renouncing all their 'Meeting'-gotten valiance,
To crawl before a handful of Italians![3]

1. See dedication of Satirical Poems in 'Collected Poems' The Author
foresaw the British International Brigade and its surrender at San Mateo,
long before the Spanish War, in a vision: and he actually dedicated his
prisoners to his wife in a poem printed before the war! Prince Rospigliosi,
now a British subject, can witness to this scene.
2. Day Lewis, the Rearguard poet, who 'fee-foh-fummed' so ferociously
in peacetime and then spent the war in an armchair wrote this line: 'Why,
when I meet a Communist, do I feel small?'
3. They were far too scared to surrender to the Spaniards who sent me over

Whose plight, electrocuted half by fear,
Must be my mandate to their Country's Ear –
That huge spittoon of webbed and scarlet gristle,
Credulity's Lofoden, the Niagara
Of Suction, where the lies like whirlwinds whistle,
And to uphold whose weight, a drunken staggerer
Revolving to its windmill-like career,
The Nation groans, the Atlas of its Ear!
And well might Lenin shout, such lugs to spy,
'Well-used, our Mightiest Weapon is the Lie':
With Kosher-cooked Alcazars to be blasted
As badly as the real one was devasted,
Its huge defenceless target weakly wags
And streams in tatters like a hundred flags
For all to spit in – journalists or 'highbrows'
(If guaranteed no brain behind the eyebrows)
For Defrocked Scoutmasters and wheedling Jews
The dumb receptacle of doctored news,
Of prophecies so stubbornly perverse
That they work out inspired – in the reverse,
(Like Lockhart's Prague and Strachey's Teruel
No sooner to be published than they fell)
And all those plans that democrats expound
To boomerang, in life, the wrong way round.
Where wowsers may discharge their wondrous lore
Who'll 'fight for peace,' and yet disarm for war –
This Ear, Public Convenience number One,
For all who rave or froth beneath the Sun,
Which sucks in all that's said, or thought, or written,
And loves by Hebrews to be mauled or bitten,
Yet when I near it, gives a threatening wag,
'For MEMBERS ONLY' running up the flag,
Because I've got the future in my bag
And by the tail can swing that howling cat about,
Who live the things they only chew the fat about,

---

to interpret: they knew what they had asked for! They said they wished to
surrender *en bloc*, to the Italians, but would otherwise 'have to fight' as
they knew what they deserved from the Spanish!

Since my existence has been lived and fought
As theirs at Oxford ready-made was bought
And in my teens I'd shed like threadbare trousers
Every experience possible to Wowsers;
I know what wrings their withers night and morn
To wish (quite rightly) they had not been born
Since of the English poets on your shelf
The only sort of 'Worker' is myself,[1]
Grown wiser in the company of mules
Than they with learned pedantries of fools,
And, since I was not sent with foreign cash,
Like some, to spread the bolshevistic rash,
Able both to explain the 'Spanish Worker'
From the inside, as to expound the Shirker,
The Communist, whose bungling Left we fight
With this Right hand – in every sense the Right!
So that when I approach that Red Left Lug
And honourably would discharge my plug
Of truth, the buckshot of my deadly mug,
To pepper with reality its dream –
Like an anemone, with folding seam,
Into its neck it tries to disappear,
And where it wagged the Man, he wags the ear, –
Who every time contrives to swing the lead
When I would raise my trumpet to his head,
Though in this cud of victory that I chew
There's balsam for the spittle of the Jew:
Since in a land where everything's called New
That's ready to dilapidate in two –
With 'New Verse' and 'New Statesman' to be new with
Alas, it's a New Newness they could do with!
All things that date the most, this label means,

1. At the time of the great popular National Uprising in Spain, I was the only foreign writer to be properly affiliated to a union of skilled workers – the 'Union de Vaqueros' – in Spain and I rose with my comrades, the agricultural workers, that is the lowest-paid and hardest-working *majority*, against the highly paid minority of miners and factory-workers, whose work is done for them by machines. It was from the agricultural peasants that Lenin and Stalin got the greatest opposition in Russia.

To-day's boneshakers, last night's crinolines,
That with the latest fashion and the mode
Still to the scrap-heap point the shortest road –
So I must strive its meaning to re-New,
And stir the fossils in their rancid stew,
By showing them a thing they've seldom seen –
A writer who is not a dead machine
Turned out like Ford cars in a time of crisis
From Charlie-factories of Cam or Isis[1]
And only guaranteed to run down-hill
Where failure can be headed for a spill.
For naught have they espoused in prose or rhyme
But perished through incompetence or crime:
What they uphold of its own self will fall
And out the Blums and Beneshes will crawl;
Though Lenin triumphed, into fullness blowing,
Ere these lugubrious Mascots could get going,
That was his luck, for Luck where they appear,
As from a Bunyip,[2] howling flies in fear –
And now poor Lenin's cherished dream of Spain,
Through their support, has gurgled down the drain.
When from his eminence Azaña fell,
It was upon the day they wished him well;
A letter came, from Woolfs and Huxleys sent
Support and sympathy to represent,
And straightway all his energies expired,
Something collapsed in him, he went all tired
And from the State executive was fired:
And flawlessly this axiom has been kept
What Auden chants by Spender shall be wept –
Go, ask the poor old Negus if I lie,
And Largo Caballero, by and by!
For they've signposts that always point the path
First to Geneva, afterwards to Bath,

1. Charlie Chaplin, the clown, with his outsize feet, stands to the author as the symbol of *pedestrian* commercial civilization.

2. Australasian Bogey-Man, which, from all accounts of it, must be rather terrifying.

When, crunched by the Right-handedness they lack,
Each Thug or slaver takes the scrap-yard track,
With these funereal croakers at his back;
Vultures and crows so rally to the field
And where they 'group' you know the doom is sealed,
Before it hits our nostrils ripe and hot
They've long ago divined the inward rot,
And as by sympathy I sense the rose
Of Victory before its buds unclose,
So they (before it trumpets to the nose)
Anticipate the maggot on its way,
With it co-operate in swift decay,
And so with one more carcass strew the way:
Which you may spoor, by no exception crossed –
One trail of causes villainously lost!
See, how they come 'Democracy' to save
The moment it begins to dig its grave,
While jutting bonework corrugates the scurf,
With murderous paws to shovel its own turf
A starved hyena at whose sapless dugs
The Russian Romulus in frenzy tugs,
While Spanish Remus has the brighter wheeze
To polish off its last remaining fleas –
Till even such a chump as Herbert Read
Woke up to it that things had gone to seed,
And chose the next most mouldy thing he could
That promised nits and jiggers in the wood,
Who now in Anarchism's foetid cell
The elixir of life pretends to smell.
Decrepitude for them's the only Right,
Though as 'humanitarians' they write
With greasy Tartuffades to slime the cause
That has more victims in its murderous jaws
Than ever were destroyed in mortal fight,
Blasted with bombs, or heaved with dynamite,
Or executed here, to serve them right:
Not only that, but if we well examine,
Invariably they side with filth and famine,

431

Morality for them has never mattered,
Except when crime or failure must be flattered:
For all their talk of what is Right or Wrong,
What matters most to them is – 'Does it Pong?'
For they'll have nothing but what's stale or late
And to be 'modern' must be out of date.
They bury facts as crocodiles their meat
Returning later to 'debunk' the treat
Which most they live for; like their friends, the Reds
Who pulled the mouldering corpses from their beds,
Who in Huesca's graveyard raised a Bar,
And drummed with thighbones to the shrill guitar,
Doomed by the same sub-realistic curse
In living bodies to forestall their hearse,
A doomed and dying species, with their cause
Condemned by the inexorable laws,
Who only by inversion can exist
As perverts, in a charnel-breathing mist,
From Death and Sin their scrawny themes to twist –
And with such bards to trumpet them to battle
No wonder British Reds stampede like cattle!
Their 'Progress' is to shunt along a track
Where 'Left' means left-behind and 'Front' means back
When was a Front so definitely split
As this fat Rump they have mistook for it,
And shown us little else as we advance
Our proper *Front* from Portugal to France:
And if they're facing 'Front'-wards, I'll not quiz
What must the tail be like, if that's the phyz?
With them, for opposites we have to hunt –
'Backwards' 's the word, when Popular the 'Front.'
From Seville to Toledo, every day,
They write up their advances all the way:
With victories they fill their daily sheet,
Woe to our cause, then, if they should retreat –
God save us from their ultimate defeat!
In a whole year when they would do or die
Their sole Alcazar still has been the LIE,

There all their foes are routed, only there
Pusillanimity can fight with prayer!
Put France and England's might upon the main,
The Gold of Moscow, and the loot of Spain,
Have all your mobs from arsenals prepared
Against a cause already thrice despaired,
A country prostrate, so that Moscow's powers,
Can say 'Within a fortnight Spain is ours' –
Add but their vows – and all is ineffectual
Once smiled on by the British Intellectual:
For they have spat on Life, the valiant Friend,
Who must be our companion to the end,
And he, no Red-Neck to forgive such fun,
From where they look, will turn away the Sun!
This, which I only whisper to my gun,
To the dry grass, and to a broken tree,
Long after may be heard beyond the sea
When nations catch their ancient health again
From the new might of Resurrected Spain,
That like a miracle, from nothing born,
To nightmare-ridden Europe shows the Morn
And stands between her and the living Hell
No liberal Democracy could quell –
But let these prisoners speak for my precision
And answer for my range and drive of Vision,
Who promised this before the war begun,
And drilled them with my pen before my gun
To dance in dudgeon what I wrote in fun:
And come like 'Calais Burghers,' as I planned,
'With their pink halters tamely brought to hand'[1]
In every detail fleshed, as fancied then,
When first the Sword was fathered by the Pen:

1. The Pink halter, the ringworm of sunburn, with which the God of poets and herdsmen, Apollo, brands the necks of Britishers. The Author had never been to San Mateo yet he saw in a vision the whole scene and dedicated the British prisoners which he later took there to his wife in a hermetic poem which was printed and published two years before the event ('Mithraic Emblems'). This is a perfect description of what happened and couldn't have been bettered had I written it retrospectively.

Surrendering without a single blow
For nothing, save that I foretold it so –
To make this great round-up at San Mateo
A film of my original rodeo –
To see them act down to its quaintest antic
The verse they dared to dream of as 'Romantic,'
When (ere they dreamed of it) I had portrayed
The British International Brigade,
And twice predicted clearly in advance
Lest any fool should foist it on to chance
If only once I'd whirled the whistling line
To get them hog-tied with iambic twine,
Preventing all suggestions of coincidence
When the live words should burgeon into incidents,
As in a tame hypnotic trance they follow
My verse, the flaming lariat of Apollo.
See now, like filings to its powerful magnet,
Like barbels gasping in its mighty drag-net,
Daring all likelihood of place or time
To prove my sure trajectory in rhyme,
Trampling geography, deriding space,
To fetch these grapenut-crunchers face to face,
I haul them out of their sub-human trance
Before a true reality to dance.
For the first time by a creative thought
Their Joadified existence has been caught,
Their miserable can-can they rehearse
As margin illustrations to my verse,
Projected by its force, gambol by gambol,
Through its side-splitting rigmarole to scramble,
And learn the difference if they didn't know it
Between a left-wing pedant and a poet!
Some fools may find Romantics in my Obra –
But where's a Realism that is sob'rer
When heroes Rooperted in Spauden's line
As dying stoics, nonchalant and fine,
Like numbed, frostbitten bullfrogs to a Cobra,
Galvanically volted through the spine,

Confront the cold Reality of mine?
I warned John Bull to fatten up his son[1]
And Jackie Veal-Calf to be underdone
When with their stainless cutlery and steel
Like waiters they would serve their own cold veal,[2]
Yes, even blobbed with mustard-coloured hair,
Which I'd forgot to order – all was there
A prophet's feast of laughter to prepare!
And Vain were all their boycotts to deflect
My prophecies that hiss their hair erect,
Who guaranteed their Popular Behinds
To show a pair of cheeks to all the winds,
And could as easily, in my Delphic rapture,
Have prophesied their slaughter as their capture,
But here the very Quarter-masters vex
For Turkey-food to redden up their necks
Till, all unhurt, we ship them to their shops
With grapenuts still distended in their crops
If we can find any – treating them kindly
To send them home from where they rushed so blindly
To fling their scraping curtseys to the Wops,
After they'd sacked the Churches, looted farms,
And raised us angry cattlemen in arms –
Leftness of Hand (the shame of work and war)
Disgracing England on a foreign shore,
Whose honour here I battle to restore
From such unholy ridicule to save her.
And when I Bolshevize for Royal Favour
Amongst her Modern Southeys, henna-tressed,
By watering down the Vodka like the rest,
May my Right hand lose cunning, flinch, and waver,
Salaaming there for baksheesh with their best,

1. 'John Bull, go fatten up your son – against my passing by And Jackie
Calf be underdone – whether you roast or fry!' So certain was the author
before the war that his vision would come true that he not only described the
surrender as it afterwards happened but issued prophetic orders to John Bull
to send out his sons to be captured: and was on the spot at the rendezvous
three years after publication.

2. See 'Mithraic Emblems', 'John Bull, go fatten up your son.' 1934.

435

Who'll call you honest, daring, fearless, bold,
For blacking boots and doing what you're told,
 If only you upclench that 'no' to life
And wish your Father hadn't took a wife,
If only you renounce all Faith and Vision
Foresentencing your manhood to derision.
For King's Gold Medals when I strive to please
Their winning will require a sterner test,
No defrocked Scoutmaster could Tupper these
That jingle with the Cross upon my chest:
When Britain and her poets stand for causes
That aren't foredoomed by foul subhuman crime
They'll change their present sanctions to applauses
And own me for the prophet of my time,
Since the whole trouble with the other chaps is
Whatever cause they flunkey for collapses
However well it flourished at the time:
For I foretold La Mancha's Knight would prance
With Charlie like a cockroach on his lance
Which I was called Romantic to believe:
Around the Fates to play at pitch and toss
Like kittens with the skein of Atropos
My devil-daring prophecies had leave;
So happy were the Fates at last to weave
A prophecy that wasn't pusillanimous,
And when they saw my program, were unanimous
I'd come a tedious chapter to relieve:
So merry hummed the wheel and clashed the shears
Was never such a miracle for years
Materialists and wowsers to aggrieve:
For when our cause was scarce a handsbreadth grown
And theirs in blood and arson towered alone
And Absolute from Portugal to France,
With flawless certitude I flung defiance
At all our pundits, bards, and men of Science,
Who've always viewed my gasconades askance,
Since well they know, those paladins of failure!
They've backed no cause from Greenland to Australia

But petered out for fear of worse mischance.
For still the 'Southern Stranger' of their theme,[1]
My 'Southern Gestures Modify' their dream –
And well may they beware: for from her chain
A 'Southern Gesture' liberated Spain.[2]
For where they doze in faint Utopian steam
Among their vicious languors and their lilies,
My Hand will pepper them with Southern chillies
Whenever I can spare it from my team,
As these found out, these gutless weary-willies
Who but that I had called this dance of wowsers
Would still be hiking in their sawn-off trousers
Or climbing grapenut-trees in some green lane –
But that I gave the rendezvous in Spain,
And came to greet them, shouting from my mule,
'Woodley! Old Woodley! welcome Home to School!'
One votive goat, had they but spared my kraal
Would have been worth this batch, their kit, and all,
Who had not even the guts to run away
When their Red Paradise behind them lay
And not a single man to bar their way –
Inviting them with all its charms untold,
The New Jerusalem, the Age of Gold,
Where loving 'comrades' howl for gory tripes
And pay their services with shots and swipes.
But take them, Muse, since they were in our contract,
Forgiving me the horseplay of this Entre-Acte,
And oh, sweet sister of Right-handed men,
Be ready to direct my willing pen
With the same constant certitude as when
Though years and seas and lands between us lay,
It goaded them my summons to obey:
And as it then Collectivized one Fool
Out of these Tomboys of the Summer School
Grant that it now may move as many minds
As here it chivvied prominent Behinds –

1. See Auden's Poem.
2. A literal fact, Franco flew from exile at Tenerife.

'Popular Fronts' – ahem! I meant to say
For we can euphemize as well as they –
And so collectivize a Wiser Man
Out of the better specimens of this Clan
Till England is unpommified once more
And poets grace her God-forsaken shore.
For just as ably, and with equal vision,
As I forecapture pommies with precision
And with a breath can puff to non-existence
Three years of time, a thousand miles of distance,
I can distinguish Right from Crying Wrong
And that's the theme and purpose of my song.
So sun my couplets with your radiant smiles
And ride with me these long Castilian miles
Your weight upon the croup behind me swinging,
Your Open Palm upon my thorax clinging,
That palm of victory in whose warm hold
To lullaby a wound my heart is singing
Like a red bird within its frond of gold;
While lovely as the lilt of the guitar
The silence of my rifle sounds afar,
Your jet-blue curls and lips like burning chillies,
Your beauty, like the Giantess of lilies,
Respiring fragrance as we ride along,
The one-horse cavalry whose charge is song,
Two voices underneath a single hat,
Two singers on the same bay bronco sat,
Two melodies in love with the same tune,
That runs in gold and silver to the moon.
Now like the rushing Tagus let us sing
How houses from their blasted ruins spring,
For one bombarded town how twenty rise
And float those long-lost colours to the skies:[1]

1. The Republicans ('patriots' as they were called by the liars of Fleet Street) abolished the Spanish flag – for the Hammer and Sickle, a ridiculous tricolor with a liver-coloured stripe, and the red and black 'skull and cross-bones' of the anarchists. They never had the effrontery to call themselves 'patriots'. They shot people for shouting 'Viva España'.

How kneeling crowds receive our marching hosts
As if we had been dear, departed ghosts:
As if they had forgot that wine is red
And dazzled by the whiteness of our bread.
The loaves and fishes of an 'outworn creed'
Suffice the starving multitude to feed,
And that is wrought by the mere faith of Spain
For which the purse-proud nations strove in vain.
Shiploads from Britain, loaded trains from France
Served but the march of hunger to advance,
As Bread to famine, water turned to thirst,
The miracles of Jesus were reversed:
In vain the Gaucho toiled for their relief
On Pampas thundering with tons of beef –
Round up the plains, or trawl the teeming sea
Where the Red Curse is, there will Hunger be!
The cargoes of a myriad trains and boats
Shrunk to a spider's breakfast in their throats.
They gasp to see our half-ton bullocks bleed
Whom wealth of mighty nations failed to feed,
To see the flocks of fat merinos spring
From some poor provinces where Christ is King,
Where loaves are multiplied from scanty grain
And fishes seem deserters from the main.[1]
Now through the Nation as our legions spread
The richer by the poorer half is fed:
Beside the lewd inscription, where they sprawl,
From loafing idly charcoaled on the wall
Hammer and Sickle to their labour fall.
Storks to the steeples, rollers to the wires
Return, and swallows to the broken spires –
And men to the religion of their Sires!

1. Alas! this was true when written in '38. It was only on the collapse of the Red front that the amazing achievements of the Nationalists in husbandry were all drained away to feed the starving multitudes who had suffered Red rule for close on three years, with four years of republican incompetence before that. The Russian dictator of Red Spain then decamped with the largest gold deposit in Europe (the property of the Spanish nation) and the present régime was blamed for the poverty of Spain!!

Over the blood of martyrs scarcely dry
Toledo, there, against the morning sky
Like some great battle-cruiser from the fight
Returned with Victory (terrific sight!).
God's flagship, she, with shattered sides, presents
Her leaning funnels and her gaping rents,
In high salute uplifts her steepled guns,
And far the deep reverberation runs –
Through echoing gorges of the hills it roars
The listening plain receives it and adores
And at her mast the Royal Ensign soars,
Where one ecstatic eagle soars and faints,
And morning like a red and golden banner
Is roaring in the hurricane hosanna
Of the Heroes, and the Martyrs, and the Saints!

ROY CAMPBELL

The Talking Bronco

A Review of Roy Campbell, *Flowering Rifle*, 1939

The great difficulty in creating any work of art about a subject chosen directly from the contemporary scene is to give it such coherence of theme, imagination and plot, that the whole work seems to exist independently of the reality by which it is inspired. A work that makes one constantly refer back to the outside reality, remains journalism or pamphleteering – however ingenious and excellent it may be in detail. Satire is bound to contain certain elements of reportage, because the whole point lies in its reference to external events: but the greatest satires of Swift, Dryden and Pope survive because, in spite of their references to contemporary figures and events of varying importance, these poets managed to create legends and symbols which still hold our interest.

So the question one must ask concerning Mr Campbell's poem is: What is it about? In the first place, it is an incoherent, biased, unobjective, highly coloured and distorted account of one man's experiences of the Spanish war, seen through the eyes of a passionate partisan of Franco. Although I strongly disagree with Mr Campbell's politics, I do not think that a work of this kind should be condemned either on the poet's opinions or even the degree of objective truth he attains, if he creates some artistic unity which has an existence of its own. But beyond this mass of reportage, what does Mr Campbell offer us? Very little, I am afraid. The poem, as a whole, has no unity of design, no sustained argument, no plot, no single vision. It is a kind of three-decker sandwich consisting of one layer of invective against the intellectuals of the Left, the International Brigade, the Spanish Republican Army, etc.; a second layer of autobiography concerning the exploits of Mr Campbell and his flowering rifle; and a top layer of rhapsody about Franco and his colleagues, who are treated as nothing less than angels. The transitions from one motif to another seem to spring from no inner logic in the poem itself, and, particularly when he is being autobiographical, the actual circumstances of the poem are often very obscure. Mr Campbell relies far too much on the reader's knowledge of the Spanish War.

A fellow-reviewer had the temerity to accuse Mr Campbell of automatically equivocating 'Right' and 'Wrong' with 'Right' and 'Left'. In a long reply, Mr Campbell explained that the 'reiterated and monotonous theme of the whole thing . . . is the Harvest'. Reiterated and monotonous this deathly Harvest certainly is, but a mere symbol of Franco's Victory does not provide the poem with a unifying theme, which it lacks. What it does have, is passages of violent and sometimes effective satire, and occasional rhapsodic passages of a certain power, in which Mr Campbell has always excelled. Here is a good example of the rhapsodic style:

> And so must Spain to passing stars appear
> Two-thirds illumed as in the lunar sphere
> And all the rest besmeared with greed and lust,
> But there a scythe of light the darkness reaping
> And there a sword with dented edges sweeping:
> And often have I blest her humble dust
> Sure of the sacred treasure in its keeping,
> That holy, holy, holy was the rust
> Wherein those twin Excaliburs were sleeping.

Admirers of Mr Campbell's earlier work may notice here a certain falling off in the intensity of his glowing repertoire of images, so I quote an example of the satire at its best:

> And, see, the Bullring to its use restored,
> Where late the loud, half-hourly 'Meeting' roared
> For every time the bolsheviks are routed,
> Why, sure, a meeting must be held about it,
> Which held, and many resolutions passed,
> They seek a bigger trouncing than the last,
> And then a bigger meeting than the beating,
> And so the endless rigmarole repeating,
> From meeting to defeat, defeat to meeting,
> From rout to rout so rapidly they switch
> That nobody could tell you which was which.

But these passages are exceptions, they are stones of a certain lustre buried under ignoble sweepings of every kind of anti-Semitic and atrocity propaganda, of boasting and bullying from the *Stü[r]mer* and the speeches of dictators. Mr Campbell lacks the swaggering impertinence of the Italian bully, which takes pleasure in violence for its own sake; he excels rather in the Saxon and Anglo-Saxon form which seeks to justify itself, so that whilst he repeats every exploded propagandist rationalization of the Cause to which he adheres, every inversion of the witnessed fact (such as that the 'Reds' destroyed Guernica), he also indulges in the degrading abuse of a Julius Streicher:

> The least fastidious Element we knew,
> That loves the chill, webbed hand-clasp of the Jew.

There are several passages in this book which make me feel physically sick. Finally, the undiscriminating abuse of the enemy defeats its own ends, because if we are to believe Mr Campbell, there can be little merit in defeating an army which never does anything but run. All sense of conflict is lost when his verminous adjectives culminate in the defiant:

> The bronco Life, with angry snort of fire,
> Has ever boomeranged four feet entire
> And stamped him like a cockroach in the mire.

Mr Campbell indignantly repudiates the accusation that he is a Romantic. He is quite right, for the Romantics were distinguished by their disinterested passion for truth, equalled only by their love of freedom and justice. The bronco Life! Perhaps that phrase gets nearer the mark. Mr Wyndham Lewis diagnosed the Dumb Ox in Hemingway's novels. Here we have the Talking Bronco, the Brute Life armed with abusive words and, most unfortunately, not with Mr Campbell's Flowering Rifle, but with Flowering Machine Guns, Flowering He[i]nkels, Flowering Capronis.

STEPHEN SPENDER

'Flowering Rifles'
A Reply to Stephen Spender's Review

Sir, – Since diligent lying to appeal to harrowed sentiment is openly exhorted in propaganda by nearly all Red Spanish manuals on the subject, and by Left leaders from Lenin downwards, I need not challenge Mr Spender (supporting as he does the side in Spain which preaches lying and which lays so much importance on propaganda as to devote two enormous skyscraper buildings to nothing else) to show by what monopoly of grace he entitles himself to treat me to hypocritical Tartuffades about 'disinterested truth', 'witnessed fact', and other sanctimonious blarney about 'freedom' and 'justice', which have long ago been degraded from their use as human speech by the ghoulish babooneries of the Reds which have come to be associated with them. As I am far nearer to common humanity than the orchidacious poets of Bloomsbury, I don't need to ask him from what standard of happy and healthy normality he treats me to Stiffkeyisms and sanctimonious phrases about 'distortion' or 'inversion'. Are the majority of Spaniards, then, distorted and inverted to feel like I do for their cause? As he seems to warn his readers against my personal experience of both regimes in Spain as if it were (*per se*) a serious disqualification and a handicap – he exposes himself too laughably for any comment as to what the real meaning of 'witnessed fact' is for him – since either way he shows he disapproves of it whether as being of intrinsic weight or of being the dangerous form of lying which carries most weight in England and which is recommended by his own side as of vital necessity! In either case he is equally suspicious of it. Luckily for him, however, no nationalist can dirty his lips with such phrases as 'witnessed fact' or 'disinterested truth' after the use that has been made of them. Let us cut out these degrading tartufferies which defile the lips, and appeal to those events which need no 'witnesses', to decide whether Mr Spender has any more right than a discredited and broken down fortune-teller, or a convicted palmist, in the presence of an exact astronomer, to mention the word 'truth' in my presence. Let us examine whether the Truth has ever come within fifty miles of Mr Spender and his colleagues other than as an avenging, ·punitive, and hostile Force, with nose held between finger and thumb, to kick their mouldy day-dreams into smithereens and trample their fungoid proliferations whenever they got too 'ripe'. It is by now an axiom that whatever Mr Spender and his colleagues support, even if it were the Pyramids themselves, would collapse like rotten, worm-eaten cheeses within a few hours of the manifestation of their sympathy. This happened in the case of Azaña's, Caballero's, and finally Negrin's Government which collapsed on the day of the joint manifestation of the British poets with their Poems for Spain. The form of collective bedroom palmistry which they mistake for poetry can be guaranteed to work out inversely and reversely to a hair. So he has no right to talk of 'inversion'. What but a rapacious appetite for, and a continuous diet of lies or inversions of fact, could produce such a flawless and continuous inversion of their day-dreams in real life: it is surely what they live on that causes them to live in a perpetual state of abortion. It is surely an *innate falsehood* in themselves, coupled with a degrading credulity, that enables them to bring out, without any conscious shame, a book in support of a Spain which never existed, when even the judo-masonic Babel they mistook for it had collapsed a week before; with the cowardly desertion of their dupes by leaders (who had sworn their 'last drop of blood') into the wallow of infra-civil strife between 'comrades', which was the last of my series of flawless prophecies that yet remained to be fulfilled (p. 129). Even before this war I had so much of the living *truth* in me that I had already galloped through Mr Spender and his fellow-Roopertisers of this war and planted our colours at the summit of triumph when events are only just reaching them. In *Broken Record*, 1933, I delineated to a hair the role of Mr Spender and his colleagues with their antics and defeat as the Rooperts of this next war to end war – and how they would be more tamely dragooned than ever into a war for 'Peace' (as they call the international judo-masonry) to be dumped and disillusioned worse than before. I was even able prophetically to dedicate a bunch of their Rooper-tées in advance, as later captured on the Castilian veld, to my wife (see *Dedication of Mithraic Emblems*) long before a Brigade of Rednecks had ever been envisaged by the cynical humorists that sent them out here. At the beginning of the war, when 'freedom and justice' were supremely wallowing throughout the peninsula, in a worse carnage than the war itself, and when they were all toasting a Red Spain, I printed a poem, 'Hard Lines, Azaña', in the first weeks of the war, flawlessly adducing the inevitable failure of the Red cause to the support of the British Intellectuals. In all I have written I have been able prophetically to anticipate and proclaim victory years beforehand when I was supposed to be as wrong about what matters most (then a 'technical impossibility'), the victorious event, as Mr Spender tries to pretend I am about the details. In view of her treatment of him and his cronies it is laughable of Mr Spender to pretend to be on speaking terms with Truth; even if she hadn't been obscured for three years by the most gigantic campaign of lies the world has yet seen, he could never have found her except as she raids his mouldy Utopias as an angry, outraged, and punitive force! It requires a really perverse and passionate craving for inversion to arrive where Mr Spender is with regard to events; since if ever a crowd of silly, dishonest, bungling, and pretentious mountebanks have been mauled, trampled, and spat on by the falseness of their day-dreams and aspirations it is these same Rooperts of the War of 1939! This type of antediluvian lounge-lizard is now extinct in Spain and will soon be in England: but when one remembers the delighted response of Mr Spender and his cronies to the gloating exhortations of Sender and Maurin to 'monstrous crimes' and the wholesale 'sticking of bellies' – now that the boot is on the other foot, the shameless, whining, and hypocritical tartufferies of Mr Spender about 'brutality', 'justice' and 'freedom' have a very queer smell and a very plaintive sound. For him to talk about truth when the sawdust is visibly running out of him in the shape of appeals to a bourgeois morality which he has always pretended to deride is an abject confession of the final abortion in defeat of all he pretended to stand for. If he did not live on lies his dreams would come true: if I lived on anything but truth my otherwise risky long-range prophecies would fail as hopelessly and humiliatingly as he.

> One must choose between the bronco life
> And the Manso death who feeds on lies.

13 Airogas, Toledo.

ROY CAMPBELL

BUT SOME REMEMBER SPAIN

'But some remember Spain and the black spots
They shouted "Bombers" at.'
(Bernard Gutteridge, 'In September 1939')

Two Days

I

'The Negrin Government has fallen,' News Item, 7th March 1939

And so it ends. Three years of straining hope . . .
O the first surge of spring through spume of snow,
the uncertain cry of the first blackbird groping
hoarsely for the full song of summer flow,

the tight buds tapping on the windowpane
out of the wind's pursuit, the scummed earth waking
through mists of glass with sudden clash of green,
through smear of brown decay the spring's spear breaking,

and all the tattered flowers, shrivelled early,
wasting their bells of sweetness on bleak valleys,
lost children of the year, raggedly daring
the barricades of wind, the swivelling volleys.

Summer has the victory-flag, the clap of glory,
only for that we face the winter's roar;
and yet, and yet, my heart is with the unwary,
the fearless salliers, who will laugh no more.

O summer strews the happy lap with plenty
and that's the only goal to lead us straight;
and yet . . . the seeds that burst where soil was flinty,
frail windflowers holding spring's siege-battered gate.

Now come the hooves of darkness on the grass,
the spurs slice through the flanks that labour and heave.
I see mad eyes of stone. The riders pass.
Slowly the torn earth, bulling, bleeds, beneath.

No horror have I known, no horror imagined
like that dark silence left upon the earth
scarred with an echo of moans forgotten, ravaged
with memories of that hope, that broken birth –

A glare of lightning on the jagged scene,
the grinding swell cracking the earth in waves
of desolation, the uplifted arms of green,
the arms of drowners sinking, whom nothing saves.

2

*Sitting in a bus, March 8th in the morning, and listening to two
busmen talking about horse racing and about the virtues of the
Royal Family of England.*

Shame is the dark reverberation. Vainly,
Citrine and Bevin are to blame, we say.
They have obstructed unity,
they have delivered up the body of Spain.

Only for thirty pieces, a regular salary,
condescending backslaps in the millionaire press,
they have delivered up the fool of a Saviour,
their bureaucratic hearts are craven and yellow.

But to blame them is no answer. Strip the mask.
They were but images of our grovelling spirits.
Citrine is only my cowardice in a discreet mask,
Bevin is only my bull-smugness behind a desk.

The betrayal is mine, the betrayal is yours, comrades.
Dalton is only my stupidity with an academic voice.
Atlee is only my weakness meaning the best.
In this moment of our shame, let us stand dumbly.

We are the broken body, we are the corrupted
out of whose lack of unity these maggots are bred.
Let us not evade our shame by blaming.
Let us stand dumb a moment, shamed abruptly.

That afternoon, back in my cottage:

How far does anger go, how far remorse?
I sat today in a budding fruit-tree lane
in Devon, I heard girls go lithely laughing.
How far away is Spain?

How far goes the pang, how far the songbeat
throbbing in baby buds, the faces smug as pearls?
What have I done to save you, comrades dead
under the heels of heedless girls?

And yet the laughter was lovely and unstained
as poplar-fountains flutterleafed with blue.
It was their scream I heard upon the day
when fear comes true.

They do not know the barrier's down that kept
the blackbird whistle safe, the cherry-snow.
They do not know what foulness roots the earth,
but soon they'll know.

Sitting in Torquay on the sea-front, on a park-bench: News Item,
8th March: 'Communist Troops refusing to accept the coup against
Negrin were bombed in Madrid by forces who included Anarchists.'

And while I lingered O regard repentance
seeking high tones of intricate lament:
beyond all shame the larksong of humanity,
beyond all failure the bloodspout through the teeth.

Words cannot utter what these integrate
in the white noon of man. Now let the living
each make his peace the best way that he can,
strike each his compact, turn to starker war.

There is no more to say. The hour is come,
is past upon this chime of searing death.

Fellowship is completed. Hark the larksong
beyond all shame; beyond all failure, love.

Out of the newsprint blows this wind of honour,
pause reading amid the traffic blast. Seal down,
red as the heart, the oath which we must swear
if we are still to live on such an earth.

And so it ends and ending so begins.

JACK LINDSAY

(Written 7–8 March 1939)

Memory

Do you remember Calabria
And the stately hills beyond?
Do you remember Huesca
In the sun-baked blòody land?

Do you remember men who fought
And men who died, and those
Who came back, lame, dispirited,
Broken, alone and sad?

Yes, I remember war in Spain,
And old wounds open up again,
Lifting their mouths in anguish
And the burnt blood boils again.

J. T. RODERICK

In the Interval

Again this circle of trees and houses, the Waldrons,
    And again the rain.
Landmarks of the spirit have since fallen
    As Prague or Spain.

Searchlights now wipe the windscreen of the sky,
    Which once was clear,
When from the garden we saw planes go by
    Not dulled by fear.

Our guests did not leave early, before dark:
    We all made plans.
Time walked gently through our lazy park
    And shook our hands.

Again these faces and these neighbours, older now:
    And a new face.
Time, rough and in haste, a frown upon his brow,
    Now owns the place.

                                        H. B. MALLALIEU

from *Autumn Journal*

VI

   And I remember Spain
2   At Easter ripe as an egg for revolt and ruin
   Though for a tripper the rain
4   Was worse than the surly or the worried or the haunted
     faces
   With writing on the walls –
6   Hammer and sickle, Boicot, Viva, Muerra;

7   With café-au-lait brimming the waterfalls,
8   With sherry, shellfish, omelettes.
9   With fretted stone the Moor
           Had chiselled for effects of sun and shadow;
       With shadows of the poor,
           The begging cripples and the children begging.
       The churches full of saints
           Tortured on racks of marble –
       The old complaints
           Covered with gilt and dimly lit with candles.
       With powerful or banal
18   Monuments of riches or repression
       And the Escorial
           Cold for ever within like the heart of Philip.
       With ranks of dominoes
22   Deployed on café tables the whole of Sunday
       With cabarets that call the tourist, shows
           Of thighs and eyes and nipples.
       With slovenly soldiers, nuns,
26   And peeling posters from the last elections
       Promising bread or guns
           Or an amnesty or another
29   Order or else the old
           Glory veneered and varnished
       As if veneer could hold
           The rotten guts and crumbled bones together.
       And a vulture hung in air
           Below the cliffs of Ronda and below him
       His hook-winged shadow wavered like despair
           Across the chequered vineyards.
       And the boot-blacks in Madrid
38   Kept us half an hour with polish and pincers
       And all we did
           In that city was drink and think and loiter.
       And in the Prado half-
42   wit princes looked from the canvas they had paid for
43   (Goya had the laugh –
44   But can what is corrupt be cured by laughter?)

454

And the day at Aranjuez
46   When the sun came out for once on the yellow river
47 With Valdepeñas burdening the breath
48   We slept a royal sleep in the royal gardens;
And at Toledo walked
50   Around the ramparts where they throw the garbage
And glibly talked
    Of how the Spaniards lack all sense of business.
And Avila was cold
    And Segovia was picturesque and smelly
And a goat on the road seemed old
    As the rocks or the Roman arches.
And Easter was wet and full
58   In Seville and in the ring on Easter Sunday
A clumsy bull and then a clumsy bull
    Nodding his banderillas died of boredom.
And the standard of living was low
    But that, we thought to ourselves, was not our business;
All that the tripper wants is the *status quo*
64   Cut and dried for trippers.
And we thought the papers a lark
66   With their party politics and blank invective;
And we thought the dark
    Women who dyed their hair should have it dyed more
      often.
And we sat in trains all night
    With the windows shut among civil guards and peasants
And tried to play piquet by a tiny light
72   And tried to sleep bolt upright;
And cursed the Spanish rain
    And cursed their cigarettes which came to pieces
75 And caught heavy colds in Cordova and in vain
76   Waited for the right light for taking photos.
And we met a Cambridge don who said with an air
    'There's going to be trouble shortly in this country',
And ordered anis, pudgy and debonair,
    Glad to show off his mastery of the language.
But only an inch behind

This map of olive and ilex, this painted hoarding,
Careless of visitors the people's mind
   Was tunnelling like a mole to day and danger.
And the day before we left
   We saw the mob in flower at Algeciras
87 Outside a toothless door, a church bereft
88   Of its images and its aura.
And at La Linea while
   The night put miles between us and Gibraltar
91 We heard the blood-lust of a drunkard pile
   His heaven high with curses;
And next day took the boat
94   For home, forgetting Spain, not realising
That Spain would soon denote
   Our grief, our aspirations;
Not knowing that our blunt
   Ideals would find their whetstone, that our spirit
Would find its frontier on the Spanish front,
100   Its body in a rag-tag army.

LOUIS MACNEICE

'Having felt for Spain, what further can we feel?'

Having felt for Spain, what further can we feel?
Acted out is the tragedy of our day.
Staled and dull gesturings of the old evil
only remain, a hollow world, sordidly grey.
Find even agony a boredom ticking
mindless as a clock. Face on to bleakness,
the foregone struggle accepted, but something lacking,
the sweet light quencht, while madmen fight in darkness.

So I said, but forgot how the earth's daffodil-spear
splits winter's iron mail, and thrushsong wakes

out of black frost of silence. Listen now.
Across war's thickening storm the life-beat breaks:
Red Army match or budpulse on the bough?
unconquerable Spring or the Soviet Star?

JACK LINDSAY

Postscript for Spain

Spain in her struggle breached no frontier.
The ingenuous battle raging through that land
Hardly disturbed us. We could understand
The roistering roundhead and the cavalier.

Where are the happy emblems of that war?
Under what terrace, crumbling at the gun,
Bursts the delicious grape? Against the sun
What orange blossoms in a bomb of fire?

This was a nation that we little knew,
The long vendetta, and the fatal wind
Under the Pyrenees. The cancer grew
Bitterly in the European wound.

Out of the dancing and the singing came
Civil dissension, bitter deeds and cruel;
Out of the poet and the murdered fool
The blood leapt rigid in a rage of shame.

J. C. HALL

Times of War and Revolution

The years reveal successively the true
Significance of all the casual shapes
Shown by the atlas. What we scarcely knew
Becomes an image haunting as a face;
Each picture rising from neglected place
To form the dial of our cursor hopes,
As that undreamt-of frontier slowly writhes
Along the wishes of explosive, lives.

The pages char and turn. Our memories
Fail. What emotions shook us in our youth
Are unimaginable as the truth
Our middle years pursue. And only pain
Of some disquieting vague variety gnaws,
Seeing a boy trace out a map of Spain.

ROY FULLER

Aftermath

The conferring of the Freedom of Guernica on Generalissimo Francisco Franco

Through the undisputed heaven,
Bent on hopes of greater glories
Than the battle fronts had given
Came the fascist trimotores,
On Guernica loosed their venom,
Hammered helpless men and women
Into pulped and writhing earth.
Thus they brought the blitz to birth.

458

Gaudily across the passes
Now no longer barricaded,
White hope of the ruling classes
Since all other hopes have faded,
Franco rides with pomp and pageant,
Little salesman, foreign agent,
Rides between the flags and vistas
Staged by anxious falangistas
To receive the freedom ordered
From the city that he murdered.

Eyes in all the darker places,
Round the door, behind the pillar,
Eyes gleam from hidden faces,
Eyes are levelled at the killer.
Fear of what's to come is stirring,
Tyrants' deaths are squalid, gory,
Mussolini, Hitler, Goering
Left him to complete the story.
Here, in eyes that have no pity
He may read the final chapter:
Thus within the murdered city
Freedom waits to greet her captor.

Scorched and splintered lie its stones,
Blood is dust with flesh and hair,
Whiter runs the street for bones –
El Caudillo's welcome there.
There the friendly maggot fêtes him
With his pomp and pinchbeck fasces,
There the city's freedom waits him
Where he left its dust and ashes.

MILES TOMALIN

Notes

Collections are referred to in the Notes by initials or date of publication. Full titles will be found in the list given at the beginning of the notes to each poem.

The Map of Pain

W. H. AUDEN: 'SPAIN'

Spain (1937); *Poems for Spain* (1939), pp. 55–8;= 'Spain 1937', *Another Time* (1940), pp. 103–6; *Collected Poetry* (New York, 1945), pp. 181–5; *Collected Shorter Poems* (1950), pp. 189–92.

Original published text.

7   *cartwheels*] cart wheels *(PS)*   cart-wheels *(1940, 1945, 1950)*
8   *Horses. Yesterday*] *(PS)*   Horses; yesterday *(1940, 1945, 1950)*
9   *giants,*] *(PS)*   giants; *(1940, 1945, 1950)*
12   *alarming*] *(PS)*   of frightening *(1940, 1945, 1950)*
16   *witches;*] *(PS)*   Witches. *(1940, 1945, 1950)*
    but] *(PS)*   But *(1940, 1945, 1950)*
    (Here and throughout) to-day] *(PS, 1940, 1950)*   today *(1945)*
17   *turbines,*] *(PS)*   turbines; *(1940, 1945, 1950)*
21   *Greece,*] *(PS)*   Greek; *(1940, 1945, 1950)*
23   *sunset*] *(PS)*   sunset, *(1940, 1945, 1950)*
25   *pines,*] *(PS)*   pines *(1940, 1945, 1950)*
26   *Or . . . sings*] *(PS)*   Or, . . . sings, *(1940, 1945, 1950)*
32   *inquire. I*] *(PS)*   inquire, I *(1940, 1945, 1950)*
33   *lodgings,*] *(PS)*   lodgings *(1940, 1945, 1950)*
34   *loss,*] *(PS)*   loss. *(1940, 1945, 1950)*
36   *Organiser,*] *(PS, 1945, 1950)*   Organiser. *(1940)*
40   *found the*] *(PS)*   found once the *(1940, 1945, 1950)*
43   *O descend*] *(1940, 1945, 1950)*   Oh, descend *(PS)*
44   *engineer,*] *(PS)*   engineer: *(1940, 1945, 1950)*
47   *mover;*] *(PS)*   Mover, *(1940, 1945, 1950)*
48   *Not to-day;*] *(PS)*   Not to-day, *(1940, 1950)*   Not today, *(1945)*
    To you,] *(PS)*   To you *(1940, 1945, 1950)*
49   *easily-duped;*] *(PS)*   easily-duped: *(1940, 1945, 1950)*
50   *do.*] *(PS)*   do; *(1940, 1945, 1950)*
51   *story.*] *(PS)*   story; *(1940, 1945, 1950)*
52   *voice.*] *(PS)*   voice; *(1940, 1945, 1950)*

53 *just city?*] *(PS)*   Just City? *(1940, 1945, 1950)*
56 *decision. Yes,*] *(PS)*   decision: yes, *(1940, 1945, 1950)*
58 *fisherman's islands*] *(PS)*   fishermen's islands, *(1940, 1945, 1950)*
59 *Or*] *(PS)*   In *(1940, 1945, 1950)*
    city,] *(PS)*   city; *(1940, 1945, 1950)*
61 *birds*] burrs *(PS, 1940, 1945, 1950)*
64 *passes. All presented*] *(PS)*   passes: they came to present *(1940, 1945, 1950)*
66 *Europe;*] *(PS)*   Europe, *(1940, 1945, 1950)*
68–69 *Our thoughts have bodies; the menacing shapes of our fever / Are precise and alive.*] *(PS)*   Our fever's menacing shapes are precise and alive. *(1940, 1945, 1950)*
70–76 *For the fears . . . people's army.*] *(PS)*   deleted *(1940, 1945, 1950)*
77 *(Here and throughout) To-morrow*] *(PS, 1940, 1950)*   Tomorrow *(1945)*   *To-morrow, perhaps the future. The*] *(PS)*   To-morrow, perhaps, the future: the *(1940, 1950)* Tomorrow, perhaps, the future: the *(1945)*
81 *love,*] *(PS)*   love; *(1940, 1945, 1950)*
84 *musician,*] *(PS)*   musician. *(1940, 1945, 1950)*
85–88 *The . . . struggle*] *(PS)*   deleted *(1940, 1945, 1950)*
89 *To-morrow for the young*] *(PS, 1940)*   Tomorrow, for the young, *(1945)*   To-morrow, for the young, *(1950)*
90 *weeks*] *(PS)*   winter *(1940, 1945, 1950)*
92 *evenings. But*] *(PS)*   evenings: but *(1940, 1945, 1950)*
93 *deliberate . . . death,*] *(PS)*   inevitable . . . death; *(1940, 1945, 1950)*
94 *necessary murder;*] *(PS)*   fact of murder; *(1940, 1945, 1950)*
97 *consolations:*] *(PS)*   consolations; *(1940, 1945, 1950)*
    cigarette,] *(PS)*   cigarette; *(1940, 1945, 1950)*
98 *candlelit barn,*] *(PS)*   candle-lit barn *(1940, 1945, 1950)*
101 *dead. The*] *(PS)*   dead; the *(1940, 1945, 1950)*
    look.] *(PS)*   look: *(1940, 1945, 1950)*
102 *short,*] *(PS)*   short *(1940, 1945, 1950)*
104 *nor*] *(PS)*   or *(1940, 1945, 1950)*

W. H. AUDEN: 'IMPRESSIONS OF VALENCIA'

New Statesman (30 January 1937), p. 159.

H. B. MALLALIEU: 'THE FUTURE IS NEAR US'

Poets of Tomorrow: First Selection (Hogarth, 1939), pp. 34–5; *Poems for Spain* (1939), pp. 59–60.

Poets of Tomorrow text.

5 *dead,*] dead *(PS)*
7 *Spain. Over*] Spain: over *(PS)*
10 *air:*] air. *(PS)*

13 *Earth;*] earth, (*PS*)
16 *cut off:*] cut off (*PS*)
18 *fight;*] fight: (*PS*)
20 *sets*] has set (*PS*)
21 *in*] for (*PS*)
23 *shall have . . . chorus:*] must have . . . chorus, (*PS*)

STEPHEN SPENDER: 'THE LANDSCAPE'

New Stateman (4 December 1937), p. 929.

CHARLES DONNELLY: 'HEROIC HEART'

Ireland Today, II, No. 7 (July 1937), p. 30.

GEORGE BARKER: FROM 'CALAMITERROR'

Calamiterror (1937), Section X, pp. 51–3.

STEPHEN SPENDER: 'THE MOMENT TRANSFIXES THE SPACE WHICH DIVIDES'

New Statesman (21 August 1937), p. 280.

CHARLES DONNELLY: 'THE TOLERANCE OF CROWS'

Ireland Today, II, No. 2 (February 1937), p. 50; *The Book of the XV Brigade* (Madrid, 1938; republished Newcastle upon Tyne, 1975), p. 118; *Poems for Spain* (1939), pp. 50–51.

Ireland Today text.

In *The Book of the XV Brigade* the poem is introduced thus: 'This prophetic poem was written by Charles Donnelly before he had decided to leave Ireland and join the International Brigade in Spain. He fell charging the Fascist trenches at Jarama on February 27, 1937. His body, shattered by two explosive bullets, was recovered four days later.'
11 *collapse is*] collapse's (*PS*)

EDGAR FOXALL: 'SPAIN AND TIME'

Water-Rat Sonata and Other Poems (Fortune Press, 1941), p. 30.

CHARLES DONNELLY: 'POEM'

Ireland Today, II, No. 1 (January 1937), pp. 48–9.

GEORGE BARKER: 'O HERO AKIMBO ON THE MOUNTAINS OF TOMORROW'

Poems for Spain (1939), p. 59.

JOHN CORNFORD: 'POEM'

New Writing, IV (Autumn 1937), p. 39; *Poems for Spain* (1939), p. 21; = 'To Margot Heinemann', *John Cornford: A Memoir*, ed. Pat Sloan (1938), pp. 248–9; = 'Huesca', *Penguin New Writing*, No. 2 (January 1941), p. 73.

JOHN CORNFORD: LETTERS TO MARGOT HEINEMANN

John Cornford: A Memoir, ed. Pat Sloan (1938), pp. 236–43.

JOHN CORNFORD: 'A LETTER FROM ARAGON'

Left Review, II, No. 14 (November 1936), p. 771; *John Cornford: A Memoir*, ed. Pat Sloan (1938), pp. 247–8.

JOHN CORNFORD: 'DIARY LETTER FROM ARAGON'

John Cornford: A Memoir, ed. Pat Sloan (1938), pp. 197–211.

H. B. MALLALIEU: SECTION 4 OF 'POEM IN SPRING'

Letter in Wartime and Other Poems (Fortune Press, 1941), p. 30.

J. BRONOWSKI: 'GUADALAJARA'

New Writing, new series, I (Autumn 1938), pp. 134–5; *Spain 1939: Four Poems* (Hull, 1939), pp. 1–2; *Poems for Spain* (1939), pp. 84–5.

New Writing text.

20   *besides*] beside (*1939; PS*)

JOHN CORNFORD: 'FULL MOON AT TIERZ: BEFORE THE STORMING OF HUESCA'

Left Review, III, No. 2 (March 1937), pp. 69–70; *John Cornford: A Memoir*, ed. Pat Sloan (1938), pp. 244–6; *Poems for Spain* (1939), pp. 26–9.

Left Review text.

7   source,] (*PS*)   source (*1938*)
8   hands] hand's (*1938; PS*)
9   plasticene] (*PS*)   plasticine (*1938*)
16 *Where in the fields by Huesca*] Where, in the fields by Huesca, (*1938; PS*)
21 *All round,*] All round (*1938; PS*)
25 mausers'] (*PS*)   mauser's (*1938*)
29 death,] (*PS*)   death (*1938*)
31 fight.] (*PS*)   fight, (*1938*)
40 party] Party (*1938; PS*)
46 O be] (*1938*)   Oh, be (*PS*)
48 O let] (*1938*)   Oh, let (*PS*)
60 Here too] (*PS*)   Here, too, (*1938*)
61 O understand] (*1938*)   Oh, understand (*PS*)
66 plain,] (*PS*)   plain (*1938*)

JOHN LEPPER: 'BATTLE OF JARAMA 1937'

Poems for Spain (1939), pp. 33–4.

STEPHEN SPENDER: 'AT CASTELLON'

New Writing, new series, I (Autumn 1938), p. 25; *Poems for Spain* (1939), pp. 30–31; *The Still Centre* (1939), pp. 67–8.

New Writing text.

2   head lamps] (*PS*) headlamps (*1939*)
10 ember.] (*1939*)   ember (*PS*)
12 rifle butt] (*PS*)   rifle-butt (*1939*)
22 him.] (*1939*)   him (*PS*)

SYLVIA TOWNSEND WARNER: 'WAITING AT CERBERE'

Poems for Spain (1939), pp. 86–7.

Title. Cerbere is clearly a misprint for Cerbère: which is how Sylvia Townsend Warner spoke of the poem (e.g. in correspondence with me).

SYLVIA TOWNSEND WARNER: 'BARCELONA'

Left Review, II, No. 15 (December 1936), pp. 812–16.

TOM WINTRINGHAM: 'BARCELONA NERVES'

Volunteer for Liberty, I, No. 23 (Madrid, 15 November 1937), p. 7; *Poems for Spain* (1939), pp. 29–30.

Poems for Spain text.

In *VL* the poem is dated September 1936.
1   *longer :*] longer, (*VL*)
3   *stranger :*] stranger, (*VL*)
8   *for.*] for ... (*VL*)
9   *buried :*] buried; (*VL*)
10 *brothels*] brothels, (*VL*)
17 *children*] children, (*VL*)
19 *We*] We'll (*VL*)
    what can wreck others] what wrecks these others (*VL*)

LOUIS MACNEICE: 'TODAY IN BARCELONA'

Spectator (20 January 1939), pp. 84–5.

EWART MILNE: 'THE HOUR GLASS (1)'

Letter from Ireland (Dublin, 1940), p. 34.

EWART MILNE: 'THE HOUR GLASS (2)'

Letter from Ireland (Dublin, 1940), p. 35.

LAURIE LEE: 'A MOMENT OF WAR'

The Sun My Monument (1944), pp. 9–10; *The Sun My Monument* (2nd impression (reset), 1961), pp. 13–14.

1944 text.

7   *soil,*] soil (*1961*)
12 *pity,*] pity (*1961*)

TOM WINTRINGHAM: 'THE SPLINT'

Poems for Spain (1939), pp. 94–5.

TOM WINTRINGHAM: 'BRITISH MEDICAL UNIT – GRANIEN'

Left Review, II, No. 16 (January 1937), p. 873; = 'Grañen' (dated 'British Hospital, Aragon Front, September 1936'), *Volunteer for Liberty*, I, No. 24 (Madrid, 17 November 1937), p. 3; = 'Granien', *Poems for Spain* (1939), p. 41.

Left Review text.

1 *Death*] death (*VL, PS*)
3 *Acknowledge*] Consider (*VL, PS*)
6 *No inverted commas in VL and PS*
7 *different*] (*VL*)   sharper (*PS*)
   close by] close-by (*VL*)   near by (*PS*)
8 *lamp*] (*VL*)   torch (*PS*)
   lighting] (*VL*)   lighting, (*PS*)
9 *glinting*] searching (*VL, PS*)
   probe] (*PS*)   knife (*VL*)
12 *the night*] this night (*VL, PS*)
13 *This*] The (*VL, PS*)
   yet] but (*VL, PS*)
14 *fingers. We*] (*VL*)   fingers; we (*PS*)

SYLVIA TOWNSEND WARNER: 'BENICASIM'

Left Review, III, No. 14 (March 1938), p. 841; *Poems for Spain* (1939), pp. 87–8.

Left Review text.

4 *a*] *This and all first letters are capitalized in PS*
14 *halt.*] halt: (*PS*)

LAURIE LEE: 'WORDS ASLEEP'

The Sun My Monument (1944), p. 11; *The Sun My Monument* (2nd impression (reset), 1961), p. 15.

L. J. YATES: 'POEM'

New Writing, new series, I (Autumn 1938), p. 232.

STEPHEN SPENDER: 'TILL DEATH COMPLETES THEIR ARC'

New Writing, new series, I (Autumn 1938), p. 27.

Junker Angels in the Sky

GEORGE BARKER: 'ELEGY ON SPAIN'

Lament and Triumph (1940), pp. 71–6; *Collected Poems 1930–1955* (1957), pp. 98–103.

Collected Poems text.

45, 71 *tomorrow*] to-morrow (*1940*)
107 *morning*] morning, (*1940*)

MILES TOMALIN: 'WINGS OVERHEAD'

Volunteer for Liberty, I, No. 28 (Madrid, 27 December 1937), p. 10.

RUTHVEN TODD: 'JOAN MIRÓ'

Poets of Tomorrow: First Selection (Hogarth, 1939), p. 58; = 'Poem for Joan Miró', *Poems for Spain* (1939), pp. 95–6.

STEPHEN SPENDER: 'THE BOMBED HAPPINESS'

New Statesman (4 February 1939), p. 167; *The Still Centre* (1939), pp. 69–70.

JACQUES ROUMAIN: 'MADRID: TO RAMON SENDER'

Translated by Nancy Cunard.

Left Review, III, No. 15 (April 1938), pp. 909–10.

HERBERT READ: 'BOMBING CASUALTIES IN SPAIN'

Collected Poems (1966), p. 149; = 'Bombing Casualties', *Poems for Spain* (1939), pp. 41–2.

Collected Poems text.

4 *blench'd*] blenched (*PS*)
8 *spatter'd*] spattered (*PS*)
11–12 *PS divides this second stanza into two at this point*

F. L. LUCAS: 'PROUD MOTHERHOOD (MADRID, A.D. 1937)'

Poems for Spain (1939), p. 78.

A. S. KNOWLAND: 'GUERNICA'

Spain at War, No. 8 (November 1938), p. 307.

ALBERT BROWN: 'FROM A PAINTING BY PICASSO'

Poems for Spain (1939), pp. 64–5.

NANCY CUNARD: 'TO EAT TO-DAY'

New Statesman (1 October 1938), p. 488. The last stanza appeared separately, entitled 'In Spain It is Here', in *Voice of Spain* (incorporating *Spain at War*), No. 1 (January 1939), p. 13, with the appended date 'Barcelona, September 13, 1938'.

C. DAY LEWIS: 'BOMBERS'

Overtures to Death (1938), p. 15; *Poems for Spain* (1939), pp. 82–3; *Collected Poems* (1954), pp. 170–71.

Collected Poems text.

4	*deepsea*] (*1938*)	deep-sea (*PS*)
19	*answered*] (*1938*)	answered – (*PS*)
20	*delivered*] (*1938*)	delivered, (*PS*)
22	*guilt*] (*PS*)	gilt (*1938*)
	children] (*1938*)	sons (*PS*)

W. H. AUDEN: 'EPITAPH ON A TYRANT'

New Statesman (21 January 1939), p. 81; *Another Time* (1940), p. 95; *Collected Shorter Poems* (1950), p. 112; *Collected Shorter Poems 1927–1957* (1966), p. 127.

New Statesman text.

6 *And, when he cried,*] And when he cried (*1940, 1950, 1966*)

He is Dead and Gone

DONAGH MACDONAGH: 'HE IS DEAD AND GONE, LADY ... (FOR CHARLES DONNELLY, R.I.P.)'

Ireland Today, II, No. 7 (July 1937), p. 30; = 'He is dead and gone, Lady ...' *Voice of Scotland*, I, No. 3 (Dec. 1938–Feb. 1939), p. 7.
Ireland Today text.

Title. 'He is dead and gone, Lady' is from Ophelia's song, *Hamlet* Act IV scene 5.
4 *Keats.*] Keats, (*VS*)
10 *Jack-o-Lantern*] Jack-o'-Lantern (*VS*)
16 *repents.*] repents? (*VS*)
17 *quietus,*] quietus (*VS*)
22 *integrity*] integrity, (*VS*)
23 *us; somewhere ... charted –*] us. Somewhere ... charted, (*VS*)
24 *Something has been gained by this mad missionary.*] Time will remember this militant visionary. (*VS*)

BLANAID SALKELD: 'CASUALTIES'

The Criterion, XVII, No. 66 (October 1937), p. 53.

EWART MILNE: 'THINKING OF ARTOLAS'

Letter from Ireland (Dublin, 1940), pp. 27–9.

JACK LINDSAY: 'REQUIEM MASS: FOR THE ENGLISHMEN FALLEN IN THE INTERNATIONAL BRIGADE'

New Lyrical Ballads, ed. Maurice Carpenter, Jack Lindsay, Honor Arundel (Poetry London, 1945), pp. 104–10.

STEPHEN SPENDER: 'TO A SPANISH POET (*To Manuel Altolaguirre*)'

The Still Centre (1939), pp. 105–7; *Selected Poems* (1940), pp. 66–8; *Collected Poems* (1955), pp. 108–9.

Collected Poems text.

Dedication. (*To Manuel Altolaguirre*)] (for Manuel Altolaguirre) (*1939, 1940*)
2 *exploding;*] exploding: (*1939, 1940*)
4 *Blown to one side by*] Blasted sideways by (*1939, 1940*)
5 *being alone*] loneliness (*1939, 1940*)
6 *Drained*] Was drained (*1939, 1940*)
    mind.] mind (*1939, 1940*)

7   *There was no fixed object for the eye to fix on.*] By the lack of any motionless object the eye could find. (*1939, 1940*)

8   *You became*] You were (*1939, 1940*)

9   *how the worst things happen.*] things happen. (*1939, 1940*)

10   *stucco pigeon*] sulphur stucco (*1939, 1940*)

11   *On the gable roof that was*] Fixed to the gable above (*1939, 1940*)

12   *Parabolized before your window*] Swooped in a curve before the window (*1939, 1940*)

13   *Uttering (you told me later!) a loud coo.*] Uttering, as it seemed, a coo. (*1939, 1940*)

14   *Alone to your listening self, you told the joke.*] When you smiled, (*1939, 1940*)

15   *broke.*] was shattered; (*1939*)   was shattered, (*1940*)

16   *But you remained whole,*] Only you remained whole (*1939, 1940*)

17   *Your own image unbroken in your glass soul.*]
In frozen wonder, as though you stared
At your image in the broken mirror
Where it had always been silverly carried. (*1939, 1940*)

18   *Having heard this all from you, I see you now*] Thus I see you (*1939, 1940*)

19   *– White astonishment haloing irises*] With astonishment whitening in your gaze (*1939, 1940*)

20   *retain in their centres*] retains in the black central irises (*1939, 1940*)

21-22   *Black ... stories*] Laughing images (*1939, 1940*)

23   *an aristocrat*] a man (*1939, 1940*)

24   *Where he had got*] Having got (*1939, 1940*)

25   *And, for a whole week, followed, on foot, a partridge.*] And spent a week following a partridge; (*1939, 1940*)

26   *Stories of that general, broken-hearted*] Or of that broken-hearted general (*1939, 1940*)

27   *Because he'd*] Who (*1939, 1940*)

28-30   *But ... dread?*]
Beyond the violet violence of the news,
The meaningless photographs of the stricken faces,
The weeping from entrails, the vomiting from eyes,
In all the peninsular places,
My imagination reads
The penny fear that you are dead. (*1939, 1940*)

31   *we – the living – who are dead*] we who are unreal and dead, (*1939, 1940*)

32   *revolves and dissolves*] revolves, dissolves and explodes (*1939, 1940*)

33   *set ... earth's lid.*] lay ... ground/Just beneath the earth's lid, (*1939, 1940*)

34-37   *The eyes ... plaster.*]
And the flowering eyes grow upwards through the grave
As through a rectangular window
Seeing the stars become clear and more clear

In a sky like a sheet of glass,
Beyond these comedies of falling stone. (*1939, 1940*)

38 *ribs –*] body, (*1939, 1940*)

39 *Oiled axle through revolving spokes.*] Like axle through the turning wheel, (*1939, 1940*)

40–42 *Unbroken . . . world.*]
With eyes of blood.
Unbroken heart,
You stare through my revolving bones
On the transparent rim of the dissolving world
Where all my side is opened
With ribs drawn back like springs to let you enter
And replace my heart that is more living and more cold.

Oh let the violent time
Cut eyes into my limbs
As the sky is pierced with stars that look upon
The map of pain,
For only when the terrible river
Of grief and indignation
Has poured through all my brain
Can I make from lamentation
A world of happiness,
And another constellation,
With your voice that still rejoices
In the centre of its night,
As, buried in this night,
The stars burn with their brilliant light. (*1939, 1940*)

HERBERT READ: 'THE HEART CONSCRIPTED'

Poems for Spain (1939), pp. 39–40; *Collected Poems* (1966), p. 174.

Collected Poems text.

5 *exact remorse*] poetic pride (*PS*)
9 *hear only*] only hear (*PS*)

MARGOT HEINEMANN: 'FOR R.J.C. (SUMMER, 1936)'

New Writing, IV (Autumn 1937), pp. 59–60; *Poems for Spain* (1939), pp. 44–5. 'R.J.C.' is John Cornford.

MARGOT HEINEMANN: 'GRIEVE IN A NEW WAY FOR NEW LOSSES'

New Writing, IV (Autumn 1937), pp. 60–61; *Poems for Spain* (1939), pp. 45–6.

MAURICE CARPENTER: 'LAMENT FOR A LOVER'

New Lyrical Ballads, ed. Maurice Carpenter, Jack Lindsay, Honor Arundel (Poetry London, 1945), pp. 99–100.

ROY FULLER: 'POEM (FOR M.S., KILLED IN SPAIN)'

New Writing, V (Spring 1938), pp. 233–5; *Poems for Spain* (1939), pp. 47–9; = 'To M.S., Killed in Spain', *Collected Poems 1936–1961* (1962), pp. 20–22.

New Writing text.

1   *Great cities,*] (*PS*)   Great cities (*1962*)
3   *Knew how to rub the flesh from fable:*] (*PS*)   Knew how to tell the fable from the flesh: (*1962*)
5   *In all preserving larva her thigh bones*] (*PS*)   Her thigh bones in immortal larva (*1962*)
7   *The necks bent looking for the geese,*] (*PS*)   Necks bent to look for the seditious geese, (*1962*)
8   *over blocks*] (*PS*)   over blocks, (*1962*)
9   *The heads were all*] (*PS*)   Heads all (*1962*)
11   *The wrists were thick, the finger-pads worn down,*] (*PS*)   Wrists thick, the finger pads worn down (*1962*)
20   *gold.*] (*PS*)   gold; (*1962*)
21   *We*] (*PS*)   And (*1962*)
27   *towards the spring*] (*PS*)   to war with wrong (*1962*)
47   *Spain*] (*PS*)   SPAIN (*1962*)
49   *half raised*] (*PS*)   half-raised (*1962*)
50   *waxwork*] (*PS*)   waxwork, (*1962*)
53   *position*] (*PS*)   position, (*1962*)
57   *silver-green*] (*PS*)   silver green (*1962*)
59   *gestured*] (*PS*)   labourer's (*1962*)
62   *natural*] (*PS*)   all natural (*1962*)
67–68   *Take ... dream*] (*PS*)   The scalpel in my back / That broke my uneasy dream (*1962*)
73   *Eyes open*] (*PS*)   The future (*1962*)

BILL HARRINGTON: 'TO A FALLEN COMRADE'

Volunteer for Liberty, II, No. 31 (Barcelona, 5 September 1938), p. 3.

T. A. R. HYNDMAN: 'JARAMA FRONT'

Poems for Spain (1939), p. 40; *The Distant Drum: Reflections on the Spanish Civil War*, ed. Philip Toynbee (1976), p. 129 (where *comrades*, line 15, is reprinted *Comrades*).

A. M. ELLIOTT: 'JARAMA'

The Book of the XV Brigade (Madrid, 1938; republished Newcastle upon Tyne, 1975), p. 112.

T. E. NICHOLAS: 'IN REMEMBRANCE OF A SON OF WALES (WHO FELL IN SPAIN)'

Daily Worker (8 February 1938), p. 2; *Spain at War*, No. 5 (August 1938), p. 178.

W. B. KEAL: 'FOR THE FALLEN'

Daily Worker (29 October 1937), p. 4.

STEPHEN SPENDER: 'IN NO MAN'S LAND'

Collected Poems (1955), p. 101.

PABLO NERUDA: 'TO THE MOTHERS OF THE DEAD MILITIA'

Translated by Nancy Cunard.

Left Review, III, No. 3 (April 1937), pp. 140–41.

STEPHEN SPENDER: 'THE WORD DEAD AND THE MUSIC MAD'

Spectator (29 July 1938), p. 204.

The Crime was in Granada

ANTONIO MACHADO: 'THE CRIME TOOK PLACE IN GRANÁDA: TO FEDERICO GARCÍA LORCA'

Translated by D. Trevor and ?. Neumann.

Left Review, III, No. 8 (September 1937), pp. 459–60.

GEOFFREY PARSONS: 'LORCA'

Poems for Spain (1939), pp. 103–4.

J. BRONOWSKI: 'THE DEATH OF GARCIA LORCA'

Spain 1939: Four Poems (Hull, 1939), pp. 3–4; *Poems for Spain* (1939), pp. 104–5.

Prisoner

CLIVE BRANSON: 'ON BEING QUESTIONED AFTER CAPTURE. ALCANIZ'

Previously unpublished.

CLIVE BRANSON: 'DEATH SENTENCE COMMUTED TO THIRTY YEARS'

Previously unpublished.

CLIVE BRANSON: 'THE NIGHTINGALE'

Previously unpublished.

CLIVE BRANSON: 'PRISONERS'

Previously unpublished.

CLIVE BRANSON: 'THE AEROPLANE'

Previously unpublished.

CLIVE BRANSON: 'SAN PEDRO'

New Writing, new series, II (Spring 1939), p. 53.

Title in MS is 'British Prisoners in San Pedro', and the poem is dated 'San Pedro De Gardena, 1938'. The poem is divided into four stanzas in MS, and the final line reads 'barren hell' for 'empty hell'.

CLIVE BRANSON: 'TO THE GERMAN ANTI-FASCISTS IN SAN PEDRO'

= 'The German Prisoner & the Nightingale in San Pedro', *Poetry and the People*, No. 11 (*Poems for May Day*), 1939, pp. 6–7.

Text from manuscript.

PP capitalizes the first word of each line.

1   *us*]   us. (*PP*)
1–2; **17–18**   At these points *PP* makes stanza breaks.
5   *Nazis . . . home.*]   NAZIS . . . home (*PP*)
15   *corner.*]   corner (*PP*)
21   *nightingale?*]   night-bird? (*PP*)
27   *the captive*   this captive (*PP*)
33   *promise*]   promises (*PP*)
34   *sometime*]   Sometimes (*PP*)
36   *murder*]   murder, (*PP*)

CLIVE BRANSON: 'IN THE CAMP'

Previously unpublished.

CLIVE BRANSON: 'BY THE CANAL CASTILLA'

Previously unpublished.

CLIVE BRANSON: 'THE PRISONER'S OUTLOOK'

Previously unpublished.

CLIVE BRANSON: 'SUNSET'

Previously unpublished.

CLIVE BRANSON: 'A SUNDAY AFTERNOON'

Previously unpublished.

CLIVE BRANSON: 'ON DREAMING OF HOME'

Previously unpublished.

CLIVE BRANSON: 'ON THE STATUE OF CHRIST, PALENCIA (1)'

Previously unpublished.

CLIVE BRANSON: 'ON THE STATUE OF CHRIST, PALENCIA (2)'

Previously unpublished.

CLIVE BRANSON: 'LINES WRITTEN IN A BOOK OF DRAWINGS DONE BY THE ORDER OF THE COMMANDANT OF THE ITALIAN CAMP'

Previously unpublished.

CLIVE BRANSON: 'ON BEING ORDERED TO COPY A LARGE SIGNATURE OF MUSSOLINI UNDER A SLOGAN WRITTEN ON THE CAMP WALL'

Previously unpublished.

Ballads of Heroes

RICHARD CHURCH: 'THE HERO'

Listener (12 January 1939), p. 61; *Collected Poems* (1948), p. 219.

Collected Poems text.

8   *deeds,*] deeds; (*Listener*)
10 *child-bed*] childbed (*Listener*)
14 *saw, too*] saw too (*Listener*)

MILES TOMALIN: 'MAY DAY'

Previously unpublished.

MILES TOMALIN: 'SELF-DESTROYERS'

Volunteer for Liberty, II, No. 4 (Barcelona, 5 February 1938), p. 8.

MILES TOMALIN: 'CHRISTMAS EVE 1937'

Previously unpublished.

CHRISTOPHER CAUDWELL: 'LAST LETTERS OF A HERO'

News Chronicle (28 June 1937), p. 10. This page of the *News Chronicle* was subsequently reprinted as part of a pamphlet to raise funds for sending a Sprigg Memorial Ambulance to Spain.

ZOFIA SCHLEYEN: 'PLAZA DE ESPAÑA'

Translated from the Polish volunteers' paper *Dabrowszak*. Adapted into English by Miles Tomalin.

Volunteer for Liberty, I, No. 27 (Madrid, 20 December 1937), p. 5.

RICHARD CHURCH: 'THE MADRID DEFENDERS'

New Statesman (5 December 1936), p. 886; *Poems for Spain* (1939), pp. 25–6.
New Statesman text.
5   *rung;*] rung. (*PS*)

SYLVIA TOWNSEND WARNER: 'HARVEST IN 1937'

New Statesman (31 July 1937), p. 184.

C. DAY LEWIS: 'THE NABARA'

Overtures to Death (1938), pp. 41–52; *Collected Poems* (1954), pp. 191–200.

MARGOT HEINEMANN: 'THIS NEW OFFENSIVE (EBRO, 1938)'

Poems for Spain (1939), pp. 24–5.

MILES TOMALIN: 'THE GUNNER'

Volunteer for Liberty, II, No. 35 (Barcelona, 7 November 1938), p. 9.

H. G. SUTCLIFFE: 'ASTURIAS'

Volunteer for Liberty, I, No. 26 (Madrid, 13 December 1937), p. 8.

HERBERT READ: 'A SONG FOR THE SPANISH ANARCHISTS'

Poems for Spain (1939), p. 93; *Collected Poems* (1966), pp. 149–50.

STEPHEN SPENDER: 'SPAIN'S AIR CHIEF IN A MECHANIC'S BLUE DUNGAREES'

Daily Worker (19 April 1937), p. 4.

MARGOT HEINEMANN: 'ON A LOST BATTLE IN THE SPANISH WAR'

New Writing, IV (Autumn 1937), p. 61.

CHARLOTTE HALDANE: 'PASSIONARIA' [*sic*]

Left Review, III, No. 15 (April 1938), p. 926.

JACK LINDSAY: 'ON GUARD FOR SPAIN'

Left Review, III, No. 2 (March 1937), pp. 79–86.

The following 'adagio passage' was specially written by the author at the request of the declaimers and the Unity Theatre producer 'so that there would be a period of rest, a slow dirge, as contrast with the movement of the rest of the declamation' (information in a private communication to me by Jack Lindsay). These stanzas are now published for the first time.

> Mourn for the workers fallen at Badajoz
> When night flows on us and the cold stars bubble,
> In that dark width of silence, drown, go down,
> Mourn for the workers fallen, the best sons of Spain.
> Mourn for the workers fallen, the best sons of Spain.
>
> Mourn for the workers fallen in Seville
> In that dark pause that makes dark earth a stone
> Graven with the names of our beloved dead,
> Go down into the dark earth, remember them.

Mourn for the workers fallen before Madrid
Mourn for the workers fallen at Málaga
Mourn for the women's bodies quenched like broken moons
Mourn for the children, their lives snapped at flower-time.

Mourn for the workers fallen before Irun.
Their strong hands clenched upon the last defiance
Their sinewy bodies gay with all freedom's promise,
Wasted, defaced, thrust down from the lap of summer.

Mourn for the workers fallen, the best sons of Spain.
Mourn for the workers fallen, the best sons of Spain.

(Inserted between lines 246 and 247.)

STEPHEN SPENDER: 'THE WILL TO LIVE'

New Statesman (12 November 1938), p. 772.

A review of *John Cornford: A Memoir*, ed. Pat Sloan, 1938.

Romanceros

ANON: 'SPANISH FOLK SONG OF THE WAR'

Translated by Langston Hughes.

Daily Worker (16 July 1938), Supplement, p. 2.

RAFAEL ALBERTI: 'A SPECTRE IS HAUNTING EUROPE'

Translated by A. L. Lloyd.

Daily Worker (14 October 1936), p. 7. (There's another version: translated by D. Trevor and ?. Neumann, *Left Review*, III, No. 8 (September 1937), pp. 457–8.)

MANUEL ALTOLAGUIRRE: 'THE TOWER OF EL CARPIO'

Freely translated by Isidor Schneider and Stephen Williams.

International Literature, No. 7 (July 1937), pp. 32–3.

STEPHEN SPENDER: 'MY BROTHER LUIS'

Translated from the Spanish of Manuel Altolaguirre.

New Statesman (30 October 1937), p. 681.

STEPHEN SPENDER: 'MADRID'

Translated from the Spanish of Manuel Altolaguirre.
New Statesman (9 July 1938), p. 73.

STEPHEN SPENDER: 'I DEMAND THE ULTIMATE DEATH'

Translated from the Spanish of Manuel Altolaguirre.
New Statesman (8 January 1938), p. 39.

PLÁ Y BELTRAN: 'BALLAD OF LINA ODENA'

Adapted by Rolfe Humphries.
International Literature, No. 3 (March 1937), pp. 35–6.

FRANCIS FUENTES: 'REVOLUTIONARY MADRID'

Translated by Sylvia Townsend Warner.
Previously unpublished.

PEDRO GARFIAS: 'SINGLE FRONT'

Translated by Tom Wintringham.
Poems for Spain (1939), pp. 93–4.

JULIO D. GUILLÉN: 'LA PEÑA'

Translated by Sylvia Townsend Warner.
Previously unpublished.

MIGUEL HERNÁNDEZ: 'HEAR THIS VOICE'

Translated by Inez and Stephen Spender.
New Writing, V (Spring 1938), pp. 56–8; *Poems for Spain* (1939), pp. 21–4.
New Writing text.
4   *heart.*]heart, (*PS*)
58   *of innocence*] innocence (*PS*)

MIGUEL HERNÁNDEZ: 'THE WINDS OF THE PEOPLE'

Translated by A. L. Lloyd.
Poems for Spain (1939), pp. 37–9.

ANTONIO GARCÍA LUQUE: 'YO ESTAR UN ROJO!'

Translated by D. Trevor and ?. Neumann.
Left Review, III, No. 8 (September 1937), p. 458.

ANTONIO GARCÍA LUQUE: 'THE MOORISH DESERTER'

Translated by Rolfe Humphries from the French version of Roland-Simon.
International Literature, No. 3 (March 1937), p. 38.
(A second version of Luque's romancero.)

FELIX PAREDES: 'ENCARNACION JIMENEZ'

Translated by Sylvia Townsend Warner.
Previously unpublished.

JOSÉ HERRERA PETERE: 'AGAINST THE COLD IN THE MOUNTAINS'

Translated by A. L. Lloyd.
New Writing, III (Spring 1937), pp. 49–50; *Poems for Spain* (1939), pp. 91–2.

JOSÉ HERRERA PETERE: 'EL DIA QUE NO VENDRA'

Translated by Sylvia Townsend Warner.
Previously unpublished.

LUIS DE TAPIA: 'SALUD'

Freely translated by Isidor Schneider.
International Literature, No. 10–11 (1937), p. 191.

GONZÁLEZ TUÑÓN: 'LONG LIVE THE REVOLUTION'

Translated by A. L. Lloyd.
New Writing, III (Spring 1937), p 51. A shortened version, entitled 'Hail the Revolution', translated by Rolfe Humphries from the French version, appeared in *International Literature*, No. 3 (March 1937), pp. 38–9.

LORENZO VARELA: 'POEM'

Translated by A. M. Elliott.
Daily Worker (21 May 1938), Supplement, p. 2.

JOSÉ MORENO VILLA: 'MADRID FRONT'

Translated by Stanley Richardson.

New Writing, new series, I (Autumn 1938), pp. 34–5.

The Internationals

NANCY CUNARD: 'SONNET IN FIVE LANGUAGES:
THE INTERNATIONALS'

Nancy Cunard, ed. Hugh Ford (1968), p. 172.

Nancy Cunard added explanatory notes for each line (p. 173):

1 At this time comes another pause in history, but where is its Dante (to chronicle it)?

2 If the fire burn low (the spirit perforce be dim, inarticulate) it is the same fire, I see.

3 Muted art thou (Spain), but strivest ever forward

4 And all that happened before might well come here again

5 Some of the 'Moor-Soldiers' still live. 'Die Moorsoldaten' was the name given them by the inhabitants near the Nazi concentration camps in the nineteen-thirties, to the men they saw returning from the enforced, utterly senseless work with pick and shovel, digging dry ground, carting stones, making tracks, putting up yet more barbed wire etc. These men formed themselves into marching units, singing as they came and went in all that misery – songs of courage, of unending defiance. Alejo Carpentier, the Cuban musician, recorded one: 'Die Moorsoldaten' and another, both in German; 'Die Thaelmann Kolonne in den Strassen von Madrid' is its first line.

6 They, and other Germans of the same feeling, would be ready to fight again (in the case of need, against the Fascists)

7 As would many another man, from far away and near;

8 If such be not spoken of, yet it is well known.

9 Upsurge of tongues comes ever, mixed with hope, wherever one goes;

10 'I treni misti' in Italian means part-goods, part-passenger, and they go very far ...

11 May our own (British) feelings coincide with all this (if it should come to pass),

12 Though who can tell me the date of the year wherein such might be?

13 Courage endures if the heart clings to its aces ...

14 Ah (Spain) when thine own turn comest, much much shallst thou harvest!

CLIVE BRANSON: 'THE INTERNATIONAL'

= 'International', *Poetry and the People*, No. 17 (February 1940), p. 18.

Text of manuscript.

8, 24 *PP attaches these lines to the stanzas following.*
17 *I*] I've (*PP*)
26 *Time*] Time, (*PP*)
27 *humanity*] humanity, (*PP*)

TOM WINTRINGHAM: 'MONUMENT'

Left Review, III, No. 9 (October 1937), pp. 517–19; *Volunteer for Liberty*, II, No. 35 (Barcelona, 7 November 1938), p. 18.

Left Review text.

40 *Extramadura*]   Extremadura (*VL*)
45–46 *VL makes a stanza break at this point*
71 *No space after line 71 in VL*
81 future,]   futures (*VL*)

TOM WINTRINGHAM: 'COMRADES OF JARAMA'

Volunteer for Liberty, No. 2 (February 1940), p. 4.

GEORGE ORWELL: 'THE ITALIAN SOLDIER SHOOK MY HAND'

From 'Looking back on the Spanish War', *New Road* (1943), p. 157; *Such, Such Were the Joys* (New York, 1953), pp. 152–3; *Collected Essays, Journalism and Letters of George Orwell*, ed. Sonia Orwell and Ian Angus (4 vols., 1968), II, pp. 266–7.

New Road text.

9 *fly-blown*] flyblown (*1953, 1968*)

HUGH MACDIARMID: 'AN ENGLISH WAR-POET'

The Voice of Scotland, IX, No. 1 (1958), pp. 17–19.

C. DAY LEWIS: 'THE VOLUNTEER'

Overtures to Death (1938), p. 40; *Collected Poems* (1954), pp. 190–91.

TOM WINTRINGHAM: 'IT'S A BOHUNK'

New Writing, new series, II (Spring 1939), pp. 54–60.

AILEEN PALMER: 'THAELMANN BATTALION'

Poetry and the People, No. 12 (June 1939), p. 12.

L. KENDALL: 'TO THE HEROES OF THE INTERNATIONAL BRIGADE IN SPAIN'

Poetry and the People, No. 4 (October 1938), p. 7; *Volunteer for Liberty*, IV, No. 5 (1943), p. 14.

ERIC EDNEY: 'THE BATTALION GOES FORWARD'

Volunteer for Liberty, No. 2 (February 1940), pp. 4–5.

ANON: 'SALUD, BRIGADE – SALUD!'

Volunteer for Liberty, No. 4 (April 1940), pp. 4–5.

ERIC EDNEY: 'SALUD!'

Volunteer for Liberty, No. 5 (May 1940), p. 7.

W. B. KEAL: 'BUT NO BUGLES'

Daily Worker (29 October 1937), p. 4.

R. GARDNER: 'INTERNATIONAL BRIGADE'

Poetry and the People, No. 7 (January 1939), p. 10.

LUIS PEREZ INFANTE: 'VOLUNTEERS FOR LIBERTY'

Translated by Hans Kahle and Leslie Phillips.
Kingdom Come, III, No. 9 (1941), pp. 20–21.

Unheroic Notes

STEPHEN SPENDER: 'TWO ARMIES'

New Statesman (8 May 1937), p. 770; *The Still Centre* (1939), pp. 55–6; *Selected Poems* (1940), pp. 39–40; *Collected Poems* (1955), pp. 97–8.

Collected Poems text.

1   *plain,*] (*1939, 1940*)   plain (*NS*)
2   *machinery,*] (*1939, 1940*)   machinery (*NS*)
5   *leave;*] (*1939, 1940*)   leave (*NS*)
9   *That*] Which (*NS, 1939, 1940*)
10 *song,*] (*1939, 1940*) song (*NS*)
11 *their salute;*] (*NS*)   the salute; (*1939, 1940*)
12 *fell,*] (*1939, 1940*)   fell (*NS*)
14 *harvest,*] harvest (*NS, 1939, 1940*)
16 *the revolver.*] a revolver. (*NS, 1939, 1940*)
20 *Finally,*] (*1939, 1940*)   Finally (*NS*)
21 *with hail*] like hail (*NS, 1939, 1940*)
22 *Or shoots*] Or pours (*NS, 1939, 1940*)
     at,] (*1939, 1940*)   at (*NS*)
25 *those*] these (*NS, 1939, 1940*)
26 *night,*] night (*NS, 1939, 1940*)
34 *this plain*] the plain (*NS, 1939, 1940*)
35 *shadows*] (*NS*)   shadow (*1939, 1940*)
     thousand] (*1939, 1940*)   million (*NS*)
36 *No-Man's-Land*] no man's land (*NS*)   no-man's-land (*1939, 1940*)
38 *destroy.*] kill life. (*NS, 1939, 1940*)

STEPHEN SPENDER: 'HEROES IN SPAIN'

New Statesman (1 May 1937), pp. 714–15.

STEPHEN SPENDER: 'THE COWARD'

The Still Centre (1939), pp. 59–60; *Selected Poems* (1940), pp. 43–4; *Collected Poems* (1955), pp. 102–3.

Collected Poems text.

3 *This is wiser*] It is easier (*1939, 1940*)
4 *After line 4, 1939 and 1940 insert*   Of death plunged in their willed desire
6 *These blood-dark*] Its opened (*1939, 1940*)
7 *shame.*] shame (*1939, 1940*)
   After line 7, 1939 and 1940 insert   Whose inexpiable blood/For his unhealing wound is food.

8   *Here one died,*] A man was killed, (*1939, 1940*)
9   *Of lead, but of lead rings of terror.*] With lead but with rings of terror; (*1939, 1940*)
10   *His final moment*] To him, that instant (*1939, 1940*)
11   *Of naked revelatory truth:*] Of the final hidden truth (*1939, 1940*)
12   *He saw the flagship*] When the troopship (*1939, 1940*)
13   *His . . . his*] The . . . the (*1939, 1940*)
14   *white accompaniment*] following handkerchiefs (*1939, 1940*)
15   *Lead to*] All led to (*1939, 1940*)
16   *muscle, eyes,*] muscle and eyes (*1939, 1940*)
17   *Built in their noble tower of lies,*] Assembled in a tower of lies (*1939, 1940*)
18   *Scattered on the*] Were scattered on an (*1939, 1940*)
19   *Him their false promises betrayed.*] When the deceiving past betrayed (*1939, 1940*)
20   *All the bright visions in one instant*] All their perceptions in one instant, (*1939, 1940*)
21-22 *Changed . . . trees.*] And his true gaze, the sum of present,/Saw his guts lie beneath the trees. (*1939, 1940*)
23-25 *There's . . . here*]
           Lest every eye should look and see
           The answer to its life as he,
           When the flesh prizes are all lost
           In that white second of the ghost
           Who grasps his world of loneliness
           Sliding into empty space: –
           I gather all my life and pour
           Out its love and comfort here. (*1939, 1940*)
26   *loneliness*] loneliness, (*1939, 1940*)
27   *release*] release, (*1939, 1940*)
28   *Love and pity dare not*] My love and pity shall not (*1939, 1940*)
29   *lifetime, at the least.*] lifetime at least. (*1939, 1940*)

EWART MILNE: 'SIERRAN VIGIL'

New Writing, new series, II (Spring 1939), pp. 34-5; *Letter from Ireland* (Dublin, 1940), pp. 32-3.

New Writing text.

(*1940* text, unlike the *New Writing* text, begins *each* line with a capital letter.)

12   *ill-starred*] illstarred (*1940*)
20   *river.*] river (*1940*)
34   *unalterably!*] unalterably. (*1940*)
35   *war?*] War? (*1940*)
37   *chico's . . . chica's*] Chico's . . . Chica's (*1940*)

STEPHEN SPENDER: 'ULTIMA RATIO REGUM'

The Still Centre (1939), pp. 57–8; *Selected Poems* (1940), pp. 41–2; *Collected Poems* (1955), p. 99; = 'Regum Ultima Ratio', *New Statesman* (15 May 1937), p. 811; *Poems for Spain* (1939), pp. 43–4.

Text of *Collected Poems*.

2 *Spring*] spring (*NS, PS, 1939, 1940*)
  hillside] (*NS, 1939, 1940*)   hill-side (*PS*)
7 *lived, tall*] (*1939, 1940*)   lived tall (*NS, PS*)
  him] (*NS, PS*)   him. (*1939, 1940*)
8 *in*] (*NS*)   in; (*PS*)   in. (*1939, 1940*)
11 *well,*] (*1939, 1940*)   well (*NS, PS*)
12 *intangible as a Stock Exchange rumour*] (*1939, 1940*)   intangible as rumour (*NS, PS*)
13 *O too*] (*NS, 1939, 1940*)   Oh, too (*PS*)
15 *guns,*] (*1939, 1940*)   guns; (*NS, PS*)
16 *Machine-gun*] (*PS, 1939, 1940*)   Machine gun (*NS*)
21 *Consider. One*] (*1939, 1940*)   Consider: only one (*NS, PS*)
22 *Ask. Was*] (*1939, 1940*)   Ask: was (*NS, PS*)
23 *young, and*] young and (*NS, PS, 1939, 1940*)
24 *Lying*] (*1939, 1940*)   Stretched (*NS, PS*)
  O world, O death?] (*NS, 1939, 1940*)   Oh, world, Oh, death? (*PS*)

EWART MILNE: 'ESCAPE'

Ireland Today, II, No. 12 (December 1937), pp. 49–55.

STEPHEN SPENDER: 'THOUGHTS DURING AN AIR RAID'

The Still Centre (1939), p. 45; *Selected Poems* (1940), p. 38; *Collected Poems* (1955), p. 96.

Collected Poems text.

1 *oneself*]   myself (*1939, 1940*)
4 *Well, well, one carries on.*] Well, well, I carry on (*1939, 1940*)
5 *this thing 'I'*]   the great 'I' (*1939, 1940*)
  up on]   upon (*1939, 1940*)
6 *so like*]   more like (*1939, 1940*)
7 *the wall-paper*]   flowering wallpaper (*1939, 1940*)
8 *Blowing smoke-wreaths of roses, one*]   Which rings in wreathes above, I (*1939, 1940*)
9 *the fingers*]   my fingers (*1939, 1940*)
10–11 *Indented . . . wireless.*]   Heavy and black as I rustle the paper, / The wireless wail in the lounge margin (*1939, 1940*)

13 *one*]   me (*1939, 1940*)
14 *thought's*]   thought is (*1939, 1940*)
15-16 *For . . . indeed.*]   To whom my death would only be a name,/One figure in a column. (*1939, 1940*)
17 *every 'one'*]   all the 'I's (*1939, 1940*)
18 *roses*]   flowers (*1939, 1940*)
20 *Piecemeal for each,*]   For everyone (*1939, 1940*)
21 *That wreath of*]   And drags him to that (*1939, 1940*)

STEPHEN SPENDER: 'FALL OF A CITY'

New Statesman (6 August 1938), p. 219; *Poems for Spain* (1939), pp. 85-6; *The Still Centre* (1939), pp. 65-6; *Selected Poems* (1940), pp. 47-8; *Collected Poems* (1955), pp. 104-5.

Collected Poems text.

1 *walls,*] (*NS*)   walls (*PS, 1939, 1940*)
2 *streets*] (*PS, 1939, 1940*)   streets, (*NS*)
3 *destroyed,*] destroyed (*NS, PS, 1939, 1940*)
4 *tears,*] (*NS, 1939, 1940*)   tears (*PS*)
5-6 *Skins peeling from their bodies/In*] (*NS, 1939, 1940*)   Bodies with paper skins peeled/By (*PS*)
7 *hall*] (*PS, 1939, 1940*)   hall, (*NS*)
8 *the feet thundered*] (*NS, 1939, 1940*)   feet stamped (*PS*)
    roared, (*NS, PS, 1939, 1940*)
9 Fox *and* Lorca] (*PS, 1939, 1940*)   *Fox* and *Lorca* (*NS*)
10 *furiously deleted*] angrily deleted, (*NS*)   angrily deleted (*PS, 1939, 1940*)
11 *to dust*] (*NS, 1939, 1940*)   in dust (*PS*)
    their gold] their dust, (*NS, 1939, 1940*)   to dust, (*PS*)
12 *From praise*] From golden praise (*NS, PS, 1939, 1940*)
13 *and salutes*] (*NS, 1939, 1940*)   and the signs (*PS*)
14 *hands,*] hands (*NS, PS, 1939, 1940*)
15 *wore,*] (*NS*)   wore; (*PS*)   wore (*1939, 1940*)
16 *Or in*] (*PS, 1939, 1940*)   Or to (*NS*)
17 *with a smile*] (*NS, 1939, 1940*)   by a smile (*PS*)
18 *victors where*] victors when (*NS, 1939, 1940*)   tyrants when (*PS*)
22 *tune*] (*NS, 1939, 1940*)   music (*PS*)
23 *Following the donkey's bray;*] (*1939, 1940*)   Following the donkey bray – (*NS*)   Accompanying the donkey's bray, (*PS*)
24 *These only remember to forget*] (*NS, 1939, 1940*)   Only remembering to forget (*PS*)
26 *In the high door*] In the high shelf (*NS*)   On the high door (*PS, 1939, 1940*)
27 *irrefrangible eye*] (*1939, 1940*)   irrefragable eye, (*NS, PS*)
28 *child*] (*PS, 1939, 1940*)   child – (*NS*)

29 – *Spark . . . liberty.*] Spark . . . potency: (*NS*)   Spark . . . energy,
(*PS*)   – Spark . . . energy. (*1939, 1940*)
30 *bitter toy.*] (*1939, 1940*)   wicked toy. (*NS, PS*)

H B MALLALIEU: 'SPAIN'

Letter in Wartime and other Poems (Fortune Press, 1941), p. 14; = 'Spain,
1938', in *Poets of Tomorrow: First Selection* (Hogarth, 1939), p. 33, and in
Poems for Spain (1939), p. 34.

1941 Text.

2 *dead,*] (*1939*)   dead (*PS*)
5 *nor*] (*PS*)   or (*1939*)
8 *deserted*] deserted, (*1939, PS*)
9 *use. Those who mourn grown mad.*] use: and those who mourn grow mad.
(*1939*)   use, the suffering mind is mad. (*PS*)
10 *May*] (*1939*)   Let (*PS*)
13 *will, then let us show*] (*PS*)   will. Now let us show (*1939*)

STEPHEN SPENDER: 'A STOPWATCH AND AN ORDNANCE MAP (TO SAMUEL BARBER)'

(Without dedication) *The Still Centre* (1939), p. 61; *Selected Poems* (1940),
p. 45; (with dedication) *Collected Poems* (1955), p. 100.

Text of *Collected Poems.*

7, 14, 21 *All under the olive trees.*] not in italics (*1939, 1940*)
12 *Opening*] That opened (*1939, 1940*)
20 *Space*] The space (*1939, 1940*)

STEPHEN SPENDER: 'THE ROOM ABOVE THE SQUARE'

The Still Centre (1939), p. 40; *Selected Poems* (1940), p. 37; *Collected Poems*
(1955), p. 95.

Text of *Collected Poems.*

2 *When*] Where (*1939, 1940*)
3 *glowed*] flowered (*1939, 1940*)
8 *That through us*] Which through me (*1939, 1940*)
9 *high*] dark (*1939, 1940*)
10 *Above the darkened*] Which hangs above the (*1939, 1940*)
11 *roots,*] roots (*1939, 1940*)
12 *Unshattered*] Peaceful (*1939, 1940*)

STEPHEN SPENDER: 'PORT BOU'

Poems for Spain (1939), pp. 89–90; *The Still Centre* (1939), pp. 71–3;
Selected Poems (1940), pp. 49–50; *Collected Poems* (1955), pp. 106–7; =
'Port Bou – Firing Practice', *New Writing*, new series, I (Autumn 1938),
pp. 26–7.

Collected Poems text.

3   *looks through*] stares at (*NW*)   watches (*PS, 1939, 1940*)
4   *freedom animal*] freedom in animal (*NW, PS, 1939, 1940*)
5   *earth-and-rock arms*] earth-and-rock flesh arms (*NW, PS, 1939, 1940*)
     this small harbour] this harbour (*NW, PS, 1939, 1940*)
6   *encircle*] enclose (*NW, PS, 1939, 1940*)
7   *Which, through a gap,*] (*PS, 1939, 1940*)   Which through a gap (*NW*)
     into the ocean,] to the Mediterranean (*NW*)   to the open sea (*PS,
     1939, 1940*)
8   *Where dolphins swim and liners throb.*] Where ships and dolphins swim
     and above is the sun. (*NW, PS, 1939, 1940*)
9   *bright winter sunlight*] (*PS, 1939, 1940*)   winter sunlight (*NW*)
     parapet] stone parapet (*NW, PS, 1939, 1940*)
10   *circling*] (*PS, 1939, 1940*)   encircling (*NW*)
11   *And my mind is empty*] Empty in my mind (*NW, PS, 1939, 1940*)
     glittering stone] (*PS, 1939, 1940*)   glaring stone (*NW*)
12   *While*] Because (*NW, PS, 1939, 1940*)
13   *(The one written above) and the words (written above)*] And seeing an
     image I coin out the words (*NW*)   And seeing an image I count out the
     coined words (*PS, 1939, 1940*)
14   *To set down*] To remember (*NW, PS, 1939, 1940*)
.   *Port Bou.*] this harbour. (*NW, PS, 1939, 1940*)
16   *warm downwards-looking*] warm waving flaglike (*NW*)   waving flag-
     like (*PS*)   warm waving flag-like (*1939, 1940*)
17   *militia men*] militiamen (*NW, PS, 1939, 1940*)
     (French)] French (*NW, PS, 1939, 1940*)
18   *write of our struggle*] speak of our struggle, (*NW, PS, 1939, 1940*)
19   *paper, but they cannot read it,*] paper but they refuse it (*NW*)   paper
     but they refuse, (*PS, 1939, 1940*)
20   *They . . . cigarettes.*] They did not ask for anything so valuable/But only
     for friendly words and to offer me cigarettes. (*NW*)   They did not ask for
     anything so precious/But only for friendly words and to offer me cigarettes.
     (*PS, 1939, 1940*)
21   *waving flag-like*] smiling (*NW, PS, 1939, 1940*)
     peace. The] peace, the (*NW, PS, 1939, 1940*)
22   *Of rusted carbines lean against their knees,*] Of the rusty carbines brush
     against their trousers (*NW, PS, 1939, 1940*)
23   *Like . . . reeds.*] Almost as fragilely as reeds, (*NW*)   Almost as
     fragilely as reeds; (*PS, 1939, 1940*)

24 *Wrapped in cloth – old granny in a shawl –*] And wrapped in cloth, like a mother in a shawl (*NW*)　　And wrapped in a cloth – old mother in a shawl – (*PS, 1939, 1940*)

25 *stuttering*] terrible (*NW, PS, 1939, 1940*)

26 *shout – salute*] wave (*NW*)　　shout, salute (*PS, 1939, 1940*)
forward] (*1939, 1940*)　　forwards (*NW*)　　forward. (*PS*)

28 *mouth dribbling,*] laughing mouth (*NW*)　　running mouth, (*PS, 1939, 1940*)

29 *From . . . pom'.*] With three teeth like yellow bullets, spits 'bang-bang-bang!' (*NW*)　　With three teeth like bullets, spits out 'pom-pom-pom.' (*PS, 1939, 1940*)

30 *The children*] (*PS, 1939, 1940*)　　Children (*NW*)
women;] women (*NW, PS, 1939, 1940*)

31 *skirts, trail over the horizon.*] clothes, follow over the hill (*NW*) clothes, follow over the hill. (*PS*)　　clothes, follow over the hill; (*1939, 1940*)

32 *Now . . . practice.*] To the firing practice, till the village is empty. (*NW*) Till the village is empty, for the firing practice (*PS, 1939, 1940*)

33 *I*] (*NW*)　　And I (*PS, 1939, 1940*)
on the parapet at the exact centre] at the port's exact centre (*NW*)　　on the bridge at the exact centre (*PS, 1939, 1940*)

34 *Above . . . saliva.*] Where the cleaving river trickles like saliva. (*NW, PS, 1939, 1940*)

35 *The exact centre, solitary as the bull's eye in a target.*] I on the bridge solitary as a target (*NW*)　　At the exact centre, solitary as a target, (*PS, 1939, 1940*)

36 *Nothing*] Where nothing (*NW, PS, 1939, 1940*)
the background] a background (*NW, PS, 1939, 1940*)
stage-scenery houses] cardboard houses (*NW, 1939, 1940*)　　cardboard houses, (*PS*)

37 *Save the skirring mongrels.*] Except disgraceful scurring dogs. (*NW*) Except the disgraceful scurring dogs; '(*PS*)　　Except the disgraceful skirring dogs; (*1939, 1940*)
The firing now begins] Then the firing begins (*NW*)　　and then the firing begins, (*PS*)　　and the firing begins (*1939, 1940*)

38 *mouth,*] mouth (*NW, PS, 1939, 1940*)

39 *flecks of foam*] (*PS, 1939, 1940*)　　flecks (*NW*)
whipped] are gashed (*NW*)　　gashed (*PS, 1939, 1940*)
from the sea.] in the sea. (*NW*)　　in the sea (*PS*)　　in the sea; (*1939, 1940*)

40 *An echo spreads its cat-o'-nine tails*] The echo trails over like an iron lash (*NW*)　　And the echo trails over like an iron lash (*PS*)　　And the echo trails over its iron lash (*1939, 1940*)

41 *Thrashing*] Whipping (*NW, PS, 1939, 1940*)
neighbour hills.] the circling hills. (*NW*)　　the surrounding hills. (*PS, 1939, 1940*)

43 *is paper on which*] seems of paper where (*NW*) seems paper where (*PS, 1939, 1940*)

  dust and words sift,] dust and ink fall, (*NW, 1939, 1940*) dust and ink falls, (*PS*)

44 *assure*] tell (*NW, PS, 1939, 1940*)

  practice] practice, (*NW, PS, 1939, 1940*)

45 *But I am the coward of cowards. The machine-gun stitches*] But my body seems a rag which the machine-gun stitches, (*NW*) But my body seems a cloth which the machine-gun stitches (*PS*) And my body seems a cloth which the machine-gun stitches (*1939, 1940*)

46 *My intestines with a needle, back and forth;*] Like a sewing-machine, neatly, with cotton from a reel; (*NW, PS, 1939, 1940*)

47 *The solitary, spasmodic, white puffs*] And the solitary, irregular, thin 'paffs' (*NW, 1939, 1940*) And the solitary, irregular thin 'paffs' (*PS*)

48 *Draw fear in white threads back and forth through my body.*] Draw on long needles white threads through my navel. (*NW, PS, 1939, 1940*)

EWART MILNE: 'THE STATUE'

Ireland Today, III, No. 3 (March 1938), pp. 231-8.

MILES TOMALIN: 'AFTER BRUNETE'

Previously unpublished.

MILES TOMALIN: 'NICHOLAS'

Previously unpublished.

Insensible at Such a Time

CLIVE BRANSON: 'SPAIN. DECEMBER 1936'

Previously unpublished.

VALENTINE ACKLAND: 'INSTRUCTIONS FROM ENGLAND. (1936)'

Previously unpublished.

MILES TOMALIN: 'TO ENGLAND FROM THE ENGLISH DEAD'

Volunteer for Liberty, II, No. 35 (Barcelona, 7 November 1938), p. 9.

EDGELL RICKWORD: 'TO THE WIFE OF ANY NON-INTERVENTION STATESMAN'

Left Review, III, No. 14 (March 1938), pp. 834–6; *Poems for Spain* (1939), pp. 74–7.

Left Review text.

23 *a husband*] your husband (*PS*)
32 *our*] our (*PS*)
65 *Teruel,*] Teruel (*PS*)
76 *Robbed*] Rob (*PS*)
83 *Would she not have its sponsor*] Should not its sponsor be (*PS*)

GEOFFREY GRIGSON: 'THE NON-INTERVENERS'

Several Observations: Thirty-Five Poems (1939), pp. 32–3.

SAGGITARIUS: 'DULCE ET DECORUM EST'

New Statesman (16 January 1937), p. 76.

BRIAN HOWARD: 'FOR THOSE WITH INVESTMENTS IN SPAIN'

Poems for Spain (1939), pp. 77–8. According to *Brian Howard, Portrait of a Failure*, ed. M.-J. Lancaster (1968), p. 595, this poem was first published in *Les Poètes du Monde defendent le peuple espagnol*, and *PS* transposed the ends of the last two lines (originally '... shooting from breaking rooms', '... grieving in falling homes').

ALBERT BROWN: 'THEY DON'T KNOW'

New Writing, new series, I (Autumn 1938), p. 193.

PABLO NERUDA: 'ALMERIA'

Translated by Nancy Cunard.

Left Review, III, No. 7 (August 1937), p. 407; *Poems for Spain* (1939), pp. 73–4.

Left Review text.

2 *tears,*] tears. (*PS*)
12 *soigne*] soigné (*PS*)
19 *fete*] fête (*PS*)

SAGITTARIUS: 'THEY GOT WHAT THEY WANTED'

New Statesman (13 May 1939), p. 734.

STANLEY RICHARDSON: 'TO A CERTAIN PRIEST'

Spain at War, No. 3 (June 1938), p. 112.

ELISABETH CLUER: 'ANALOGY IN MADRID'

New Statesman (8 April 1939), p. 536.

HERBERT L. PEACOCK: 'SHIP FOR SPAIN'

Poetry and the People, No. 6 (December 1938), pp. 5–6.

MILES TOMALIN: 'DOWN THE ROAD'

Volunteer for Liberty, No. 1 (January 1940), p. 6.

REDMAYNE FITZGERALD: 'THE VICTORS'

Poems for Spain (1939), p. 83.

SOMHAIRLE MACALASTAIR: 'BALLYSEEDY BEFRIENDS BADAJOZ'

Left Review, II, No. 15 (December 1936), p. 817.

REX WARNER: 'ARMS IN SPAIN'

Left Review, III, No.3 (April 1937), p. 139; *Poems for Spain* (1939), p. 50.
Left Review text.

4 *these*] These (*PS*)
4 and 12 *machine guns*] machine-guns (*PS*)

SOMHAIRLE MACALASTAIR: 'BATTLE SONG OF "IRISH CHRISTIAN FRONT": "OFF TO SALAMANCA"'

Peadar O'Donnell, *Salud! An Irishman in Spain* (1937), pp. 251–2.

That Fighting was a Long Way Off

BERNARD SPENCER: 'A THOUSAND KILLED'

New Verse, No. 20 (April–May 1936), p. 11; *The Years's Poetry* (1937), ed.
D. K. Roberts and G. Grigson, p. 104; *Aegean Islands and Other Poems*
(1946), p. 43; *Collected Poems* (1965), p. 14.

RICHARD CHURCH: 'GRIEF'S REFLECTION'

Collected Poems (1948), pp. 220–21.

REX WARNER: 'THE TOURIST LOOKS AT SPAIN'

New Writing, IV (Autumn 1937), pp. 229–31; *Poems for Spain* (1939), pp. 65–9.

New Writing text.

69   *sea*] the sea (*PS*)

JACK LINDSAY: 'LOOKING AT A MAP OF SPAIN ON THE DEVON COAST (AUGUST, 1937)'

Poems for Spain (1939), pp. 60–64.

BERNARD SPENCER: 'A COLD NIGHT'

New Verse, No. 24 (Feb.–March 1937), pp. 8–9; *Aegean Islands and Other Poems* (1946), p. 39; *Collected Poems* (1965), p. 10.

H. M. KING: 'COLD IN ENGLAND'

Daily Worker (22 December 1938), p. 7.

KATHLEEN RAINE: 'FATA MORGANA'

New Verse, No. 25 (May 1937), pp. 7–9; *The Year's Poetry* (1937), ed. D. K. Roberts and G. Grigson, pp. 91–5.

30   For *allhallowed*, *New Verse* reads: unhallowed.

HANS HAFLIN: 'THE NEWS'

Daily Worker (18 December 1936), p. 4.

EDGAR FOXALL: 'POEM' ('HE AWOKE FROM DREAMS OF THE FORTUNATE ISLES')

Proems (The Fortune Press, 1938), p. 70.

RUTHVEN TODD: 'IN SEPTEMBER'

The Listener, XVIII (27 October 1937), p. 899; *Proems* (The Fortune Press, 1938), p. 54; *Poets of Tomorrow: First Selection* (Hogarth, 1939), pp. 50–51.

22   The *Proems* text ends this line with a comma.

RUTHVEN TODD: 'POEM (FOR C.C.)'

Twentieth-Century Verse, No. 9 (March 1938), p. 15; *Proems* (The Fortune Press, 1938), p. 52; *Poets of Tomorrow: First Selection* (Hogarth, 1939), p. 57.

Photogenic War

C. DAY LEWIS: 'NEWSREEL'

Left Review, III, No. 13 (February 1938), p. 794; *Overtures to Death* (1938), p. 17; *Collected Poems* (1954), pp. 171–2.

Collected Poems text.

4 *a fur*] (*OD*)　　the fur (*LR*)
9 *this common*] (*OD*)　　a common (*LR*)

BERNARD GUTTERIDGE: 'SPANISH EARTH'

New Writing, new series, III (Christmas 1939), p. 59. *Spanish Earth* was the film by Joris Ivens which Hemingway helped to make.

STEPHEN SPENDER: 'WAR PHOTOGRAPH'

New Statesman (5 June 1937), p. 922; *The Still Centre* (1939), pp. 62–3; *Selected Poems* (1940), p. 46.

New Statesman text.

1–3]　*Omitted from 1939 and 1940.*
6 *frond.*] frond, (*1939, 1940*)
16 *changes*] changes, (*1939, 1940*)
　　tense] tense, (*1939, 1940*)
17 *moon,*] moon (*1939, 1940*)
22 *snow's*] snows' (*1939, 1940*)

BERNARD GUTTERIDGE: 'IN SEPTEMBER 1939'

Traveller's Eye (1947), p. 30; *Old Damson Face* (1975), p. 41; = 'In 1939', *Listener*, XXII (19 October 1939), p. 769.

Traveller's Eye text.

2 *Illustrated London News:* 'Illustrated London News' (*Listener*)　　Illustrated London News (*ODF*)
3 *bloody*] (*ODF*)　　bloody, (*Listener*)
8 *path:*] (*ODF*)　　path, (*Listener*)

9 *Between lines 9 and 10, Listener has a row of asterisks, breaking the poem clearly into two halves.*
10–12 *Now . . . moons*] (*Listener*)   *deleted ODF*
12 *zany moons.*] many moons. (*Listener*)
13 *window*] (*ODF*)   windows (*Listener*)

STEPHEN SPENDER: 'PICTURES IN SPAIN'

Spectator (30 July 1937), p. 199.

J. F. HENDRY: 'PICASSO: FOR GUERNICA'

Seven, No. 4 (Spring 1939), p. 18.

STEPHEN SPENDER: 'GUERNICA'

New Statesman (15 October 1938), pp. 567–8.

Talking Bronco

ROY CAMPBELL: 'A LETTER FROM THE SAN MATEO FRONT'

Collected Poems(1949–1960), Vol. II (1957), pp. 38–54. The poem is Part One of *Flowering Rifle: A Poem from the Battlefield of Spain* (1939), plus the footnotes.

STEPHEN SPENDER: 'THE TALKING BRONCO'
(Review of *Flowering Rifle*)

New Statesman (11 March 1939), p. 370.

ROY CAMPBELL: 'FLOWERING RIFLES'
(Letter in reply to Spender's review of *Flowering Rifle*)

New Statesman (8 April 1939), pp. 540–41.

But Some Remember Spain

JACK LINDSAY: 'TWO DAYS'

Previously unpublished.

J. T. RODERICK: 'MEMORY'

Seven, II, No. 3 (October–November 1941), p. 21.

H. B. MALLALIEU: 'IN THE INTERVAL'

Letter in Wartime and Other Poems (Fortune Press, 1941), p. 35.

LOUIS MACNEICE: FROM 'AUTUMN JOURNAL'

Part VI, *Autumn Journal* (1939), pp. 26–9; *Poems 1925–1940* (New York, 1940), pp. 182–5; *Collected Poems* (1949), pp. 130–32; = 'Remembering Spain', *Poems for Spain* (1939), pp. 97–100.

Collected Poems text.

2 *ruin*] (*1939, 1940*)   ruin, (*PS*)
4 *or the haunted faces*] (*1939, 1940*)   of the haunted faces. (*PS*)
6 *sickle, Boicot, Viva, Muerra:*] (*1939, 1940*)   Sickle, Boicott: Viva · Muerra; (*PS*)
7 *waterfalls,*] (*1939, 1940*)   waterfalls; (*PS*)
8 *shellfish*] (*1939, 1940*)   shell-fish (*PS*)
9 *fretted stone the Moor*] (*1939, 1940*)   fretwork that the Moor (*PS*)
18 *riches or repression*] (*1939, 1940*)   riches and repression, (*PS*)
22 *Sunday*] Sunday; (*1939, PS, 1940*)
26 *elections*] (*1939, PS*)   election (*1940*)
29 *Order*] (*1939, 1940*)   Order, (*PS*)
38 *pincers*] (*1939, 1940*)   pincers, (*PS*)
42 *for*] (*1939, 1940*)   for; (*PS*)
43–44 (*Goya . . . laughter?*)] (*1939, 1940*)   And Goya . . . laughter? (*PS*)
46 *river*] (*1939, 1940*)   river, (*PS*)
47 *Valdepeñas*] (*1939, 1940*)   Valdepenas (*PS*)
48 *gardens;*] (*1939, 1940*)   gardens. (*PS*)
50 *throw*] (*1939, 1940*)   threw (*PS*)
58 *Seville*] (*1939, 1940*)   Seville, (*PS*)
64 *Cut and dried for*] (*1939, 1940*)   That hands a pass to (*PS*)
66 *invective;*] (*1939, 1940*)   invective (*PS*)
72 *upright;*] (*1939, 1940*)   upright, (*PS*)
75 *Cordova*] (*1939, 1940*)   Cordova, (*PS*)
76 *right light*] (*1939, 1940*)   light to be right (*PS*)
87 *Outside a toothless door, a church bereft*] (*1939, 1940*)   Outside a church bereft (*PS*)
88 *aura.*] (*1939, 1940*)   aura; (*PS*)
91 *blood-lust*] (*1939, 1940*)   bloodlust (*PS*)
94 *realising*] (*1939, 1940*)   realizing (*PS*)
100 *rag-tag*] (*1939, 1940*)   rag-time (*PS*)

JACK LINDSAY: 'HAVING FELT FOR SPAIN, WHAT FURTHER
CAN WE FEEL?'

After the 'Thirties: The Novel in Britain and its Future (1956), p. 65.

J. C. HALL: 'POSTSCRIPT FOR SPAIN'

Kingdom Come, I, No. 4 (1940), p. 135.

ROY FULLER: 'TIMES OF WAR AND REVOLUTION'

Collected Poems 1936–1961 (1962), p. 154.

MILES TOMALIN: 'AFTERMATH'

Previously unpublished.

Index of Authors

Ackland, Valentine, 372
Alberti, Rafael, 270
Altolaguirre, Manuel, 271, 274–6
Anon, 269, 326
Auden, W. H., 97, 100, 171

Barker, George, 104, 110, 157
Branson, Clive, 211–22, 303, 371
Bronowski, J., 129, 208
Brown, Albert, 168, 378

Campbell, Roy, 423, 443
Carpenter, Maurice, 188
Caudwell, Christopher, 228
Church, Richard, 225, 232, 391
Cluer, Elisabeth, 382
Cornford, John, 110–28, 130
Cunard, Nancy, 169, 303

Donnelly, Charles, 104, 107, 108

Edney, Eric, 324, 326
Elliott, A. M., 194

Fitzgerald, Redmayne, 385
Foxall, Edgar, 107, 405
Fuentes, Francis, 279
Fuller, Roy, 190, 458

Gardner, R., 328
Garfias, Pedro, 280
Grigson, Geoffrey, 376
Guillén, Julio D., 281
Gutteridge, Bernard, 412, 414

Haflin, Hans, 404
Haldane, Charlotte, 252
Hall, J. C., 457
Harrington, Bill, 192
Heinemann, Margot, 185–8, 245, 251
Hendry, J. F., 418
Hernández, Miguel, 282–7
Howard, Brian, 378
Hyndman, T. A. R., 193

Infante, Luis Perez, 329

Keal, W. B., 195, 327
Kendall, L., 323
King, H. M., 400
Knowland, A. S., 167

Lee, Laurie, 147, 151
Lepper, John, 133
Lewis, C. Day, 170, 236, 314, 411
Lindsay, Jack, 179, 253, 396, 449, 456
Lucas, F. L., 166
Luque, Antonio García, 287–8

Macalastair, Somhairle, 387
MacDiarmid, Hugh, 310
MacDonagh, Donagh, 175
Machado, Antonio, 205
MacNeice, Louis, 142, 453
Mallalieu, H. B., 102, 128, 352, 453
Milne, Ewart, 145–7, 177, 339, 342, 355

Neruda, Pablo, 197, 379
Nicholas, T. E., 195

Orwell, George, 309

Palmer, Aileen, 322
Paredes, Felix, 289
Parsons, Geoffrey, 206
Peacock, Herbert L., 382
Petere, José Herrera, 290–93
Plá y Beltran, 276

Raine, Kathleen, 401
Read, Herbert, 165, 185, 248
Richardson, Stanley, 381
Rickword, Edgell, 373
Roderick, J. T., 452
Roumain, Jacques, 164

Sagittarius, 377, 380
Salkeld, Blanaid, 176

501

Index of First Lines

This index contains first lines of poetry only; prose pieces are given in the Index of Titles.

Index of Titles

(P) = prose piece

INDEX OF TITLES